W9-CDC-078

POLITICAL DISQUISITIONS

VOLUME III

A Da Capo Press Reprint Series

THE ERA OF THE AMERICAN REVOLUTION

GENERAL EDITOR: LEONARD W. LEVY
Claremont Graduate School

POLITICAL DISQUISITIONS

An Enquiry into Public Errors, Defects, and Abuses

Calculated to Draw the Timely Attention of Government and People to a Due Consideration of the Necessity, and the Means, of Reforming Those Errors, Defects, and Abuses; of Restoring the Constitution, and Saving the State

By James Burgh

VOLUME III

DA CAPO PRESS • NEW YORK • 1971

A Da Capo Press Reprint Edition

This Da Capo Press edition of
Political Disquisitions
is an unabridged republication of
the first edition published in London
in 1774 and 1775.

Library of Congress Catalog Card Number 78-146144
SBN 306-70101-4

Published by Da Capo Press
A Division of Plenum Publishing Corporation
227 West 17th Street, New York, N.Y. 10011

Manufactured in the United States of America

POLITICAL DISQUISITIONS, &c.

Μετα τον περι Θεων λογον, κ. τ. λ. After treating of our duty to the *Gods*, it is proper to teach that which we owe to our *Country*. For our Country is, as it were, a *secondary* God, and the first and greatest *Parent*. —It is to be *preferred* to Parents, Wives, Children, Friends, and all things, the Gods only excepted.—And if our Country perishes, it is as impossible to save an *Individual*, as to preserve one of the fingers of a mortified hand.

HIEROCL.

POLITICAL DISQUISITIONS:

OR,

An ENQUIRY into public ERRORS, DEFECTS, and ABUSES. Illustrated by, and established upon FACTS and REMARKS, extracted from a Variety of AUTHORS, ancient and modern.

CALCULATED

To draw the timely ATTENTION of GOVERNMENT and PEOPLE to a due Consideration of the Necessity, and the Means, of REFORMING those ERRORS, DEFECTS, and ABUSES; of RESTORING the CONSTITUTION, and SAVING the STATE.

By J. B. Gent. Author of the DIGNITY of HUMAN NATURE, and other Tracts.

VOLUME THE THIRD AND LAST.

LONDON:
Printed for EDWARD and CHARLES DILLY.
MDCCLXXV.

ADVERTISEMENT.

WHEN the Author wrote the General Preface to theſe Diſquiſitions, he propoſed to lay before the Public more than three volumes of the materials he had collected. What theſe three volumes contain, is the moſt intereſting to the Public; and his health daily breaking, diſqualifies him for proceeding farther at preſent.

CONTENTS

OF VOLUME III.

BOOK I.

Of Manners.

CONTENTS.

POLITICAL

POLITICAL DISQUISITIONS, &c.

BOOK I.

Of Manners.

CHAP. I.

Importance of Manners in a State.

THIS work professes itself to be an inquiry into public errors, deficiencies, and abuses. And surely there is no grosser error, no deficiency more fatal, no abuse more shameful, than a nation's losing the proper delicacy of sentiment with regard to right and wrong, and deviating into a general corruption of manners. Has ambition raised a tyrant, a *Cæsar*, or a *Charles*, to despotic power? The sword of a *Brutus*, or the axe in the hand of the man in the mask, in a moment sets the people free. Has an aristocracy of thirty tyrants, as at *Athens*, seized the liberties of a country? A bold *Thrasybulus* [*] may be found, who com-

[*] *Corn. Nep.* VIT. THRASYB.

ing upon them in their secure hour, shall, by means perhaps seemingly very inadequate, blast all their schemes, and overthrow the edifice of tyranny they had set up, burying them in its ruins. The people thus set free, if the spirit of liberty be not extinct among them, and their manners generally corrupt, will preserve their recovered liberties. If their manners be so universally debauched, as to render them uncapable of liberty, they will, as the degenerate *Romans*, upon the fall of *Julius*, set up an *Augustus* in his place. It is impossible to pronounce with certainty concerning any country, as the angel did of the devoted cities, that the decline of manners in it is universal and irretrievable. But where that is the case, the ruin of that country is unavoidable, the disease is incurable. For vice prevailing would destroy not only a kingdom, or an empire, but the whole moral dominion of the Almighty throughout the infinitude of space.

The excellent *Montesquieu* [a] teaches the necessity of manners, in order to gain the effect proposed by laws; and brings several instances where the manners defeated the purpose of laws. Nothing, he says, could appear to the *Germans* more unsupportable than *Varus's* tribunal. They cut out the tongues of the advocates, who pleaded at the bar, with these sarcastic words, as related by *Tacitus*, 'Viper! give over hissing.' The trial ordered by the emperor *Justinian*, on occasion of the murder of the king of the *Lazians*, appeared to that people a horrible and barbarous thing. *Mithridates*, king of *Pontus*, haranguing against the *Romans*, reproaches them, above all things, with the formalities of their courts of justice. The *Parthians* could not endure a king, set over them by the *Romans*, because, having been educated in a commonwealth, he was

[a] *Montesq.* II. 119.

was free and affable. Even liberty and virtue to an enslaved and vicious people, become odious and insupportable, as a pure air is disagreeable to those who have lived in a marshy country. No people ever lost the spirit of liberty but through the fault of their government.

Liberty cannot be preserved, if the manners of the people are corrupted; nor absolute monarchy introduced, where they are sincere, says *Sidney* ON GOVERNMENT.

When *Antigonus*, and the *Achaians*, restored liberty to the *Spartans*, they could not keep it; the spirit of liberty was gone.

When *Thrasybulus* delivered *Athens* from the thirty tyrants, liberty came too late; the manners of the *Athenians* were then too far gone into licentiousness, avarice, and debauchery. There is a time, when a people are no longer worth saving.

When the *Tarquins* were expelled, *Rome* recovered her liberty. When *Julius* was stabbed, *Rome* continued in slavery. What occasioned such different consequences from the same measure in this same country at different periods? In the times of the *Tarquins*, *Rome* was incorrupt; in those of *Cæsar*, debauched. Even in the dictators' times, a few more *Catos* and *Brutuses* would have restored liberty. For the people are always interested against tyranny, if they can but be properly headed. Half the firmness the *Dutch* shewed against the *Spanish* tyranny, would emancipate *France*.

When the *Romans* were defeated by *Hannibal*, most of their allies forsook them. But *Hiero* king of *Sicily* saw that the constitution of the republic was still sound, and rightly concluded, that she would recover. He would not have thought so in the times of *Lucullus*, of

Cinna, *Sylla*, &c. when corruption was wasting all like a pestilence.

'*Il ne faut pas beaucoup de probite*, *&c.* Great pro-'bity is not essentially necessary for the support of a 'monarchy, or despotic government. The force of 'laws in the former, in the latter the arm of the prince 'lifted up, commands all. In a popular government, 'another engine is necessary, viz. virtue; because no-'thing else will keep up the execution of the laws, 'and the practice of what is right[a].' This sentiment is oracular. And what then is the prospect we have before us?

Where the manners of a people are gone, laws are of no avail. They will refuse them, or they will neglect them. There are in our times more of the laws ineffectual, than those that operate. And on every occasion of misbehaviour, we hear people cry, there ought to be such or such a *law* made; whereas, upon inquiry, it is perhaps found that there are already several unexceptionable laws upon the head standing; but, through want of manners, a mere dead letter.

'If all parts of the state do not with their utmost 'power promote the public good; if the prince has 'other aims than the safety and welfare of his coun-'try; if such as represent the people do not preserve 'their courage and integrity; if the nation's treasure 'is wasted; if ministers are allowed to undermine the 'constitution with impunity; if judges are suffered to 'pervert justice and wrest the law; then is a mixed 'government the greatest tyranny in the world: it is 'tyranny established by a law; it is authorised by con-'sent, and such a people are bound with fetters of their

[a] *Montesq.* I. 31.

'their own making. A tyranny that governs by the 'ſword, has few friends but men of the ſword; but 'a legal tyranny, (where the people are only called to 'confirm iniquity with their own voices) has on its 'ſide the rich, the timid, the lazy, thoſe that know 'the law, and get by it, ambitious churchmen, and 'all thoſe whoſe livelihood depends upon the quiet 'poſture of affairs: and the perſons here deſcribed 'compoſe the influencing part of moſt nations; ſo 'that ſuch a tyranny is hardly to be ſhaken off. Men 'may be ſaid to be enſlaved by law or their own con'ſent under corrupt or degenerate republics, ſuch as 'was the *Roman* commonwealth from the time of *Cinna* 'till the attempts of *Cæſar*; and under degenerate 'mixed governments, ſuch as *Rome* was, while the 'emperors made a ſhow of ruling by law, but with an 'influenced and corrupted ſenate, to which form of 'government *England* was almoſt reduced, till the King 'came over to put our liberties upon a better foot[a]."

Plato[b] calls virtue the health of the mind, and vice its diſeaſe and diſorder. Αρετη μεν γαρ ὡς εοικεν, κ. τ. λ. That nation is in a dreadful way, in which almoſt every mind is *diſeaſed* and *diſordered*.

The ancient politicians placed their whole dependence for the ſafety of their governments, on the virtue and patriotiſm of their people. Now we place our ſecurity in our commerce, our fleet, our treaſures, our miniſtry's ſkill in managing a houſe of commons. Formerly the fortunes of private men were the ſtrength of the ſtate. Now the public money is the object of the general avarice. The great kingdoms and ſtates of antiquity had the ſame internal force of men and mo-

 ney,

[a] *Daven.* II. 300.

[b] DE REPUBL. IV. *in fine.*

ney, after they loſt their liberties, as when they had them. But a nation of men, who only fight for their country, or undertake the adminiſtration of their country, becauſe they are paid for it, are very different from a nation of men who are willing to die for their country.

'*Elle* [*Athenes*] *conſiderait*, &c. The Athenians 'conſidered, that in a republic manners were above all 'things neceſſary[a].' In *England* we never conſider this.

The *Athenians* did not ſuffer thoſe who frequented lewd women, to harangue the people. *Demoſthenes* highly approves this law[b].

'It is of great conſequence (ſays *Solon* in his letter 'to *Epimenides*), of what diſpoſitions thoſe are, who 'influence the common people[c]."

A magiſtrate overtaken in liquor was ſeverely puniſhed; the firſt archon, though accidentally, with death.

It was impoſſible for any man at *Athens* to live a diſſolute life unreproved: for every man was liable to be ſent for by the Areopagites, to be examined, and puniſhed, if guilty. At *Rome* the cenſors had the ſame power[d]. We Chriſtians may be as wicked as we pleaſe. Our governments encourage vice for the benefit of the revenues.

Emmius[e] accounts for the long duration of liberty in the *Athenian* republic, by obſerving that the people were of a ſublime, bold, and penetrating genius, as much ſuperior to the other ſtates of *Greece*, as the other ſtates of *Greece* were to the barbarous people. That there

---

[a] *Monteſqu.* III. 32.

[b] Ant. Univ. Hist. vi. 314.

[c] Ibid. xli.

[d] Ibid. vi. 330.

[e] De Rep. Athen. i. 107.

there was continually rising among them a succession of men eminent for political wisdom and integrity, who planted in the minds of the people sentiments of true patriotism, and inspired them with such a love of liberty, that every *Athenian* was ready to pour out his best blood for its preservation. That the people were, by *Solon*, taught, that the strength of a free state consists in its laws; that laws are nothing, unless they be obeyed; that laws will not be obeyed, unless honour be given to the obedient, and punishment inflicted on transgressors; that the laws are not to be subjected to the government, but the government to the laws; that riches, interest, and party are to yield to the laws, not the laws to them. That therefore in the best times of that commonwealth, honours and rewards were given in such a manner, as tended to lead the persons honoured and rewarded to gratitude rather than to ambition, which *Demosthenes* exemplifies in the case of *Miltiades*, *Cimon*, *Themistocles*, and others. And on the contrary, whoever made himself obnoxious to the laws of his country, was to expect no alleviation on account of his riches, his family, or even of his former meritorious actions. Accordingly *Miltiades*, *Themistocles*, *Cimon*, and others, though eminent for their public services, were not spared, when thought to have violated the laws. For the *Athenians* considered, that it is the duty of a citizen to behave well, not on one occasion only, but at all times; not to be at first zealous, faithful, and obedient, and afterwards a lawless plunderer; for that this is not the behaviour of men of principle, who are uniform in their conduct, but of artful and insidious men, who study only to surprise the public opinion, that they may deceive with the better success. That the *Athenians* were, above all other nations, severe against corruption above all other

 offences,

offences, as what tends moſt directly to the deſtruction of ſtates. The *Athenians*, therefore, puniſhed this crime with a fine to ten times the value of the bribe, or with outlawry, or death; ſome of which puniſhments were inflicted even on thoſe, who had on other occaſions deſerved well of their country, as *Timotheus*, *Epicrates*, *Thraſybulus* the younger, and others. Another cauſe of the flouriſhing ſtate of the *Athenian* republic, was the encouragement given to marriage and population. Another was the wiſe ſeverity of *Solon*, in bringing upon the offences of magiſtrates a ſwifter puniſhment than on thoſe of private perſons; for that the latter might be delayed; but if the former was put off, things might quickly come into ſuch diſorder, that it would be too late to think of puniſhing powerful offenders; beſides, that the offences of private perſons may be compared with thoſe of the common ſailors, on board of a ſhip, which may not prove fatal to the crew; but the crimes of magiſtrates are like thoſe of the maſter, or pilot, which endanger the loſs of ſhip, loading, crew, and paſſengers. That *Solon* likewiſe laid great ſtreſs on the education of youth, that they might be habituated to virtue, induſtry, courage, and love of their country. That his laws tended to honour wiſdom and virtue, and to bring diſgrace on the contrary characters, by refuſing to men of profligate lives all honours in the ſtate, and even forbidding them to ſpeak in the εκκλησια, or aſſembly of the people. For the wiſe legiſlator thought there was little probability, that he, who could not manage his own private eſtate, would adminiſter that of the public with frugality and wiſdom; and that the people would not, or however ought not, to pay any regard to the patriotic harangues of a man, who ſtudied more to poliſh his ſpeeches, than to regulate his life.

While

While all *Europe* groaned under the chain of *Roman* tyranny, the *Germans*, and northern nations, preserved their liberty.

Tacitus ſays, nobody among the *Germans* laughs at vice, or apologiſes for corruption, by ſaying, it is univerſally practiſed [a]. But the *Germans* were barbarous heathens; we are polite chriſtians.

Hannibal, when prætor of *Carthage*, ſet about reforming abuſes, regulated the finances, reſtrained the injuſtice of the judges, and peculation of the grandees, and collectors of the revenues, who were got to ſuch a degree of open corruption, that they pretended a lawful title to whatever they could plunder from the people. The many proved of courſe too hard for one. Yet (ſuch is the advantage of integrity) they had no means for this purpoſe, but exciting the *Romans* againſt him. The conſequence was, that this illuſtrious warrior and reformer, who had bled for his country, and had laboured for its reformation, was driven into exile, and hunted from country to country, like a felon, and at laſt beſet in his retirement by his enemies, and only eſcaped the cruelties, they would have inflicted on him by deſtroying himſelf.

Every page of the hiſtory of the great revolution of *Rome* ſhews ſome inſtance of the degeneracy of the *Roman* virtue, and of the impoſſibility of a nation's continuing free after its virtue is gone.

It is thought by many of the authors of this part of the *Roman* hiſtory, that ſuch was the corruption of manners, that the greateſt part of thoſe who oppoſed *Julius*, were enemies to the man rather than to his cauſe [b].

Would

---

[a] De Mor. Germ.

[b] Ant. Univ. Hist. xiii. 410.

Would the *Romans* in the times of *Scipio*, have suffered *Cæsar* to keep his government in *Gaul*, to debauch the army, and openly corrupt the people? No. There were times when ten *Pompeys* and twenty *Cæsars* could not have enslaved the *Roman* people.

A tender virgin of eighteen years of age, has but little strength of body, compared with that of an athletic ravisher inflamed with lust. Yet we find she can preserve her honour safe, if she pleases, even against his utmost strength; and in fact, scarcely any woman loses her virtue, no nation its liberties, without their own fault. What *Milton* says of one is true of both.

——————Chastity!
She who has that, is clad in complete steel,
And like a quiver'd nymph, with arrows keen
May trace huge forests, and unharbour'd heaths,
Infamous hills, and sandy perilous wilds,
Where through the sacred rays of chastity
No savage fierce, bandit, or mountaineer
Will dare to soil her virgin purity.
Yea there, where every desolation dwells
By grots and caverns shagg'd with horrid shades,
She may pass on with unblanch'd majesty,
Be it not done in pride, or in presumption.
——————But when lust,
By unchaste looks, loose gestures, and foul talk,
But most by lewd, and lavish act of sin,
Lets in defilement on the inward parts,
The soul grows clotted by contagion,
Embodies and embrutes, till she quite lose
The divine property of her first being.

MILT. COMUS.

Nothing is more essentially necessary to the establishment of manners in a state, than that all persons employed in stations of power and trust be men of exemplary characters.

'Let

'Let *Valerian* [afterwards emperor] be cenſor,' ſaid the *Roman* ſenators, 'who has no faults of his own [a].'

The *Roman* cenſors had authority over all perſons, except only the governor of *Rome*, the conſuls in office, the *rex ſacrorum*, and the ſuperior of the veſtal virgins. This office, ſo uſeful in the republican times, was neglected under almoſt all the emperors [b].

The *Roman* cenſors uſed to ſtrike out of the liſt thoſe ſenators, who ſeemed to them not to ſupport, with proper dignity, their illuſtrious ſtation. We find ſixty-four thus diſgraced, in the times of *Sylla*, when it may be ſuppoſed the manners were greatly degenerated.

It is to be doubted that thoſe old-faſhioned heathen cenſors would, if they were employed among us, take umbrage at our chriſtian foibles of adultery, gambling, cheating, rooking, bribing, blaſphemy, ſodomy, and the other frolics which ſo elegantly amuſe our ſenatorial men and women of pleaſure.

The *Romans* to the laſt ſhewed their opinion of the uſefulneſs of the office of cenſors. We find it, after a long interruption by the civil wars, reſtored, and ſixty-four ſenators immediately ſtruck out of the liſt [c].

Scipio was not chaſte from ſtupidity; for it is recorded of him, that he was a great admirer of beauty.

Socrates acknowledged, that he was naturally inclinable to ſenſuality, but that he had, by philoſophy, corrected the bent of his nature.

The public cannot be too curious concerning the characters of public men; ſo common is it for them to change upon preferment, according to the old adage, *honores mutant mores*.

Sylla,

[a] Ant. Univ. Hist. xv. 416.
[b] Ibid. [c] Ibid. xii. 151.

Sylla, who, in his youth, was of ſo tender a heart, as to weep for very ſlight occaſions, became one of the moſt cruel of men; ordered *Granius* to be ſtrangled in his preſence, as he lay a dying[a], and deluged *Rome* with the blood of her citizens.

Nero, when he was to ſign a dead-warrant, in his earlier years, often wept, and wiſhed he had never learned to write. Yet the very name of that prince afterwards became the proverb for cruelty.

That ſtate is going to ruin, ſaid *Antiſthenes*, in which the honours due to merit, are beſtowed on the artful and deſigning, or on the tools of power.

The *Athenian* archons, before they entered upon their office, were obliged to ſwear, that if ever they were convicted of bribery, they would ſend to *Delphi*, as a fine, a ſtatue of gold of their own ſize[b].

The antient *Spartans* choſe their ephori out of any rank indifferently; which policy *Ariſtotle* prefers to that of the *Cretans*, who elected their coſmi only from certain particular orders.

Ariſtotle ſays, that in 400 years there was neither ſedition, nor tyranny, in *Carthage*; a proof of a good conſtitution, good adminiſtration, and virtuous manners.

Ariſtotle commends the *Carthaginian* wiſdom, for that they choſe their men of authority rather according to their perſonal characters, than according to family. 'Men of great power, and of no character, are very 'hurtful, and actually have very much prejudiced the '*Spartan* republic.' Και βελτιον δε τυς βασιλεις, κ. τ. λ[c]. And afterwards in the ſame chapter, he blames their policy in confining authority only to the rich.

[a] Ant. Univ. Hist. xiii. 96.

[b] *Ub. Emm.* De Rep. Athen. i. 27.

[c] Arist. Pol. ii. 11.

rich. For that this naturally leads the people to the admiration and purſuit of riches, rather than the ſtudy of virtue. Whilſt it is impoſſible that a ſtate ſhould be ſecure, where virtue is not ſupremely honoured. Παρεκ βαινει δε, κ. τ. λ.

The manners of the upper ranks will deſcend to the loweſt. When *M. Antonius*, grandfather of the triumvir of the ſame name, was accuſed, his ſlave bore the torture with heroic fortitude [a].

It was to keep up a ſenſe of national honour, that there was a law made, forbidding a *Roman* citizen to be ſcourged [b].

'*Ad illa mihi pro ſe quiſque*, &c.

'Let every reader of hiſtory (ſays *Liv. Proœm.*) apply his mind to obſerve the manners and characters of our anceſtors; by what ſort of men, and by what arts of peace and war, the commonwealth was raiſed; and let him attend to the cauſes of its decline, viz. the neglect of diſcipline, and degeneracy of manners; and let him obſerve how this degeneracy has increaſed in an accelerated proportion, till we are now fallen into ſuch a condition, that we can neither bear our vices, nor the reformation of them.'

When the firſt triumviri, *Cæſar*, *Pompey*, and *Craſſus*, were laying the foundation for the ruin of *Roman* liberty, and had ſo debauched the people (a people cannot be enſlaved while they continue honeſt), that candidates, inſtead of depending on their ſervices and merits, openly bought votes; and afterwards, improving upon corruption, inſtead of purchaſing ſingle votes, went directly to the triumviri, and paid down the ready money; when all was thus going headlong to ruin, *Cato* attempted to put ſome check to the torrent of wickedneſs.

[a] Ant. Univ. Hist. xii. 453. [b] Ibid. xii. 342.

wickedneſs. What was the conſequence? He only got himſelf the ill-will of both rich and poor. All love of country was then loſt in a general ſcramble for the ſpoils of their country[a].

The reſemblance between the diſpoſition of the *Roman* people of thoſe degenerate days, and that of a certain country in our times, is ſtriking enough to freeze the blood in the veins of every friend to that country.

The *Romans* ſeem to have loſt their national character from the time of the fall of their rival *Carthage*. Time was, when hardly a *Roman* could have been found capable of the villanous proceedings of *Cæpio*[b].

And it was not till the *Roman* virtue was degenerated, that the republic was capable of baſely violating a ſolemn treaty with the *Numantians*, though that unhappy people had actually complied with the conditions.

As if the ſuperior powers had intended a leſſon for all mankind, not to trifle with ſolemn treaties, the *Romans* are defeated by the *Numantians* (even the women lending their aſſiſtance, and attacking the *Romans* with unuſual valour), though their army was 30,000 againſt only 4000. Of the *Romans*, 20,000 were cut in pieces in the purſuit, their courage failing them, as through ſenſe of the guilt of an unjuſt and cruel war. The *Numantians* would not afterwards treat with the *Roman* general; ſo infamous was the character of thoſe who formerly reproached the *Carthaginians* with their national treachery, at laſt they agreed to treat with *Tib. Gracchus*, whoſe reputation for probity was eminent. The wicked ſenate, as if determined ſtill farther to make good the ſuſpicions, which the *Numantians*

---

a ANT. UNIV. HIST. XIII. 170. b Ibid. XII. 392.

tians had of them, again violates the new treaty with the *Numantians*, though that people (called by the destroyers of mankind, barbarous) had generously spared 10,000 *Romans*, whom they had in their power. The *Romans*, who boasted their justice and clemency in war, were not to be satisfied but with the destruction of those who had saved them. Nor did their sufferings for their treachery end here. *Tib. Gracchus*, who had made the treaty with the *Numantians*, being offended at the disgrace brought on him by the senate's basely violating it, begun that fatal sedition, distinguished by the name of the *Gracchi*, which drew after it the most destructive consequences [a].

The *Romans* at the time of *Sylla*'s voluntary resignation, had it in their power to recover their liberties. But corruption was even then too far gone [b].

My much esteemed friend and relation Dr. *Robertson* thinks, the *Roman* empire must have sunk, though the *Goths* had never invaded it, because the *Roman* virtue was sunk [c]. They were so debauched, that among the northern nations it was usual to call a person of a flagitious character, a *Roman*, as among us, a *Jew*. The destruction of eternal *Rome* was completed in less than two centuries from the first irruption of the barbarians [d]. *Rome* destroyed by *Goths* and *Vandals*, resembled a lion devoured by vermin.

The degeneracy of the *Roman* senate appeared shockingly conspicuous on occasion of the prosecution of *Jugurtha*. When that bloody tyrant, the murderer of his benefactors two sons, came to *Rome* to answer for his innumerable crimes, after having for several years neglected

[a] Ant. Univ. Hist. xii. 392, *et seq.*

[b] *Plut.* in Syll.

[c] Hist. Ch. V. i. 3.

[d] Ibid. 7.

neglected the summons, and carried on war against the *Roman* generals; he frees himself from the deserved censure, by bribing one of the ten tribunes; who accordingly in open senate stops the examination of the king, when questioned by the others concerning certain senators, whom he had corrupted [a].

Jugurtha returning home after an acquittance obtained by money, cries out, 'O city ready for sale, 'if a buyer rich enough can be found [b]!'

Corruption ruins the whole proceedings of a state, both in peace and war.

Jugurtha, notwithstanding his atrocious villanies, continued unpunished, and baffled the vengeance of the mighty *Roman* commonwealth for several years, because corruption protected him. He had bribed the senate, and the commanders who went against him. But whenever the war was put into the hands of *Metellus* and *Marius*, men of honour, he was presently crushed.

'Ουδεν γαρ οφελος της πολεως, κ. τ. λ. It is a great 'evil in a state, when there is not power to curb offend- 'ers [c].'

The *Roman* senate, whose decrees formerly shook three quarters of the world, sneak to *Pompey*, all but *Hortensius* and *Catulus* [d].

The *Roman* people, lost to the true republican spirit, confer on *Pompey* voluntarily more power than *Sylla* obtained by force of arms.

When inconsiderable merits obtain high rewards, it is to be presumed, that real merit is scarce in that country, and contrarywise.

Calpurnius

---

a See *Sallust*. BELL. JUGURTH. b Ibid.

c *Anon*. ap. *Ub. Emm*. DE REP. ATHEN. I. 125.

d ANT. HIST. XIII. 131.

Calpurnius Flamma, for ſaving the whole *Roman* army at the *Furcæ Caudinæ*, was rewarded with the elegant ornament of a wiſp of hay put round his head.

Aul. Poſthumius miſbehaved, or was unfortunate in one battle; gained a victory in another. The ſtern *Roman* people did not however allow, that the ſucceſs ſhould expiate for the miſcarriage. He could not obtain the honour of a triumph; but was obliged to content himſelf with an ovation [a].

Horatius Cocles was rewarded with a contribution of victuals and a bit of land [b].

The *Greeks* would not have the names of their commanders mentioned on occaſion of victories; but aſcribed them to the army in general. We find *Demoſthenes* afterwards blaming the honours ſhewn to the generals, by aſcribing ſuch and ſuch victories to ſuch and ſuch commanders. At length they became ſo exorbitant in conferring honours, that *Demetrius Phalerius* had 300 ſtatues in *Athens*.

Mr. *Hume* obſerves, that the *Romans* were very *vicious* in the times of the *Punic* wars, when the commonwealth was moſt flouriſhing [c]. But they were not corrupt or diſhoneſt to their country, or luxurious or extravagant. Theſe are the manners which chiefly tend to bring ruin upon ſtates. Theſe are political vices. And yet every able ſtateſman will guard againſt the prevalency of other vices, as well as theſe. For there is a connexion between vices, as well as between virtues, and one opens a door for the entrance of the other.

If *Cæſar* and *Pompey* (ſays the author of GRAND. ET DECAD. DES ROM. p. 229.) had been very *Catoes*, there would

[a] ANT. UNIV. HIST. XI. 380. [b] Ibid. XI. 370.
[c] POL. ESS. IV. 39.

would have been other *Cæsars* and other *Pompeys*, and the republic, deſtined to ruin, [through corruption] would have been dragged to the precipice by other hands.

A remain of virtue among the *Romans* in *Catiline's* time, kept the ſtate afloat, in ſpite of his traitorous attempts to ſink it. That being at the time of *Cæſar's* attack extinct, he was enabled to finiſh what his predeceſſor attempted in vain. *Catiline* was defeated and killed. His deſign is branded with the infamous name of a conſpiracy. *Cæſar* conquered his oppoſers, and for a ſhort time triumphed over liberty. His attempt is called a civil war; and himſelf reckoned among the heroes.

Cicero accuſes *Catiline* to his face in the open ſenate; but dares not exert the conſular power to apprehend or puniſh him, though in the ſenate-houſe he threatened deſtruction to the ſenate[a].

A ſtate muſt be weak, or its government incapable, when one deſperado is too mighty for the laws.

Cæſar advances all his partiſans to poſts and honours[b]. With what view? Manifeſtly with the ſame which moves our court to give places to members of the houſe of commons, viz. to bias them from the intereſt of their country, and bribe them to do their dirty work. When *Brutus* had executed the law on the deſtroyer of his country's freedom, he ſcorned to harangue the people, in order to reconcile them to the meaſure. Much leſs could he have brought himſelf to bribe them, even to allure them to their intereſt.

Pompey barefacedly gets himſelf propoſed for dictator, at a time when there was no uſe of a dictator. That is,

a *Sal.* Bell. Catil.

b Ant. Univ. Hist. xiii, 225.

is, he plainly told his countrymen, he ſhould be much obliged to them, if they would give him leave to do with them whatever he pleaſed. For a dictator's power was abſolute. *Cato*, however, had influence enough to retard *Pompey*'s ſcheme [a], and to get him made ſole conſul, the firſt of the kind, which likewiſe was a groſs violation of the conſtitution [b]. A ſtanding army is appointed him, and his government in *Spain* continued. The *Romans* ſeem to have been at this time weary of liberty and happineſs.

It is a prognoſtic of the downfall of a ſtate, when ſalutary regulations are unneceſſarily broke through.

Marius was choſen conſul four times ſucceſſively, notwithſtanding the law forbidding any man's being twice conſul in leſs than ten years [c].

When *Marius* treacherouſly endeavoured to enſnare the brave *Metellus*, the latter ſhewed a firmneſs worthy of univerſal imitation. 'To do a baſe action, ſays he, 'is, under all circumſtances, ſhameful. To do well, 'when no danger is nigh, is common. But to do well 'in ſpite of danger, is the part of a brave man [d].'

Sylla was created, through fear, perpetual dictator. *Rome* was ripe for ſlavery, before *Julius* wreathed her chains. All the inteſtine confuſions in *Rome* were owing to a conſtitution originally ill-balanced. A ſtatue was erected to the conqueror of his country in the very forum which he had ſo lately drenched with the nobleſt blood of *Rome*. He himſelf publickly expreſſes his contempt for the ſlaviſh diſpoſition ſhewn in his own favour, by the degenerate ſons of the brave *Romans*. They even pay diſtinguiſhed honours to his memory, after his death. Yet it is certain, that *Tarquin*, whom their anceſtors

 expelled,

[a] Ant. Univ. Hist. xiii. 171. [b] Ibid. 173.
[c] Ibid. 9. [d] Ibid. 24.

expelled, and for his ſake rejected regal government, was not ſo bloody a tyrant as *Sylla*.

When the efficiency of government goes from where the conſtitution placed it, into hands which have no right to it, that ſtate is far gone toward ruin.

The *Roman* conſuls became at laſt ſlaves to the triumviri, *Cæſar*, *Pompey*, and *Craſſus* [a].

When the houſes of parliament are ſeen to be the tools of the miniſtry, the liberties of *Britain* are near their end.

Cæſar bribes all *Rome* againſt *Pompey*, ſay the ancient univerſal hiſtorians [b]. Then all *Rome* muſt have been corrupt. For *Pompey* was certainly the better man of the two.

With the power which *Julius* had, he might have reformed, inſtead of enſlaving, his country. That it was not by the wiſeſt men thought impracticable, appears from *Brutus*'s and *Cicero*'s endeavours for that purpoſe, from *Auguſtus*'s propoſing (however inſincerely) to reſtore the republican government, and even from *Tiberius*'s affected deſign of quitting the throne. Therefore the apology for *Auguſtus*'s continuing *Julius*'s tyranny, viz. That *Rome* was become unfit for republican government, is falſe and ſlaviſh [c].

Here a diſtinction is to be made between a people incapable of free government, and a people among whom the ſpirit of liberty is got to ſo low an ebb, that they have not the courage to ſeize it, when put within their reach, or to reſiſt the attempts of thoſe who would deprive them of it. Any people are capable of enjoying liberty, when procured for them. The *Romans*, if *Auguſtus* had reſtored the republican government, would have

---

[a] Ant. Univ. Hist. xiii. 154. [b] Ibid. 174.

[c] *Gord.* Disc. on Tacit. i. 68.

have been free; and there is no doubt, but he had it in his power to reſtore it, and probably to keep it up, during his life (as *Epaminondas* made his ſtupid countrymen the *Bœotians* great in ſpite of themſelves during his life), and he is inexcuſable for neglecting the opportunity, and inſtead of purſuing the glorious views of *Brutus*, rivetting the chain which *Julius* had faſtened but ſlightly; and flattering the ſenators, that he underwent ſo many labours and perils only to reſtore peace to the *Romans*. Thoſe abject ſlaves decree him honours for daſhing out of their hands their liberties, when within their graſp [a].

The *Romans*, it is true, at the time of *Cæſar*'s execution, were ripe for ſlavery. None to ſeize liberty, when put in their hands. 'They were no longer 'that nation of heroes, to whom liberty was dearer 'than life. They were become effeminate, debauched, 'and accuſtomed to live by the price of their votes, 'which they ſold to the beſt bidder [b].' Time was, and continued for many ages, when it would have been no diſputable point, whether a tyrant was to be extirpated or not, as it was on this occaſion [c]. There was indeed no room for diſputing the point. From the time of the expulſion of the *Tarquins*, by the *Roman* conſtitution, it was unlawful for any perſon to aſſume ſingular power. *Julius*, therefore, who did this, was legally executed by *Brutus*, excepting that he had no regular trial.

It may, therefore, be ſaid of a people, that they are at the ſame time capable and incapable of liberty. The *French*, for inſtance, are incapable of liberty, inaſmuch as they cannot find a ſet of men capable of

C 3 overſetting

a Ant. Univ. Hist. xiii. 462. b Ibid. 283, 4, 5.

c Ibid. 286. the various opinions of the ſenators, concerning the deſtroyers of *Cæſar*.

overſetting the tyranny under which they groan, and of reſtoring and eſtabliſhing, inſtead of it, a free government, which ſhall keep itſelf up for ages, in ſpite of any attempts to overthrow it, and to reſtore the preſent ſyſtem of deſpotiſm. At the ſame time there is no doubt, but the *French* are ſo far capable of liberty, that if the neceſſary deliverers and defenders could be found, they would be actually delivered, and would be actually free. But to return;

Atrocious crimes unpuniſhed, as well as inconſiderable merits over-rewarded, and honeſt men perſecuted, are bad ſymptoms in a ſtate.

Murders became, in the times of *Sylla* and *Marius*, common, and often eſcaped unpuniſhed, as of *Aul. Sempronius*, *Pomponius Rufus*, &c.

A decline of manners threatens a decline of empire [a].

When *Rome* became to ſuch a degree corrupt, that the rapacious publicans in *Aſia* had intereſt enough to get *Rutilius Rufus*, their enemy, baniſhed, that brave detector of villany betook himſelf to *Greece*, and lived among the philoſophers. After ſome time, the *Romans* were deſirous of recalling him. But he refuſed to return to a place, where knaves had got ſuch an aſcendancy as to be able to bring puniſhment upon honeſt men [b].

'The once illuſtrious *Roman* ſenate became, under 'the emperors, an aſſembly of mean-ſpirited wretches, 'entirely devoted to corruption and ſervitude. For 'this execution [of *Octavia*, the innocent wife of *Nero*] as for ſome notable deliverance, they pompouſly 'decreed gifts and oblations to the gods. Such was 'the debaſement of the once great and venerable *Roman* ſenate. Fear had ſtopped their mouths, or 'opened them only to the moſt ſcandalous ſtrains of 'flattery.

[a] Ant. Univ. Hist. xiii. 42, *et paſſ.* [b] Ibid. 33.

'flattery. Our hiſtorian obſerves here to their eternal 'infamy, that as often as any cruel ſentence was pro-'nounced by the prince, as often as murders or ba-'niſhments were by him commanded, ſo often were 'acknowledgments and thankſgivings, by the autho-'rity of the ſenate, paid to the deities [a].'

'*Dio Caſſius* deſcribes at large an entertainment, to 'which the emperor [*Domitian*] invited the principal men 'among the ſenators and knights. An entertainment, 'ſays that writer, which more than any thing elſe, diſ-'plays his tyrannical temper, and how wantonly he 'abuſed his power. At the entrance of the palace the 'gueſts were received with great ceremony, and con-'ducted to a ſpacious hall hung round with black, and 'illuminated with a few melancholy lamps, which were 'only ſufficient to diſcover the horror of the place, and 'the ſeveral coffins, upon which were written in capi-'tals the names of the ſeveral ſenators and knights in-'vited. Great was their fright and conſternation at the 'ſight of ſo diſmal a ſcene; for the emperor had often 'publickly declared that he could not think himſelf ſafe 'ſo long as one ſenator was left alive, and that amongſt 'the knights there were few, whom he did not look 'upon as his enemies. After they had long waited 'expecting every moment their laſt doom, the doors 'were at length all on a ſudden burſt open, when a 'great number of naked perſons, having their bodies 'all over dyed black, entered the hall, with drawn 'ſwords in one hand, and flaming torches in the other. 'The gueſts, at this dreadful appearance, giving them-'ſelves up for loſt, already felt all the agonies of death. 'But thoſe whom they looked upon as their execu-'tioners, having for ſome time danced round them,

[a] Ant. Univ. Hist. xiv. 407.

'at once set open the doors, and acquainted them that 'the emperor gave the company leave to withdraw. 'Thus did *Domitian* insult these two illustrious orders, 'shewing, says *Dio Cassius*, how little he feared them, 'and at the same time, with how much reason they 'might dread his resentment, since it was in his power 'to cut them all off without exposing himself to the 'least danger[a].'

A slavish submission to the commands even of the lawful prince, is a mark of a decline of the spirit of liberty.

One of *Solyman Shah*'s generals voluntarily offered to kill himself, to divert the prince and his court[b]. Twenty officers, commanded by *Hasan khan* to kill themselves, to shew the sultan's ambassadors their submission, immediately obey[c].

'How was the *Roman* spirit sunk when *Tiberius* wrote 'to the senate, desiring the tribunitial power for *Drusus*; 'which the fathers granted with the more refined flat-'tery, as they had foreseen this request. Statues were 'decreed both to *Tiberius* and *Drusus*; altars were 'erected to the gods; arches raised, &c. *M. Silanus* 'moved, that for the future not the names of the con-'suls, but of those who exercised the tribunitial power, 'should be prefixed to all public and private records. '*Haterius Agrippa*, that the decrees of that day should 'be written in letters of gold, and hung up in the se-'nate. Thus the lords of the *Roman* senate, who once 'headed mighty armies, raised and deposed great kings, 'bestowed or took away empires, were by degrees 'changed into mean slaves, and become, by their infa-'mous behaviour, an object of derision and contempt 'to

---

a ANT. UNIV. HIST. XV. 69.

b MOD. UNIV. HIST. VI. 17. c Ibid. III. 277.

'to all foreign nations; nay, to that very tyrant whoſe 'favour they ſtrove to gain by diſgracing themſelves. '*Druſus*, who was then in *Campania* probably with his 'father, wrote to the ſenate, returning them thanks for 'the tribunitial power with which they had inveſted 'him; but did not condeſcend to come to *Rome*, as was 'expected, to receive it[a].'

'*Non eſt noſtrum æſtimare*, &c. it does not become 'us to judge of the perſons you are pleaſed to ad-'vance, nor of the reaſons for your advancing them. 'The gods have given you ſovereign power; to us 'remains the glory of obedience.' The ſcoundrel ſpeech of *M. Terentius* to *Tiberius*, acknowledging his connexion with *Sejanus*, the moſt odious miniſter of the moſt odious emperor [b].

When *Libo Druſus*, in the reign of *Tiberius*, was unjuſtly tried upon the *lex majeſtatis*, and his eſtate to be divided among his accuſers; which, as *Amm. Marcellinus* ſays, was ſounding a trumpet to aſſemble the odious *dilatores* againſt the beſt men in *Rome*; the degenerate ſenators ſtrove which ſhould moſt groſsly flatter the cruel emperor, by declaring the deceaſed *Libo* (for he laid violent hands upon himſelf before his condemnation) guilty of treaſon. The firſt lords of the ſenate were not above taking upon themſelves the vile office of informers. The metropolis of the world often in thoſe times ſaw her public dignities beſtowed as rewards upon thoſe execrable parricides who had ſpilt her beſt blood. One ſenator made one motion, and another made another propoſal, all diſgraceful to the unhappy deceaſed, but flattering to the tyrant. So miſerable was the ſervility of the once venerable

[a] Ant. Univ. Hist. xiv. 169.

[b] *Tacit.* Ann. vii.

nerable *Roman* senate so early as the beginning of *Tiberius*'s reign[a].

Valerian the *Roman* emperor, about the middle of the third century, was conquered by *Sapor* king of *Persia*, dragged chained through all the cities of that vast kingdom, and treated with greater indignity than the meanest slave. For that haughty conqueror made him his footstool when he mounted his horse. He flayed him (alive, some say), dressed his skin, dyed it red, hung it up, and shewed it to all strangers. And the wretched fallen *Romans* were obliged to bear all this unresented; which patience brought on them attacks from the barbarous nations[b].

At last the *Roman* empire was fairly put up to auction by the soldiery, and purchased by the highest bidder, *Didius Julianus*, who reigned two months and six days, hated, cursed, and stoned by the people, and at last put to death by order of the senate, and whose most remarkable action was causing a number of children to be murdered, that he might have their blood to use in his magic rites[c]. And though other emperors might not so openly purchase the imperial diadem, it is certain that they generally made a present, on their accession to the soldiery, which was the *sine quâ non* of their preferment.

The western or proper *Roman* empire, was annihilated by *Odoacer* the *Goth*, who takes the throne from *Augustulus*, and makes himself king of *Italy*, *A. D.* 476, 507 years after the battle of *Actium*, which terminated the *Roman* republican or free state, and begun the monarchy; after which fatal period, public virtue declined continually, and the vast dominion of the *Romans*

---

[a] *Tacit.* ANNAL. II.

[b] ANT. UNIV. HIST. XV. 425. [c] Ibid. 282.

mans was by degrees mutilated of *Britain*, *Spain*, *Africa*, and *Gaul*; the greateſt ſtate the world ever beheld, demoliſhed by its own luxury and depravity, by the hand of a contemptible barbarian, a perſon ſo obſcure, that his family, and the country he came from, are ſcarce known[a]. From the foundation of *Rome* to *Odoacer*'s conqueſt, was 1324 years.

How were the mighty fallen, when the emperor *Valentinian* II. ſent an embaſſy to deprecate the wrath of *Attila* coming againſt him, and at the head of the embaſſy, the biſhop of *Rome*[b]. Poor *Roman* emperor!

——Quantum mutatus ab illo
Cæſare! VIRG.

Afterwards the *Saracens*, the *Nubians*, the moſt contemptible nations, broke into the empire. Like the dying lion in the fable, ſhe was expoſed to all diſgraces. '*Attila*, my maſter and yours,' are the words of that barbarous monarch's ambaſſador to the fallen *Roman* emperor[c]. *Alaric*, the *Goth*, depoſes the *Roman* emperor twice, and afterwards ſhews him publicly in the dreſs of a ſlave[d]. The mighty *Rome*, the ſeat of liberty, the miſtreſs of the world, 'the nurſe of 'heroes, the delight of gods, which humbled the 'proud tyrants of the earth, and ſet the nations free,' was taken by *Alaric* the *Goth*, *A. D.* 410, and plundered for three days. What nation could have taken *Rome* in the days of the *Scipios* and the *Fabii*[e]?

So lately as *A. D.* 1347, an attempt was made to reſtore liberty to the *Romans* by *Nicolas Gabrini de Rienzo*,

---

[a] ANT. UNIV. HIST. XVI. 597. [b] Ibid. 569.
[c] Ibid. XIX. 226. [d] Ibid. XVI. 513.
[e] Ibid.

Rienzo, the ſon of a miller. He propoſes to reſtore to the people their ancient republican government. Puniſhes with baniſhment and death ſome of the ancient nobility convicted of oppreſſion. Invites all the citizens of *Italy* to liberty. Foreign princes ſeek his alliance. Pope *Clement* is glad to countenance him, and deſires him to govern *Rome* in his name. Becomes quickly intoxicated with his authority, diſdains to depend on the pope. Loſes the people's favour. For in thoſe times no people would be free, unleſs the pope gave them leave. *Rienzo* aſſumes ſwelling titles. Irritates ſeveral princes needleſsly. The pope thunders out bulls againſt him. The bigotted people abandon him. He makes his eſcape, and ſculks about long in the habit of a pilgrim. The people, unworthy of liberty, ſink again into ſlavery [a].

Let us hear the excellent *Davenant* on this ſubject. 'And now to recapitulate the reaſons of this great 'people's ruin, firſt, their luxuries extinguiſhed an'cient honour, and in its room introduced irregular 'ambition; ambition brought on civil wars; civil 'war made ſingle perſons too conſiderable to remain 'afterwards in a private condition; ſo that the foun'dation of their deſtruction was laid in the century 'wherein *Cæſar* invaded their liberties: however, they 'might have continued a powerful and flouriſhing na'tion for many ages, if the ſucceeding princes had 'imitated either *Julius* or *Auguſtus*. But many of 'thoſe that followed, aſſumed to themſelves unlimited 'authority; and when bad emperors came, they 'pulled down what had been building up by the wiſ'dom of all their predeceſſors. They ſeized upon 'that treaſure which the frugality of preceding times 'had

[a] MOD. UNIV. HIST. XXVI. 43.

'had ſet aſide for urgent occaſions. They accounted 'the public revenues to be their own particular pro-'perty, and to be diſpoſed of at their pleaſure. Such 'as were laviſh, ſquandered away among their minions 'and favourites, that which was to maintain the dig-'nity of the ſtate. When their profuſion had reduced 'them to neceſſities, they fell to laying exorbitant 'taxes, and to pillage the remote provinces: when 'theſe provinces were haraſſed and exhauſted by con-'tinual payments, they became weak and unable to 'reſiſt foreign invaſions. In theſe naked and defence-'leſs provinces the barbarians neſtled themſelves, and 'when they were grown ſtrong and powerful, from 'thence they made irruptions into *Italy*, till at laſt 'they came to invade and conquer *Rome* itſelf, the 'very head and ſeat of the empire. From this brief 'account of the *Roman* affairs, perhaps it will appear, 'that to let miniſters waſte the public revenues, or 'to ſuffer any negligence and profuſion of the like 'nature, is of dangerous conſequence both to the 'prince and people[a].'

God forbid that ever any future political writer ſhould have occaſion to deſcribe and account for the decline and fall of the *Britiſh* empire, as *Davenant* has that of the *Roman*.

'It is of great conſequence to a kingdom, that reli-'gion and morals be conſidered as worthy the atten-'tion of perſons of high rank. There is no doubt, 'whatever might be pretended, theſe troubles [in 'France during the minority of Lewis XIV.] which 'were fatal to the lives of many, to the fortunes of 'more, and to the liberties of the whole nation, ſprung 'from the coquetries of half a dozen great ladies, who 'with

a *Daven.* III. 56.

'with light heads, and bad hearts, sacrificed every 'thing to their pleasures, according to the nature of 'the sex, who having forfeited one virtue, seldom re- 'spect any other[a].'

The welfare of all countries in the world depends upon the morals of their people. For though a nation may get riches by trade, thrift, industry, and from the benefit of its soil and situation; and though a people may attain to great wealth and power either by force of arms, or by the sagacity of their councils; yet when their manners are depraved, they will decline insensibly, and at last come to utter destruction. When a country is grown vicious, industry decays, the people become effeminate and unfit for labour. To maintain luxury, the great ones must oppress the meanest; and to avoid this oppression, the meaner sort are often compelled to seditious tumults or open rebellion. Such, therefore, who have modelled governments for any duration, have endeavoured to propose methods by which the riotous appetites, the lusts, avarice, revenge, ambition, and other disorderly passions of the people might be bounded[b].

To the sobriety, and temperate way of living, practised by the Dissenters retired to *America*, we may justly attribute the increase they have made there of inhabitants, which is beyond the usual proportion to be seen any where else. The supplies from hence do by no means answer their present numbers. It must then follow, that their thrift and regular manner of living incline them more, and make them more healthful for generation, and afford them better means of having the necessaries to sustain life, as wholesome food, and cleanly dwelling

[a] MOD. UNIV. HIST. XXV. 41.

[b] *Daven.* II. 41.

dwelling and apparel; the want of which, in other countries, is a high article in the burials of the common people.

Where riot and luxuries are not discountenanced, the inferior rank of men become presently infected, and grow lazy, effeminate, impatient of labour, and expensive, and, consequently, cannot thrive by trade and tillage; so that when we contemplate the great increase and improvements, which have been made in *New England*, *Carolina*, and *Pensylvania*, we cannot but think it injustice not to say, that a large share of this general good to these parts is owing to the education of their planters; which, if not entirely virtuous, has a show of virtue; and, if this were only an appearance, it is yet better for a people that are to subsist in a new country by traffic and industry, than the open profession and practice of lewdness, which is always attended with national decay and poverty[a].

Burnet is excellent, in the conclusion to his history of his own times, on the moral character of the people. He observes[b], that those of the commonalty of *England*, who attend the church, are grossly ignorant in matters of religion; the Dissenters more knowing; which is not owing to want of capacity, but of teaching. To cure this evil, the Bishop, very judiciously, advises the clergy to use two courses, *viz.* catechising, that is, explaining to young people, in a familiar manner, the first principles of religion, and of morality; and preaching in the same manner on the same subjects; applying their discourses to the characters of their audience, setting before them the evil nature and consequences of the vices they know them to be particularly addicted to.

---

[a] *Daven.* II. 33. [b] *Burn.* p. 428.

He

He gives a ſad account of the gentry of his times; which, it is to be hoped, would be too ſevere, if applied to thoſe of the preſent age. 'They are, ſays he, for 'the moſt part the worſt inſtructed, and the leaſt know-'ing of any of their rank I ever went among. The '*Scotch*, though leſs able to bear the expence of a learned 'education, are much more knowing.—A gentleman 'here is often both ill-taught, and ill-bred. This 'makes him haughty and inſolent. The gentry are not 'early acquainted with the principles of religion. So 'that after they have forgot their catechiſm, they ac-'quire no more new knowledge, but what they learn 'in plays and romances. They grow ſoon to find it a 'modiſh thing that looks like wit and ſpirit, to laugh 'at religion and virtue, and ſo they become crude and 'unpoliſhed infidels.—In the univerſities, inſtead of be-'ing formed to love their country and its conſtitution, 'laws, and liberties, they are rather diſpoſed to love 'arbitrary government, and to become ſlaves to ab-'ſolute monarchy[a].' He ſays, he has ſeen the nation three times in danger of ruin from men thus tainted, *viz.* 1. After the Reſtoration. 2. Under *James* II. And, 3. Under Queen *Anne*'s Tory miniſtry. If ſo, manners are of great conſequence in a ſtate; which likewiſe farther appears from what follows:

That excellent Prelate thought liberty a thing very eaſily loſt. 'I have ſeen, ſays he, the nation thrice on 'the brink of ruin, by men tainted with wrong prin-'ciples. After the Reſtoration, all were running faſt 'into ſlavery. Had *Charles* II. been, on his firſt re-'turn, attentive to thoſe bad deſigns, which he purſued 'afterwards with more caution, ſlavery and abſolute 'power might then have been ſettled into a law, with

[a] *Burn.* p. 439.

'a reve-

'a revenue able to maintain them. He played away 'that game without thought; and he had then honeſt 'miniſters, who would not ſerve him in it. After all 'that he did, during the courſe of his reign, it was 'ſcarce credible, that the ſame temper ſhould have re-'turned in his time: yet he recovered it in the laſt four 'years of his reign; and the gentry of *England* were as 'active and zealous to throw up all their liberties, as 'their anceſtors had ever been to preſerve them. This 'diſpoſition continued above half a year in his bro-'ther's reign; and he depended ſo much upon it, that 'he thought it could never go out of his hands. But 'he, or rather his prieſts, had the dexterity to play this 'game away likewiſe, and loſe it a ſecond time; ſo 'that at the Revolution, all ſeemed to come again to 'their wits. But men who have no principles, cannot 'be ſteady. Now, *A. D.* 1708, the greater part of 'the capital gentry ſeem to return again to a love of ty-'ranny, provided they may be the under-tyrants them-'ſelves; and they ſeem to be uneaſy at the court, when 'it will not be as much a court as they will have it. 'This is a folly of ſo ſingular a nature, that it wants 'a name. It is natural for poor men, who have little 'to loſe, and much to hope for, to become the inſtru-'ments of ſlavery; but it is an extravagance peculiar 'to our age, to ſee rich men in love with ſlavery and 'arbitrary power. The root of all this is, that our 'gentry are not betimes poſſeſſed of a true meaſure of 'ſolid knowledge and ſound religion, with a love to 'their country, a hatred of tyranny, and zeal for li-'berty [a].' He then gives ſome directions for improving our gentry's education.

[a] *Burnet*, IV. 431.

'Wherever the ſtate has, by means, which do not 'preſerve the virtue of the ſubject, effectually guarded 'its ſafety, remiſſneſs, and a neglect of the public, are 'likely to follow, and poliſhed nations of every de-'ſcription appear to encounter a danger on this quarter, 'proportioned to the degree in which they have, du-'ring any continuance, enjoyed the uninterrupted poſ-'ſeſſion of peace and proſperity [a].'

Il y a des mauvais examples, &c. 'Some bad ex-'amples are more miſchievous than crimes; and more 'ſtates have periſhed becauſe the people violated mo-'rals, than becauſe they broke the laws.' A people's being obliged to obſerve ſtrictly the laws and conſtitution of their country, is no ſign of a failure of liberty. 'Obſerve the power which the *Roman* cenſors had in 'the freeſt times of that commonwealth, even to the 'moſt ſevere reſtriction of private luxury in furniture, 'tables, clothing, and every article of living, which 'yet produced no complaint from the people; and, on 'the contrary, obſerve the unbridled licentiouſneſs of 'manners in the times of the moſt tyrannical of the 'emperors [b].

Nations have often been deceived into ſlavery by men of ſhining abilities. Miſerable is the ſpirit of a nation, that ſuffers itſelf to be enſlaved by ſhining metal. The *Romans* under *Julius* were delicately enſnared, and groſsly bribed. The *Engliſh* under *Walpole* were clumſily bought. The hero, the orator, the gentleman in *Julius* captivated many, and concealed the tyrant and uſurper. *Walpole* told his hirelings, 'I know your price; here it is.' A nation deceived into ruin, is like a fond but artleſs virgin debauched by her

[a] *Ferguſon's* Hist. Civ. Soc. 404.

[b] Grand. et Decad. des Rom. 96.

her lover on promiſe of marriage. Our caſe is that of a worthleſs bold wench, who *ſells* her maidenhead for a piece of money, or ſo much a year.

The collector of *Alm.* Deb. Com. writes very juciouſly on this ſubject, as follows:

'The profligacy of the common people, at this 'time, [about *A. D.* 1751,] called for ſome legal re'ſtraint; for not only every city and town, but al'moſt every village had aſſemblies of muſic, dancing, 'and gaming. This occaſioned a prodigious diſſipa'tion of the time, money, and morals of the lower 'people. Robberies were ſo frequent, that the enor'mity of the crime was almoſt effaced in the minds 'of the people; and nothing was more common than 'to advertiſe in the news-papers, an impunity to any 'perſon who could bring to a party that was robbed, 'the effects that had been taken from them, and that 'too with a reward according to the value. Thoſe 'diſorders were very juſtly aſcribed, in a great meaſure, 'to the extravagance of the common people, and there'fore a bill was brought in for the better preventing 'thefts and robberies, and for regulating places of pub'lic entertainment, and puniſhing people keeping diſ'orderly houſes. The operation of this bill, when it 'paſſed the houſe of commons, was confined to *Lon'don* and *Weſtminſter*, and twenty miles round; and 'all perſons within that circuit were required to take 'out licences from the juſtices of the peace of the 'county, aſſembled at their quarter ſeſſions, before 'they could open any room or place for public dancing, 'muſic, or any other entertainment of the like kind. 'Several other regulations regarding idle, diſorderly, or 'ſuſpected perſons and houſes, were inſerted in the 'ſame act, and pecuniary as well as corporal penal'ties were affixed to the tranſgreſſors. When this 'bill went to the house of lords, they thought so well 'of it, that they extended the operation of it all over '*England*. But as a tax was laid by it upon the sub-'ject, when they returned the bill to the house of com-'mons, their amendments were unanimously disagreed 'to, because they would not suffer the lords to alter 'any bill that was to affect the purse of the subject. 'They therefore desired a conference of the lords, and 'appointed a committee to draw up reasons against 'the amendments. The lords, on the other hand, 'having never formally given up their right to amend 'money bills, could not receive the true reason of the 'dissent of the commons, without giving up that 'right, or coming to an open breach with them. 'The commons therefore, to avoid so disagreeable an 'emergency, drew up reasons against the amendment, 'which had no regard or connection with the true rea-'son of their disagreeing with them; and the lords ra-'ther than so good a bill should be lost, agreed not to 'insist upon their amendments; and thus the bill 'passed, and received the royal assent [a].'

'Few crimes either private, or relating to the pub-'lic, can be committed by those whose minds are early 'seasoned with the principle of loving and promoting 'the welfare of their native country. For, generally 'speaking, all our vices whatsoever turn to her pre-'judice; and if we were convinced of this betimes, 'and if from our very youth we were seasoned with 'this notion, we should of course be virtuous, and 'our country would prosper and flourish in proportion 'to this amendment of our manners. Wherever pri-'vate men can be brought to make all their actions 'and counsels thoughts, and designments, to center in 'the

[a] *Alm.* DEB. COM. v. 29.

'the common good, that nation will ſoon gather ſuch 'ſtrength as ſhall reſiſt any home-bred miſchief, or 'outward accident. No great thing was ever done, 'but by ſuch as have preferred the love of their coun- 'try to all other conſiderations; and wherever this 'public ſpirit reigns, and where this zeal for the com- 'mon good governs in the minds of men, that ſtate 'will flouriſh, and increaſe in riches and power, and 'wherever it declines, or is ſet at nought, weakneſs, 'diſorder, and poverty muſt be expected. This love 'to their native ſoil, where it has been deeply rooted, 'and where it could be preſerved, has made little ci- 'ties famous and invincible, as *Sparta*, *Corinth*, *Thebes*, 'and *Athens*; and from thence all the *Roman* great- 'neſs took its riſe. But where they are wretchedly 'contriving their own ends, without any care of their 'country's profit, or trafficking its wealth and liberties, 'for rewards, preferments, and titles; where every 'one is ſnatching all he can; and where there is a ge- 'neral neglect of national intereſt, they grow luxuri- 'ous, proud, falſe, and effeminate; and a people ſo 'depraved, is commonly the prey of ſome neighbour 'ſeaſoned with more wiſe and better principles. In a 'kingdom but too near us, we may ſee all ſorts of 'men labouring for the public welfare, and every one as 'vigilant in his poſt, as if the ſucceſs of the whole 'empire depended on his ſingle care and diligence; ſo 'that, to the ſhame of another place, they ſeem more 'intent upon the proſperity and honour of their coun- 'try, under a hard and oppreſſive tyranny, than the in- 'habitants of ſome free nations, where the people have 'an intereſt in the laws, and are a part of the conſti- 'tution. *Homer* in his two poems ſeems to intend but 'two morals. In the ILIAD, to ſet out how fatal 'diſcord among the great ones is to ſtates and armies,

'And in his ODYSSEY, to show that the love of our 'own country ought to be stronger than any other 'passion; for he makes *Ulysses* quit the nymph *Calypso* 'with all her pleasure, and the immortality she had 'promised him, to return to *Ithaca*, a rocky and barren 'island. The affairs of a country relating either to 'civil government, war, the revenues, or trade, can 'never be well and prosperously conducted, unless the 'men of principal rank and figure divest themselves of 'their passions, self-interest, overweening opinion of 'their own merits, their flattery, false arts, mean am-'bition, irregular appetites, and pursuits after wealth 'and greatness. No people did ever become famous 'and powerful, but by temperance, fortitude, justice, 'reverence to the laws, and piety to the country. 'And when any empire is destined to be undone, or 'to lose its freedom, the seeds of this ruin are to be 'first seen in the corruption of its manners. In vi-'cious governments, all care of the public is laid aside; 'and every one is plundering for himself, as if the 'commonwealth were adrift, or had suffered ship-'wreck; and where a people is thus depraved, their na-'tional assemblies have the first open marks of the in-'fection upon them, from whence spring all disorders 'in the state whatsoever. For then such as have most 'eloquence, valour, skill in business, and most interest 'in their country, throw off the mask of popularity, 'which they had put on for a time, and in the face of 'the world desire wealth, honours, and greatness, upon 'any terms; and this ambition leads them to corrupt 'others, that their own natural vices may be the less 'observed; so that in a constitution ripe for change, 'those who are best esteemed, and most trusted, begin 'to buy the people's voice, and afterwards expose to 'sale their own suffrages; which practice is always

'attended

'attended with utter destruction, or the loss of liberty. 'This error in the first concoction does presently de'prave the whole mass; for then the dignities of the 'commonwealth are made the reward of fraud and 'vice, and not the recompence of merit. All is 'bought and sold, and the worst men who can af'ford to bid highest, are accepted; and where the ma'nagement is once got into such hands, factions are 'suffered to grow; rash counsels are embraced, and 'wholesome advices rejected; every one is busy for 'himself, and careless of the common interest; 'treachery is winked at, and private persons are al'lowed to become wealthy by the public spoils; all 'which is followed with the loss of reputation abroad, 'and poverty at home [a].'

Mr. *Sydenham*, in the debate, *A. D.* 1744, on the motion for annual parliaments, argues, that long parliaments produce, and increase corruption of manners in the people. 'Sir, says he, the middling people in 'this country have always, till of late years, been re'markable for their bravery, generosity, and hospita'lity, and those of inferior rank for their honesty, 'frugality, and industry. These are the virtues which 'raised this nation to that height of glory, riches, and 'power it had once arrived at; but these virtues are every 'one of them in danger of being utterly extinguished 'by ministerial corruption at elections, and in par'liament. For proving this, I have no occasion to 'appeal to any thing but experience under the late ad'ministration, the decay of every one of these virtues, 'and the causes of that decay became so visible to 'every thinking man in the kingdom, that the whole 'nation, except the very tools of the minister, joined 'in putting an end to his power, and thank God, with 'the help of a very extraordinary conjuncture at court;

[a] *Daven.* II. 48.

'we at last in some degree succeeded in our endeavours. 'For this reason I say I need not appeal to any thing 'but experience, for shewing what an effect public 'corruption has upon private as well as public vir- 'tue; but as it may be proved by reason, as well as 'experience, and as I think it necessary to take ad- 'vantage of every argument that can be thought of 'for establishing the truth of this proposition, I shall 'beg leave to consider separately every one of the vir- 'tues I have mentioned, in order to shew from the 'reason of things how necessarily it must decay, in pro- 'portion as public corruption is introduced. And first 'with regard to courage or bravery. Though courage 'or resolution, Sir, depends in some measure upon the 'nature or constitution of the man, yet it may be very 'much increased or diminished by custom and educa- 'tion, and especially by public rewards bestowed upon, 'or refused to those who have shewn any remarkable 'degree of it in the service of their country. In for- 'mer times, and when we had an honest and wise ad- 'ministration, the chief method by which our nobi- 'lity and gentry could recommend themselves to the 'esteem of their country, or the favour of their so- 'vereign, was by their courage, and military capacity; 'and the same consideration made them take notice of 'those that were in any station below them, which 'propagated a brave and military spirit among all ranks 'of men in the kingdom. In those days our ministers 'did not desire any man in parliament to vote as they 'directed. They desired no man to vote, but accord- 'ing to the dictates of his own conscience, and there- 'fore they never thought of rewarding those who ap- 'proved, much less of punishing those who disapproved, 'of their measures in parliament. At elections again, 'though a seat in parliament was always reckoned ho-

'nourable

'nourable, yet as it was in ancient times reckoned rather burdensome than profitable, there was never any violent competition at the election, and consequently the person chosen never thought himself much obliged to those who voted for him, nor did they so much as expect any favours from him upon that account alone. But no sooner did ministers begin to solicit the votes, instead of convincing the reason of the members of parliament, then they began to think themselves obliged to reward those who complied with their solicitations; and soon after this practice was introduced, a seat in parliament became profitable as well as honourable, which of course begot violent competition at elections; and this made voters begin to claim a merit with those in favour of whom they gave their vote at any election.

Hinc prima mali tabes. VIRG.

'From henceforth, Sir, the natural channel through which all public honours and preferments flowed, began to be disused, and betraying our country to the will of a minister in parliaments or at elections, began to be the only channel through which a man could expect any honours or preferment. When this began, or whether it has not met with some interruptions since it first began, I shall not determine; but this I will say, that it never became so apparent as it did under the late administration; and I wish we may not fatally feel the consequence of it in the war we are now engaged in. The natural courage of Englishmen is not by any discouragements to be absolutely extinguished; but I wish it may not have taken a wrong turn: I wish we may not find that the courage of our men is become rather an avaricious than an ambitious courage, and that men now seek to raise by their courage their private fortunes rather than 'their own or their country's glory; for if that be the 'case, we may make good pirates or maroders, but we 'shall never, while this spirit remains, make good sol- 'diers or seamen; and no man, I believe, can expect 'that we should be able to put a glorious end to the 'war either by piracy or maroding. Courage, Sir, 'like many other good qualities, becomes laudable only 'according to the use that is made of it, and the mo- 'tives upon which it is founded; for a man who ven- 'tures his life with no other view but that of raising 'his own private fortune, differs from a common high- 'wayman in nothing but this, that the one plunders 'according to law, the other against it. When I say 'this, Sir, I hope it will not be thought, that I intend 'to reflect upon any of those brave men who have 'ventured their lives in taking prizes from the enemies 'of their country: for as they thereby weaken the 'enemy, it is a public service as well as a private ad- 'vantage; and when the first of these motives is their 'chief inducement, which I hope it always is with re- 'gard to the officers at least, they deserve the esteem and 'applause of their country. From such gentlemen we 'may expect an equal behaviour, where nothing but 'blows and triumphs are to be got from the enemy; 'but this is not to be expected from those who have 'nothing but the prize in view. This sort of courage, 'which proceeds from sordid avarice, I have mentioned, 'Sir, only to shew that we are not to suppose, that all 'the bold actions we read of in our journals, proceed 'from that true and generous spirit of courage by 'which our ancestors were actuated; nor are we to 'judge of the spirit of a people from what appears in 'their regular armies or navies, because a spirit of 'courage may for some time be preserved in the armies 'or navies of a country, after it has been industriously 'depressed

'depreſſed among all other ranks of men. The only 'way to judge in this caſe, is to conſider the conduct 'and behaviour of the gentlemen of fortune in that 'country, the methods they take to recommend them-'ſelves to the eſteem of their country, and the qualifica-'tions which recommend thoſe of inferior rank to their 'favour; and from theſe conſiderations we muſt conclude, 'that the ancient ſpirit of the people of this nation is now 'almoſt entirely extinct. Do we now ſee any gentleman of 'fortune who is not of the army or navy, endeavouring 'to recommend himſelf by his courage or military 'knowledge? Do we now hear of the armies of foreign 'princes being encouraged by the example of a crowd 'of Engliſh volunteers? Do we now hear of any 'gentleman's encouraging his tenants and ſervants to 'make themſelves maſters of military diſcipline, or 'conferring diſtinguiſhing favours upon thoſe who have 'ſhewn great courage and reſolution upon any occa-'ſion? Few ſuch examples are to be met with in our 'preſent ſtory; and the reaſon is plain: All public fa-'vours are now beſtowed upon voting, not fighting. 'If a man be qualified to vote, he has no occaſion for 'any other qualification; and of late years, even in 'our army or navy, it has appeared to be the beſt qua-'lification for entitling a man to preferment. We 'muſt therefore demoliſh this ſuperſtructure, which has 'been raiſed by corruption. We muſt render it im-'poſſible for a miniſter to expect to gain a majority in 'parliament, or at election, either by bribery or by a 'proper diſpenſation of places and preferments. I ſay, 'we muſt do this, if we intend to reſtore that ſpirit of 'bravery by which our anceſtors preſerved their liber-'ties, and gained ſo much glory to their country; and 'for this purpoſe nothing can, in my opinion, be ſo 'effectual as the reſtoration of annual parliaments.

'Then,

'Then, Sir, as to the generosity and hospitality of our 'nobility and gentry, every one knows, that by long 'parliaments and corrupt elections, they have been 'banished almost entirely out of the country; for I hope 'it will not be called generosity, to give a country 'fellow, by express bargain, five or ten guineas for his 'vote; and as little will it, I hope, be called hospitality 'to make a county or borough drunk once in seven 'years, by way of preparation for an ensuing election. 'In former times most of our noblemen and gentlemen 'lived at their country seats, where they often gene-'rously relieved such of the poor in the neighbourhood 'as were in real distress; and they daily entertained 'their friends and neighbours at their houses, not with 'luxuries and extravagant feasts, but with a plentiful 'and hospitable table. By these methods they recom-'mended themselves to the favour of their country, or 'of some neighbouring city or borough, and in return, 'if they desired it, they had sometimes the honour con-'ferred upon them of representing it in parliament, 'which being but of short duration, it never induced 'them to think of altering their method of living, or of 'leaving their seat in the country. But since the in-'troduction of septennial parliaments, and with them 'of course the practice of downright bribery at all 'elections, this method of living has been entirely 'altered, and no wonder it should be so; for suppose a 'gentleman to have lived in the most generous and 'hospitable manner in his country, or in the neigh-'bourhood of his borough; suppose such a gentleman 'sets up for their representative, down comes a cour-'tier with his pockets full of public money, and offers 'the electors, or such of them as will vote for him, seven 'guineas a man: by such an offer the country gentle-'man's friendship, his generosity, his hospitality, are

'all

'all at once effaced out of the memories of many of 'them, and he is thereby defeated of his election. Is it 'not natural for ſuch a gentleman to reſolve, not to 'put himſelf any more to the trouble and expence of 'being generous and hoſpitable? The favour of his 'countrymen he ſees muſt be purchaſed, not won; 'therefore he reſolves to contract his expence, in order 'to prepare the proper ammunition for the next elec-'tion; and if he ſucceeds, being then aſſured of his ſeat 'in parliament for ſeven years, and ſenſible that being 'in the country can be of no ſervice to him on any 'future election, he retires with his family to *London*, 'and reſolves to depend upon bribery alone for his ſuc-'ceſs in every future election. Thus, Sir, an end is 'put to the generoſity and hoſpitality of that gentle-'man, and thus an end has already been put to the 'generoſity and hoſpitality of moſt of the noblemen and 'gentlemen of the kingdom. But this is not the only 'evil, for this change of a country life into a town life, 'has introduced a new ſort of expence, which is of the 'moſt pernicious conſequence to the kingdom in ge-'neral, and to the landed intereſt in particular. By 'the ancient country hoſpitality a great deal was, it is 'true, conſumed, but the conſumption was all our 'own: almoſt the whole, excepting a few ſpiceries, was 'the produce of our own farmers; whereas the expence 'attending a town life is moſtly laid out on things 'of foreign importation, and moſt of them of ſuch a 'a nature as tend to deprive us of every good quality 'we have left among us. One modern polite ſupper 'in town, with a ſet of Italian muſicians to entertain 'the company, will now coſt as much as would formerly 'have hoſpitably entertained a whole country for a 'week; with this difference, that the expence of the 'latter centered chiefly in the pocket of the neighbour-'ing

'ing farmers, whereas the expence of the former centers chiefly in the pocket of foreigners, and thoſe foreigners, perhaps, who are our moſt dangerous enemies. When I conſider this, Sir, I do not wonder at the heavy complaints we hear among the farmers in all parts of the kingdom, for want of a market for their goods, nor do I wonder at ſo many of them becoming bankrupt. A man of fortune who lives in *London*, may, in plays, operas, routs, aſſemblies, French cookery, French ſauces, and French wines, ſpend as much yearly as he could do, were he to live in the moſt hoſpitable manner at his ſeat in the country; but will any one ſuppoſe, that there is as much malt, meat, bread, or poultry conſumed in his family? Will any one ſuppoſe, that the poor, or even the farmers and tradeſmen, in the neighbourhood of his country-ſeat conſume as much, when they have nothing but what they take from their own table, as when they had his hall to feaſt in? What a diminution then in country conſumptions muſt the retiring of one great family make? What a diſtreſs muſt be brought upon a country, eſpecially if remote from *London*, when all its rich families repair to live conſtantly in this city? Sir, the fatal conſequences brought upon our land eſtates by thus tempting our rich families to live conſtantly in *London*, are ſo glaring, that I ſhall wonder to ſee any landed gentleman in this houſe oppoſe the motion; and if any of them do, I ſhall be very apt to ſuppoſe they have ſome other income leſs honourable, though perhaps more punctual; for that annual parliaments would ſend moſt of our rich families to the country, and reſtore our ancient generoſity and hoſpitality, is a queſtion that can admit of no diſpute; becauſe no gentleman could then preſerve his intereſt in his 'country, city, or borough, but by going to live 'amongst them; and if by neglecting to live there he 'should be turned out of parliament, I believe the most 'courtly dame could hardly prevail upon the most uxo- 'rious husband to live in *London*, after having nothing to 'do there but to see her play at quadrille. I now come, 'Sir, to those good qualities or virtues for which the 'inferior rank of our people were very remarkable. 'These, I said, were honesty, frugality, and industry. 'As to every one of these, the manners of our people 'have been very much altered by the introduction of 'septennial parliaments, and the corruption and vio- 'lent contestation at elections, which have thereby of 'course been propagated through the whole king- 'dom. With regard to the honesty of the people, 'perhaps an instance may be here and there found of a 'man who acts honestly in private life, and yet has 'made it his practice to sell his vote to the best bidder. 'But I will say, that such a man's honesty proceeds 'more from the fear of the gallows than from any na- 'tural disposition; and it is well known that few men 'jump at once into the height of wickedness. They 'generally begin with little venial sins, and move by 'degrees to the most aggravating crimes. Do not 'most of the wretches that suffer at Tyburn tell us, 'that they began their wicked course with a breach of 'the sabbath? This is none of the most heinous sort of 'crimes; but the danger consists in the first encroach- 'ment upon conscience; for being once got into a 'wicked course they seldom stop at the threshold. In 'the same manner a man who sells his vote at an elec- 'tion, to a candidate who he thinks will sell his coun- 'try in parliament, must be sensible he has committed 'a crime: In so doing he certainly acts against his 'conscience, and by this means his acting against his 'conscience,

'conſcience, becomes familiar to him, which prepares 'him for the committing of any crime he thinks he may 'be ſafe in, and then if he commits no crime in private 'life, it is not for want of will, but for want of oppor-'tunity. He is honeſt, juſt as ſome women are chaſte, 'only becauſe they never had an opportunity of being 'otherwiſe. The only difference is, that he becomes 'wicked by cuſtom, whereas they are ſo by nature. 'We ſhould, therefore, in order to preſerve the honeſty 'of our people, prevent, as much as poſſible, a man's 'being tempted to ſell his vote at an election, and the 'beſt method for doing this will be to reſtore annual 'parliaments, becauſe no candidate will then be at the 'expence of corrupting, eſpecially as he cannot expect 'to be corrupted by a miniſter after he is choſen. 'Now, Sir, with regard to the frugality of the people, 'we know by experience, that what people get by ſell-'ing their votes at an election, is generally ſpent in 'extravagance; and being once led into an extravagant 'manner of living, few of them ever leave it, as long 'they have a penny to ſupport it. By this means they 'are led into neceſſities, and having once broke in upon 'their conſcience, by ſelling their vote at an election, 'they are the leſs proof againſt thoſe temptations they 'are expoſed to by their neceſſities; ſo that I am per-'ſuaded, many a poor man in this kingdom has been 'brought to the gallows by the bribe he received for his 'vote at an election. Beſides, as all the little places 'under the government have of late been beſtowed 'upon pliable voters at elections, without requiring 'any one other quality to recommend them, ſuch 'voters generally diſſipate their own ſubſtance, in 'hopes of being afterwards provided for by ſome little 'place in government; and, by the example of ſuch 'voters, many of their neighbours are led into the

'ſame

'same extravagant course of living, which, I believe, 'is one great cause of that luxury which now so gene-'rally prevails among the lower sort of people. The 'same causes, Sir, that promote the people's extrava-'gance prevent their being industrious. Whilst a 'little country freeholder or tradesman is spending in 'extravagance his infamous earnings at an election, he 'disdains to think of honest industry or labour; and 'being once got out of the road of industry, many of 'them cannot find their way into it again. If such 'fellows are not provided by the court candidate who 'was chosen by their venality, with some little post in 'the government, which all expect, but few are so 'lucky as to meet with, they soon become bankrupts, 'are thrown into prison, and their families a burden 'upon the country which they have sold and betrayed. 'This is the fate of most of them; and as to those who 'happen to be provided for, their good luck is of the 'most pernicious consequence in the neighbourhood, 'because it encourages others to become venal, in 'hopes of meeting with the same good fortune; for 'in this case it is the same as in a lottery, people over-'look the thousands that are unfortunate, and take no-'tice only of the happy few that get the great prizes: 'If it were not for this unaccountable humour in man-'kind, no man would be an adventurer in a lottery; no 'man, even in this corrupt age, would sell his vote at 'an election. But whilst this humour remains, which 'it will do as long as the race of man subsists, there 'will be adventurers, there will be sellers. There is 'no preventing it, but by demolishing the market; 'and this, I think, will be the effect of the bill now 'proposed to you, if it be passed into a law: it will de-'molish the market of corruption, both in this house 'and at every election in the kingdom, for ministers 'will not then corrupt, because they can expect no 'success by corruption; and though little contests 'may now and then happen among country gentlemen, 'yet they will never be so violent as to occasion cor-'ruption on either side of the question. On the con-'trary, Sir, I believe very few contests will ever happen 'among the country gentlemen; for in every county, 'city, and borough in the kingdom, the chief families 'will come to a compromise amongst themselves, and 'agree to take the honour by turns, of representing it 'in parliament. No man will grudge his neighbour the 'honour for one year, when he knows he is to have the 'same honour the next year, or in a year or two after, 'especially when that honour is to be attended with no 'expectation of any post, place, or pension from the 'crown, unless he can recommend himself to it by some 'other qualification: whereas, when a gentleman is to 'be chosen into parliament for seven years, and when 'his being a member, without so much as the appear-'ance of any other qualification, is known to be suffi-'cient for recommending or rather enlisting him to some 'place of great profit under the crown, I do not wonder 'at his often meeting with a violent opposition. The 'length of the term makes any such compromise as I have 'mentioned impossible, which of course creates him an-'tagonists among those who are only ambitious of the 'honour; and the expectation of advantage creates 'him antagonists, among those who are resolved to 'make their market. This generally begets a violent 'opposition; and if the antagonist be one of the better 'sort, he generally has recourse to bribery; for as he is 'resolved to sell, he makes no scruple to purchase, if 'he thinks he can purchase for less than he may sell. 'These, Sir, are the causes why we find such violent 'contests about elections to septennial parliaments;

'and

'and as all these causes would cease the moment we 'made our parliaments annual, I think it is next to a 'demonstration, that in elections for annual parliaments there could be no violent opposition, and much 'less any bribery or corruption. Therefore, if we have 'a mind restore the practice of these virtues, for which 'our ancestors were so conspicuous, and by which they 'handed down to us riches, glory, renown, and liberty, 'we must restore the custom of having parliaments not 'only annually held but annually chosen.'

Very excellent is the speech of Sir *J. Philips* in the house of commons, *A. D.* 1745, on this subject [a].

SIR,

'The opinion my honourable friend has of what we 'ought to do upon this occasion, and the addition he 'has proposed to be made to our address, viz. promising the king, that the house would frame bills for 'checking abuses, and restraining corruption, are so 'agreeable to my way of thinking, that I cannot avoid 'standing up to second his motion, I shall readily concur with those gentlemen who think that we ought 'upon this occasion to express, in the warmest terms, 'our loyalty to our king, and our steady resolution to 'support him against all his enemies, both foreign and 'domestic; and I hope they will concur with me, and 'I believe many other gentlemen in this house, that we 'ought at the same time, and with the same energy, to 'express our fidelity to our country, and our steady resolution to support the liberties of the people against 'the fatal effects of corruption, which, in my opinion, 'are as much to be dreaded as any effects that can ensue from the success of the present rebellion. From 'arbitrary power established in our present royal family,

[a] *Alm.* Deb. Com. 11. 336.

'and supported by a corrupt parliament, and a mercenary standing army, I shall grant, Sir, we are in no immediate danger of popery; but the certain consequence will be a general depravity of manners, and a total extinction of religion of every kind; and then if chance, or any foreign view should make some future king even of our present royal family, turn papist, which is far from being impossible, how could we guard against the introduction and establishment of popery? To a man who has no religion at all, it signifies nothing what sort of religion is established; for he will always make that sort or sect his profession, which he finds most suitable to his interest, consequently such a king would meet with no opposition from the people; and our laws against popery would be no bar to his intentions, because every one of them would at his desire be repealed by a corrupt parliament; therefore the only sure and lasting fence we can have against popery is, the preservation of our constitution. Whilst the people continue to have any religion, and are generally sincere protestants, no king, should he turn papist himself, can have it in his power to introduce, much less establish popery amongst us, if the people be freely and fairly represented in parliament; but a government that proposes to support itself by corruption, must at the same time endeavour to abolish all principles of honour and religion; for a man who has any principle of either, will never frame any selfish motive, give his vote in parliament, or at elections, against what he knows to be the true interest of his country. Such a government must necessarily conduct itself in direct opposition to all the maxims of true policy. Merit of every kind will be disregarded, religion will be laughed at, and patriotism turned into ridicule. Libertinism will

'be

'be encouraged, avarice will be fed, and luxury will 'be propagated, in order to render the operation of 'corruption the more easy, and its effect the more cer- 'tain. And when the people are generally and tho- 'roughly corrupted, which, because of our frequent 'elections, they must be before the government can 'for its support depend upon corruption alone, the 'church of *Rome*, whose politicks we have more rea- 'son to dread than her power, will have a much more 'easy and certain game to play, than that of forcing 'the Pretender upon us. This, Sir, they can never do 'as long as we have any religion, virtue, or courage 'amongst us, and should they by an extraordinary 'mischance succeed, the Pretender and they together, 'would find it a very difficult task to convert a whole 'nation of religious and sincere protestants to popery: 'besides, they could not be sure of the Pretender's not 'serving them as *Henry* II. of *France* served the pro- 'testants of that kingdom: after they had helped him 'to the throne, supposing him to be a man of sense 'and no bigot, he might very probably for his own 'ease and security, declare himself of the same religion 'with the majority of his subjects. But should we 'lose our liberties by corruption, and of course our 'religion and virtue, if the church of *Rome* could find 'means to convert our king then upon the throne, their 'business would be done. Our nobility having no 'religion, would in complaisance, or in order to re- 'commend themselves to their sovereign, declare 'themselves papists; and the majority of the people 'having as little religion as they, would follow their 'example. Surely, Sir, it will not be said to be impos- 'sible to suppose that any future king, even of our pre- 'sent royal family, can ever be converted to popery. 'How many kings have been persuaded to change their 'religion by a favourite wife or mistress? How many 'from political views? The crown of *Poland*, but of 'late years made one protestant prince declare himself 'papist, though all his then subjects were protestants 'too. The imperial crown of *Germany* we know is 'elective; and a view to that crown may induce some 'future king of *Great Britain* to declare himself papist; 'if he has a corrupt parliament, they will be ready at 'his desire, to repeal that law by which papists are ex- 'cluded from the crown and government of these 'realms. We have therefore no infallible security 'against popery, but the preservation of our constitu- 'tion, and for this reason, nothing can be more pro- 'per than to declare our resolution, that we will take 'care to frame such bills as are necessary for the pre- 'servation of our constitution against corruption, at 'the same time, that we declare our resolution to sup- 'port his majesty against a popish Pretender. This is 'not only proper, Sir, but necessary upon the present 'occasion, in order to convince the world that we are 'true protestants, as well as loyal subjects, and that 'therefore we are resolved to keep every door bolted, 'by which popery can make its way into this king- 'dom; and if we are resolved to frame and pass, in 'this session, any bills that may be effectual against 'corruption, I am sure no objection can be made against 'our declaring in our address that we will do so. I 'hope we are all now convinced that some such bills 'are necessary. The danger we are now exposed to, 'and the present unlucky circumstances of *Europe* must 'convince every man of the necessity of our having 'such bills passed into laws; for the danger our liber- 'ties are now exposed to, and the danger to which the 'liberties of *Europe* are now exposed, are both evi- 'dently owing to the measures of a late administra- 'tion.

'tion. Meaſures that could never have been approved 'of by a Britiſh parliament, if the eyes of ſome gentle- 'men's underſtandings had not been blinded by the 'lucrative places they expected, or thoſe they were 'afraid to loſe. The fatal conſequence of thoſe mea- 'ſures were then foretold, and are now ſo plainly ſeen, 'that thoſe who approved of them, if they ſpeak in- 'genuouſly, muſt confeſs their having been miſled. I 'am far from ſaying, Sir, that any gentleman who had 'the honour to repreſent his country in parliament, 'voted againſt the dictates of his conſcience; but it is 'a failing of human nature to judge weakly, in caſes 'where our private intereſt is concerned, which we 'may be daily convinced of by many law-ſuits, that 'are obſtinately carried on by men even of the beſt ſenſe 'in the kingdom. We muſt therefore baniſh, as much 'as poſſible, all private intereſt from this houſe, other- 'wiſe we can never expect to have the queſtions that 'come before us impartially conſidered, or rightly de- 'termined. For this purpoſe, Sir, I hope every gen- 'tleman is now convinced, that ſome new bills are ne- 'ceſſary, and if we are reſolved to frame any ſuch in 'this ſeſſion, why ſhould we not ſay ſo in our addreſs 'upon this occaſion? I can ſuggeſt to myſelf no rea- 'ſon againſt it, and I am very ſure it will give great 'ſatisfaction without doors. From hence, I muſt ſup- 'poſe, that my honoured friends motion will meet 'with no oppoſition, and therefore I ſhall add no more; 'but conclude with heartily ſeconding it.'

A bill was brought in *A. D.* 1659, under the com- commonwealth, that no man ſhould ſit in the houſe of commons, who was looſe in his morals, or profane in his behaviour.'

One would imagine, that, at all times, thoſe who have the weight of government upon their ſhoulders, ſhould be particularly anxious about the public favour, with a view to the cheerful obedience of the ſubjects. But in modern times (the preſent always excepted) courts, miniſters, and parliaments ſeem to have given up the eſteem of the people, as an object of no conſequence; for every body knows, the eſteem of the people can only be kept by keeping incorrupt characters. At the ſame time our governors (the preſent always excepted) affect to wonder at the diſobedience of the people.

'In bad times, men of bad morals have ever been 'picked out, as the fitteſt inſtruments of enſlaving 'others; and in free ſtates the men of virtue have been 'the known preſervers of the public liberty [a].' 'Thoſe 'who are guilty of fraud or oppreſſion in their private 'capacity, are never to be depended on in a public [b].' 'The Marquis of *Halifax* [c] ſays, great drinkers ought 'not to ſerve in parliament.'

When men have intereſt to get themſelves choſen to places and employments, for which they are totally unfit, there is reaſon to fear the government, under which that happens, is corrupt.

Cæſar had intereſt to get himſelf choſen *pontifex maximus*. A hopeful archbiſhop! Strongly accuſed of the moſt ſhameful of vices, and notoriouſly guilty of every kind of injuſtice, rapine, and violence. *Pompey* uſed to call him the *Roman Ægyſthus*. And we know, that *Ægyſthus*, after debauching *Agamemnon*'s queen, procured him to be murdered [d].

Abilities are undoubtedly of great conſequence in a public character. But virtue is infinitely more important. An honeſt man of moderate abilities may fill a moderate

[a] Serious Address, &c. 10. [b] Ibid. [c] Ibid. 11.

[d] Ant. Univ. Hist. xii. 145.

moderate station with advantage. A knave confounds whatever he meddles with, and therefore cannot safely be employed. But in a corrupt state, that which should give a man the greatest consequence, I mean integrity, gives him the least. Both abilities and integrity are eclipsed by riches. For want of the proper abilities, the same person may be a good man, and a bad king, magistrate, or general. But it is a horrid reproach to a public man, to say, he has a bad private character; because his example will produce infinite mischief, and because the man who as an individual is wicked, is not likely to be good as a prince, a minister, a magistrate, &c. Employing in stations of power and trust men of notorious bad characters, is disgracing the age in which it was done; for it supposes a want of better men, and endangers the state.

The great and good *Sertorius* would not suffer *Mithridates* king of *Pontus* to re-conquer those parts of *Asia*, which, in virtue of his treaty with *Sylla*, he had been forced to give up to the Romans. *Sertorius* would have been a great gainer, by only conniving at this injury to his country, which he might have done in such a manner, as to avoid suspicion. But that brave *Roman* would not know himself to be false to his country, for any consideration whatever [a]. The employers of worthless men are disgraced; and bad men advanced to high stations, are pilloried, that they may be the more effectually pelted.

"Men will never [if they be wise] trust the important concerns of society to one, who they know will do what is hurtful to society for his own pleasure:" A sentiment of Mr. Boswell's, in his Account of Corsica, p. 302. N. B. Mr. Boswell, when he wrote that book,

[a] *Plut.* in *Sertor.* Πεμπει δε πρεσβεις ὁ Μιθριδατες εις Ιβεριαν, κ.τ.λ.

book, was but just of age, and was employed in improving himself by study and travel, while many of his equals in years and fortune were in pursuit of debauchery.

Let no bad man be trusted. *Aurelian* gave up *Heraclammon*, who had betrayed his country to him, to be cut to pieces, saying, It was vain to expect fidelity in the man who had betrayed his own country[a]. He gave the traitor's estate to his family, lest it should be alleged, that he ordered him to be made away with for the sake of his money.

It was enacted in the time of *Henry* VI, that no keepers of public stews in Southwark should be impannelled upon juries, because supposed to be unconscientious persons[b]. I do not pretend to support the character of the persons who kept those famous houses of reception, which, by the bye, are said to have been under the government of the good bishops of Winchester; but thus far I will venture to say, that it would be a very difficult task for a worthy lord, or an illustrious patriot, who, for the sake of pleasure merely, keeps a wh—— in open violation of the most solemn vows a man can make, and in direct defiance of damnation, to shew that he is more worthy of being impannelled on a jury, as being a more conscientious person than the poor keeper of a bawdy-house, who may be faithful to his own spouse, who never had taken a vow upon him at the altar never to keep a bawdy-house, and who keeps it merely for the sake of getting a livelihood.

See *King*'s very judicious and learned ESSAY ON THE ENGLISH CONSTITUTION AND GOVERNMENT, printed for *White*, in which the author shews, by observations

[a] ANT. UNIV. HIST. XV. 456.

[b] PARL. HIST. II. 235.

ſervations on a number of ſtates, ancient and modern, that freedom or ſlavery will prevail in a country according as the diſpoſitions and manners of the inhabitants render them fit for one or the other. And to the ſame purpoſe, *Hurd's* DIALOGUES, *Hume*, *Monteſquieu*, *Rollin*, &c,

---

CHAP. II.

Luxury hurtful to Manners, and dangerous to States.

THE wiſe ancients thought luxury more dangerous to ſtates, than the attacks of foreign enemies.

——— ſævior armis
Luxuria incubuit. LUCAN.

For that a brave people will find that in themſelves which will repel foreign force; whilſt a people enervated by luxury are but a nation of women and children,

The hardy *Spartans*, a handful of men, but thoſe true *men*, baffled the attacks of *Xerxes*'s world in arms. The *Romans*, while they kept up their martial ſpirit and diſcipline, were too hard for all the nations around them, and conquered almoſt as often as they fought. Afterwards, being debauched by the Emperors, they fell an eaſy prey to the hardy *Goths*, *Alans*, *Hunns*, &c. The inconſiderable ſtates of *Holland*, a handful of people living in a marſh, reſiſted for ſeventy years, and at laſt baffled the mighty *Spaniſh* monarchy, and forced them to give up all claim to ſuperiority over the *Netherlands*; which was, in fact, conquering *Spain*, and ſtripping her of part of her former dominion. *Spain* was enervated by luxury, the effect of the introduction of gold from the mines of *South America*, whilſt the hardy

hardy *Dutch*, unexperienced in the enfeebling arts, fought for civil and religious liberty, with an obſtinacy never to be tamed or tired out.

It may therefore be ſtarted by ſome readers, that however dangerous luxury may be, we have nothing to fear from that quarter; for that in the late war the *Britiſh* arms were univerſally victorious, beyond all paſt example. That therefore luxury can as yet have produced no material effect in this happy country, and cannot be counted among the abuſes, of which thoſe collections profeſs to be a ſurvey, and an inquiry into the means for correcting.

But to ſet this matter in its true light, there are ſeveral particulars reſpecting the conduct of the late war, to be recollected, as, for inſtance, that the expence laid out by *Britain* in the late war, was beyond all example; which gives us a *claim* to extraordinary ſucceſs; that we took upon *ourſelves* the whole weight of the war, truſting nothing to *allies*; that, according to Lord *Chatham*'s account of the matter [a], who himſelf conducted the war in its moſt glorious times, our ſucceſs was chiefly owing to the hardy *Scots*, among whom it is certain, that luxury has yet made no conſiderable progreſs.

But beſides all this, it is to be remembered, that there are other effects naturally to be expected from the prevalency of luxury in a country, altogether as dangerous as this, of its tendency to break the martial ſpirit of a people. Every man, in proportion to his degeneracy into luxury, becomes more and more obnoxious to bribery and corruption. He finds wants and deſires before unknown; and theſe wants and deſires being *artificial* merely, are without all *bounds* and *limits*. For the whole world is not enough for one fantaſtic voluptuary; while a very little ſatisfies nature.

Then

[a] See his ſpeech on the *American* ſtamp-act.

Then he becomes an eaſy prey to the bribing candidate at an election; then he is ready to ſell his ſoul to the enemy of mankind, and his country to the French king, in obedience to the order from the miniſter, who pays him the damning penſion, and directs when he is to vote evil to be good, and darkneſs to be light.

Again, it is notorious, that luxury and expenſive living, produce infinite peculation of the public money, and infidelity in thoſe employed by the public.

It has been diſputed, but, I think, with little force of argument on one ſide of the queſtion, Whether the avaricious man or the ſpendthrift is the worſe member of ſociety?

The avaricious man is ever ſcraping and heaping up, and what he ſaves perhaps he locks up in his ſtrong box, to the prejudice of commerce and the injury of thoſe, whom he ruins by cheating, uſury, pettifogging, &c. But he will not venture upon any bold and extenſive miſchief. He keeps within the letter of the law, however he may overleap the bounds of juſtice; for he has the fear of the pillory and the gibbet before his eyes.

With the prodigal, on the contrary, it is always neck or nothing. He will commit the moſt daring villany, for the ſake of making the figure in life which he aſpires at.

The prevalency of luxury in a country, produces multitudes of this atrocious ſpecies, of which we ſee many inſtances daily. It follows, therefore, that, notwithſtanding our late ſucceſſes in war, indicating a happy ſuperiority to the enervating effects of luxury upon our national courage, or at leaſt upon the courage of our northern people, we have ſtill a great deal to fear from that formidable internal enemy to manners and principles.

Luxury has been ſometimes defended upon the pretence of its being favourable to commerce. But there are facts in hiſtory, which ſhew, that it is even capable of ruining commerce. About the time of the Emperor *Juſtinian*, his ſubjects, who are commonly diſtinguiſhed by the name of the Eaſtern or *Greek* Empire, the capital of which was *Conſtantinople*, poſſeſſed a very advantageous trade to India, which they loſt through their luxury and idleneſs, and the States of *Italy* gained it by their ſhrewdneſs, induſtry, and frugality. This is explained by the authors of the MODERN UNIVERSAL HISTORY [a] as follows:

The decline of the empire of the *Greeks*, while in the full poſſeſſion, and that in a more abſolute degree than any other nation whatever, of this lucrative trade of the *Indies*, ſeems to be a ſtrong objection to the principle laid down at the beginning and maintained through the courſe of this chapter. But this, as the reader will ſee, is fully accounted for by their conduct; for while in their hands this commerce was really the ſource of vaſt riches and great power, a great part of the former the *Greeks* retained; the remainder, together with the naval force, they abandoned. The objection then vaniſhes; for it is impoſſible to furniſh a wanton, idle, and profligate nation with power of any kind, and leaſt of all with a naval force.

Thus luxury is capable of deſtroying commerce, its parent. Which ſhews the wiſdom (the *neceſſity*, I had almoſt ſaid) of ſetting bounds, as the ancients did, by their oſtraciſms and petaliſms, to the effects of exorbitant wealth in individuals.

It

---

[a] MOD. UNIV. HIST. IX. 216.

It was a cuſtom at the new-year's luſtration at *Rome*, for the conſul ſolemnly to pray, that the gods would increaſe the *Roman* ſtate. But one of thoſe conſuls, wiſer than the reſt, inſiſted, that the *Roman* ſtate was already great enough, and declared, that he would only pray, that the gods would keep the commonwealth as it then was; for that it was already great enough. *Horace* in his times, which were later, and more corrupt, ſaw plainly that *Rome* was too great.

Suis et ipſa Roma viribus ruit.

'From the riches, and at the ſame time the frugality of the *Dutch*, it will appear (ſays Sir *William Temple*) that ſome of our maxims are not ſo certain as they are current in our common politics. As that the example and encouragement of exceſs and luxury if employed in the conſumption of native commodities, is of advantage to trade. It may be ſo, to that which impoveriſhes, but not to that which enriches a country. It is indeed leſs prejudicial, if it lies in native than if in foreign wares; but the humour of luxury and expence cannot ſtop at certain bounds; what begins in native, will proceed in foreign commodities: and though the example ariſes among idle perſons, yet the imitation will run into all degrees, even of thoſe men by whoſe induſtry the nation ſubſiſts. And beſides, the more of our own we ſpend, the leſs we ſhall have to ſend abroad; and ſo it will come to paſs, that while we drive a vaſt trade, yet, by buying much more than we ſell, we ſhall come to be poor[a].'

Some apologiſe for luxury as ſerving to promote arts and taſte. On the contrary, *Polybius*, ſpeaking of the ignorance of *Mummius*, caſts a reflection on the arts, as if

[a] *Anderſ.* Hist. Com. I. 186.

if taste made people extravagant and dishonest. But he might as well say, we ought not to love women, because that passion often hurries us into folly and vice. It is not too much taste, but too little prudence and virtue, that produces degeneracy in a people. The truth is, it is only *occasionally*, not necessarily, that commerce, arts, and taste do harm. And the same spendthrift, who in a polished age and country breaks for half a million, would, in a time and place of less cultivation and and less ostentation, have broke for 10,000l.

Montague observes, that the *Carthaginians*, though enriched by commerce, were not effeminated by it [a].

Riches do not *necessarily* enervate a people, unless there be a relaxation of discipline, and degeneracy of manners. The *Florentines*, (though they had been at war 50 years, with almost all the states of *Italy*, and several powerful princes) were 'by means of their extensive commerce, encouragement of ingenious arts, '*strictness* of *discipline*, and *regularity* of *government*, 'prodigiously rich; and their riches, far from enervating them, inspired them with ideas of rivalling the 'old *Romans*, not only in sentiments, but in power [b].' In the time of their war with *Scaliger* prince of *Verona*, they were cultivating the arts of peace at home. *Giotto*, a famous architect and painter, worked at this time in *Florence*; and built the square tower of *Florence*, said to be 144 ells high [c].

The *Romans* did not think of paving streets, till 500 years after the building of the city [d]; the æra of their greatest glory, their greatest virtue, courage, public spirit, liberty, &c. but of their greatest ignorance of the

---

[a] Ant. Rep. p. 338.

[b] Mod. Univ. Hist. xxxvi. 100.

[c] Ibid. 101.

[d] Ant. Univ. Hist. xii. 358.

the polite arts, as appears from the famous inſtance of the conſul *Mummius*, and others.

Excudent alii ſpirantia, &c. VIRG.

The *Athenians* were but clumſy artiſts, while they were a free people. They did not take to the fine arts, till they loſt their liberties.

The *French* are thought to excel us as much in painting, ſtatuary, engraving, and ſome other elegancies, as they fall ſhort of us in freedom. It muſt be confeſſed, that we have carried muſic and poetry much farther, than they.

It has often been ſaid, that liberty encourages the arts, and that ſlavery depreſſes them. And it is certain, that men, whoſe minds are debaſed and diſpirited by actual cruelty exerciſed againſt them by their ſovereign, are not likely to enjoy that tranquil mind, which is ſo neceſſary for the free play of imagination.

But, on the other hand, there is generally found, in a free people, a certain ferocity, (the very cauſe of their being free; for kings and miniſters are always ready to enſlave all who will permit them) which ferocity is ſcarcely conſiſtent with the turn of mind that is neceſſary for a proficient in the elegant arts. Add, that a certain degree of luxury, the forerunner of ſlavery, is neceſſary for the ſupport of the fine arts.

In our times the rapacity for riches is got to an unexampled height. We have not, like the *Romans* [a], a temple dedicated to *Juno Moneta*; but every man and every woman ſeems to have erected a temple to money in their hearts. Not that hoarding is the vice of the times. But the caſe is worſe. For the voracity of thoſe who diſgorge their money as faſt as they ſwallow it, is the moſt inſatiable. Like the gluttons ſatyrized by

[a] ANT. UNIV. HIST. XII. 54.

by *Juvenal*, who forced themselves to bring up one supper, that they might have the filthy pleasure of eating two, the same evening, our nobility and gentry, who repeatedly beggar themselves at Mrs. *Cornely*'s, and *Arthur*'s, are incomparably more insatiable than misers, who have no call upon them, but that of their avarice merely. *Catiline*'s character, in *Salust*, suits a great multitude in our times. *Alieni appetens*; *sui profusus*. Rapacious, yet profuse.

The *English* are probably the most luxurious people now in the world; and the *English* are the most given to suicide of any people now in the world. Does not this remarkable coincidence give ground to presume, that there is a connexion between luxury and self-murder? That a people enslaving themselves to luxury, grow extravagant and expensive in their living; and, not being able to bear the expence of their way of living, and growing effeminate, impotent, and impatient of disappointment, they suffer despair to hurry them into the crime, which admits of no repentance or reformation. Ought not then every wise and good government to suppress luxury? Ought not every individual to set up an example against it?

Wherever luxury has prevailed, it may be traced by its mischievous effects.

The *Ionians* were once as valiant as the other *Greeks*. But they degenerated through luxury, the ruin of all bravery and public virtue. *Maximus Tyrius* says, the *Crotonians* loved the Olympic games, the *Spartans* fine armour, the *Cretans* hunting, the *Sybarites* dressing, and the *Ionians* lascivious dances. The *Ionians* accordingly joined *Xerxes* against their countrymen the *Athenians*. It is true, after they saw themselves taken to task by *Themistocles*, they deserted the *Persians*, and gave the *Greeks*

Greeks an opportunity of gaining the important victory of *Salamis*.

The fall of *Athens* is, by some writers, ascribed to *Pericles*'s contriving to bring the court of *Areopagus* into disgrace, because he was refused admission into it[a].

The conquering of *Antiochus* was the first introduction of luxury into the commonwealth[b].

Hannibal probably would have overset *Rome*, and saved his country from the horrible cruelty of the *Romans*, if he had not himself been overset by faction. Thus faction was the ruin of *Carthage*, and riches probably were the cause of faction[c].

Scarce any of the ancient *Numidians* died of any thing, but old age, says *Salust*.

Alexander's ministers, and generals, were corrupted by his profusion in enriching them out of the spoils of the conquered nations[d]. Hence factions and conspiracies. At length he himself became infected. Then he must wear the *Persian* dress, and mimick the oriental effeminacy. At last he sunk into a beastly sot, and is thought, by some authors, to have fallen, at *Babylon*, a sacrifice to ebriety, though others ascribe his death to poison.

The author of GRAND. ET DECAD. DES ROM. ascribes the ruin of *Carthage* in great measure to the exorbitant riches of some individuals, p. 33.

Alexander and *Kouli khan* thought it necessary (the same author observes, p. 46.) to retrench the growing riches of their armies.

The great, but effeminate empire of *China*, said to contain innumerable cities, some of which inhabited by two millions of people, besides 4,400 walled, and 2,920

---

a ANT. UNIV. HIST. VI. 331.
b Ibid. IX. 270.
c Ibid. XVIII. 110.
d Ibid. VIII. 562.

open towns, an army of 2,659,191 men; and in all about 12 millions of families, or 60 millions of people, the first establishment of which is too ancient for history, was conquered by the warlike *Tartars*, in as many single years, as it had stood thousands [a].

The *Tartar* princes, enervated by the pleasures of the fine country of *China*, degenerated from the valour of their ancestors [b]. So *Capua* proved a *Cannæ* to *Hannibal*.

Don Pelayo, when he recovered the *Asturias* from the *Moors*, walled no towns, built no castles, fortified no passes, thinking all such proceedings encouragements to laziness, and detrimental to courage [c].

At the battle of *Bretinfeld*, between the Imperialists and the Swedes, and their allies, *A. D.* 1642, in which the former were defeated, the regiment of *Madlon*, of the Imperial side, fled without striking a blow, and occasioned the confusion, which proved fatal. After the decision they were surrounded by six regiments, disarmed, their ensigns torn, their disgrace published, the regiment erased from the muster-roll, and their sentence read, viz. That the colonel, captains, and lieutenants, should be beheaded, the ensigns hanged, the soldiers decimated, and the survivors driven with disgrace out of the army [d].

The *Lusitanians* gained victories over the *Romans* [e]. Any nation in *Europe* can beat the modern *Portuguese*.

Hear the excellent *Mountague* on the prevalency of luxury among the *Romans*, and its effects [f].

'If we connect the various strokes interspersed 'through what we have remaining of the writings of '*Salust*,

[a] Mod. Univ. Hist. viii. 15. [b] Ibid. viii. 4;0.
[c] Ibid. xix. 494. [d] Ibid. xxx. 260.
[e] Ant. Univ. Hist. xii. 363.
[f] *Mountag.* Ant. Republ. 269.

'*Saluſt*, which he levelled at the vices of his country-'men, we ſhall be able to form a juſt idea of the man-'ners of the *Romans* in the time of that hiſtorian. 'From the picture thus faithfully exhibited, we muſt 'be convinced, that not only thoſe ſhocking calamities, 'which the republic ſuffered during the conteſt between '*Marius* and *Sylla*, but thoſe ſubſequent and more fa-'tal evils, which brought on the utter extinction of the '*Roman* liberty and conſtitution, were the natural ef-'fects of that foreign luxury, which firſt introduced 'venality and corruption. Though the introduction 'of luxury from *Aſia* preceded the ruin of *Carthage* in 'point of time, yet as *Saluſt* informs us, the dread of 'that dangerous rival reſtrained the *Romans* within 'the bounds of decency and order. But as ſoon as 'ever that obſtacle was removed, they gave a full ſcope 'to their ungoverned paſſions. The change in their 'manners was not gradual, and by little and little, as 'before, but rapid and inſtantaneous. Religion, 'juſtice, modeſty, decency, all regard for divine or 'human laws, were ſwept away at once by the irre-'ſiſtible torrent of corruption. The nobility ſtrained 'the privileges annexed to their dignity, and the peo-'ple their liberty, alike into the moſt unbounded li-'centiouſneſs. Every one made the dictate of his 'own lawleſs will, his only rule of action. Public 'virtue, and the love of their country, which had 'raiſed the *Romans* to the empire of the univerſe, were 'extinct. Money, which alone could enable them to 'gratify their darling luxury, was ſubſtituted in their 'place. Power, dominion, honours, and univerſal 'reſpect were annexed to the poſſeſſion of money. Con-'tempt, and whatever was moſt reproachful, was the 'bitter portion of poverty; and to be poor, grew to 'be the greateſt of all crimes, in the eſtimation of 'the *Romans*. Thus wealth and poverty contributed 'alike to the ruin of the republic. The rich employed 'their wealth in the acquisition of power, and their 'power in every kind of oppression, and rapine for the 'acquisition of more wealth. The poor, now dissolute 'and desperate, were ready to engage in every seditious insurrection, which promised them the plunder 'of the rich, and set up both their liberty and country to sale, to the best bidder. The republic, which 'was the common prey to both, was thus rent to 'pieces between the contending parties. As an universal selfishness is the genuine effect of universal 'luxury, so the natural effect of selfishness is to break 'through every tye, both divine and human, and to 'stick at no kind of excesses in the pursuit of wealth, 'its favourite object. Thus the effects of selfishness 'will naturally appear in irreligion, breach of faith, 'perjury, a contempt of all the social duties, extortion, frauds in our dealings, pride, cruelty, universal venality and corruption. From selfishness arises 'that vicious ambition, if I may be allowed the term, 'which *Salust* rightly defines, the lust of domination. 'Ambition is a passion which precedes avarice; for 'the seeds of ambition seem almost to be innate. The 'desire of pre-eminence, the fondness for being distinguished above the rest of our fellow-creatures, 'attends us from the cradle to the grave. Though as 'it takes its complexion, so it receives its denomination 'from the different objects it pursues, which in all 'are but the different means of attaining the same end. 'But the lust of domination here mentioned by *Salust*, 'though generally confounded with ambition, is in 'reality a different passion, and is strictly speaking only a different mode of selfishness. For the chief end 'which we propose by the lust of domination, is to

'draw

'draw every thing to center in ourſelves, which we 'think will enable us to gratify every other paſſion. 'I confeſs it may be alleged that ſelf-love, and ſelfiſh-'neſs, both ariſe from the general law of ſelf-preſerva-'tion, and are but different modes of the ſame prin-'ciple. I acknowledge that if we examine ſtrictly 'all thoſe heroic inſtances of love, friendſhip, or pa-'triotiſm, which ſeem to be carried to the moſt exalted 'degree of diſintereſtedneſs, we ſhall probably find the 'principle of ſelf-love lurking at the bottom of many 'of them. But if we rightly define theſe two prin-'ciples, we ſhall find an eſſential difference between 'our ideas of ſelf-love and ſelfiſhneſs. Self-love, with-'in its due bounds, is the practice of the great duty of 'ſelf-preſervation regulated by that law, which the 'great Author of our being has given for that very end. 'Self-love, therefore, is not only compatible with the 'moſt rigid practice of the ſocial duties, but is in fact a 'great motive and incentive to the practice of all moral 'virtue. Whereas ſelfiſhneſs, by reducing every thing 'to the ſingle point of private intereſt, a point which it 'never loſes ſight of, baniſhes all the ſocial virtues, and 'is the firſt ſpring of action, which impells to all theſe 'diſorders which are ſo fatal to mixed government in 'particular, and to ſociety in general. From this poi-'ſonous ſource *Saluſt* deduces all thoſe evils which ſpread 'the peſtilence of corruption over the whole face of the 'republic, and changed the mildeſt and moſt upright 'government in the univerſe, into the moſt inhuman 'and moſt inſupportable tyranny. For as the luſt of 'domination can never poſſibly attain its end without the 'aſſiſtance of others, the man who is actuated by that 'deſtructive paſſion, muſt of neceſſity ſtrive to attach 'himſelf to a ſet of men of ſimilar principles for the ſub-'bordinate inſtruments. This is the origin of all thoſe

 'iniquitous

'iniquitous combinations which we call factions. To 'accomplish this, he must put on as many shapes as '*Proteus*; he must ever wear the mask of dissimula-'tion, and live a perpetual lie. He will court the 'friendship of every man, who is capable of promoting, 'and endeavour to crush every man who is capable of 'defeating his ambitious views. Thus his friendship 'and his enmity will be alike unreal, and easily con-'vertible, if the change will serve his interest. As 'private interest is the only tie which can ever con-'nect a faction, the lust of wealth, which was the 'cause of the lust of domination, will now become the 'effect, and must be proportionable to the sum total of 'the demands of the whole faction; and as the latter 'know no bounds, so the former will be alike insatiable. 'For when once a man is inured to bribes in the service 'of faction, he will expect to be paid as well for acting 'for, as for acting against the dictates of his con-'science. A truth which every minister must have 'experienced, who has been supported by a faction, 'and which a late great minister, as he frankly con-'fessed, found to be the case with him during his long 'administration. But how deeply soever a state may be 'immersed in luxury and corruption, yet the man who 'aims at being the head of a faction for the end of do-'mination, will at first cloak his real design under an 'affected zeal for the service of the government. 'When he has established himself in power, and formed 'his party, all who support his measures will be re-'warded as the friends; all who oppose him will be 'treated as enemies to the government. The honest 'and uncorrupt citizen will be hunted down, as 'disaffected, and all his remonstrancs against mal-ad-'ministration, will be represented as proceeding from 'that principle. The cant term *disaffection*, will be

'the

'the watch-word of the faction; and the charge of 'disaffection, that constant resource of iniquitous mi-'nisters, that infallible sign that a cause will not stand 'the test of a fair inquiry, will be perpetually employed 'by the tools of power to silence those objections which 'they want arguments to answer. The faction will esti-'mate the worth of their leader, not by his services to his 'country; for the good of the public will be looked 'upon as obsolete and chimerical; but his ability to 'gratify or screen his friends; and crush his opponents. 'The leader will fix the implicit obedience to his will 'as the test of merit to his faction: consequently all 'the dignities and lucrative posts will be conferred upon 'persons of that stamp only, whilst honesty and public 'virtue will be standing marks of political reprobation. 'Common justice will be denied to the latter in all con-'troverted elections, whilst the laws will be strained 'or over-ruled in favour of the former. Luxury is the 'certain forerunner of corruption, because it is the cer-'tain parent of indigence: consequently a state so 'circumstanced will always furnish an ample supply of 'proper instruments for faction. For as luxury con-'sists in an inordinate gratification of the sensual 'passions, the more the passions are indulged, they grow 'the more importunately craving, till the greatest for-'tune must sink under their insatiable demands. Thus 'luxury necessarily produces corruption. For as 'wealth is essentially necessary to the support of luxury, 'wealth will be the universal object of desire in every 'state where luxury prevails: consequently, all those who 'have dissipated their private fortunes in the purchase of 'pleasure, will be ever ready to inlist in the cause of 'faction for the wages of corruption. A taste for 'pleasure immoderately indulged, quickly strengthens 'into habit, eradicates every principle of honour and

'virtue,

'virtue, and gets poſſeſſion of the whole man. And 'the more expenſive ſuch a man is in his pleaſures, the 'greater lengths he will run for the acquiſition of 'wealth for the end of profuſion. Thus the conta- 'gion will become ſo univerſal that nothing but an 'uncommon ſhare of virtue can preſerve the poſſeſſor 'from infection. For when once the idea of reſpect 'and homage is annexed to the poſſeſſion of wealth 'alone, honour, probity, every virtue and every amiable 'quality will be held cheap in compariſon, and looked 'upon as aukward and quite unfaſhionable. But 'as the ſpirit of liberty will yet exiſt in ſome degree, in 'a ſtate which retains the name of freedom, even 'though the manners of that ſtate ſhould be generally 'depraved, an oppoſition will ariſe from thoſe virtuous 'citizens who know the value of their birth-right, li- 'berty, and will never ſubmit tamely to the chains of 'faction. Force then will be called in to the aid of 'corruption, and a ſtanding army will be introduced. 'A military government will be eſtabliſhed upon the 'ruins of the civil, and all commands and employ- 'ments will be diſpoſed of at the arbitrary will of law- 'leſs power. The people will be fleeced to pay for 'their own fetters, and doomed, like the cattle, to 'unremitting toil and drudgery, for the ſupport of their 'tyrannical maſters. Or if the outward form of civil 'government ſhould be permitted to remain, the people 'will be compelled to give a ſanction to tyranny by 'their own ſuffrages, and to elect oppreſſors inſtead of 'protectors. From this genuine portrait of the *Roman* 'manners, it is evident to a demonſtration, that the 'fatal cataſtrophe of that republic, of which *Salluſt* 'himſelf was an eye-witneſs, was the natural effect of 'the corruption of their manners. It is equally as 'evident from our author and the reſt of the *Roman* 'hiſtorians,

'hiſtorians, that the corruption of their manners was 'the natural effect of foreign luxury, introduced and 'ſupported by foreign wealth. The fatal tendency of 'theſe evils was too obvious to eſcape the notice of 'every ſenſible *Roman*, who had any regard for liberty 'and their ancient conſtitution. Many ſumptuary 'laws were made to reſtrain the various exceſſes of 'luxury; but theſe efforts were too feeble to check the 'overbearing violence of the torrent. *Cato* propoſed 'a ſevere law, enforced by the ſanction of an oath, 'againſt bribery and corruption at elections; where the 'ſcandalous traffic of votes was eſtabliſhed by cuſtom, 'as at a public market. But as *Plutarch* obſerves, he 'incurred the reſentment of both parties by that ſa-'lutary meaſure. The rich were his enemies, becauſe 'they found themſelves precluded from all pretenſions 'to the higheſt dignities; as they had no other merit 'to plead but what aroſe from their ſuperior wealth. 'The electors abuſed, curſed, and even pelted him, as 'the author of a law which deprived them of the wages 'of corruption, and reduced them to the neceſſity of 'ſubſiſting by labour. But this law, if it really paſſed, 'had as little effect as any of the former; and like the 'ſame laws in our own country upon the ſame occaſion, 'was either evaded by chicane or over-ruled by power. 'Our own ſeptennial ſcenes of drunkenneſs, riot, bri-'bery, and abandoned perjury, may ſerve to give an 'idea of the annual elections of the *Romans* in thoſe 'abominable times. Corruption was arrived at its 'laſt ſtage, and the depravity was univerſal. The 'whole body of the unhappy republic was infected and 'the diſtemper was incurable. For theſe exceſſes 'which formerly were eſteemed the vices of the people, 'were now, by the force of cuſtom fixed into a habit,

'become

'become the manners of the people. A moſt infallible 'criterion by which we may aſcertain the very point 'of time when the ruin of any free ſtate, which labours 'under theſe evils, may be naturally expected. The 'conſpiracies of *Catiline* and *Cæſar* againſt the liberty 'of their country, were but genuine effects of that cor'ruption which *Saluſt* has marked out as the imme'diate cauſe of the deſtruction of the republic. The 'end propoſed by each of theſe bad men, and the means 'employed for that end, were the ſame in both. The 'difference in their ſucceſs aroſe only from the difference 'of addreſs and abilities in the reſpective leaders. 'The followers of *Catiline*, as *Salluſt* informs us, were 'the moſt diſſolute, the moſt profligate, and the moſt 'abandoned wretches, which could be culled out of the 'moſt populous and moſt corrupt city of the univerſe. '*Cæſar*, upon the ſame plan, formed his party, as we 'learn from *Plutarch*, out of the moſt infected and 'moſt corrupt members of the very ſame ſtate. The 'vices of the times eaſily furniſhed a ſupply of pro'per inſtruments. To pilfer the public money, and 'to plunder the provinces by violence, though ſtate 'crimes of the moſt heinous nature, were grown ſo 'familiar by cuſtom, that they were looked upon as no 'more than mere office perquiſites. The younger 'people who are ever moſt ripe for ſedition and inſur'rection, were ſo corrupted by luxury, that they might 'be deſervedly termed an abandoned race, whoſe diſſi'pation made it impracticable for them to keep their 'own private fortunes; and whoſe avarice would not 'ſuffer their citizens to enjoy the quiet poſſeſſion of 'theirs.'

'Though there is a concurrence of ſeveral cauſes 'which brings on the ruin of a ſtate, yet, where luxury

'prevails,

'prevails, that parent of all our fantaſtic imaginary 'wants, ever craving and ever unſatisfied, we may 'juſtly aſſign it as the leading cauſe: ſince it ever was 'and ever will be the moſt baneful to public virtue. 'For as luxury is contagious from its very nature, it 'will gradually deſcend from the higheſt to the loweſt 'ranks, till it has ultimately infected a whole people. 'The evils ariſing from luxury have not been peculiar 'to this or that nation; but equally fatal to all where-'ever it was admitted. Political philoſophy lays this 'down as a fundamental and inconteſtible maxim, that 'all the moſt flouriſhing ſtates owed their ruin, ſooner 'or later, to the effects of luxury; and all hiſtory, from 'the origin of mankind, confirms by this truth the 'evidence of facts, to the higheſt degree of demonſtra-'tion. In the great deſpotic monarchies it produced 'avarice, diſſipation, rapaciouſneſs, oppreſſion, perpe-'tual factions amongſt the great, whilſt each endea-'voured to engroſs the favour of the Prince wholly to 'himſelf; venality, and a contempt for all law and 'diſcipline, both in the civil and military departments. 'Whilſt the people, following the pernicious example 'of their ſuperiors, contracted ſuch a daſtardly effe-'minacy, joined to an utter inability to ſupport the 'fatigues of war, as quickly threw them into the hands 'of the firſt reſolute invader. Thus the *Aſſyrian* em-'pire ſunk under the arms of *Cyrus*, with his poor but 'hardy *Perſians*. The extenſive and opulent em-'pire of *Perſia* fell an eaſy conqueſt to *Alexander*, and a 'handful of *Macedonians*. And the *Macedonian* empire, 'when enervated by the luxury of *Aſia*, was compelled 'to receive the yoke of the victorious *Romans*. Luxu-'ry, when introduced into free ſtates, and ſuffered to be 'diffuſed without control through the body of the 'people, was ever productive of that degeneracy of

'manners

'manners which extinguishes public virtue, and puts a 'final period to liberty. For as the incessant demands 'of luxury quickly induced necessity, that necessity 'kept human invention perpetually on the rack, to find 'out ways and means to supply the demands of luxury. 'Hence the lower classes at first sold their suffrages in 'privacy and with caution; but as luxury increased, 'and the manners of the people grew daily more cor- 'rupt, they openly set them up to sale to the best bid- 'der. Hence too the ambitious amongst the higher 'classes, whose superior wealth was frequently their 'only qualifications, first purchased the most lucrative 'posts in the state by this infamous kind of traffic, 'and then maintained themselves in power by that 'additional fund for corruption, which their employ- 'ments supplied, till they had undone those they had 'first corrupted. But of all the ancient republics, '*Rome*, in the last period of her freedom, was the scene 'where all the inordinate passions of mankind operated 'most powerfully and with the greatest latitude. 'There we see luxury, ambition, faction, pride, re- 'venge, selfishness, a total disregard to the public 'good, an universal dissoluteness of manners, first make 'them ripe for, and then complete their destruction. 'Consequently that period, by shewing us more striking 'examples, will afford more useful lessons than any 'other part of their history[a].'

Great must have been the frugality and moderation of the *Romans*, when *Attilius Regulus* warring at the head of the *Roman* legions abroad, wrote home to the senate, desiring to be recalled, because his farm being, in his absence, neglected, his wife and children were in danger of starving[b]. And by the same rule, the

[a] *Mountag* Ant. Rep. 221.

[b] Ant. Univ. Hist. vol. xii. p. 178.

the ſtate might be thought on the decline, when the ladies ſolicited a repeal of the *Oppian* law, by which they were, in times of extremity, reſtrained in their expences as to dreſs, chariots, &c[a].

In the conteſt between *Craſſus* and *Pompey*, we ſee the former catching the favour of the people by entertaining them at 10,000 tables, and giving them largeſſes of corn. Well might it be pronounced, that the *Roman* ſpirit was on the decline, when ſuch a baſe art was found ſucceſsful. Very different were the times, when *Curius Dentatus* rejected the *Samnite* preſent of plate; or when the *Roman* ambaſſadors ſet the golden crowns, they had ſent them by king *Ptolemy*, on the heads of his ſtatues.

We ſee luxury gradually increaſing and prevailing over the *Roman* ſpirit and virtue, till at length, in the imperial times, the contagion even reached ladies of the greateſt diſtinction, who, in imitation of the prince and his court, had their aſſemblies and repreſentations too, in a grove planted by *Auguſtus*, where booths were built, and in them ſold, whatever incited to ſenſuality and wantonneſs. Thus was even the outward appearance of virtue baniſhed the city, and all manner of avowed lewdneſs, depravity, and diſſoluteneſs, introduced in its room, men and women being engaged in a contention to outvye each other in glaring vices, and ſcenes of impurity. At length *Nero* could forbear no longer; but took the harp, and mounted the public ſtage, trying the ſtrings with much attention, and care, and ſtudying his part. About him ſtood his companions, and a cohort of the guards, with many tribunes and centurions, and *Burrhus* their commander, ſad on this infamous occaſion; but praiſing *Nero*, while he grieved for him. At this time he inrolled a body of *Roman*

[a] Ant. Univ. Hist. xii. 342.

Roman knights, entitled the knights of *Augustus*; young men distinguished by the bloom of their years, and strength of body, but all professed profligates. As the emperor spent whole days and nights in singing, and playing upon the harp; the sole business of these knights was, to commend his person and voice, to extol the beauty of both, by names and epithets peculiar to the gods, and to sing his airs about the streets.

It may be questioned whether there is in history any example more striking of the excess, to which luxury may be carried in a country, than the following of the ancient inhabitants of *Tarentum*[a]:

'The heat of the climate, the fruitfulness of the 'country, and the opportunity of supplying themselves 'by sea, with all the delights of *Greece*, sunk the *Tarentines* into idleness, and all the vices that attend it. 'Their whole life was spent in feasts, sports, and public entertainments. Buffoons and prostitutes governed the state at their pleasure, and often determined the most important affairs by a joke, or an indecent gesture. They bore a mortal hatred to the '*Romans*, and dreaded their dominion, not so much 'out of fear of losing their liberty, as of being disturbed 'by that warlike and rough people, in the pursuit of 'their pleasures. They therefore employed all their '*Grecian* subtilty, to draw such a number of enemies 'upon them, as still to keep them at distance from 'themselves, and this without appearing to be concerned.

'The *Tarentines* imagining that *Rome* having at last 'discovered their secret plots, had sent that fleet to 'punish them, they all, with one consent, ran down 'to the port, fell upon the *Roman* fleet with the fury 'of madmen, sunk one ship, and took four, the other 'five escaping. All the prisoners fit to bear arms, 'were

[a] Ant. Univ. Hist. xii. 143. 146. 148.

'were put to the ſword, and the others ſold for ſlaves 'to the beſt bidder. The *Romans*, upon the news of 'this act of hoſtility, ſent a deputation to *Tarentum*, 'to demand ſatisfaction for the inſult offered to the 'republic; but the *Tarentines*, inſtead of hearkening to 'their demands, inſulted the ambaſſadors in the moſt 'outrageous manner. They admitted them to an au-'dience in the theatre, where *Poſthumius*, who was at 'the head of the embaſſy, and had been thrice conſul, 'harangued the aſſembly in *Greek*. His advanced age, 'his perſonal merit, and above all, the character of an 'ambaſſador, from a powerful people, ought to have 'gained him reſpect; but the *Tarentines*, heated with 'wine, not only gave no attention to his diſcourſe, but 'burſt into loud laughter, and impudently hiſſed him, 'whenever he dropped an improper expreſſion, or pro-'nounced a word with a foreign accent. Nor was 'this all. When he began to ſpeak of reparation of 'injuries, they flew into a rage, and rather drove him 'out of the aſſembly, than diſmiſſed him. As he was 'walking off with an air of gravity and dignity, which 'he preſerved, notwithſtanding the reception they gave 'him, a buffoon named *Philonides*, coming up to him, 'urined upon his robe; a new ſource of immoderate 'laughter to the mad and drunken multitude, who 'clapped their hands, applauding the outrageous inſo-'lence. *Poſthumius* turning about to the aſſembly, 'ſhewed them the ſkirt of his garment ſo defiled; 'but when he found that this had no effect, but to in-'creaſe the loudneſs of their contumelious mirth, he 'ſaid without the leaſt emotion, Laugh on *Tarentines*, 'laugh on now while you may; the time is coming 'when you will weep. It is not a little blood that 'muſt waſh and purify this garment. This ſaid, he 'withdrew, left the city, and embarked for *Rome*.

 'When

'When the *Tarentines* came to themſelves, and began 'to reflect on the enormity of their conduct, and at the 'ſame time, on the inability of their neighbours to 'defend them againſt ſo powerful a republic, they caſt 'their eyes upon *Pyrrhus* king of *Epirus*, whoſe great 'reputation for valour and long experience in war, had 'gained him the reputation of one of the heroes of '*Greece*. They therefore immediately diſpatched am-'baſſadors to him, but rather to ſound his diſpoſition, 'and obſerve the ſituation of his affairs, than to enter 'without farther deliberation into any engagements 'with him. As *Pyrrhus* naturally loved action, and 'the buſtle and hurry of war, the ambaſſadors found 'him in a diſpoſition to hearken to any propoſal, which 'would furniſh him with employment worthy of his 'ambition.

'*Meton*, on the day that a public decree was to paſs 'for inviting *Pyrrhus* to *Tarentum*, and when the peo-'ple were all placed in the theatre, putting a withered 'garland on his head, and having a flambeau in his 'hand, as was the manner of the drunken debauchees, 'came dancing into the midſt of the aſſembly, accom-'panied by a woman playing on the flute. This ſilly 'ſight was ſufficient to divert the *Tarentines* from their 'moſt important deliberations. They made a ring and 'called out to *Meton* to ſing, and to the woman to 'play; but when they expected to be entertained with 'a ſong, and were all ſilent, the wiſe citizen aſſuming 'an air of great ſeriouſneſs, You do well *Tarentines*, 'ſaid he, not to hinder thoſe from diverting themſelves, 'who are diſpoſed to mirth; and if you are wiſe, you 'will yourſelves take advantage of the preſent liberty 'you enjoy, to do the ſame. When *Pyrrhus* comes, 'you muſt change your way of life; your mirth and 'joy will be at an end. Theſe words made an im-

'pression upon the multitude, and a murmur went 'about that he had spoken well; but those who had 'some reason to fear, that they should be delivered up 'to the *Romans*, in case of an accommodation, being 'enraged at what he had said, reviled the assembly for 'suffering themselves to be so mocked and affronted; 'and crowding together, thrust *Meton* out of the as-'sembly.'

Heliogabalus never wore a suit, or a ring, twice. He gave away always to his guests the gold plate used at supper. Oftentimes he distributed among the people, and soldiery, gold, silver, and tickets, entitling them to receive large sums, which were regularly paid. He had his fish-ponds filled with rose-water, and the naumachia (a bason large enough for fleets to exhibit mock-fights) with wine. Tongues of peacocks and nightingales, and brains of parrots and pheasants, were his dishes, and his dogs were fed with the livers of geese, his horses with raisins, and the wild beasts of his menagerie with partridges and pheasants [a]. Yet this effeminate wretch was as cruel as the roughest soldier [b].

Davenant [c], thinks the *Spaniards* laziness came upon them in the time of *Philip* II. when they got their new world in *America*, which brought among them immense treasures of gold and silver, and damped the spirit of industry. It is to be feared, that the Nabob fortunes lately acquired in *India*, and brought hither, may have some such effect on the disposition of the *English*.

Commerce established by the czar *Peter*, introduced luxury. 'Universal dissipation took the lead, and pro-'fligacy of manners succeeded. Many of the lords be-'gun to squeeze and grind their peasants, to extort

a Ant. Univ. Hist. xv. 551. b Ibid. 352.
c *Davenant*, i. 382.

'fresh supplies for the incessant demands of luxury [a].' If luxury has produced corruption among the poor *Russians*, what may it not be expected to do among the rich *English*?

The extreme poverty occasioned by idleness and luxury in the beginning of *Lewis* XIII. of *France*, filled the streets of *Paris* with beggars. The court (which then resided at the Louvre) disgusted at this sight, which indeed was a severe reproach on them, issued an order, forbidding all persons, on severe penalties, to relieve them, intending thereby to drive them out of town, and not caring though they dropped down dead, before they could reach the country towns and villages [b].

The Moors possessed, for a long time, the richest parts of *Spain*, and the Christians the least fertile. The consequence was, that hard labour strengthened the former, and easy living enfeebled the latter. Accordingly, the Christians in the last and decisive battle between them and the Moors at *Tolosa*, killed 200,000 of the infidels [c].

Scarce half the army, who, under *Bourbon*, sacked *Rome*, in the time of *Charles* V. got out of that city alive. They fell the victims of their own debauchery.

The nobles of *Spain* grew so effeminate in the time of *Ferdinand* and *Isabella*, that they would not ride upon horses; but chose mules; because their motion is gentler and easier. So that the breed of horses would have been lost, if the king had not given an order about preserving it [d].

So *Horace* complains of the *Roman* youth of his times;

Nescit hærere equo ingenuus puer.

The

---

a Pref, to the Czarina's instruction for a code of laws, p. 11.

b Mod. Univ. Hist. xxiv. 451.

c Ibid. xx. 171.

d Ibid. xxi. 186.

The danger of a people's ſliding into luxury and corruption, is thus deſcribed by my worthy friend Mr. profeſſor *Ferguſon* of *Edinburgh* [a].

'The increaſing regard with which men appear in 'the progreſs of commercial arts, to ſtudy their profit, or 'the delicacy with which they refine on their pleaſures, 'even induſtry itſelf, or the habit of application to a 'tedious employment, in which no honours are won, 'may perhaps be conſidered as indications of a grow'ing attention to intereſt, or of effeminacy contracted 'in the enjoyment of eaſe and conveniency. Every 'ſucceſſive art by which the individual is taught to 'improve on his fortune, is in reality an addition to 'his private engagements, and a new avocation of his 'mind from the public. Corruption however does not 'ariſe from the abuſe of commercial arts alone; it re'quires the aid of political ſituation; and is not pro'duced by the objects that occupy a ſordid and a mer'cenary ſpirit, without the aid of circumſtances, that 'enable men to indulge in ſafety any mean diſpoſition 'they have acquired. Providence has fitted mankind 'for the higher engagements, which they are ſome'times obliged to fulfil; and it is in the midſt of ſuch 'engagements, that they are moſt likely to acquire or 'to preſerve their virtues. The habits of a vigorous 'mind are formed in contending with difficulties, not 'in engaging the repoſe of a pacific ſtation; penetration 'and wiſdom are the fruits of experience, not the 'leſſons of retirement and leiſure; ardour and gene'roſity are the qualities of a mind raiſed and animated 'in the conduct of ſcenes that engage the heart, not 'the gifts of reflection or knowledge. The mere in'termiſſion of national and political efforts is, notwith-

 'ſtanding,

[a] *Ferguſon*'s Hist. Civ. Soc. 392.

'standing, sometimes mistaken for public good; and 'there is no mistake more likely to foster the vices, or 'to flatter the weakness of feeble and interested men. 'If the ordinary arts of policy, or rather if a growing indifference to objects of a public nature, should 'prevail, and under any free constitution, put an end 'to their disputes of party and silence, that noise of 'dissension which generally accompanies the exercise of 'freedom, we may venture to prognosticate corruption 'to the national manners, as well as remissness to the 'national spirit. The period is come, when no engagement remaining on the part of the public, private interest, and animal pleasure, become the sovereign objects of care. When men being relieved 'from the pressure of great occasions, bestow their attention on trifles; and having carried what they are 'pleased to call sensibility and delicacy on the subject 'of ease or molestation, as far as real weakness or folly 'can go, have recourse to affectation, in order to enhance the pretended demands, and accumulate the 'anxieties of a sickly fancy, and enfeebled mind. In 'this condition, mankind generally flatter their own 'imbecillity under the name of politeness. They are 'persuaded, that the celebrated ardour, generosity and 'fortitude, of former ages bordered on frenzy, or 'were the mere effects of necessity on men, who had 'not the means of enjoying their ease or their pleasure. They congratulate themselves on having 'escaped the storm, which required the exercise of such 'arduous virtues; and with that vanity which accompanies the human race in their meanest condition, 'they boast of a scene of affectation of languor, or of 'folly, as the standard of human felicity, and as furnishing the properest exercise of a rational nature. 'It is one of the least menacing symptoms of an age, prone

'prone to degeneracy, that the minds of men become 'perplexed in the diſcernment of merit, as much as 'the ſpirit becomes enfeebled in conduct, and the heart 'miſled in the choice of its objects. The care of 'mere fortune is ſuppoſed to conſtitute wiſdom; re-'tirement from public affairs, and real indifference to 'mankind, receive the applauſe of moderation and 'virtue. Great fortitude and elevation of mind, have 'not always indeed been employed in the attainment 'of valuable ends; but they are always reſpectable, 'and they are always neceſſary when we would act for 'the good of mankind, in any of the more arduous 'ſtations of life. While therefore we blame their miſ-'application, we ſhould beware of depreciating their va-'lue. Men of a ſevere and ſententious morality, have 'not always ſufficiently obſerved this caution; nor have 'they been duly aware of the corruptions they flattered, 'by the ſatire they employed againſt what is aſpiring 'and prominent in the character of the human ſoul.'

Harrington, in his OCEANA[a], writes, in a very edifying manner, on this ſubject, as follows:

'*Rome* was never ruined, till her balance being 'broken, the nobility forſaking their ancient virtue, 'abandoned themſelves to their luſts; and the ſenators, 'who, as in the caſe of *Jugurtha*, were all bribed, 'turned knaves; at which turn all their ſkill in go-'vernment (and in this never men had been better 'ſkilled) could not keep the commonwealth from over-'turning. *Cicero*, an honeſt man, laboured might and 'main; *Pomponius Atticus*, another, deſpaired; *Cato* 'tore out his own bowels; the poignards of *Brutus* and '*Caſſius* neither conſidered prince nor father; but the

G 4 commonwealth

[a] *Harrington*'s OCEANA, p. 323.

'commonwealth had ſprung her planks, and ſplit her 'ballaſt; the world could not ſave her.'

'When governors,' ſay the authors of the UNIVERSAL HISTORY[a], 'either through want of thought, or, 'which is often the caſe, from a wrong turn of 'thought, ſuffer thoſe of whom they have the care, to 'ſink into all the exceſſes of debauchery, they muſt 'not expect from theſe wicked and effeminate men 'either generous thoughts or gallant actions. When 'a people become ſlaves to their luſts, they are in the 'faireſt train imaginable of becoming ſlaves to their 'neighbours. Politicians may for a time indeed ward 'off the blow; but how? Why, by making uſe of 'mercenary troops. Thus the cowardly ſpendthrift 'pays a bully to fight his quarrels, and when he pays 'him no longer, is beaten by him himſelf. This was 'the fate of the *Perſians*; they hired *Greek* troops; 'maintained them in the exerciſe of their diſcipline; 'made them perfectly acquainted with their country 'and manners; ſuffered them to ſee and conſider thoſe 'errors in their government which made it, in ſpite of 'its grandeur, appear contemptible; and then theſe 'very *Greeks*, on their return home, were continually 'prompting their countrymen to go and pull down that 'empire, whoſe weight ſcarce permitted it to ſtand. 'If the *Perſian* emperors had always encouraged feuds 'in *Greece*, the *Greeks* could never have turned their 'arms upon them; for we ſee that till one ſtate ſubdued 'the reſt, an expedition into *Aſia* might be talked of, 'but could not be executed. Inſtead of this, the neceſſity we before mentioned compelled the *Perſians* to 'compoſe the quarrels of the *Grecians*, that they might 'furniſh him with troops. Peace enervated the *Greeks*; 'the

[a] ANT. UNIV. HIST. VIII. 480.

'the facility of recruiting their mercenaries, made the 'Persians neglect all martial discipline. In the mean 'time Philip, blessed with an excellent education, ex-'ercised with early troubles, endowed with invincible 'fortitude, and full of as restless ambition, raised the 'nation he governed from an indigent and dependent 'state to be, first, the terror of its neighbours, then 'the mistress of Greece, last of all a match for Persia. 'On this foundation stands the fame of Philip. These 'were the causes of his being in a condition to pass in-'to Asia, and these the sources of that weakness and 'inability to resist, which afterwards appeared in the 'Persian administration.'

The same authors explain as follows[a], the submission of the once brave and free Spartans to a set of lawless tyrants, for a long course of years.

'It may seem strange, that the Spartans, who had 'entertained such generous notions of liberty submitted 'patiently, for so long a tract of time, to the arbitrary 'commands of lawless tyrants; but this wonder will in 'a great measure be taken off, if we consider two 'things; first, that the manners of the Lacedemonians 'were greatly corrupted; which is indeed the very 'basis of slavery. There can be no such thing as 'bending the necks of virtuous people; but when once 'men are abandoned to their vices, and become slaves 'to their passions, they readily stoop to those who can 'gratify them; and this was the case of the majority 'of the inhabitants of Sparta at this time. Secondly, 'those amongst them, who were distinguished by their 'merit and their morals, were, on this very account, 'proscribed by the tyrants, and hated by their creatures; 'so that they were forced to forsake their country, and 'leave

[a] Ant. Univ. Hist. vii. 158.

'leave it to groan under a power, which they were un-'able to resist. To this we may add, that such as were 'of mild dispositions, flattered themselves with the 'hopes of seeing better times; and even in these con-'soled themselves with the thoughts, that *Sparta* yet 'retained her independency, and was not subjected by 'another state.'

What then avails civilisation? How are nations gainers by improving in arts and sciences, if they improve at the same time in all that is selfish, base, and sordid? Our untutored ancestors in the forests of *Germany* two thousand years ago, had a high relish for patriotism, liberty, and glory; of which we their improved posterity talk with contempt and ridicule[a]. Their pride was to bear cold, hunger, and thirst, with a manly fortitude. Ours to have fifteen dishes of meat, and six different sorts of wine, on our tables every day. Their pride was to defend themselves against their enemies: ours to hire a mercenary army, who have only to turn their swords upon us, instead of our enemies, and we are their slaves. Their pride was, to shew themselves faithful, constant, and disinterested, in serving their country: ours to fill our pockets with the spoils of our country, and then cry, It will hold my time. To them honour was the reward for serving the public: we have no conception of any reward, but yellow dirt.

Of the mischievous effects of luxury, thus writes the humane and pious Dr. *Price*[b].

'I have represented particularly the great difference 'between the probabilities of human life in towns and 'in

[a] *Jul. Cæs.* DE BELL. GALL. and *Tacit.* DE MOR. GERM. *pass.*

[b] *Price* ON ANNUITIES, p. 274.

'in country pariſhes; and from the facts I have recited, 'it appears, that the farther we go from the artificial 'and irregular modes of living in great towns, the 'fewer of mankind die in the firſt ſtages of life, and the 'more in its laſt. The lower animals, except ſuch as 'have been taken under human management, ſeem in 'general to enjoy the full period of exiſtence allotted 'them, and to die chiefly of old age: and were any 'obſervations to be made among the ſavages, perhaps the 'ſame would be found to be true of them. Death is 'an evil to which the order of Providence has ſubjected 'every inhabitant of this earth; but to man it has been 'rendered unſpeakably more an evil than it was deſign-'ed to be. The greateſt part of that black catalogue 'of diſeaſes which ravage human life, is the offspring 'of the tenderneſs, the luxury, and the corruptions in-'troduced by the vices and falſe refinements of civil 'ſociety. That delicacy which is injured by every 'breath of air, and that rottenneſs of conſtitution which 'is the effect of intemperance and debauchery, were 'never intended by the author of nature; and it is 'impoſſible that they ſhould not lay the foundation of 'numberleſs ſufferings, and terminate in premature 'and miſerable deaths.—Let us then value more the 'ſimplicity and innocence of a life ſo agreeable to na-'ture; and learn to conſider nothing as ſavageneſs but 'malevolence, ignorance, and wickedneſs. The order of 'nature is wiſe and kind. In a conformity to it conſiſts 'health and long life, grace, honour, virtue, and joy. 'But nature turned out of its way will always puniſh. 'The wicked ſhall not live out half their days. Cri-'minal exceſſes embitter and cut ſhort our preſent 'exiſtence; and the higheſt authority has taught us to 'expect, that they will not only kill the body but the 'ſoul; and deprive it of an everlaſting exiſtence.'

The

The ſame writer, in his 62d page, makes the following obſervations:

'Calves are the only animals taken under our peculiar care immediately after birth; and in conſequence of our adminiſtering to them the ſame ſort of phyſic that is given to infants, and treating them in other reſpects in the ſame manner, it is probable that more of them die ſoon after they are born than of all the other ſpecies of animals, which we ſee in the ſame circumſtances. See THE COMPARATIVE VIEW OF THE STATE AND FACULTIES OF MAN WITH THOSE OF THE ANIMAL WORLD, p. 23. It is indeed melancholy to think of the havock among the human ſpecies by the unnatural cuſtoms, as well as the vices, which prevail in poliſhed ſocieties. I have no doubt but that the cuſtom in particular of committing infants, as ſoon as born, to the care of foſter mothers, deſtroys more lives, than the ſword, famine, and peſtilence, put together. The ingenious and excellent writer quoted in the laſt note, obſerves, that the whole claſs of diſeaſes which ariſe from catching cold, are found only among the civilized part of mankind, p. 51. And concerning that loſs of all our higher powers, which often attends the decline of life, and which is often humiliating to human pride, he obſerves, That it exhibits a ſcene ſingular in nature, and that there is greateſt reaſon to believe that it proceeds from adventitious cauſes, and would not take place among us if we led natural lives.'

All wiſe ſtates have guarded againſt luxury as a ruinous evil. At *Athens*, the court of *Areopagus* was to take care, that no perſon lived in idleneſs, and that no man carried on two employments. If a father did not take care to have his ſon inſtructed in ſome art, by which he might

might live, the ſon was not obliged to maintain the father, when paſt labour a.

It was with a view to manners, and for preventing luxury and corruption, that the wiſe ancients of *Athens*, *Sparta*, *Rome*, *Carthage*, &c. appointed cenſors, and ſumptuary laws, public meals, &c.

When a country is overwhelmed by luxury, the patriot is the man, who, by his example, and by promoting good police and the execution of good laws, ſtems the tide of theſe vices. He who does other accidental ſervices, is ſo far laudable; but not a patriot.

O qui vult pater urbium
Suſcribi ſtatuis, &c. HOR.

The patriot is he who delivers his country from that which would otherwiſe bring certain ruin upon it.

Lycurgus allowed no ſtrangers at *Sparta*, nor allowed the *Spartans* to travel, leſt the manners of the people ſhould be corrupted. There is reaſon to expect, that all wiſe governments ſhould forbid their ſubjects coming into *England*, eſpecially during the life of Mrs. *Cornellys*.

Valerius Maximus tells us, that an old *Roman*, on occaſion of a ſumptuary law, mounted the roſtra, and told the people, It was time to demoliſh the commonwealth; ſince they were no longer to have the liberty of living as luxuriouſly as they pleaſed.

When the ſalutary *Licinian* law for reſtraining luxurious tables, was propoſed, the people (even in the degenerate times of the *Jugurthine* war) received it before it was confirmed.

We cannot prevail with the good people of *England* to keep from eating veal and lamb in a time of ſcarcity, though the deſtruction of young animals is manifeſtly of prejudice to the neceſſary quantity of proviſions.

It

a ANT. THYS. DE REP. ATHEN. 250.

It was a good law of the Emperor *Adrian*, that he who ſquandered away his eſtate, ſhould be publickly whipped and baniſhed [a].

The good Emperor *Aurelius* ſold the plate, furniture, jewels, pictures, and ſtatues of the imperial palace, to relieve the diſtreſſes of the people, occaſioned by the invaſion of barbarians, peſtilence, famine, &c. the value of which was ſo great, that it maintained the war for five years, beſides other ineſtimable expences [b].

A law was made in the beginning of *Tiberius*'s reign, That no man ſhould diſgrace his ſex by wearing ſilk [c].

Of ſuch importance were the *Roman* cenſors, that when the office fell into deſuetude for ſeventeen years, the conſequence was, great diſorders in the ſtate [d].

Edward King of *Portugal* propoſed laws againſt luxury, promiſing, that he and his nobles would give a ſtrict attention to their execution, by which he meant, that they would obſerve them. For it was a maxim of his, That whatever is amiſs in the manners of the people, either proceeds from the bad example of the great, or may be cured by the good [e].

Sumptuary laws were univerſal among the ancients. In *England* we ſhould have ſome difficulty in procuring obedience to them; ſuch are our *Engliſh* notions of liberty. But able ſtateſmen know how to conquer thoſe difficulties [f].

Peter, to recall his ſubjects' deviating into luxury, juſt after they had emerged from barbarity, makes a public wedding at his court, to which every body was invited. The entertainment was very plain, and there were no liquors but mead and brandy. Hearing that complaints were made, he obſerved to them, that their anceſtors

[a] Ant. Univ. Hist. xv. 181. [b] Ibid. 217. [c] Ibid. 122.
[d] Ibid. xi. 503. [e] Mod. Univ. Hist. xxi. 135.
[f] Ant. Univ. Hist. xiii. 252.

anceſtors had, for many ages, regaled on theſe liquors. This ſtopped the mouths of the *Ruſſians*, who had often ſhewn, to the Emperor's no ſmall trouble, a fooliſh attachment to the *bad* cuſtoms of their anceſtors; but (like ſome other nations) were too ready to ſhake off the *good* ones [a].

Charlemagne made ſumptuary laws to reſtrain the luxury of his nobility and gentry; and made uſe of a whimſical contrivance to ſhew them, that ſilk cloaths are not fit for men. He drew them along with him a hunting, one rainy day, through woods and rugged places; and when they returned, he permitted none of them to change their dreſs, ſaying, their cloaths would dry beſt on their backs by the fire, which ſhrivelled all their furs, torn before in the woods. He ordered them to come to court the next day in the ſame cloaths. When the court was full, looking round upon them, 'What a tattered company have I about me,' ſays he, 'while my ſheep-ſkin cloak, which I turn this way or 'that, as the weather ſets, is not at all the worſe for 'yeſterday's wear. For ſhame, learn to dreſs like men, 'and let the world judge of your ranks from your me'rit, not from your habit. Leave ſilks and finery to 'women, or to thoſe days of pomp and ceremony, 'when robes are worn for ſhow, and not for uſe [b].

The great and good *Lewis* XII of *France*, at his acceſſion, was attacked by the wits for his frugality. When he was told of it, he only ſaid, 'I had rather 'hear my people laugh at my parſimony, than weep at 'my oppreſſion [c].'

The Emperor *Maximilian* II, never purchaſed a jewel for himſelf [d].

Kong-ti,

---

[a] Mod. Univ. Hist. xxxv. 420. [b] Ibid. xxiii. 161. Ibid. xxiv. 134. [d] Ibid. xxx. 86.

Kong-ti, one of the *Chinese* Emperors, demolished the imperial palace, because it was too magnificent, and likely to effeminate the Emperors[a]. *Yivn-Tsong*, another of those laudable Princes, to check, by example, luxury, in his attendants, ordered all his embroidered cloaths to be publicly burnt[b].

The *Chinese* Emperor *Ching-Tsu*, about *A. D.* 1403, ordered a diamond mine to be shut up. 'The digging 'up of these glittering baubles,' says he, 'fatigues and 'kills my people, and the stones they find are neither 'food nor clothing[c].'

In the war between *Ferdinand* and the *Moors*, the King's equipage was remarkably plain. This being taken notice of to the grandees, by the Queen *Isabella*, they imitated it; and, without law, frugality prevailed by the more potent influence of fashion[d].

When the daughter of the brave Admiral *Coligni* (who was murdered on account of religion, in the horrible massacre of St. *Bartholomew)* went to be married to the Prince of *Orange*, at the *Hague*, her carriage was a covered cart, in which she sat on a board[e].

The ancient *Portuguese* would not let the banks of the golden *Tagus* be searched for that fatal metal, wisely preferring agriculture to mines[f].

It would be of great service to lay a very heavy tax on saddle-horses and carriages, kept by people for their own use. To disable nine in ten, of those who keep horses and carriages, would be a great advantage. People in middling stations would then be enabled to lay down their carriages and saddle-horses without shame,

---

a Mod. Univ. Hist. viii. 442. b Ibid. 446.
c Ibid. viii. 472. d Ibid. xxi. 172.
e *Volt.* Ess. sur l'Hist. iii. 304.
f Anc. Univ. Hist. xviii. 467.

ſhame, or loſs of credit. The number of horſes, which at preſent devour the nation, would be leſſened. All luxury would be diminiſhed. For ſaddle-horſes and carriages are connected with other expences, and muſt be kept up, or fall with them. Many thouſands of hands would be uſefully employed in agriculture and the manufactures, which are now driving people in coaches, chariots, and whiſkies, to bankruptcy. The nobility and gentry would recover that ſuperiority over the bourgeoiſe, which they ſo much deſire.

See the ſtatutes 37 *Edw.* III. cap. 8—14. for regulating 'the diet and apparel of ſervants, handicraftſ-'men, yeomen, their wives and children, of gentle-'men under the eſtate of knights, of eſquires of 200 'mark-land, &c. their wives and children; of mer-'chants, citizens, burgeſſes; of knights who have lands 'within the yearly value of 200 marks, and of kinghts 'and ladies, who have 400 mark-land; of ſeveral ſorts 'of clerks; of ploughmen, and others of mean eſtate [a].' And ſee 3 *Edw.* iv. cap. 5 [b]; ſee a proclamation by *James* I, commanding the great men to keep to their country ſeats, for reviving the old *Engliſh* hoſpitality at the approaching *Chriſtmas* [c]; and another by *Charles* I, *A. D.* 1632, commanding the gentry to keep their reſidence at their manſions in the country, and not at *London* [d].

A Duke of *Bedford* was degraded from his nobility for the ſmallneſs of his income; becauſe it was thought, his having a title and not a ſuitable fortune to maintain it, might be of bad conſequence [e]. I think all noble perſons who impoveriſh themſelves by extravagance, ought to be degraded.

[a] STAT. AT LARGE, I. 298. [b] Ibid. 609.
[c] ACT. REG. IV. 312. [d] *Rym.* FOED. XIX. 374.
[e] *Blackſt.* COM. I. 403.

Lord *Chesterfield*, *A. D.* 1773, left his estate to his nephew, but under the prudent restriction, that, if ever he be seen at *Newmarket* during the races, he shall forfeit 5000l. and the same sum for every 100l. lost by him at play. The Dean and Chapter of *Canterbury* to sue and apply the money to the use of that church[a].

CHAP. III.

Of the public Diversions, and of Gaming, and their Influence on Manners.

FEW things have a more direct influence upon the manners of the people, than the public diversions, and gaming. Of the former, the chief are theatrical exhibitions, which ought to be very carefully attended to by the rulers of all states. Accordingly, when *Solon* observed with how much avidity the people listened to old *Thespis*'s mean compositions, whose theatre was a cart, and who, instead of giving out tickets at so much money each, was paid with a goat given by the neighbourhood or quarter where he had entertained the people, from whence the word Tragedy (a Goat-song) was derived; *Solon*, I say, when he observed how greedily the people listened to *Thespis*'s low stuff, struck the ground with his staff, not without indignation, crying out, that he foresaw that these trifling amusements would come to be matter of great importance in life. This was thoroughly verified afterwards among both *Greeks* and *Romans*, insomuch that concerning the latter it was proverbially alleged, A *Roman* wanted nothing but bread and the *Circensium*

[a] WHITEHALL EVEN. POST, *March* 27.

Circensian games. The theatre, with certain management, might undoubtedly be made a very powerful instrument for cultivating either virtue or vice in the minds of a people, as it exhibits an assemblage of what is most elegant in the fine arts, poetry, painting, music, speaking, action, &c. and as the story is drawn from what is the most striking in history and in life. It is reckoned by some, that the first dramatic pieces were written and performed as acts of religion in honour of the gods. Our modern productions have, generally speaking, as little tincture of religion as can well be imagined. And yet I must observe, to the honour of the *people*, not the *government* of our times, that scarce any age ever deserved more praise on account of the decency and chastity of its theatrical compositions, and the behaviour of the actors and actresses upon the stage, than the present, if you except the female dancers, whose immodest curvetting in the air, and exposing of their limbs as they do, are both consummately ungraceful, as every female motion, that is not gentle, and soft, and tender, like the sex, must be; but likewise shockingly offensive to modest eyes, and fatally alluring to those already familiarized to vice. This is an evil which merits reformation. But it will be much better corrected by the public disapprobation, than by law. We had a licenser of plays in the time of *Walpole*, but he only inquired, whether a new play was anti-ministerial or not. If it contained any satire on *corruption*, the *index expurgatorius* was applied to it by the Lord Chamberlain without mercy. So wretchedly do ministers discharge their duty; so miserably do they fill their important station.

Demosthenes severely blamed the degenerate *Athenians* for diverting the public money raised for the defence of the state, to shews and plays, by which the people were enervated.

'A very wise man said, he believed, if a man were 'permitted to make all the ballads, he need not care 'who made the laws of a nation. The ancient legis'lators did not pretend to reform the manners of the 'people without the help of the poets[a].'

How austere must the manners of the *Romans* have originally been, which did not allow a person of character to *dance!* It was a saying among them, *Nemo fere*, &c. 'No body dances unless he be either drunk 'or mad[b].' The *Greeks*, however, had no objection to this art.

There must have been a considerable falling off, when *Sylla* won that popular favour by a shew of lions, which in better times he could only have obtained by substantial services[c].

The *Olympic* games are to be looked upon in a very different light from all other public diversions, shows, &c. They gave an opportunity to all persons to exhibit their skill and abilities in all the accomplishments which were esteemed in those days. They kept up a laudable emulation to excel; for, a prize gained on account of the meanest accomplishment, as swiftness of foot, for instance, was a matter of great honour, as a man's being victor in that contest, supposed him to be a better runner than any other within the *Olympian*, *Nemæan*, *Elean*, or *Isthmian* circles. The contests were also useful for keeping up in the people a pleasure in manly and warlike exercises, which was absolutely necessary

[a] *Fletcher*, p. 372.

[b] See *Cicero*'s ORATION in defence of a man of consular rank accused of the crime of dancing.

[c] ANT. UNIV. HIST. XIII. 33.

necessary in those times, when personal valour was of such consequence, which now is nothing, since the art of war has, by the invention of gun-powder, been wholly changed[a].

The combats of *Athletæ* were first introduced at *Rome* when the manners of the people were considerably corrupted, of which these diversions, with the shows of gladiators and the like, were the causes and symptoms[b].

As for these last, which prevailed more and more as the manners degenerated more, they are a disgrace to human nature, and only *Milton*'s devils[c] ought to be capable of being diverted with the sight of men tormenting, cutting with swords, tearing to pieces by wild beasts, and destroying their wretched fellow-creatures. The government which suffered such abominations to prevail for so many ages, must have been very barbarous. For it is not necessary, in order to make a people martial and brave, to make them infernal furies.

We find, that players, on account of their debauchery, were banished from *Italy* in the debauched times of *Tiberius*[d]; and that games of hazard, and concerts of music, were forbidden[e]. It is not known what the harm of those musical entertainments might be. Perhaps they were of the same kind with the music-houses in Holland, which are public brothels.

---

a See the learned account of the *Olympic* games, prefixed by my late esteemed friend *Gilbert West*, Esq; to his TRANSLATION OF PINDAR.

b ANT. UNIV. HIST. XII. 354.

c Referring to the poet's account of the diversions with which the dæmons amused themselves during *Satan*'s absence. PARAD. LOST, Book II.

d ANT. UNIV. HIST. XIV. 184. e Ibid. XII. 450.

Antoninus led a private life in the imperial court of *Rome*[a]. *Aurelius* hated the public diverſions, and talked with his miniſters about the public buſineſs the whole time of his attending them[b]. *Conſtantine* put a ſtop to the ſhows of gladiators[c]. The Emperor *Honorius* totally aboliſhed the ſhows of gladiators[d].

A motion was made, *A. D.* 1735, in parliament, for reſtraining the number of playhouſes[e]. It was obſerved, that there were then in *London*, the opera-houſe, the *French* playhouſe in the *Haymarket*, and the theatres in *Covent-Garden*, *Drury-lane*, *Lincoln's-inn-fields*, and *Goodman's-fields*; and that it was no leſs ſurpriſing than ſhameful to ſee ſo great a change for the worſe in the temper and inclinations of the *Britiſh* nation, who were now ſo extravagantly addicted to lewd and idle diverſions, that the number of playhouſes in *London* was double to that of *Paris*. That we now exceeded in levity even the *French* themſelves, from whom we learned theſe and many other ridiculous cuſtoms, as much unſuitable to the manners of an *Engliſhman* or a *Scot*, as they were agreeable to the air and levity of a *Monſieur*: That it was aſtoniſhing to all *Europe*, that *Italian* eunuchs and ſingers ſhould have ſet ſalaries equal to thoſe of the lords of the treaſury, and judges of *England*. After this it was ordered, *nem. con.* that a bill be brought in, purſuant to Sir *John Barnard*'s motion, which was done accordingly: but it was afterwards dropt, on account of a clauſe offered to be inſerted in the ſaid bill, for enlarging the power of the lord chamberlain, with regard to the licenſing of plays.

Plays

[a] Ant. Univ. Hist. xv. 197. [b] Ibid. 209.
[c] Ibid. 581. [d] Ibid. xvi. 492.
[e] Deb. Com. ix. 93.

Plays and other public diverſions were ſtopped by parliament, *A. D.* 1647, for half a year. Several lords proteſted becauſe it was not for perpetuity[a].

Petitions were preſented, *A. D.* 1738, from the city, univerſity, and merchants of *Edinburgh*, againſt licenſing a playhouſe[b].

The reader ſees, that, though I have mentioned the entertainments of the theatre among thoſe abuſes of our times, of which this work exhibits a general ſurvey; I have not abſolutely condemned them: on the contrary, I have confeſſed the uſe, which a ſet of able ſtateſmen might make of them in reforming and improving the manners of the people: the particulars of which I leave to be found and applied by men of wiſdom and of public ſpirit.

The moſt faſhionable of all diverſions in our time, is maſquerading; on which I have a few thoughts to offer.

Shame is the moſt powerful reſtraint from bad actions. To put on a maſk is to put off ſhame. And what is a human character without ſhame?

It was obſerved long ago by the excellent *Tillotſon*, on another account, that the people of *England* are but too tractable in imitating ſome of their worſt neighbours in ſome of their worſt cuſtoms. The *French* taught us maſquerading, which has been an amuſement of that fantaſtical people ever ſince the days of *Charles* VI, if not earlier. For in his time there was exhibited a moſt dreadful ſcene of that kind, which, one would have expected to cool a little their eagerneſs for maſquerades ever after. The king and five of the court, on occaſion of a marriage, diſguiſed themſelves like ſatyrs, by covering their naked bodies with linen

H 4 habits,

[a] PARL. HIST. XVI. 112. [b] DEB. COM. X. 9.

habits, close to their limbs, which habits were bedaubed with rosin, on which down was stuck. One of the company, in a frolick, running a light against one of them, as they were dancing in a ring, all the six were instantly enveloped with flames, and the whole company in a consternation, lest the fire should be communicated to all. Nothing was to be seen or heard but flames and screams. Four of the six died two days after, in cruel agonies; and the King, who was subject to a weakness of brain, was overset by the fright, so that he was ever after outrageous by fits, and incapable of government.

There are few entertainments more unmeaning, to say the least, than masquerades. For the whole *innocent* pleasure of them must consist in the ready and brilliant wit of the masks, suitable to the characters they assume. But it cannot be supposed, that among a thousand people, there are fifty persons capable of entertaining by the readiness of their wit, and their judgment in sustaining assumed characters. Accordingly we hear of much stupidity played off on those occasions; and yet the rage after them continues. Wit must indeed be at a low ebb, when it is thought witty for a nobleman to assume at a masquerade the dress of a turkey-cock. This piece of wit, I am informed, was really exhibited at a late masquerade at Mrs. *Cornellys*'s. As we know of nothing characteristical in a real turkey-cock, but his gabbling, it is not easy to imagine what entertainment a man of quality should propose to give a company by assuming that character. If he had taken the likeness of a rook, he might have been a visible satire on gamesters, placemen, &c. if that of an owl, he might have said he was a deep statesman; or if he chose a quadrupedal transformation, as that of an ass, for instance, or of a stag, a bull, or any of the horned fraternity, he might have told those who questioned

him,

ſm, that he was their repreſentative in parliament, &c. Obſerving the frequency of violated marriage-beds of late years, and the frequent celebrations of maſquerades, it requires a conſiderable ſtretch of charity to avoid ſuſpecting a connexion between maſquerading and intriguing, which may account for the eagerneſs ſhewn by the quality for that ſpecies of diverſion, in direct oppoſition to the known diſapprobation of both King and Queen; no great proof of politeneſs in our courtiers.

'Maſquerades (ſays Mr. *Gordon*[a]) are a market for 'maidenheads and adultery, a dangerous luxury oppo-'ſite to virtue and liberty. There was ſomething like 'them formerly in the reigns of our worſt Princes, by 'the name of maſks. As the preſent reign reſembles 'theſe in nothing elſe, ſo neither would I have it re-'ſemble them in this. They were revived, or rather 'introduced, after the *French* way, by a foreign ambaſſa-'dor, whoſe only errand then in *England* could be but 'to corrupt and enſlave us, and for that end this mad 'and indecent diverſion was practiſed and exhibited by 'him, as a popular engine to catch looſe minds, or to 'make them ſo with great ſucceſs. What good pur-'poſe they can ſerve now, I would be glad to know: 'The miſchief of them is manifeſt both to public 'and private perſons; a handle is taken from them to 'traduce ſome great characters, whom I would have 'always reverenced; and they are viſibly an oppor-'tunity and invitation to lewdneſs. If people will 'have amuſements, let them have warrantable and de-'cent ones; as to maſquerades, they are ſo much the 'ſchool of vice, that excepting a law to declare it 'innocent and ſafe, I queſtion whether human inven-'tion

[a] TRACTS, I. 32.

'tion can contrive a more successful method of propagating it. The practice of the commonalty is formed upon the example of the great, and what the latter do the former think they may do. If a city wife has it in her head against her husband's inclinations, to take the pleasures of the masquerade, she has but to tell him, that my Lady Dutchess ——— is to be there (no doubt upon the same errand), and the poor, sober, saving man must submit, and be content to be in the class of his betters. From this source of prostitution, I fear many a worthy man takes to his arms a tainted and vicious wife, and finds in her a melancholy reason both, for himself and his posterity, to curse and detest masquerades and all those that encourage them.

Severe and cutting is Mr. *Gordon's* remonstrance to *Sherlock* Bishop of *London* [a], on his lordship's politeness in passing over masquerades, when enumerating, in his LETTER ON OCCASION OF THE EARTHQUAKES, *A. D.* 1750, the national vices, which those awful phænomena suggested the necessity of reforming.

'You come, my lord,' says he, 'in all humility, not as our accuser, but as our faithful servant and monitor in Jesus Christ, and tell us, that your heart's desire and prayer to God is for us, that we may be saved. Whom do you mean to save, my good lord? Those who frequent plays, operas, music, dancings, gardens, cock-fighting, and prize-fighting? And why not those who frequent masquerades and *Venetian* balls? Surely your lordship cannot be a stranger to the frequent legal presentments, which, founded on the declared sense of all sober men, have stigmatized these dissolute assemblies with the severest 'public

[a] *Gord.* TRACTS, II. 268.

'public censure; nor can you be ignorant, that *Venetian* 'balls, in their own native soil, exhibit on occasion, the 'most various scenes of exaggerated lewdness, which 'that most lewd and effeminate of all regions, *Italy*, 'can produce? Or did you, in the innocence of your 'heart, take it for granted, that our imitations of these 'balls were so purified by the presence of the greatest, 'as to make you fear the censure of uncharitableness, 'at least of indelicacy, had they been included in 'your black catalogue of sinful recreations? Who 'knows, my lord, that your courtly omission of this 'new imported diversion, has not been the means of 'sanctifying its further use; for the very next day after 'the expected earthquake, I observed one of these *Ve*-'*netian* balls advertised in the public papers, as the 'first place for our affrighted countrymen to assemble 'and rejoice in after the dissipation of their fears.'

A certain late king was fond to distraction of masquerading. And he set before his people another execrable example, viz. the violation of the matrimonial vow.

His present majesty, whom God preserve, has acted a contrary part in both respects. This, however, is no comparison between them as kings; but as men only; and I mention it merely to introduce the following anecdote, which ought to be kept in remembrance.

A grand masquerade was given out in the last reign for a certain evening. Some well-disposed persons, taking into consideration the mischievous tendency of those diversions, ordered hand-bills to be scattered about the streets, advising the ladies to keep at home; for that the people, displeased with the indecency of masquerades, had determined to prevent any of the fair sex from going, and that there would probably be mobbing and quarrelling in the streets. Whether there was any thing more in this, than that those gentlemen hoped to intimidate the ladies, and keep them at home, I never learned. But, rather than the court ſhould loſe the night's entertainment, a very great commander gave notice that he would order out a ſufficient body of the military to keep the peace; ſo that the ladies might go to the virtuous rendezvous without fear of interruption from the people. This was making our ſtanding army uſeful.

At the marriage of *Tamerlane's* grand-children, the people aſſembled were allowed, by the emperor's proclamation, to purſue whatever pleaſures they thought fit, and no one was to hinder another. It is to be expected, that we ſhall ſoon have maſquradesat Mrs.—'s eſtabliſhed on this very foot[a]. The following paragraph gives an abridged account of a late celebration of that kind.

'Such a ſcene of ebriety was exhibited laſt maſ-'querade, and the behaviour of the women of the 'town, and of the bucks of diſſipation, ſo ſhocking, 'it is hoped, the enormity of it will occaſion the total 'abolition of thoſe abandoned nightly orgies[b].'

We always begin our pretended reformations of manners at the wrong end. Inſtead of making laws to reſtrain the lower people, our rulers ought to ſhew them by their example how they ought to behave. Here follows the preamble to an act, which might have been intituled, An Act to make the lower people better than their betters. The multitude of places of entertainment for the higher ſort of people is a great evil, as well as thoſe for the lower. The thefts and robberies committed by ſtateſmen are more miſchievous than the petty larceny of the lower people.

'Whereas

---

[a] MOD. UNIV. HIST. VI. 362.

[b] WHITEHALL EVEN. POST, *May* 1, 1773.

'Whereas the multitude of places of entertainment 'for the lower ſort of people is a great cauſe of thefts 'and robberies, as they are thereby tempted to ſpend 'their ſmall ſubſtance in riotous pleaſures, and in con- 'ſequence are put on unlawful methods of ſupplying 'their wants, and renewing their pleaſures, &c.' Preamble to the act 25 *Geo.* II. for preventing thefts and robberies, and for regulating places of public entertainment, and puniſhing perſons keeping diſorderly houſes[a].

The oldeſt accounts we have of diverſions bearing any reſemblance to maſquerades, and from whence the hint may have been taken, are, perhaps, thoſe of the nightly orgies upon mount *Cithæron*, the myſteries of the *Bona Dea*, and the like, which were eſtabliſhed in honour of ſundry gods and goddeſſes. Their being concealed under cloud of night, and the ſecrecy obſerved with reſpect to the tranſactions carried on in ſome of them, give them a ſuſpicious air, which increaſes the reſemblance which our maſquerades bear to them. I wiſh ſome of our learned antiquaries would inquire, whether the *Bona Dea* was not an anceſtor of our famous Mrs. *Cornellys* *. It is true, that the myſteries of

a STAT. AT LARGE, IX. 109.

* Let this page immortalize the genius of this wonderful outlandiſh old woman, who by dint of a knack ſhe has at ſticking up lamps againſt a wainſcot, in the ſhape of fans, bodkins, ſciſſars, and the like, and of ranging cakes and ſugar-plums upon the ſhelves of a lacquered cupboard, has for ſeveral years ſo drained our nobility and gentry, that they cannot pay off their playhouſe ſcores, their *Newmarket* ſcores, nor their milk ſcores. Her cuſtom is to ſtick up her lamps, and range her cakes in a certain ſet of ſhapes, (very fine, you may be ſure) and next day after ſhe has drawn together all the people of taſte to ſee them, at

of the *Bona Dea* are commonly reckoned to have been celebrated by women exclusively, while the manager of the heightened pleasures of the *English* admits a mixture of both sexes. But it is not certain, that many of the figures, which passed for females, were not in reality of the other sex in disguise, as it is not certain, that many of the virtuous-seeming ladies at our masquerades, are not rampant wh——s in disguise.

Mrs. *Cornellys* was indicted before the grand jury, *A. D.* 1771, for keeping a common disorderly house, and permitting divers loose, idle, and disorderly persons, both men and women [of quality], to be, and remain in her house the whole night, rioting, and otherwise misbehaving themselves; that she kept public masquerades without licence, and received and harboured loose and disorderly persons [of quality] in masks, with great noise and tumult, &c[a].

There was a masquerade in *Scotland*, *A. D.* 1773, the very year in which almost all credit in that country

---

the expence of 20,000 *l.* she asks pardon in the news-papers, that her show was not so fine as it ought to have been, and humbly begs the favour of their lordships and ladyships to come such a night, and they shall see what they shall see. They all go accordingly, over and over as often as she changes her lamps and her cakes, as it costs them nothing but their expences; and the outlandish old woman acts the part of the money-taker, and sweeps together the guineas. But, whatever may be the matter, whether her œconomy is bad, or that money gotten in such a way does not wear well, she not only sends many to the spunging-house, but is often obliged to take a night's lodging there herself.

——dii talem terris avertite pestem. VIRO.

[a] LOND. MAG. *Feb.* 1771, p. 109.

try was overthrown [a]; and the ſame diverſions have been exhibited at *Southampton*, *Brighthelmſtone*, *Margate*, &c. Such is the power of example, and ſo true the old adage,

> One fool makes many
> As four farthings make a penny.

'Thoſe are puny politicians, ſays *Bolingbroke* [b], who 'attack a people's liberty directly. The means are 'dangerous, and the ſucceſs precarious. Notions of 'liberty are interwoven with our very being, and the 'leaſt ſuſpicion of its being in danger, fires the ſoul 'with a generous indignation. But he is the ſtateſ-'man formed for ruin and deſtruction, whoſe wily 'head knows how to diſguiſe the fatal hook with baits 'of pleaſure, which his artful ambition diſpenſes with 'a laviſh hand, and makes himſelf popular in undoing. 'Thus are the eaſy thoughtleſs people made the in-'ſtruments of their own ſlavery; nor do they know, 'that the fatal mine is laid, till they feel the pile come 'tumbling on their heads. This is the finiſhed poli-'tician, the darling ſon of *Machiavel*.—Maſquerades, 'with all the other elegancies of a wanton age, are 'much leſs to be regarded for their expence, (great as 'it is) than for the tendency they have to deprave our 'manners.'

As to gaming, I cannot ſay, that ever I have heard a tolerable apology for it upon the ſcore of morality, or common honeſty. Is it not literally obtaining money upon falſe pretences, and without a *valuable* conſideration, when I draw 100 guineas out of my neighbour's pocket, for which I give him nothing, but vexation and repentance? And does not every body know, that obtaining money, or goods, upon falſe pretences, is puniſhable by law, as much as theft or robbery?

This

[a] WHITEHALL EVEN. POST, *Jan.* 21. 1773.

[b] POLITICAL TRACTS, 76.

This is exclusive of the loss of time, the inflaming of passion, often producing quarrels and murders, the endangering of chastity, (for it is alleged, that the ladies do often pay with their persons what they cannot with their purses) the destruction of fortunes, often ending in despair and self-murder. It is strange, that our nobility and gentry cannot be diverted at a rate somewhat cheaper than all this. How can a person of quality bear to think of himself as guilty of what would send him to *Newgate*, if he were not above law? Nobility of rank ought to suggest the necessity of *acting* in a *noble* manner. The man is what his *actions* (not his *birth* and *rank*) make him. A man of noble birth acting in a mean and sordid manner, is only the *more* mean and sordid, because he sinks below what was to have been *expected* of him. Add, that the vices of a person of rank are incomparably more criminal than those of the common people; because his example draws the multitude into guilt, and he becomes answerable for their offences. Our nobility and gentry, so far from attending to these considerations, are the great leaders of the people into this ruinous vice. Besides, the example they exhibit of an endless attachment to carding, rooking, cocking, racing, pitting, gambling, jobbing, they have introduced gaming into their system of politics, and a pack of cards is become an engine powerful enough to overthrow a kingdom.

An anonymous speaker in the House of Commons, *A. D.* 1754, on occasion of a lottery proposed by the ministry, argued as follows:

'The mortal disease of the present generation is well 'known to be the love of gaming; a desire to emerge 'into sudden riches; a disposition to stake the future 'against the present, and commit their fortunes, them'selves, and their posterity to chance. The conse-

'quence

'quence of this pernicious paſſion is hourly ſeen in 'the diſtreſs of individuals, the ruin of families, the 'extravagance and luxury of the ſucceſsful, and rage 'and fraud of them that miſcarry; this therefore is the 'vice, at leaſt one of the vices, againſt which the whole 'artillery of power ſhould be employed. From gam-'ing, the people ſhould be diſſuaded by inſtruction, 'withdrawn by example, and deterred by puniſhment. 'To game, whether with or without good fortune, 'ſhould be made ignominious; he that grows rich by 'it ought to be deemed as a robber, and he that is im-'poveriſhed as a murderer of himſelf. Yet, what are 'the men entruſted with the adminiſtration of the pub-'lic now propoſing? What but to increaſe this luſt 'of irregular acquiſition, and to invite the whole na-'tion to a practice which the laws condemn, which 'policy diſapproves, and which morality abhors? For 'what is a lottery but a game? The perſons, who 'riſque their money in lotteries, are I believe for the 'moſt part the needy or extravagant; thoſe whom mi-'ſery makes adventurers, or expence makes greedy. 'And of theſe the needy are often ruined by their loſs, 'and the luxurious by their gain. He, whoſe little 'trade, induſtriouſly purſued, would find bread for his 'family, diminiſhes his ſtock to buy a ticket, and waits 'with impatience for the hour which ſhall determine 'his lot; a blank deſtroys all his hopes, and he ſinks 'at once into negligence and idleneſs. The ſpend-'thrift, if he miſcarries, is not reclaimed; but if he 'ſucceeds, is confirmed in his extravagance, by find-'ing that his wants, however multiplied, may be ſo 'eaſily ſupplied. It is univerſally allowed that reward 'ſhould be given only to merit, and that as far as hu-'man power can provide, every man's condition ſhould 'be regulated by his merit. This is the great end of 'established government, which lotteries seem purposely contrived to counteract. In a lottery the good and 'bad, the worthless and the valuable, the stupid and 'the wise, have all the same chance of profit. That 'wealth which ought only to be the reward of honest 'industry, will fall to the lot of the drone, whose whole 'merit is to pay his stake, and dream of his ticket.

'With indignation it was observed, that no less than 'two lotteries in one year, (*A. D.* 1763,) were now, 'for the first time, without any urgent necessity, to 'be established in the days of peace, to the encourage-'ment of the pernicious spirit of gaming, which can-'not be too much discountenanced by every state that 'is governed by wisdom, and a regard for the morals 'of the people [a].'

'Gaming is so dreadful a vice (says Mr. *Gordon* [b],) 'especially in those who are any way intrusted with our 'liberties, that I cannot pass it over in silence. A man 'who will venture his estate, will venture his country. 'He who is mad enough to commit his all to the 'chance of a dye, is like to prove but a faithless guar-'dian of the public, in which he has perhaps no longer 'any stake. It is a jest, and something worse, in a 'man who flings away his fortune this way, to pretend 'any regard for the good of mankind. His actions 'give his words the lie. He sacrifices his own happi-'ness, and that of his family and posterity to a sharper, 'or an amusement, and by doing it, shews that he is 'utterly destitute of common prudence, and natural 'affection; and on the contrary, an encourager and 'example of the most destructive corruption; and after 'all this, ridiculously talks of his zeal for his country, 'which consists in good sense and virtue, joined to a 'tenderness

---

a *Speech in Parliament, Alm.* DEB, COM. VI. 198.

b TRACTS, I. 325.

'tenderneſs for one's fellow-creatures. When he has 'wantonly reduced himſelf to a morſel of bread, he 'will be eaſily perſuaded to forſake his wretchedneſs, 'and accept of a bribe. Who would truſt their pro- 'perty with one who cannot keep his own? The 'ſame vicious imbecillity of mind, which makes a man 'a fool to himſelf, will make him a knave to other 'people. So that this wicked proneneſs to play, which 'is only the impious art of undoing or being undone, 'cuts off every man who is poſſeſſed with it, from all 'pretence either to honeſty or capacity. I doubt *Eng- 'land* has paid dear for ſuch extravagances. A law- 'maker, who is at the ſame time a gameſter, is a cha- 'racter big with abſurdity and danger. I wiſh that in 'every member of either houſe, gaming were attended 'with expulſion and degradation; and in every officer, 'civil or military, with the loſs of his place. A law 'enjoining this penalty would be effectual, and no 'other can.'

One of the greateſt miſchiefs of gaming is, that the gameſter, like the dropſical patient, becomes more and more attached to it.

The ancient *Germans* became at laſt ſo bewitched to gaming, that they would play for their liberty, which liberty they yet valued ſo much, that they would ſooner die, than ſuffer it to be taken from them [a].

It is common among us for a gentleman to ſit down in eaſy circumſtances, and riſe a beggar. But among thoſe fooliſh people, it was common for the men to ſit down free, and riſe ſlaves for life. That was a wretched government, which allowed ſuch proceedings.

Caſimir II. of *Poland*, when he was prince of *Sandomir*, won a conſiderable ſum of a nobleman, with

 whom

[a] Ant. Univ. Hist. xix. 42.

whom he was at play. The nobleman, fretted at his loſs, ſtruck the prince, and immediately fled. He was apprehended, and condemned to death. But *Caſimir* would not ſuffer the ſentence to be executed. It was no wonder, he ſaid, that the nobleman, loſing his money, and enraged againſt Fortune, whom he could not come at, ſhould revenge himſelf on her favourite. He owned, that he himſelf was moſt to blame for encouraging gaming by his example. He reſtored the nobleman his money [a].

Mohammed forbid gaming and drinking [b]. *Henry* IV. of *France*, ‘ had a great paſſion for play, which had ‘ terrible conſequences, as it rendered this deſtructive ‘ vice faſhionable, which is alone ſufficient to throw a ‘ kingdom into confuſion [c].’ *John* I. king of *Portugal* uſed to ſay, ‘ converſation was the cheapeſt of all ‘ diverſions, and the moſt improving [d].’ Cards have deſtroyed all converſation in *England*. Our quality ſhew ſo little natural affection, and ſo much delight in gaming, that there is reaſon to expect they will ſoon, like the *Tonkineſe* in *India*, play away their wives and children [e]. The rage of gaming has indeed changed our great folks into another ſpecies of beings than thoſe who filled that ſtation laſt century. A ruffian lord, who will make no heſitation to bribe, and (for ought he knows) damn hundreds of electors, makes a point of paying his game debts, though it be penal by law; and yet will cheat and abuſe an induſtrious tradeſman for aſking a debt due for neceſſaries; juſt to ſharpers, who ruin him; unjuſt to honeſt men, who feed and clothe him.

The

---

[a] Mod. Univ. Hist. xxiv. 90. [b] Ibid. xviii. 413. [c] Ibid. xxxiv. 436. [d] Ibid. xxii. 126. [e] Ibib. vii. 463.

The excellent *Gordon* thus exposes the mischiefs arising from the example of the *great* encouraging this ruinous vice, at the same time that the laws (made by the *great)* point their vengeance against it.

Ridicule and contempt have been cast on the laws, and principally by those whose influence and power should have given them countenance and effect: the recent prohibition of gaming, calculated to extirpate that offspring of avarice, that parent of selfishness, that enemy to humanity, compunction, and every social virtue, has been shamefully baffled by the shelter afforded to that enormity, under the privileged roofs of the great, and met with an open and contumelious disregard from personages invested with the most sacred ensigns of authority, in places of public resort among the gay, the giddy, and the young, where the native allurements of vice have long been too prevalent to want aid and encouragement from such venerable and powerful auxiliaries: the flagrant example of those in high station, has necessarily extended its pernicious effects to the lowest; then who has most right to complain either to God or man, a people abandoned by their superiors to corruption, or those who have encouraged the example of profligacy to complain of the people? Severity and decency of manners in high life, would command a similar behaviour in the multitude; a strict execution of the laws would come in aid; since the virtuous great must know, that the due exertion of the legal power is a principal part of their duty: Idleness, debauchery, and wanton recreations, would not then have a being among us, to become the objects of animadversions and censure, which leaving the fountain-head of vice untouched, and attempting the impracticable task of restraining the torrent at a distance from its source; most clearly denote the *parade* of reformation, without the *reality*, or even the *intention*[a].

'*Si vouz supposez*, &c. Reckoning in *Paris* 2000 'persons, who lose every day three hours each at play, 'the number of lost hours in a day is 6000, which, 'employed usefully, would be worth to individuals and 'the state more than 1000 livrés a day, or 365,000 'livres a year. If you estimate *Paris* to be a seventh 'part of the kingdom, this loss amounts to 7,300,000 'livres a year[b],' which at 10*d.* ½ *per* livre, is about 304,513*l.* 1*s.* *English* money lost annually by the whole people of *France* by gaming, and nothing got, but anger, quarrels, and duels.

Our ancestors have not overlooked the dangerous vice of gaming. By 2 and 3 *Philip* and *Mary*, all licences for carrying on unlawful games are to be void[c].

See an act for preventing excessive and deceitful gaming[d]; and a bill to restrain the excessive increase of horse-races[e]; and another for preventing wagers about public affairs. Designing men injured the unwary, and many kept up unlawful correspondences on purpose to win wagers[f].

James I. granted power to the groom-porter to licence a certain limited number of taverns, in which cards and dice might be played, and a certain number of bowling allies, tennis-courts, &c. in *London* and its neighbourhood[g].

'Whereas

---

[a] *Gord.* TRACTS, II. 269.

[b] *S. Pierre* OUVR. POLIT. X. 326.

[c] STAT. AT LARGE, II. 121.

[d] DEB. COM. X. 13

[e] Ibid. XI. 296.

[f] *Tind.* CONTIN. II. 118.

[g] *Anders.* HIST. COM. II. 5.

'Whereas lawful games and exercises should not be 'otherwise used, than as innocent and moderate re-'creations, and not as trades or callings to get a living, 'or to make unlawful advantage thereby; and where-'as, by the immoderate use of them, many mischiefs 'and inconveniencies do arise, and are daily found, to 'the maintaining and encouraging of sundry idle, loose, 'and disorderly persons, in their dishonest, lewd, and 'dissolute course of life, and to the circumventing, de-'ceiving, cozening, and debauching many of the 'younger sort both of the nobility and gentry, to the 'loss of their precious time, the utter ruin of their 'estates and fortunes, and withdrawing them from no-'ble and laudable employments: be it therefore enac-'ted, &c.' Preamble to the statute 16 *Charles* II. cap. 7 [a]. It enacts, among other things, that no game debt shall be recoverable by law; and that the winner shall forfeit treble the sum won by him at play.

An Act, *A. D.* 1657, for punishing persons who live at high rates, and have no visible estate, profession or calling answerable thereunto [b].

By 18 *Geo.* II. cap. 34. restraints are laid on several games; the sums, which may be played for at one time, are limited; offenders discovering others, are discharged, &c [c]. But what do laws avail against the example of the law-makers themselves?

CHAP. IV.

Of Duels.

OUR laws forbid *murder*: our manners legitimate *duelling*.

[a] Stat. at Large, II. 655.

[b] Whitel. Mem. 662.

[c] Stat. at Large, VIII. 181.

'In deliberate duelling, says the admirable *Black-* '*stone*[a], both parties meet avowedly with an intent to 'murder; thinking it their duty as gentlemen, and 'claiming it as their right, to wanton with their own 'lives, and those of their fellow-creatures, without any 'warrant or authority from any power, either divine or 'human, but in direct contradiction to the laws both 'of God and man; and therefore the law has justly 'fixed the crime and punishment of murder on them, 'and on their seconds. Yet it requires such a degree 'of passive valour to combat the dread of even unde- 'served contempt, arising from the false notions of ho- 'nour too generally received in *Europe*, that the 'strongest prohibitions and penalties will never be 'entirely effectual to eradicate this unhappy custom, 'till a method be found out of compelling the original 'aggressor, to make some other satisfaction to the 'affronted party, which the world shall esteem equally 'reputable as that which is now given at the hazard 'of the life and fortune, as well of the person insulted, 'as of him, who hath given the insult.'

The *abbe S. Pierre* insists [b], that 'it is cruel and un- 'just to punish with loss of fortune and life an un- 'happy man, who cannot obey the law [that is, can- 'not refuse a challenge] without infamy and disgrace; 'as the law of nature, on the other hand, enjoins him 'never to dishonour himself, and to prefer death to in- 'famy. *Je soutiens qu'il est cruel, &c.*' The *abbé* therefore proposes, that there be a military academy established, before which all differences between gentlemen, on points of honour, shall be decided.

The same author proposes [c] that a solemn oath be administered to every officer, on receiving his commission,

[a] COMM. IV. 129.

[b] OEUVR. POLIT. VIII. 240.

[c] Ibid. X. 53.

fion, by which he fhould abjure duelling, and promife to difcover all fuch defigns among his acquaintance. Were duelling left off among officers, it would foon become unfafhionable every where elfe. Thefe are fome of the advantages we gain by our ftanding army. They teach us, that it is polite to lie with other men's wives, to debauch innocent virgins, and to murder one another about points of honour.

Though challenging in confequence of an infult upon a perfon's honour, or what is fo called, is a very ancient cuftom, it is not eafy to explain the *reafonablenefs* of the practice. A perfon has injured me. The laws of my country give me no redrefs. (A moft fcandalous deficiency on the part of government!) To endeavour to avenge myfelf, and to vindicate my violated honour by an attack upon him, is natural, though not magnanimous, nor chriftian. But becaufe a perfon has flightly injured me, am I to give him a chance for doing me an infinitely greater injury? Here, then, comes in, I fuppofe, the pretence, that a duel is an appeal to providence, as if it were certain, that providence would give fuccefs to the party who has the right on his fide. But who has told our duellifts, that providence will certainly give fuccefs to him, who feeks to fhed the blood of his fellow-creature, *cold*, in defence of the virtue of a wh—— or of the honour of a liar, or even in defence of the chaftity of a really virtuous woman, or of the honour of him, who has fpoken the truth? We know, that fcripture reprefents the prefent as a ftate of difcipline, not of retribution, and exprefsly warns us againft rafh conclufions concerning the different lots of men in this life. And where elfe our duellifts fhould find their doctrine, of certain fuccefs to him who has the right on his fide, I cannot imagine. For experience fhews, that in duels the best swordsman, or best marksman has the best prospect of victory; as in war, generally speaking, the ablest general, and best appointed army, gain the victory.

The grand plea for duelling is, that he, who refuses a challenge, is presently set down for a coward. And who can bear to be thought a coward? But it is very easy to escape the imputation of cowardice, and yet refuse a challenge. A hot-headed young officer sends a challenge to a gentleman, no matter whether in the army or not. The gentleman directly refuses the challenge upon principle. The officer posts him for a coward. He posts the officer for a liar. The officer must not bear this. He attacks the gentleman. The gentleman defends himself, which he has a right to do against any ruffian. He, being cool, and the officer worked up to rage, it is natural to expect victory to declare herself on his side in the scuffle. And as the officer must use no weapon, but a cane, unless the gentleman draws upon him, which he is not, by any law of honour, obliged to; there is no great danger of murder on either side. And at the same time the gentleman's honour and courage are as effectually cleared before the public, as if he had fought the officer with twenty different mortal weapons.

Conquest in single combat is no more a proof, which party was in the right, than the old superstition of trial by fire ordeal, &c.

It would not be cowardice in an officer to refuse to hazard his life, by going to sea in an open boat, by encountering a wild beast, &c. for a sum of 20 or 30 guineas. Therefore it is not always cowardice in an officer to shew a due care for his life. If one officer owed another a large sum, and the debtor proposed to try by duel, whether he should pay it or not, who would

would call the creditor a coward for refusing so ridiculous a challenge[a]?

In the affair between lord *Rea* and *Ramsay* an officer, it was declared, that the sending of a challenge is a presumption of guilt[b].

The rule, that every man who refuses a challenge, must be a coward, is very disputable. A man may refuse a challenge, not because he fears his fellow-creature, or is afraid to die; but because he fears the Almighty, and does not choose to hazard damnation for the sake of preserving the good opinion of the ladies.

This rule is of modern date. The ancients did not pronounce every man a coward who refused a challenge.

The ancient *Greeks* and *Romans*, the models of courage to all ages and nations, attached the idea of courage and cowardice to a man's readiness or reluctance to fight the enemies of his country, not to his shedding the blood of his countrymen. Highwaymen often shew great intrepidity.

Pyrrhus challenged *Antigonus* to fight him for the kingdom of *Macedon*. *Antigonus* declined the challenge. Yet we do not find the ancients have branded *Antigonus* for a coward.

Marius, challenged to single combat, flatly refuses. Yet nobody has ever thought of branding *Marius* with the name of coward[c].

The Duke of *Orleans* challenged *Henry* to single combat, or with 100 knights each side. *Henry* answers, that he cannot as a king accept a challenge from any subject; but that a time might probably come, when they

[a] *S. Pierre*, OEUVR. POLIT. X. 12.

[b] WHITEL. MEM. 16.

[c] ANT. UNIV. HIST. XIII. 13.

they might meaſure ſwords in battle. The Duke of *Orleans* ſends a bitter anſwer, calling *Henry* traitor, uſurper, and murderer of his king. *Henry*, in return, gives him the lie in form; and charges him with ſorcery, by which he had thrown his father, the *French* king, into his preſent diſtemper. *Henry* complains to the ambaſſador, but in vain [a].

We have in hiſtory the famous challenge between *Edward* III of *England*, and *Philip de Valois* of *France*; which certainly produced no fight. Yet neither of thoſe princes is accounted a coward.

Lewis VI of *France* challenged *Henry* I of *England*, to ſingle combat [b]. *Henry* laughed at the challenge. Yet nobody, even in *our times*, thinks him a coward.

Henry II of *France*, permitted a duel in his preſence between two of his lords, about a love affair. The conquered would not ſuffer his wounds to be dreſſed; and accordingly died. The king vowed to ſuffer no more duelling [c].

Chriſtian IV was challenged by *Charles* IV of *Sweden*, *A. D.* 1612. Refuſed. Yet not thought a coward [d].

Francis's ſending *Charles* V a challenge [e], promoted the folly of duelling ſo much, that war itſelf hardly made more havock of the ſpecies. Yet *Charles* did not accept the challenge. Therefore thoſe who did accept challenges, did not imitate the Emperor; nor did the example of that affair render it neceſſary to accept challenges; for the hot-brained fools ſaw, that the Emperor was not reckoned a coward, though he declined.

The lie direct was given by *Francis* of *France* to *Charles*

[a] *Rap.* I. 493.

[b] MOD. UNIV. HIST. XXIII. 298. [c] Ibid. XXIV. 199.

[d] Ibid. XXXII. 456. [e] *Robertſ.* CH. V. II. 302.

Charles V. on which *Charles* sends the *French* king a challenge. But still there was no duel fought.

Among the *Turks*, the *Chinese*, and the *Persians*, it is no disgrace for an officer to refuse a challenge, and to submit the punishment of any one who has insulted him, to his superior. On the contrary, his regularity of conduct, and his prudence are honoured. *Nul officier n' est deshonore*, &c [a].

The *Czarina* thinks all deliberate offences ought to be punishable by law, from treason down to the slightest injury or affront to an individual [b]. If that were the case, there would be no pretence for duels, as now there is. And therefore that when a duel is fought, the challenger only, and not the accepter, ought to be punished; because the latter was through fear of shame forced to do what he knew to be unjustifiable, and is therefore pitiable [c].

The great and good Duke *de Sully*, who had as just notions of the point of honour as any of our modern heroes, who are daily fighting duels, has declared himself very strongly against this practice, as inconsistent with civilisation, decency, humanity, and all the laws of God and man. He even reflects with some severity on the remissness of his patriot King *Henry* IV. in neglecting to enforce the laws already standing, or to promote the framing of others more promising of success.

Beccaria, p. 38, 39, thinks death an absurd punishment for duelling, because they that will fight, shew that they do not fear death. He thinks the aggressor should be punished, and the defendant acquitted, because the law does not sufficiently secure his honour, and

---

[a] *S. Pierre*, Oeuvr. Polit. x. 8.

[b] *Instr.* 128.

[c] Ibid. 130.

and leaves him in a ſtate of nature to defend it by himſelf. But ought not then the law rather to be amended, and duelling rendered altogether inexcuſable?

Suppoſing proper proviſion made by law for checking petulancy, giving ſatisfaction for affronts, and deciding all matters of honour, it would not be amiſs to bring in every giver and receiver of a challenge, though no blood has been ſpilt, lunatic, to ſend him by authority to Bedlam for life, and give his eſtate, real and perſonal, to his heir.

Duelling was originally an appeal to Heaven. It is highly abſurd in our times, when nobody thinks of Heaven, and eſpecially as it is commonly practiſed by thoſe who ſet Heaven at defiance[a].

Duels are ſuppoſed to have received their firſt eſtabliſhment by a poſitive *law* (the practice is immemorial), from *Gundebald* King of the *Burgundians*, *A. D.* 501. See his edict[b]. His deſign ſeems to have been, to put a check to perjury. For he ſuppoſed, that obliging all perſons to defend with their ſwords what they had ſworn, would make them more careful what oaths they took. But in this he ſhewed himſelf no great reaſoner. For the natural effect of this law was, to put all people on learning the ſword.

See a minute account of the whole ceremony of trial by combat, in *Spelm. Gloſſ. voc. Campus.*

Brady II. 147, gives a clear account of the origin and manner of duels.

The following by *Verſtegan* is very conciſe and clear[c].

'For the trial by camp-fight, the accuſer was with 'the peril of his own body to prove the accuſed guilty, 'and

---

[a] Anc. Univ. Hist. xviii. 492. [b] Ibid. xix. 435.
[c] Antiq. 64.

'and by offering him his glove, to challenge him to this 'trial, which the other must either accept of, or else 'acknowledge himself culpable of the crime whereof he 'was accused. If it were a crime deserving death, 'then was the camp-fight for life and death, and either 'on horseback or on foot. If the offence deserved 'prisonment, and not death, then was the camp-fight 'accomplished, when the one had subdued the other, 'by making him to yield, or unable to defend himself, 'and so be taken prisoner. The accused had the liberty 'to choose another in his stead; but the accuser must 'perform it in his own person, and with equality of 'weapons. No women were admitted to behold it, 'nor no men children under the age of thirteen years. 'The priests and people that were spectators did si-'lently pray that the victory might fall unto the guilt-'less; and if the fight were for life or death, a bier 'stood ready to carry away the dead body of him who 'should be slain. None of the people might cry, 'shriek out, make any noise, or give any sign whatso-'ever; and hereunto at *Hall* in *Swevia* (a place ap-'pointed for camp-fight) was so great regard taken, 'that the executioner stood beside the judges, ready 'with an ax, to cut off the right hand and left foot of 'the party so offending. He that (being wounded) 'did yield himself, was at the mercy of the other to be 'killed or to be let live. If he were slain, then he was 'carried away and honourably buried; and he that 'slew him reputed more honourable than before: but 'if being overcome, he were left alive, then was he 'by sentence of the judges, declared utterly void of all 'honest reputation; and never to ride on horseback, 'nor to carry arms.'

Time was, when the seconds were to fight, and kill one another in the quarrels of their principals. That folly is happily aboliſhed. A little firmneſs in government would aboliſh the remaining folly of the principals fighting and murdering one another.

S. Pierre eſtimates the number of duels in *France* at 600 in a year, or 30,000 in every half century [a].

Duels were got to ſuch a height in *France*, that 4000 gentlemen in a year fell by them. Laws were made againſt that deſtructive practice, which reſtrained it in ſome meaſure. But the king, very unthinkingly, though ſo wiſe a man, ſpeaking with ſome contempt of ſome who had, in conſequence of the laws, refuſed challenges, the laws preſent loſt their effect. So much more powerful is faſhion than law [b].

The wiſe and good *Guſtavus Adolphus* of *Sweden*, made ſevere laws againſt duelling [c]. Two general officers begged his leave to decide a diſpute ariſen between them by ſingle combat. The king gives them leave, and deſires to be preſent. Before the fight begun, he ſends for the executioner with his ax. The gentlemen aſking his Majeſty why he called in that efficacious officer; *Guſtavus* anſwered, 'Only to cut off the head of the conqueror. The gentlemen made up the quarrel without fighting [d].

In *Cromwell*'s parliament, *A. D.* 1654, there was an act made for preventing and puniſhing duels [e]. For challenging, or accepting, or knowingly carrying a challenge, priſon for ſix months, without bail, to give ſecurity for one year afterwards; not diſcovering in twenty-four hours, to be deemed accepting; fighting, if death enſues, to be puniſhed as murder, &c. Perſons uſing provoking words or geſtures, to be indicted and fined; to be bound to good beha-
'viour

[a] Oeuvr. Polit. x. 47.

[b] Mod. Univ. Hist. xxiv. 404.

[c] Ibid. xxxiii. 226.

[d] Ibid.

[e] Parl. Hist. xx. 311.

viour, and to make reparation according to the quality of the person insulted.

A bill for abolishing the impious practice of duelling was ordered into the house of commons, *A. D.* 1713[a]. It was twice read; but dropped after all[b].

Voltaire[c] mentions a pompous battle fought by a set of knights-errant of *France* and *England*, about the beauty of certain ladies; and observes, that if the *Scipios* and *Æmiliuses* had fought about beauty, the *Romans* had never been the conquerors and lawgivers of the world.

James I. used often to say, he could not help lamenting (like *Xerxes*, when he reviewed his army, and considered, that in 100 years not one of so many myriads would be alive) when he surveyed the noble attendance round him, that not one of them was safe for twenty-four hours together from being murdered in a duel. For if a mistake happened, affront was taken, the lie given, and immediate combat and bloodshed followed[d].

There was a legal duel fought, *A. D.* 1571, the last, I suppose, upon record[e].

In the days of chivalry, they often fought for fighting sake, to distinguish themselves. *John de Bourbonnais* came from *France* into *England*, with sixteen other cavaliers, to fight whomever he could meet, all to distinguish himself, and win his mistress's heart[f]. The tournaments in those times were often very bloody. *Henry* II. of *France*, *Henry de Bourbon*, *Montpensier*, &c. were killed at tournaments. Why could not those bloody-minded

[a] Deb. Com. iv. 338. [b] Ibid. v. 38.

[c] Ess. sur l'Hist. ii. 234.

[d] *Lord Bac.* Lett. 193.

[e] *Spelm. voc. Campus*, 103.

[f] *Volt.* Ess. sur l'Hist. iii. 37.

minded fellows hire themselves as journeymen to some honest hog-butchers? In that profession they might, without sin, have washed their hands to the elbows in blood as often as they pleased.

It is the business of parliament to redress all such grievances; and an incorrupt parliament would certainly make such laws as would effectually redress them.

CHAP. V.

Of Lewdness.

UNDER the head of MANNERS, I could not avoid making some remarks on this most epidemical vice.

The breach of the most awful vows, the debauching of a virtuous wife, the destruction of a family's peace for life, the introduction of a bastard instead of the lawful heir to an ample estate, the provocation of an injured husband to that rage which no husband can promise to restrain, the hazard of murder and of damnation—these are what we of this elegant eighteenth century call gallantry, taste, the *bon ton*, knowledge of the world, *sçavoir vivre*, &c.

No statesman will look with an indifferent eye on the prevalency of lewdness in his country, if he has any regard for his country, and knows that this vice is not less mischievous by debasing the minds, than by enervating and poisoning the bodies of the subjects. A people weakened by the foul disease, are neither fit for sea nor land service, for agriculture, manufactures, nor population.

It is notorious, as above hinted, that a certain late reign exhibited from the throne a very gross example of broken

ken matrimonial vows. The effects of that evil example remain ſtill, though the behaviour of the preſent king (whom God preſerve) is the very oppoſite of that I refer to. It will appear hereafter, that the *examples of kings* do not make *right* and *wrong*. And our wicked wits may rack their brains till doomſday; but will never be able to prove, that the promiſcuous commerce of the ſexes is conſiſtent with the order of *nature*, while the numbers of both that are born are ſo nearly *equal*, which effectually cuts off the pretext of any one to carry on a commerce with a plurality, and obliges every one to keep to *one*.

Would any of our modern wits chooſe to be thought the ſon of a wh——, rather than born in wedlock? Would any of them chooſe to have his ſiſter or his daughter debauched? Do we not pronounce the contented cuckold, the wretch, who will bear with patience the defilement of his bed, a diſgrace to the ſpecies? Is it not then manifeſt, that every man who is guilty of lewdneſs is ſelf-convicted, of doing that by others which he will not bear at the hand of any other? This is acting directly contrary to the golden rule, which all nations have adopted, viz. ‘What you would not ‘have done to you, do not that to others.’ If any man would fairly ſtand forth and declare, that he will do what he pleaſes, whether right or wrong, he declares himſelf the enemy of all order, and unfit to be ſuffered to exiſt among rational and moral beings.

That every man have his own wife, and every woman her own huſband, is the voice of nature as well as of ſcripture.

Polygamy is unnatural. By the *Mahommedan* law any man may have four wives. But few men take the advantage of the law. They who have the greateſt number, are always the moſt jealous [a].

Young men would do well to conſider, that the indulging of thoſe deſires only inflames their rage.

Remarkable is the ſtory of a beautiful *Arabian* woman, taken by force from her huſband by the governor of *Caſa*, who told the khalif, ordering him to reſtore her, that if he would give him leave to keep her one year, he would be content to have his head ſtruck off at the end of the year [b].

A man's leaving the bed of his worthy ſpouſe, who perhaps now begins to verge toward age, and his invading that of his friend, who truſts him, what does it ſhew, but that he is capable of the baſeſt treachery, to gratify the moſt unworthy appetite. And the woman, whoſe libidinous diſpoſition

(Cum tibi flagrans amor et libido,
Quæ ſolet matres furiare equorum,
Sæviet circa jecur ulceroſum
Non ſine queſtu. HOR.)

drives her from her home and her huſband, raging, as *Horace* here deſcribes ſome ladies of his times,—what elegance, what taſte, does ſhe exhibit? It is granted, that love, where the ornaments of the mind more than thoſe of the outward form are the object, is a paſſion full of elegant ſentiment. But love can have no place where one of the parties is engaged to another perſon. The only ſentiments, which can enter into ſuch a connexion are thoſe of luſt and of remorſe. Where the elegance of them lies, I own I do not underſtand. Neither

[a] MOD. UNIV. HIST. VI. 247. [b] Ibid. II. 84.

Neither party can think of the other but with disapprobation.

Our great folks seem to affect to be the contrasts of the philosopher in *A. Gellius*, who would not be conscious to *himself* of sin, though he could conceal it from both gods and men. They seem to be above regarding either self-consciousness, or the knowledge of gods or men.

By the most ancient and honourable of all law-givers, Moses, adultery, in both sexes, was made capital[a]. And if a[b] virgin was seduced, the man was obliged to marry her, or find her a husband.

Adultery by consent was punished in *Egypt*, in the man, with a thousand lashes with rods; a punishment incomparably worse than hanging or beheading; and in the woman with the loss of her nose. I don't know from whence I had this; but I know I did not write it, nor any other fact, without authority.

Solon the *Athenian* legislator, gave the court of *Areopagus* power to correct all idle persons[c]. The same lawgiver allowed a husband, or any person, who surprised an adulterer in the act, to kill him on the spot[d].

Among the *Athenians*, if a husband caught his lady tripping, he was obliged to divorce her. The law did not allow him to receive her again. An adulteress was not allowed to enter the temples. *Romulus* likewise made a law, which is recorded by *Aulus Gellius*. "PELLEX ASAM JUNONIS NE TAGITO. SI TAGET, "ARNUM FOEMINAM CAIDITO." Let not the harlot of a married man touch the altar of *Juno* [the goddess

a EXOD. XXII. 16. b LEVIT. XX. 10.

c *Ubb. Emm.* DE REP. ATHEN. I: 100.

d *Plut. in Solon*, Μοιχον μεν γαρ ανελειν, κ. τ. λ.

of marriage]. If ſhe does, let her offer a female lamb [by way of expiation]. Among the *Spartans* there was no ſuch crime as infidelity to the marriage bed, nor did *Lycurgus* uſe any precaution againſt it; but the virtuous education he preſcribed for the youth of both ſexes.

Among the *Athenians*, fornication, adultery, and celibacy, were puniſhable crimes. The debaucher of a virgin was obliged to marry her himſelf, or find her a ſuitable huſband, ſays *Potter*. And *Athenæus* tells us, that at the *Lacedemonian* religious feaſts, it was cuſtomary for the women to ſeize all the old batchelors, and drag them round the altar, beating them.

'Such as frequented infamous women, *Solon* did not 'allow to harangue the people; thinking, that men 'without ſhame were not to be ſo far truſted[a].' An archon, or magiſtrate, overtaken with liquor, he ordered to be put to death, for bringing diſgrace upon the office[b].

Romulus puniſhed adultery in women with death[c].

Domitian, in his firſt years, ſhewed an attention to the manners of the people. He reſtrained licentiouſneſs, degraded a ſenator for being too fond of dancing, deprived lewd women of the privilege of being carried in litters, or of enjoying legacies, and puniſhed adultery with death[d].

Several veſtal nuns were found guilty of lewdneſs. They were buried alive, and their gallants whipped to death[e].

The Emperor *Macrinus* made an edict, by which every adulterer and adultereſs were to be tied together, and burnt alive [to cool their luſt][f].

Manilius

[a] Ant. Univ. Hist. vi. 314. *Plut.* in *Solon.* [b] Ibid. [c] Ibid. xi. 292. [d] Ibid. xv. 52. [e] Ibid. xii. 451. [f] Ibid. xv. 344.

Manilius was ſtruck out of the liſt of ſenators for ſaluting his lady, on his return from a journey, in the preſence of his daughter. A high delicacy of manners among heathens [a]. We Chriſtians do not ſtrike a man out of any of our liſts for ſaluting his wh—— in the preſence of both wife and daughter. The *Mahommetans* puniſh ſeverely ſimple fornication [b]. Among us Chriſtians, adultery is only gallantry, an amuſement for princes and grandees.

We often meet with extraordinary degrees of modeſty in heathen countries. Young *Scipio*, by his virtue and amiable behaviour, gained over many of the little *African* kings and ſtates in *Spain*, from the *Carthaginian* to the *Roman* intereſt. The *Carthaginians* beſides, were very tyrannical to their provinces, which contraſt was of advantage to the *Roman* general [c]. We ſhall turn over hiſtory long enough, before we meet with an inſtance of as much good conſequent upon whoring, as *Scipio* and his country gained by chaſtity.

Cavades king of *Perſia* projected a law for making all women common. Produces an inſurrection, which ends in his depoſition from the throne [d].

A ſachem's wife ſhews a great regard for her honour, when taken in war by the Engliſh [e]. O ſhame to the Engliſh wh——es of quality of our enlightened days!

All public brothels were ſuppreſſed in the city of *Conſtantinople*, by order of the Empreſs *Claudia*, *A. D.* 428 [f].

The *Goths* allowed no brothels [g].

 Monteſquieu

[a] Ant. Univ. Hist. xii. 355.

[b] Mod. Univ. Hist. i.

[c] Ant. Univ. Hist. xviii. 44. [d] Ibid. xi. 98.

[e] Mod. Univ. Hist. xxxix. 284.

[f] Ant. Univ. Hist. xvi. 544. [g] Ibid. 551.

Montesquieu [a] doubts the fact reported by *Dion* of *Halicarnassus*, *Valerius Maximus*, and *Aulus Gellius*, viz. That though at *Rome* the law allowed divorce, no man took the advantage of the law during the space of 520 years. And if the fact was true, it was not, he thinks, to be wondered at, because, though the law allowed divorce, yet it clogged it with terrible inconveniencies.

Corruption of manners threatens a decline of empire. About the times of *Sylla* and *Marius*, when the *Roman* republic was tottering to its fall, it was observed, that there was an universal degeneracy of manners prevailing; particularly, that the women were very scandalous in their behaviour at *Rome*, while those of the countries, called by them barbarous, were remarkably exemplary in this respect [b].

It seems to have been an old *English* law, that an adulterer should be mutilated of the offending part. For in the year 1248, a person having been punished in that manner for *fornicatio simplex*, the King ordered by proclamation, that only adulterers should suffer emasculation [c].

By the old heathen laws of Iceland, adultery was punished with death, and even lascivious behaviour between single persons was severely punished. IONÆ ISLAND. TRACT. p. 406. Where the author observes, that our modern Christian legislators may learn, from these ignorant barbarians, a lesson useful for exciting them to restrain such behaviour between the sexes, as tends to produce effects highly prejudicial to states.

By the laws of King *Kenneth* of *Scotland*, adultery was punished

[a] L'ESPR. DES LOIX, II. 6 9.

[b] ANT. UNIV. HIST. XIII. 13.

[c] *Hody's* HIST. OF ENGL. COUNCILS, p. 330.

punifhed with the death of both the offenders [a]. About the fame time, *viz.* the ninth century, the fame crime was punifhed in *England* by fine only [b].

Adultery was made capital by the incomparable *Yncas*, who firft polifhed the *Peruvians* [c].

Among the ancient *Germans*, infidelity was punifhed with the death of the woman. *Alfred* inflicted a fine, and *Canute* fined or banifhed the man, and punifhed the woman with mutilation of nofe and ears, and lofs of her portion [d].

Adultereffes, among the *Portuguefe* 700 years ago, were burnt alive, unlefs the hufbands were pleafed to pardon them [e].

A rape committed on a woman of quality of the fame country, was punifhed with death. The ravifher of a woman of inferior rank was obliged to marry her, if both fingle, be his rank ever fo much fuperior to hers [f].

Adultery in either fex was made death *April* 1650, (in the interregnum) unlefs when the man offending did not know that the woman was married, or the woman's hufband was beyond fea, or generally fuppofed dead [g]. In thofe days they went roundly to work. Our laws are not fo fevere; for a glafier was lately fined 20 *l.* and cofts of fuit for *crim. con.* with a taylor's wife [h]. And we have feen a great perfon mulcted 10,000 *l.* for a tranfgreffion with a lady of quality: by thefe two extremes may be calculated what will

[a] *Spelm.* CONCIL. I. 341. [b] Ibid. 367.

[c] MOD. UNIV. HIST. XXXIX. 4.

[d] DISC. GOV. ENG. P. 1. p. 63.

[e] MOD. UNIV. HIST. XXII. 27. [f] Ibid.

[g] PARL. HIST. XIX. 257.

[h] WHITEHALL EVEN. POST, *June* 5th, 1773.

will be the charge of cuckolding any man according to his rank from a nobleman to a taylor. Tables of these expences might be constructed by able mathematicians, and copies of them hung up at Mrs. *Cornellys*'s on masquerade nights, in the same manner as at *Vauxhall* and *Ranelagh*, the rates of provisions.

Adultery is punished with death among the *Moguls*, though the poor women have often but the fourth part of a husband; the law allowing any man, who pleases, four wives [a].

Among the *Tonkinese* in *India*, an adulteress and her lover are both punished with death [b].

In *Persia* an adulterer is punished with emasculation; and the lady is thrown headlong from the top of a tower [c].

By the laws of *Hoel Dha* king of *Wales*, in the 10th century, a married woman might be divorced from her husband only for wantonly saluting a gentleman [d].

A widow guilty of frailty was, in the *Saxon* times, to pay 20 *s.* an unmarried woman 10 *s.*[e] These were heavy fines. For the fine for murder was, in some cases, no higher.

Incontinency in an unmarried heiress was punished with loss of her estate [f].

Adultery was always punished with death among the ancient *Goths* [g].

By the laws of *Canute*, the *Dane*, an adulteress was to lose her nose and ears, and the man was banished [h].

Among

---

[a] Mod. Univ. Hist. vi. 247. [b] Ibid. vii. 482.

[c] *De Laet* Descr. Pers. 154.

[d] *Spelm.* Concil. i. 411.

[e] *Seld.* Tit. Hon. 619.

[f] *Lord Lyttelton*'s Hist. Hen. II. iii. 119.

[g] Ant. Univ. Hist. xix. 264.

[h] *Spelm.* Concil. i. 558.

Among the ancient *Saxons*, adultery was so odious, that all the women of the neighbourhood where an adulteress lived, were used to fall upon her, and after tearing off all her cloaths above the waste, whipped and cut her with knives, till she almost expired [a].

In the old *English* laws, we find punishments for wanton behaviour, as touching the breasts of women, &c [b].

By the ancient laws of *France*, the least indecency of behaviour to a free woman, as squeezing the hand, touching the arm or breast, &c. was punishable by fine.

In *Swisserland* they executed, in *Burnet*'s times, all women, who were five times convicted of fornication, or three times of adultery [c].

See *Charles* Ist's pardon to the countess of *Castlehaven* for adultery, repeatedly committed by her [d], by which she is exempted from all ecclesiastical censures, public penances, fines, &c.

Philip le Bel of *France* had three sons, whose wives were all suspected of infidelity. Their supposed gallants were flayed alive [e]. If this were the punishment for gallantry in *England*, I should advise, that the hides be confiscated, and disposed of by public auction. They would sell at a great rate, and the money might be of service, when the house was upon ways and means. Nay, I do not know whether this elegant vice might not, supposing a due attention paid to the revenue arising from it, go some considerable length toward paying

---

[a] *Spelm.* Concil. I. 234. [b] Ibid. I. 368, 373, *et pass.*
[c] *Burn.* Trav. p. 22.
[d] *Rym.* Foed. xix. 321.
[e] Mod. Univ. Hist. xxiii. 398.

ing the debt of the nation. Let it be confidered, at what a rate a rich virtuofo, or a perfon of tafte, would value a pair of gloves made of the hide of a lady of quality, or a blood royal hide. They muft indeed be much more beautiful than the fineft *French* kid. I know not whether a pin-cufhion made of fuch rich ftuff, might not fetch 100 guineas. And a hide of any fize would make a great many pin-cufhions. It is true, the frequency of adultery among us would bring to the market a prodigious glut of the article. But our engroffers of corn would prefently fhew us the way of keeping up the price, notwithftanding the plenty of the commodity. I am likewife aware of another obvious objection to my project, viz. That hides of rank are generally liable to be tender, occafioned by a polite malady very epidemical among the great, which would render the manufacturing of them difficult. But I have not the leaft doubt, but a premium propofed would prefently find us out a method of getting over that difficulty. It would be natural for the miniftry to turn this fcheme to their advantage by fetting up a *hide-office*, with commiffioners at 2000 *l.* a year, clerks at 500 *l.* a year, &c. And I doubt not, but flaying our adulterers and adultereffes (not alive; that would be too fevere) would foon bring into the treafury as much clear revenue as we are like to get by taxing our *colonies*. And though our governments are not ufed to fhew much zeal in fuppreffing vice, on account of the mifchiefs it produces, perhaps the profpect of fomewhat to be *got* by checking of the polite fin, might excite them to exert themfelves.

Thus (to draw toward an end of this chapter) we fee, that the violation of marriage vows, which we look upon as only a piece of polite vivacity, or at worft a venial fin, has in moft ages and nations been confidered as a very ſerious affair, as ever deſerving the ſevereſt puniſhment. All which is humbly recommended to the conſideration of our ſtateſmen and governors, or whoremongers and adulterers.

Jane Shore did penance at St. *Paul's* in a ſheet, and a wax taper in her hand. A good and wholeſome diſcipline, and would be uſeful in our times [a].

When it was propoſed to puniſh adultery with death, a gentleman obſerved, that ſuch a law would only make people commit the crime with greater ſecrecy. But even with this view, ſuch a law would be uſeful. For open vice is more atrocious than ſecret, and more miſchievous by its example. It is a great evil for a people to be accuſtomed to hear often of groſs crimes committed among them. It familiariſes them to vice, and hardens them againſt the horror which every well diſpoſed mind ſhould have at wickedneſs. Wiſe ſtateſmen will therefore endeavour to keep up an outward appearance of decency in the practice of the people. We have had ſtateſmen in this chriſtian, this reformed, this proteſtant country of ours, who, ſo far from giving any attention to the general manners of the people, have themſelves been the grand corruptors and debauchers of the people, ſetting ſhame and decency at defiance.

By one of the laws of *Hoel Dha*, king of Wales, in the tenth century, a married woman might be ſeparated from her huſband if he was leprous, impotent, or had a ſtinking breath [b].

In *Riley's* Plac. Parl. p. 231, is the copy of a deed, 30 *Edw.* I. by which *John de Cameys* gives up his wife *Margaret* to *William Pagnel*, to have and to hold, with all

---

[a] *Rap.* 1. 635.

[b] *Spelm.* CONCIL. I. 410.

all property belonging to her, *Omnibus Christi fidelibus*, &c. On this account she was deprived of her dower, which she sued for after the death of *John* her husband; there being an express law to that purpose. *Quod si uxor sponte reliquerit*, &c. Ibid. 232.

A. D. 1660, under the debauched *Charles* II. a bill was brought in for preventing wives quitting their husbands, and demanding separate maintenance for frivolous reasons [a]. Such a bill seems much wanted now.

The emperor *Sigismund* often caught his empress with her gallants; but always forgave her, because he was himself guilty in the same way [b].

There is great reason to think many of the divorces of our times are obtained by mutual collusion, like *Bothwel's*, in order to get rid of his wife, and espouse queen *Mary* of *Scotland*; against which *Craig*, a *Scotch* clergyman, gave a brave and open testimony; and being called before the council, so struck them with his virtuous firmness, that they did not dare to punish him [c].

Lord *Strange*, in the debate on the divorce-bill, *A. D.* 1771, observed, that 'the only means of stopping the prevalency of adultery, is to reform the manners of the women. That whilst *Coteries*, *Cornelys*, *Almack's*, and other places of rendezvous for company were so much encouraged, reformation would be impossible.'

It is to be expected, that among our other improvements in politeness, we shall soon introduce the *Italian* elegancy of *Cicisbeos*, which was derived, says *Voltaire* [d], from

[a] Parl. Hist. xxiii. 9.

[b] Mod. Univ. Hist. xxix. 406.

[c] *Hume*, Hist. Tud. 478.

[d] Ess. sur l'Hist. iv. 87.

from the romantic times, when gallant knights defended diſtreſſed ladies; but now means rank and open adulterers, ſeen in all public places with married women. Every married lady in *Italy* has one, two, or perhaps three of theſe attendants, who is to wait on her to and from all places of entertainment with the moſt careful aſſiduity, for which ſhe rewards them in what ſhe thinks a proper manner.

One great cauſe of the groſs debauchery of our times, is the putting off of marriage to ſo late a period in life, becauſe our gentlemen muſt, when they ſet up houſekeeping, live in a certain taſte, and all are ſtriving to outvie one another in ſplendor and expence. In the mean time the calls of nature are powerful, and foul water quenches fire as well as clean, which ſends our youth raging to the brothels, though they ſoon find to their coſt that, as *Milton* ſays, it is only in virtuous wedlock that

——Love his golden ſhafts employs; here lights,
His conſtant lamp, and waves his purple wings;
Reigns here and revels: not in the bought ſmile
Of harlots, loveleſs, joyleſs, unendear'd,
Caſual fruition: not in court amours,
Mix'd dance, or wanton maſk, or midnight ball.

PARAD. LOST, B. IV. ver. 763.

But while our gentlemen are going on in this courſe of debauchery, their ſentiments with reſpect to the fair ſex become groſs and ſordid; and they come at laſt to look upon womankind as merely objects of luſt, and every handſome woman, married or ſingle, is an object of luſt.

Suppoſe the cuſtom of a country were, for every father of a ſon to marry him at the firſt riſe of deſire, and before he could have time to think of rambling after lewd women, or of debauching innocence. A youth

youth of ſeventeen or eighteen would chooſe rather to cohabit with a virtuous young lady of his own rank, than with a whore. And men ought in all countries to be reſtrained from debauching innocent virgins by a law obliging them to marry them, or find them huſbands. A youth of ſeventeen or eighteen might continue to live with his parents after marriage as before, and his young wife with hers, viſiting from time to time. The children might remain with the parents of the young woman. The expences of their maintenance to be defrayed by both parents, till ſuch time as the young couple were of age to keep houſe together. If the reader ſhould ſtart objections to ſuch a ſcheme, I will engage to find as many, and of equal weight, (to ſay the leaſt) againſt whoring, the other ſide of the alternative.

The ancient *Cretan* youth were obliged to marry as ſoon as they were of age; but they did not live conſtantly with their wives till they were both arrived at the time of life when the conſtitution is formed[a]: Every State ought to puniſh voluntary celibacy.

The *Turks* are more civiliſed in reſpect to obſervance of the matrimonial vow, than the *Engliſh* and *French*. Lady *M. W. Montague* ſays, 'A gallant (in *Turkey*) 'convicted of having debauched a married woman, is 'held in the ſame abhorrence as a proſtitute with us; 'he is certain of never making his fortune, and they 'would deem it ſcandalous to confer any conſiderable 'employment on a man ſuſpected of having committed ſuch enormous injuſtice.'

One vice introduces others, and every vice is hurtful in a State; therefore wiſe ſtateſmen diſcourage all vices.

No

[a] *Ubb. Emm.* ii. 66.

'No court (says *Voltaire*[a]) has ever given itself 'up to debauchery, but seditions have followed.'

King *Dagobert* of *France* made his first departure from virtue by repudiating his Queen, on pretence of barrenness. Afterwards he became so licentious, as to keep three wives at once. The mound once broken down, it is not easy to stop the inundation[b].

Every body knows to what wickedness this passion drove *Henry* VIII. and *Charles* II.

Governor *Baleins*, of *Gascoyne*, killed an officer, who had debauched his sister on promise of marriage. The King pardoned him.

The law of *Moses* ordains, that the seducer of a virgin shall find her a husband[c].

In *Spain*, according to *Baretti*, if a young woman is debauched, the man, whom she charges as the author of her disgrace, is by law obliged to marry her, or go to prison, and to suffer endless vexation.

In respect of seduction, our law leaves us quite lawless. A rape is death. But is not the injury to me the same in the end, whether my daughter is seduced into the arms of a whoremaster, or forced? Of the two, seduction is on some accounts a greater injury than force. A young woman deflowered by main force may still be considered as undefiled in mind; whereas she who yields, must be accounted in some degree guilty. And as the law has left us in a state of nature, with respect to the seduction of our daughters, I own, I should be inclinable to take into my own hands the punishment of the man who had ruined a daughter of mine: For I should think he had done her and me as great an injury, in some respects a

 greater,

a Ess. sur l'Hist. ii. 282.

b Mod. Univ. Hist. xxiii. 74.

c Exod. xxii. 16.

greater, than if he had murdered her. And if I were upon a jury to try a father, who had killed the ſeducer of his innocent daughter, I ſhould certainly not bring him in guilty of murder.

To the diſgrace of the preſent century, a miſcreant lord decoyed an innocent young milliner of the city from her family under pretence of buſineſs; confined her ſeveral days in his own houſe; terrified her into compliance with his villanous deſires; and was accuſed of a rape, and puniſhed, with——a hearty fright: for he knew he deſerved the death of a raviſher. But it could not legally be brought in a rape. I ſhould be glad to underſtand what difference it made to the injured young woman, to her father, or to the young man who courted her, whether ſhe was put into the ruffian's bed by force, or terrified by threats; or whether one proceeding, or the other, argued the greateſt malignity, and deſerved the ſevereſt puniſhment.

'There was (ſays Chancellor *Bacon*[a]) an excellent 'law framed under *Henry* VIII. by which the taking 'and carrying away women forcibly, and againſt their 'will (except female wards and bond-women) was 'made capital; the parliament wiſely and juſtly con-'ceiving, that the obtaining women by force into poſ-'ſeſſion (howſoever aſſent might follow afterwards by 'allurements) was but a rape drawn forth into length, 'becauſe the firſt force drew on all the reſt.' Lord *B.* did not *carry away* Miſs *W.* by force; but he *detained* her in his own houſe by force. And it was in *conſequence* of this *force*, and of his *threats*, that he would get her trapanned away out of the kingdom, and carried to *Maryland*, of which he was proprietor, that he debauched her; and yet he ſuffered *no material* puniſh-

[a] Parl. Hist. II. 435.

punishment. The jury were, I ſuppoſe, quibbled out of their ſenſes by the lawyers: for a *more atrocious rape* was never committed.

In the year 1699, there was a debate in the Houſe of Peers concerning a ſeparation, on account of cruelty, and a maintenance, for the Counteſs of *Angleſea*. Lord *Haverſham* proteſted againſt it, and ſaid, There never was ſuch a bill propoſed before[a].

It is certainly not ſound policy to ſuffer what may make the matrimonial tie ſeem leſs binding; and yet married women ought to be protected againſt the brutality of ſurly huſbands. In this our police is miſerably deficient. There ought to be a court for ſuch cauſes. And yet I think nothing leſs than infidelity, or danger of life, can warrant a ſeparation; nor can even thoſe offences (in my opinion) juſtify a divorced perſon in marrying again; the vows being abſolute, not conditional. A huſband or wife, with whom one cannot live, is a misfortune; but does not, I think, void the matrimonial vow. Beſides, it is to be conſidered, that allowing ſeparated perſons to marry again is giving them another temptation to ſeparate.

It is the intereſt of almoſt every man and woman in *England* that ſtreet-walkers be ſuppreſſed, and lewd women confined to ſome obſcure parts of great towns. Our anceſtors thought it neceſſary to licence public ſtews, for fear of violence from ſailors, and other debauched people, upon their wives and daughters. But there is no occaſion for ſuffering the main thoroughfares of towns to be infeſted with thoſe women, to the deſtruction of all ſenſe of modeſty, the diſcouragement of marriage, and drawing away into vicious courſes the younger part of the male ſex. And it is

 certain,

[a] Deb. Peers. II. 21. And ſee Parl. Hist. XXIII. 33.

certain, whatever may be pretended, that the streets may be kept clear of loose women by the same people, who now keep them clear of carts, coaches, &c. during parliament time.

The court of *Spain* observing the miserable depopulation of that country after the imprudent expulsion of the Jews and Moors, among other regulations for encouraging marriage, took care to prohibit public stews[a]. There ought to be no way of coming at women, but by marriage; and then men would find it necessary to marry.

Why should the popish police of *Paris* carry reformation farther than the protestant police of *London?* In the WHITEHALL EVENING POST, *September* 1, 1772, is the following article in a letter from *France:* 'Within these few days, near 700 women of the town 'have been confined in different hospitals and prisons; 'when cured, to be sent to *Corsica*, and the *West India* 'Islands.'

Marriage is often kept back in *England* by gentlemen's going abroad upon their travels. They set out to visit foreign countries before they have acquired any knowledge of their own, and get their minds infected with foreign vices before they have established in them any good and virtuous habits.

No nobleman, or gentleman, ought to travel, if improvement be his object, till the heat of youth be over; and as every nobleman and gentleman of fortune can afford to marry young, they may travel with their ladies along with them. It is notorious, that ladies, in our times, travel almost as much as gentlemen. Any nobleman, or gentleman, may spend two or three summers in foreign parts with his lady; and the

---

[a] *De Laet*, HISP. DESCR. 105.

the reſt of the year at home; and the buſineſs is done. So that travel need not hinder marriage.

It has been ſaid, that a toaſt has of late been commonly drunk at the other end of the town, by the men of wit and gallantry, of which Satan himſelf need not be aſhamed to be thought the inventor, viz. 'May elegant vice prevail over dull virtue.' I have, not without ſome ſtruggle, forced my pen to write it; but now I ſee it upon paper, I know not whether, for the honour of human nature, and of the eighteenth century, ſuch a ſcrap of infernality ought not to be condemned to annihilation. Every purchaſer of this book may, however, if he thinks it diſgraces the page, blot it out of his own copy. The unthinking rake, whom the purſuit of pleaſure draws into innumerable indefenſible follies, is a ſaint compared with the deliberate well-wiſher and promoter of vice in others, by which he is to gain neither pleaſure nor profit. This latter may boaſt, that he has attained the ſummit and pinnacle of moral depravity. For it is impoſſible to exceed in wickedneſs the being, who loves vice for its own ſake.

'*L'amour des femmes, &c.* The love of women can 'never be a vice, but when it leads to bad actions[a].' Is not the making a woman a whore, or continuing her in a vicious courſe, who otherwiſe would have been an honeſt woman, or a penitent, a bad action? I am afraid, our polite people think not.

Auguſtus puniſhed with death many who had received the favours of his diſſolute daughter *Julia*[b]. Our youth, if they acknowledge the guilt of debauching an innocent virgin (few of them ſhew even ſo much

 ſenti-

---

[a] VOLT. ESS. SUR L'HIST. II. 162.

[b] ANT. UNIV. HIST. XIII. 540.

ſentiment) conclude, that to encourage a proſtitute in her wicked courſe of life, is no crime.

CHAP. VI.

Influence of Education upon Manners.

IT is obſerved above, that among the ancient *Spartans* there was no ſuch crime as infidelity to the marriage-bed; and that *Lycurgus*, in framing his laws, had uſed no precaution againſt it, but the virtuous and temperate education he preſcribed for the youth of both ſexes.

And indeed the influence which education has upon the manners of a people is ſo conſiderable, that it is not to be eſtimated. But by education it is to be obſerved, we muſt underſtand not only what is taught at ſchools and univerſities, but the impreſſions young people receive from parents, and from the world, which greatly outweigh all that can be done by maſters and tutors. Education, taken in this enlarged ſenſe, is almoſt all that makes the difference between the characters of nations; and it is a ſevere ſatire on our times, that the world makes moſt young men very different beings from what their educators intended they ſhould be.

The difference between the behaviour of the grave and regular Quakers, even in youth, and that of all other ſects among us, which is brought about chiefly by the management of parents, ſhews what is in the power of parents. The Quakers hold frugality and induſtry for religious duties. They accordingly thrive better, and people more than other ſects. See an excommunication and ſeparation of *John Merrick*, a Quaker,

Quaker, from their society, on account of his irregular behaviour [a].

The authors of the ANTIENT UNIVERSAL HISTORY celebrate the wisdom of the *Persians*, in respect to education, as follows: 'As to their laws, [the *Persian*] they are greatly commended by *Xenophon*, who prefers them to those of any other nation whatsoever, and observes that other law-givers only appointed punishments for crimes committed; but did not take sufficient care to prevent men from committing them; whereas the main design of the *Persian* laws was to inspire men with a love of virtue, and abhorrence of vice, so as to avoid the one, and pursue the other, without regarding either punishment or reward: to attain this end, parents, were not, by their laws, allowed to give their children what education they pleased; but were obliged to send them to public schools, where they were educated with great care, and never suffered, till they had attained the age of seventeen, to return home to their parents. These schools were not trusted to the care of common mercenary masters, but were governed by men of the first quality, and best characters, who taught them by their example the practice of all virtues; for these schools were not designed for learning of sciences, but practising of virtue. The youths were allowed no other food, but bread and cresses, no other drink but water, at least from the age of seven to seventeen. Those who had not been educated in in these schools, were excluded from all honours and preferments [b].

Dio Cassius insists, that *Burrhus* and *Seneca* were unfaithful guides of *Nero*'s youth, in not restraining

 his

[a] LOND. MAG. *May* 1766, p. 241.

[b] ANT. UNIV. HIST. v. 136.

his licentious passion for *Acte*. Their apology was, that they were glad to divert him from greater crimes [a]. But there is no safety in doing, or in conniving at evil, that good may come.

Hormouz king of *Persia* had by nature a bad disposition; but *Buzurge Mihir*, his tutor, 'took such pains 'with him, and knew so well how to set folly and 'vice in their true lights, that he vanquished his na- 'tural proneness to evil, and made him, in spite of him- 'self, a great and good man. For the first three years 'of his reign, while his old tutor remained about his 'person, he as far transcended *Nouschirvan*, as *Nous- 'chirvan* did all his predecessors. His discourses were 'fraught with wisdom. His actions were all benefi- 'cent. He carried his respect for his tutor so far, 'that he would not wear his regal ornaments in his 'presence. And when some of the courtiers inti- 'mated, that his reverence to him was excessive, since 'it was more than was due to a parent; he answered, '*You say well, my friends. But I owe more to him, than 'I do to my father. The life and kingdom, I received 'from him, will remain with me but a few years; but 'the reputation I shall acquire in virtue of my tutor's in- 'structions, will survive to the latest times.* Happy had 'it been for this prince, had he always adhered to these 'notions. But when old age had rendered *Buzurge 'Mihir* unfit for the great employment he held, he re- 'quested, and obtained, leave to retire; and with him 'retired the happiness of his royal pupil. The young 'courtiers, who were about *Hormouz*, begun, from 'that moment to gain a visible ascendency over him, 'and to influence him to do many things alike inju- 'rious to his interest and his reputation. He after- 'wards

---

[a] Ant. Univ. Hist. xiv. 373, 390.

'wards became ſuch a tyrant, as to murder his ſub-'jects by thouſands;' the conſequences of which proceedings were the hatred of his ſubjects; revolts; invaſions; battles; and the depoſition of *Hormouz*, and putting out of his eyes [a].

If education be of ſuch conſequence, it ought to be a great object with ſtateſmen; ſo much the rather becauſe the *private* educators of youth, who *alone* have it in their power to diſcharge, in any tolerable manner, that momentous truſt, are but indifferently encouraged by thoſe who employ them.

Educators of youth had formerly, in ſome countries, the authority of miniſters of ſtate, being thought of equal conſequence; and juſtly, ſays the author. Youth ſtaid in the ſeminaries till fit to enter on public employments [b]. He who is completely qualified for educating youth (who can ſay what it is to be completely qualified?) may undertake any thing. The abilities of the angel *Gabriel* would find hard exerciſe in forming a few human minds.

The *Chineſe* laws make parents anſwerable for the miſbehaviour of children, concluding, that they muſt have neglected their education [c].

S. Pierre has reckoned up the advantages of an education in a ſchool, compared with thoſe of a home education, and has, very judiciouſly [d], given the preference to that education, which puts young people out of the way of fond parents, their greateſt enemies.

Marſhal, in his travels, ſpeaking of the *Dutch* ſeminaries of learning, obſerves, that there is not in them ſuch a variety of diſſipation and expence, as are the diſgrace

---

[a] Mod. Univ. Hist. xi. 186. [b] Ibid. xxxviii. 472.
[c] Ant. Univ. Hist. viii. 266.
[d] Oeuvr. Polit. xi. 108.

disgrace of our universities of *Oxford* and *Cambridge*. That a youth, by being placed at *Leyden*, or *Utrecht*, runs no other hazard, than that of perhaps acquiring a more studious turn, than what would be suitable to active stations in life. But that at our *English* universities, a youth will acquire such a turn to extravagance, as will ruin all prudence and œconomy in him for life. He adds, 'the morals of the youth are incomparably purer at the *Dutch* universities, than the *English*, which are little better than seminaries of vice.'

If statesmen understood rightly their proper function, they would apply a great part of their time and attention to education, as a matter of great consequence toward forming right principles and manners in persons of rank, from whom the lower people receive theirs. Universities and public schools, especially those situated in great towns, seem to be a constitution incapable of proper regulation. The multitude of the youth assembled together, makes it unreasonable to expect other than dissipation and neglect of studies, if not vice and debauchery. They consider themselves as (what they really are) formidable to their masters and governors, and they will obey only when they please. But, if we must speak the truth, the error begins earlier than schools and universities. In *England* parents encourage that in their sons, which they ought to suppress, and contrariwise. The most amiable, and most useful disposition in a young mind is diffidence of itself, a sense of its own insufficiency, and consequent need of instruction and guidance, and a constant fear of offending. But we do all we can to rub off this lovely delicacy of sentiment, and to give our sons instead of it, a bold and fearless disposition, which naturally leads them to licentiousness and disobedience,

with

with a daring contempt and reſiſtance of advice and inſtruction from thoſe who alone have a right to regulate their manners and habits.

But to point out fully the errors, deficiencies, and abuſes of the times, with reſpect to this one article of forming the manners of the youth, would fill this whole volume.

It is commonly reckoned, that kindneſs is the natural growth of the human heart. Yet we find, that ſavages are almoſt univerſally rather devils than men in reſpect of cruelty, and that they only come to acquire ſome degree of humanity, in conſequence of civiliſation.

Scalping was in uſe among the *Alans* and *Huns* [a].

In *modern* times we do not expect a whole army, or other numerous ſet of people, to be reſtrained from irregularities by principle. A man of real honour, or conſcience, is one of a thouſand. We meet with various inſtances among the *ancient Heathens*, of great multitudes reſtrained by their oath, by gratitude to a public benefactor, or by reverence for the gods. To what is it owing, that with a better religion, we ſee worſe manners prevail?

Lazy ſtateſmen excuſe their neglect of this important part of their duty by alleging, that the multitude of any people is incapable of being formed to any principles of virtue or delicacy of ſentiment. But it is not true, that the majority of a people muſt be of groſs ſentiment. The *Athenians* are a proof to the contrary. They would not agree to *Themiſtocles*'s unknown propoſal, though *Miltiades* told them it would be very ſerviceable

[a] *Clarke*'s CONNEX. OF COINS, p. 415.

viceable to the ſtate, becauſe he at the ſame time told them it was diſhonourable [a].

Plato employs a great part of the IVth dialogue of his DE REPUBL. in ſhewing what care ought, for the ſecurity of ſtates, to be taken of the education of youth, and ſpeaks of it as almoſt ſufficient of itſelf to ſupply the place of both legiſlation and adminiſtration.

And *Ariſtotle* [b] lays down very ſtrict rules concerning the company young people may be allowed to keep, the public diverſions they may attend, the pictures they may ſee, and againſt obſcenity, intempearnce, &c. Επισκεπτεον δε τοις παιδονομοις, κ. τ. λ. And the VIIIth book of his POLIT. is employed wholly on education; in which he ſhews, that youth ought to be ſtrongly impreſſed with the idea of their being members of a community, whoſe good they are to prefer to their own private advantage in all caſes where they come in competition. He commends the *Spartan* wiſdom in paying ſuch attention to this great object, Such is the delicacy of this old Heathen, that he heſitates about the propriety of young mens applying to muſic, as being likely to effeminate and enervate the mind.

We Chriſtians let our youth looſe to all encounters, and hardly teach them any thing thoroughly, but the neceſſity of getting money, in order to make a figure in life.

Lycurgus did not allow his *Spartans* to travel, leſt they ſhould be tainted with the manners of other nations. We ſhould keep our gentry from making the tour of *Europe*, in mere compaſſion to our neighbours, who

---

[a] *Cic.* OFF. *Corn. Nep.* VIT. THEMIST.

[b] POLIT. VII. 17.

who cannot afford to be as debauched as we are. Time was when the *English* went abroad to learn the continental vices; but we have outdone our masters. The *English* are not reckoned great in invention, but they are famous for improving on the inventions of others.

There ought to be a large fine imposed on every person who goes needlesly abroad, and spends his income in foreign countries. This alone, carried to a considerable excess, would ruin the nation. It has been computed, that in one year our truants of the nobility and gentry have spent, in *France* alone, to the amount of near a million. If the *French* were as foolish as we are, and would come and throw away their money among us, as we do ours with them, the account would balance itself between the nations. But they know better things.

Polymnis, the father of *Epaminondas*, spent most of what he could give his son upon his education. Let history be answerable, whether he did not lay it out to the greatest advantage[a].

The *Roman* censors expelled from the city certain unqualified schoolmasters[b]. Our law prohibits all persons educating youth (not who are ignorant, negligent, or vicious) but who will not subscribe certain self-contradictory doctrines, which every man of sense in our times gives up, and which no man ever really believed, because no man ever understood them.

Hieronymus, successor to the good king *Hiero* of *Sicily*, a wicked prince, so grieved some of his guardians, that they laid violent hands on themselves, choosing death rather than the pain of seeing the bad behaviour of their *quondom* pupil[c].

In

---

[a] Ant. Univ. Hist. vii. 205. [b] Ibid. xiii. 34.
[c] Ibid. viii. 108.

In the time of *James* I. *A. D.* 1620, a motion was made in the house of peers for an academy for the education of persons of quality. This shews, that the conduct of the Universities was, in those times, disapproved [b].

The excellent Abbe *S. Pierre* holds education to be of great consequence both to princes and subjects toward the peace and happiness of states. See particularly tom. VII. 219, where he shews the great importance of good habits and customs in a country, and the great importance of education toward forming the habits and customs of a people.

Montesquieu lays great stress on education and manners [c]. What he writes is too long to quote without prejudice to his sense.

'The Czarina does not extirpate vice by stern justice, but prevents it by the more effectual means of virtuous education [d].'

Every thing in *Poland* favours frequent robberies and murders. But such is the honesty of the people, there are very few. So much more useful are good morals than good laws [e].

S. Pierre thinks it strange, that in *England* education should be neglected by parliament [f]. However, that has not always been the case. For we find a bill ordered to be brought in, *A. D.* 1711, for preventing the education of children in popish countries [g]. But indeed, excepting the article of religion, it is to be questioned whether *English* children would be great losers by going abroad for education. The conduct of *English* parents in

---

[b] PARL. HIST. V. 337.

[c] L'ESPR. DES LOIX, I. 47. *seq.*

[d] CZARINA'S INSTR. *Pref.* XV.

[e] MOD. UNIV. HIST. XLIII. 529. [f] Ibid. 165.

[g] DEB. COM. IV. 261.

in respect of indulgence, even to the voluntary and inexcusable perverseness of their children, makes it much to be desired, that they and their children be separated as early as possible.

A noble scheme was proposed in the time of *Henry* VIII. when the crown had so much in its power, *viz.* A foundation for educating ambassadors, counsellors, and public officers. The students to be trained up in the knowledge of history and politics, and to go abroad with ambassadors. Others to write the history of all public transactions. This would, however, answer no end in our times. Our politics are reduced within a very narrow compass. Packing a house of commons [a].

Statesmen ought to keep as constant an eye upon the manners of their people, as the most prudent *parents* upon those of their *children.* The manners of a people are very changeable. One would hardly imagine any thing more remote from the national character of the *English* than inhumanity. Yet the News-papers of the beginning of *April* 1771, were filled with accounts of the most infernal cruelties committed by them in the *East Indies.*

CHAP. VII.

Of Punishments.

THERE are two principal means for drawing mankind to decency of behaviour, and deterring them from those actions which are hurtful to society, *viz.* Rewards and Punishments. As to the former of these, it is but a little way that statesmen go in confer-

ring

---

[a] *Rapin*, I. 824.

ring them. In poor countries, governments have but little in their power, and in rich ones they give the honours and emoluments not to thoſe who deſerve them, but to thoſe whom it ſuits them beſt to gratify; and then they exchange the name of rewards for that of bribes. It is therefore not neceſſary to ſay much of rewards. As to puniſhments, the moſt indiſpenſable requiſite is their being adequate. A murder committed with the ſword of juſtice, is the moſt horrid phænomenon in a ſtate. And in all well-regulated ſtates, the maxim, 'Better ten guilty eſcape, than that one 'innocent be puniſhed,' has been held unqueſtioned.

Another eſſential in puniſhments is, that they be calculated to deter offenders, and prevent farther tranſgreſſion. For this is, in fact, the ſole end of puniſhments. And if a ſanction does nothing toward preventing farther violation of the law, it is totally uſeleſs.

Malefactors in *Ruſſia* are now condemned not to *death*, but to *work* in the mines[a]. A regulation not leſs prudent than humane; ſince it renders this puniſhment of ſome advantage to the ſtate. In other countries they only know how to put a criminal to death with the apparatus, but are not able to prevent the commiſſion of crimes. The terror of death does not perhaps make ſuch an impreſſion on evil doers, who are generally given to *idleneſs*, as the fear of *chaſtiſement* and hard *labour* renewed every day.

Catharine the Czarina, on aſcending the throne, promiſed, that no perſon ſhould in her reign be puniſhed with death. We puniſh every thing with death, and with death of the ſame ſort; ſo that two fellows ſhall go together to be hanged at *Tyburn*, the one for cutting

[a] Mod. Univ. Hist. xxxv. 390.

ting his wife's throat, or worſe, ſtarving her to death, the other for taking a guinea of a rich man a ſtranger to him [a].

'*Caput amputare*, &c. Beheading, racking, mutilation, breaking on the wheel, are not legal puniſhments in *England*, and yet in no country are fewer murders committed.' *Thom. Smith.* De Repub. Angl. Perhaps it is not ſtrictly true, that there is *no country* in which fewer murders are committed, than in *England*. I imagine *Scotland* and *Holland* are exceptions; to mention no others. But be this as it will, it is certain that in no countries are atrocious crimes more frequent, than in thoſe in which the puniſhments are the moſt inhuman.

Let us hear Mr. *Fazakerly* on this ſubject, who ſpoke as follows in the houſe, *A. D.* 1744:

'Some people confeſs that forfeitures and confiſcations, when annexed to capital puniſhments, are inconſiſtent with religious juſtice, and the ſpirit of our law; but theſe additional puniſhments, ſay they, are neceſſary for the preſervation of government, and preventing conſpiracies and civil wars. Did they ever do ſo in any country? Did the ſeverity of the puniſhment ever prevent the frequency of the crime? Does breaking on the wheel prevent robberies in *France*? Do the puniſhments of treaſon prevent treaſons and rebellions in *Aſia*, where traitors are put to the moſt tormenting and cruel deaths, and their whole families deſtroyed? Sir, there is ſomething in the nature of man that diſdains to be terrified; and therefore ſevere puniſhments have never been found effectual for preventing any ſort of crime. The moſt effectual way to prevent crimes is, to prevent the temptation;

[a] Mod. Univ. Hist. xxxv. 556.

'temptation: if you would prevent thefts and robberies, you must take care to have your people educated in virtuous principles, and every man brought up and enured to labour and industry, that has no estate to subsist on: if you would prevent treasons, you must do it by the mildness of your government, in order to prevent the ambitious from having any matter to work on, or any prospect of success, and to prevent any number of men from being rendered desperate; for desperate men no laws can restrain, no punishment frighten; and no man ever yet conspired against a government, without some prospect of success. I am therefore fully convinced that punishments always promote, instead of preventing, conspiracies and civil wars; and I have the experience of all ages, and all countries, for supporting my opinion. Nay, if we have any faith in providence, we must expect that a government shall not go unpunished, which injures and oppresses the fatherless, the widow, and the orphan. These severe punishments upon treason, Sir, serve for nothing but to lull a government into a fatal and mistaken security, that no man will venture to conspire or rebel against them. In arbitrary governments, this emboldens ministers to tyrannize over, and oppress the people; and in limited governments it encourages them to encroach upon the liberties and privileges of the people. In both they continue their oppressions or encroachments, till the people are become generally discontented. Then some desperate, or some ambitious man sets fire to the train, and the ministers too often with their masters are blown up by the combustibles which they themselves have collected for their own destruction. It was to this cause chiefly, I am convinced, Sir, that we owed all the civil wars, and all the revolutions that have happened

'in

'in this country almost ever since the conquest; and 'if we remove the cause, I may venture to prophesy, 'that both our civil wars and revolutions will be less 'frequent.'

One would think nothing was more natural, than that murder be punished with death, according to *Moses*'s law, 'he, who sheddeth man's blood, by man 'shall his blood be shed[a].'

——Nec lex est justior ulla,
Quam necis artifices arte perire suâ.

It seems strange, that any nation wise enough to propose punishments, should propose any other punishment for every injury, than formal retaliation, where it can be inflicted. Why should he, who mangles an innocent person, in such a manner that he is three days in the pains of death, be neatly tucked up, and put out of pain in the time of pronouncing, one, two, three? A few years ago, a merciless monster in human shape, starved his wife to death, keeping her tied with her hands behind her in constant anguish, for many weeks, if I rightly remember. He was only hanged; that is, he was punished, as if he had only stolen a sheep. This is not common sense. His guilt was as much beyond that of a sheep-stealer, as this globe of 25,000 miles round is larger than a hillock.

'At *Taunton* a man was lately executed as usual '[that is, he was hanged] for murdering his own father[b].'

Our laws are grown to be very sanguinary. In the *Saxon* times, they were quite contrary. For the lives of all ranks of men were valued at a certain fine; though

[a] Gen. ix. 6.
[b] London Mag. 1768, p. 228.

though some authors think those fines were for accidental killing; not for murder of malice forethought *. In those times they distinguished the rank of a person by the fine for killing him. One was a 200 *s.* man; another a 300, and so on [a].

Had due care been taken, 'it is impossible, that in 'the 18th century, it could ever have been made a capital crime to break down (however maliciously) the 'mound of a fish-pond, or to cut down a cherry-tree 'in an orchard, or that it should still be felony to be 'seen for one month in company with the people called '*Egyptians*, or *Gipseys*[b].' Add to these the game-acts, the dog-act, the smuggling-acts, the penal laws against dissenting preachers officiating without subscription to human articles and creeds, &c.

By 10 *Geo.* III. c. 19, every unqualified person taking or killing a partridge in the night is to be whipped publickly. This law is so cruel, that, I suppose, no magistrate will venture to put it in execution.

The good emperor *Antoninus* was so cautious of too great severity, (the worst error of the two) that he promised never to punish capitally a senator; which promise he kept so faithfully, that he spared several murderers of that rank [c].

It

---

* See *Seld.* TIT. HON. p. 603. 'Ærcebisceopes ⁊ Eorles, '&c. The weregild [or fine for killing] an archbishop and 'an earl, is 15,000 thrymsas, [a thrymsa about a third of a '*Saxon* shilling] of a bishop and an ealdorman, 8000, of a 'holde and a highgereeve 4000, of a massethane, or spiritual 'lord, and a worldthane, or temporal lord, 2000.' And see Ibid. 619, the fines for murder committed on certain holidays.

[a] *Spelm.* GLOSS. voc. *Wera, Mægbota, Weregildum*, &c.

[b] *Blackstone*, IV. 6.

[c] ANT. UNIV. HIST. XVI. 199.

It is not the ſeverity of puniſhments, but the certainty of not eſcaping, that reſtrains licentiouſneſs [a].

When laws and ſanctions are ill contrived, it is neceſſary to make *laws* to puniſh crimes occaſioned by former *laws*: but this is the heigth of injuſtice [b].

Public executions, if they do not ſtrike the people with fear, inſtead of being exemplary, do harm, by hardening them againſt puniſhment. Whenever a people come to ſhew themſelves unmoved, or not properly affected at thoſe awful ſcenes, a government, who had common ſenſe, or any feeling of their proper function, would immediately put a ſtop to ſuch exhibitions, and confine executions to the bounds of the priſon. In *Scotland* at an execution, all appear melancholy; many ſhed tears, and ſome faint away. But executions there are very rare. It is the ſame in *Holland*.

'It may not be unſeaſonable, ſays *Devenant*, in this 'place to offer to public conſideration, whether it would 'not be more religious, [more agreeable to the ſpirit of 'chriſtianity] to tranſport many of thoſe miſerable 'wretches, who are frequently executed in this king'dom for ſmall tranſgreſſions of the law; it being 'peradventure one of the faults of our conſtitution, that 'it makes ſo little difference between crimes; for expe'rience tells us, that many malefactors have, by after'induſtry, and a reformation in manners, juſtified their 'wiſdom, whoſe clemency ſent them abroad [c].'

Voltaire ſays the *Engliſh* only murder by law. He makes repeated reflexions on this nation as bloody, cruel, rebellious, &c. More crowned heads, he ſays, have been cut off in *England*, than in all *Europe* beſides. How few kings in *Europe* have been cut off, com-

 pared

[a] *Czar.* INSTR. 127. [b] Ibid. 128.

[c] *Daven.* II. 4.

pared with those who have deserved cutting off! If the *English* have shewn less patience under tyranny, than the other nations of *Europe*, I wish they had shewn still less. That, for instance, they had unheaded *Henry* VIII. his bloody daughter *Mary*, and *James* II. tyrants and murderers all, as well as *Charles* I. on whom they did justice in an exemplary manner. I wish our law was less sanguinary in punishing theft. But it very ill becomes a *Frenchman* to reflect on *English* severity. Did not their tyrant tell them a few years ago, that the whole power, legislative and executive, is in him alone? Do the *English* ever put any person to the torture to force them to confess? On the contrary, is it not a maxim in our law, that no man is obliged to accuse himself? Do the *French* try accused persons by their peers? Has not their tyrant, or their tyrant's tool, or their tyrant's whore, power to send to the Bastile whom they please? Is there a man in *France* secure of his liberty, or his property, one day to an end?

'The severest punishment, under a mild administration, would be, to convince the offender, that he has committed a foul crime [a].' It is the fault of government, if a people are less delicate to offend against the laws of their country, and of morality, than a well-brought up son, or daughter, against those of their parents. In *England* we have little notion of obeying either our maker, our laws, or our parents.

Punishments operate according to the dispositions of the people. Severe punishments harden their tempers, and defeat their own intention. There are more offenders among the *Turks*, who bastinado their people to death for slight faults [b], than in *England*. The rigorous

[a] *Czar*. Instr. 86.

[b] Mod. Univ. Hist. xviii. 205.

gorous puniſhments of martial law do not reſtrain the ſoldiery from licentious behaviour. The youth of the public ſchools, where the diſcipline is ſevere, are more unruly, than thoſe in private houſes of education, where they are corrected with more gentleneſs.

'The only puniſhment denounced againſt the tranſ-'greſſors of the *Ogulnian* law was, that they ſhould be 'deemed guilty of a diſhonourable action. A ſlight 'puniſhment indeed for a more corrupt age; but ſuf-'ficient at this time to reſtrain the *Romans*, who piqued 'themſelves on their virtue, and were never choſen 'for great employments, unleſs they had preſerved their 'reputation pure and untainted[a].'

'A violent adminiſtration will be for ſudden and 'violent remedies, in caſe of public diſturbances; and 'by and by theſe violent puniſhments become familiar, 'and are deſpiſed[b].' A people are to be led, like rational creatures, not driven like brutes.

The ſhame of being puniſhed ought always to be the principal part of an offender's puniſhment. And a perſon, who is puniſhed, will ſuffer ſeverely from ſhame, unleſs either the puniſhment be unjuſt, which is the fault of the government, or himſelf, and thoſe, who are witneſſes of his puniſhment, be hardened and abandoned; which is a greater fault of the government. For it was the government's buſineſs to take care, that the people ſhould not become thus ill-diſpoſed.

The *Czarina* propoſes[c] that all puniſhments flow naturally from the reſpective crimes. If this rule were obſerved, thieves and highwaymen would be puniſhed with hard work and hard fare, becauſe they became guilty through idleneſs and luxury.

---

[a] Ant. Univ. Hist. xii. 115.

[b] *Czar.* Instr. 86.

[c] Ibid. 82.

If a government is mild, and a country happy under it, banishment will be a sufficient punishment for most offences.

Crimes, which tend to corrupt the morals of the people, ought always to bring this punishment upon the offenders; because the morals of the people ought above all things to be secured.

Hanging is a punishment as ancient as King *Ina*, says Sir *William Dugdale*[a]. *William* the Bastard punished with putting out of eyes, emasculation, cutting off hands or feet, &c. *Henry* I. introduced hanging for theft and robbery. Beheading criminals of quality was first practised, he thinks, in 8 *Will. Conqu.* Drowning was a punishment used in the time of *Edward* II. and before. In the county palatine of *Chester* they used beheading instead of hanging, in the time of *Edward* I. A murderer was, in those days, dragged to execution by the relations of the murdered by a long rope[b].

Among the ancient *Germans*, and, after them, among our *Saxon* ancestors, a murderer was obliged to pay damages to the King for the loss of a subject; to the Lord for the loss of a vassal; and, as *Tacitus* observes (*de mor. Germ. recipit satisfactionem, &c.*) to all the family of the deceased for the loss of their father, son, brother, &c[c].

It was enacted in this parliament that the King should not pardon murder[d].

A man was boiled to death in *Smithfield* (on an old statute since repealed) for poisoning[e].

Beccaria,

[a] Orig. Juridic. p. 88. [b] Ibid. 89.

[c] *Spelm.* Gloss. voc. *Cenegild.*

[d] *Rap.* I. 466. [e] Ibid. I. 792.

Beccaria, p. 102, holds capital punishment wholly unnecessary, excepting only where the life of the offender is clearly incompatible with the safety of the state.

When an offender is hanged, he is made an example to a few hundreds, and is forgotten. Put him in a state of slavery, confinement, or continually returning correction, during many years, or for life, and you make him a constant example to a succession of individuals during the whole period of his punishment, besides that his labour may in some degree compensate for the injury he has done society.

Too severe punishments affect the people with compassion for the sufferer, and hatred against the laws and the administrators of the laws.

There are in *England* no less than 160 crimes declared by law capital, without benefit of clergy[a].

If severity were the certain means for curing some faults in a people, it does not follow that it ought to be used, because it may leave a worse distemper than it removes. It may force them out of one wrong track into another more wrong. It may break and dastardise their spirit; or it may harden and brutify them.

The *Japanese* are afraid of hardening their children by severity; but the *Japanese* government is not afraid of hardening the people by accustoming them to rigorous punishments. Yet the maxims by which a family of children, and those by which a people are to be formed, and to be governed, are no way essentially different.

There was a bill brought into parliament under *James* I. for exempting the gentry of this realm from the slavish punishment of whipping[b].

Punish-

[a] *Blackst.* IV. 18.

[b] PARL. HIST. V. 448.

Punishments are indispensable in states; and a proper application of them produces valuable effects. *Painvine's* execution for cowardice, at the beginning of the *Dutch* war, was of considerable service. He was tried twice by his brother officers; but acquitted, to the great disgust of the states, who saw, says *Burnet*[a], that 'the officers were resolved to be gentle to one 'another, and to save their fellow-officers, how guilty 'soever they might be.' The Prince of *Orange* brought him to a third trial before himself and a court of the supreme officers, in which they had the assistance of six judges. He was cast for his life.

Nothing seems clearer, if we compare Admiral *Byng's* conduct, *A. D.* 1755, with that of *Blake*, *Vernon*, or any of our truly brave commanders, than that he deservedly suffered the punishment due to cowardice. Yet we find several of the officers, who could not decently avoid condemning him, afterwards pretending great uneasiness about his fate, and desiring to disclose their reasons for passing the sentence of death on him, which would discover, they said, such circumstances as might, perhaps, shew the sentence to have been improper[b]. The King respited *Byng*: And a motion was made for bringing in a bill for releasing the officers from the obligation of secrecy; but the Lords wisely rejected it, approving the old rule, Hang well and pay well, and you shall be well served.

We punish many very atrocious crimes too slightly, as well as several inconsiderable crimes too severely. Perjury in *England* is only the pillory. Among the *Russians*, it is punished with severe whipping, and banishment[c].

A bill

---

a Hist. own Times. i. 470.

b Alm. Deb. Com. v. 204.

c Mod. Univ. Hist. xxxv. 124.

A bill was brought in *A. D.* 1694 to make perjury felony. Thrown out. Several lords protest, because there was great need of a severer punishment for perjury [a].

Our laws are too gentle to perjury; to adultery; to seduction of modest women; to insolvency occasioned by overtrading or extravagance; to idleness in the lower people; to bribery and corruption; to engrossing and monopolizing the necessaries of life; to giving and accepting challenges; to murders with aggravations of cruelty, &c.

Preventive wisdom suggests the necessity, 1. Of an incorrupt legislature. 2. Of clear and simple laws, digested in a short code. 3. Of the certainty of punishment in case of transgressions. Pardons, even from the Throne, are of doubtful consequence. They invite offenders, especially persons of rank; for they trust they shall always have interest to obtain their pardon. Laws ought to be so just and so mild, that they may be put in execution, which would supersede the use of the royal prerogative, and save the King the trouble of much solicitation and reflection when he refuses. 4. Of liberty. A slave has no veneration for his country or its laws. His country does nothing for him, that may allure him to obedience: freemen have a hand in making the laws, and therefore may be supposed to be prejudiced in their favour. Men naturally oppose laws made by those who assume an unjustifiable authority over them. 5. Of sound education, useful public instruction, and a free press, with whatever else tends to spread light and knowledge among the people. A savage or uncultivated people are only obedient as far as fear carries them. Knowledge enlarges

---

[a] Deb. Peers, i. 434.

enlarges the mind, and leads it to the love of order and regularity. Education furnishes the mind with what takes it off from the sordid pursuit of riches, power, and sensual pleasure. 6. Of rewards rather honorary than pecuniary. 7. Of associations, as that in *Poland* called the commonwealth of *Babina*; which consisted of all the most considerable people of the country, who met from time to time to enquire into the general behaviour of the people, and promoted good behaviour by their countenance and other invitations; discouraging the contrary by general disgrace. But indeed we need go no farther than our own wise and judicious Quakers; who do more by their manner of educating their youth, and their treatment of them in consequence of their behaviour, than all the Kings of *Europe* with their laws and sanctions piled on one another to the height of mountains.

CHAP. VIII.

Able Statesmen apply themselves to forming the Manners of the People.

IF manners be, as we have seen, so essentially necessary to the safety of a State, no wise Prince, Minister, or Statesman, will neglect attending to the general manners and morals. No part of the function of Statesmen is more honourable, none more useful, none more indispensable, than a due attention to the general manners of the people. If a wise and good man were to wish to be in a high station, it would be for the sake of being thus serviceable to his fellow-creatures. But a little knowledge of the world shews us, that grandees of all denominations, as Emperors, Kings, Grand-dukes, Popes, Cardinals, Peers, Archbishops,

biſhops, Biſhops, &c. are great enemies to manners. Their height above the reſt gives them an opportunity of daring, without fear of puniſhment, or almoſt of cenſure, to ſtrike out from the limited path of virtue into the wilds of licentiouſneſs; and the ſillineſs of mankind, who admire a laced coat, whether it be a man or a monkey that wears it, leads them to imitate what reaſon teaches to abhor. There muſt be leſs of this in a well regulated republic, where all are nearly upon an equality, than in a monarchy, where the falſe glare of a court miſleads the unthinking into the paths of ambition and corruption.

Do our great men conſider how they expoſe themſelves in ſetting ſuch an example before the public?

How abſurd titles without correſponding characters! To call a drinking, wh—ring, perfidious tyrant, as *Charles* II. his ſacred, or his moſt excellent, or moſt religious Majeſty; a debauched *Villiers*, and his trull, the Counteſs of *Shrewſbury*, right honourable; what groſſer inconſiſtency in language can be imagined?

—— Grant that thoſe can conquer; thoſe can cheat,
'Tis phraſe abſurd to call a villain great.
What can ennoble ſots, or ſlaves, or cowards?
Alas, not all the blood of all the Howards. Pope.

Chartres, the baſeſt of all raſcals, was wont to ſay, he cared not one farthing for real Virtues; but he would give 10,000l. for a character, becauſe he could get by it 100,000l.

A perſon of quality thinks he may do what a cottager muſt not attempt. A worm of diſtinction crawling upon the *higher* protuberances of this dunghill may rebel againſt the eternal laws of the infinite Governor of the univerſe, while the baſe-born reptile, that is confined to the lower parts, muſt be obedient. Do our great worms conſider, that he, whoſe laws they

8 are

are resisting, has only to arm with his vengeance one atom, and a world, a system, with all its inhabitants, great and small, are destroyed? Is a King, or an Emperor, a match for such power?

Men of narrow minds, when reproached upon their want of public spirit, cry out, what shall I get by serving those who shew no inclination to benefit me in return?

It is true, that mankind in general are a worthless and ungrateful set of beings, for a man to wear himself out in serving. But I am myself a worthless being, compared with my own ideas of worth, and with those in scripture; and if I do not lay myself out in the service of mankind, whom shall I serve? My insignificant self? That would be sordid indeed. If I apply myself with diligence, I may do good to several. If I regard only my single self, I serve but *one*, and him, perhaps, one of the most indifferent of the set.

But it is not true, that there is nothing to be gained by public spirit, or lost by the want of it. For there is a very serious light in which this matter is to be viewed, viz. That we are all embarked on the same bottom; and if our country sinks, we must sink with it.

But suppose there were literally nothing to be got by serving our country, antiquity exhibits a multitude of examples of great and good men serving their country without advantage, and in spite of unjust treatment. *Phocion*, though he had often commands in the army, was condemned to an undeserved death, and died poor, at a time when corruption was at a great height at *Athens*[a]. When his friends lamented him, he comforted them by putting them in mind, that his fate was the

[a] Ant. Univ. Hist. vi. 512.

4

the ſame with that of all the great and good men of *Athens*.

Xenophon got ſo little from his churliſh countrymen, though he conducted the wonderful retreat of the ten thouſand, that he found himſelf neceſſitated to engage in the ſervice of *Seuthes* King of *Thrace*, and to ſell his horſe.

There is no end to the examples of this kind in the *Grecian* and *Roman* hiſtories.

When we urge our rulers to begin a reformation, a thouſand difficulties ſtart up immediately. But when *Lycurgus* undertook to reform *Sparta*, did no difficulties lay in the way? And was not the caſe the ſame at *Athens*, when *Solon* ſet up his legiſlation? To perſuade the great and rich to give up their poſſeſſions, and voluntarily deſcend to a level with the meaneſt, what could be more difficult? Yet *Lycurgus* accompliſhed it. The force of his legiſlation, and the manners introduced by it, are not quite vaniſhed even in our times. The modern *Spartans* have more courage than any of their neighbours[a].

Confucius, the *Chineſe* philoſopher, produced a reformation in one of the oriental kingdoms in a few months[b].

Ariſtotle thinks, a regard for the virtue of the people is an eſſential part of the duty of governors[c]. Περι δε αρετης, κ. τ. λ. It would be endleſs to quote what is written by *Plato*, and the other ancients to the ſame purpoſe.

'If government be the parent of manners, where there

---

[a] Mod. Univ. Hist. xii. 572.

[b] Mod. Univ. Hist. viii. 105.

[c] *Ariſt.* Polit. iii. 9.

'there are no heroic virtues, there can be no heroic 'government[a].'

One judicious regulation will often produce an effect of very salutary importance to a whole people; as experimental philosophy shews us, that a wire will secure a castle from the once supposed irresistible force of lightning, and that a muslin cover will stop the whole effect of a burning speculum, whose focus would melt an iron bar in a few seconds.

Human nature is originally the same in all ages and nations. Only in some it is more, in others less, debauched from its original tendencies.

It is certain, that by wise contrivance, honour might have been made, even in our luxurious and degenerate age and country, the most powerful of all incentives to good behaviour.

'An able statesman can change the manners of the 'people at pleasure[b].'

It was a saying of *Solon*, the wisest of the *Greeks*, 'That by rewards and punishments states were kept 'up[c].'

Tacitus[d] observes, '*Plus ibi bonos mores*, &c. That 'good customs were more effectual for keeping up 'good behaviour among those ancient barbarous hea'thens, than good laws among other people,' [among civilized Christians.]

When *Alexander's* men mutinied, and he could not quiet them by gentle means, he sprung from his tribunal, seized with his own hands twelve of the most outrageous, and delivered them to his generals to be put to death. The rest returned to their duty[e].

When

---

[a] *Harringt.* OCEANA, 193.

[b] *Stuart's* POLIT. OECON. I. 12.

[c] *Ubb. Emm.* II. 244.

[d] DE MORIB. GERM.

[e] *Qu. Curt.*

When *Cæsar*'s army refused to march, and to fight, he shamed them into obedience by bidding them be gone; for that he scorned their service, and would pursue his wars at the head of his own tenth legion. It so happened, that this braggadocio produced the desired effect [a].

When *Mohammed Almanzor* saw his army on the point of betaking themselves to flight, he dismounts, sits down with his arms across, and declares his determination not to fly like a coward, happen what would; that if his army chose to leave him in the hands of his enemies, they might. Shame prevailed over fear [b]. These bold strokes are only to be struck in cases otherwise desperate.

Mankind may be brought to hold any principles, and to indulge any practices, and again to give them up.

The *Thracians* allowed their daughters to debauch themselves with men before marriage as much as they pleased; and only taught the necessity of restraining lust after marriage. Yet the *Thracians* were, to say the least, not so barbarous as many other nations; *Orpheus*, *Linus*, *Musæus*, *Thamyris*, and *Eumolpus*, were *Thracians*. Some nations allowed their young women to get, by prostitution, fortunes for marriage.

Herodotus tells us of an ancient people who ordered all their young women to prostitute themselves in the temple of *Venus* as a religious rite. The priests in some countries taught, that a young woman's being debauched by a holy man, sanctified and rendered her acceptable to the gods. In some countries it is fashionable for gentlemen to offer their wives to their guests, and to take it as a slight if the stranger declines the compliment.

a *Cæs.* Comm.

b Mod. Univ. Hist. xix. 534.

compliment. In ſome countries it is not more indecent to enjoy women in public, than among us to eat and drink in public. The ancient *Thracian* and modern *Indian* women, ſtrive which ſhall be burned or buried alive with their deceaſed huſbands.

Is there any notion of right and wrong about which mankind are univerſally agreed? If not, is it not evident, that by management, the human ſpecies may be moulded into any conceivable ſhape? How come we to know that antimony, or quickſilver, may, by chemical proceſs, be changed into twenty different ſtates, and again reſtored to their original ſtate? Is it not by experiment? Are not the various legiſlations, inſtitutions, regulations of wiſe or of deſigning ſtateſmen, prieſts, and kings, a ſeries of experiments, ſhewing, that human nature is ſuſceptible of any form or character?

Romulus was ſo deſirous of peopling his kingdom, that he admitted into *Rome* all ſorts of people, even the moſt wicked[a]. Yet there was not one parricide in *Rome* for 600 years, nor, according to ſome authors, one divorce (though every huſband might put away his wife at pleaſure) in 500 years. But they had cenſors, and the ſenate gave a conſtant attention to the behaviour of the people.

The *Roman* nation (ſays the excellent *Davenant*[b]) was firſt compoſed of thieves, vagabonds, fugitive ſlaves, indebted perſons, and outlaws; and yet by a good conſtitution and wholeſome laws, they became and continued for ſome ages the moſt virtuous people that was ever known. So that as looſe adminiſtration corrupts any ſociety of men, ſo a wiſe, ſteady, and ſtrict government will, in time, reform a country, let its manners have been ever ſo depraved.

Every

---

[a] Ant. Univ. Hist. xi. 282.

[b] *Davenant*, ii. 43.

Every reader knows the ſtory of *Zaleucus*, lawgiver of the *Locrians*, who having made a law (much wanted at preſent in a certain country), that every man convicted of adultery ſhould loſe his eyes; and ſeeing his own ſon regularly condemned for that offence, that he might at the ſame time ſhew himſelf the father of his ſon, and of his people, conſented to have one of his own eyes, and one of his ſon's, put out. In *England*, we ſeem to think laws want only to be made and printed.

'The ſame wiſe legiſlator applied his chief care to 'impreſſing the minds of the people with a ſenſe of a 'Deity, the author and governor of all things; his 'attributes, goodneſs, juſtice, purity; who ſees and 'regards human characters, and loves and rewards 'good men, who are obedient to the laws, and abhors 'and puniſhes the wicked and licentious[a].' But *Zaleucus* was an ignorant *Heathen*, and imagined that men would be better ſubjects for being pious. Our governors (the reader will ſee I do not mean the preſent) are *Chriſtians*, and live in an *improved* age. Therefore they lead their people to laugh at religion and conſcience; they play at cards on *Sundays*, inſtead of countenancing the public worſhip of their Maker; they have made adultery a matter of merriment; they cheat at play whenever they can; they lead their inferiors into extravagance and diſſipation by encouraging public diverſions more luxurious and more debauched than all that ever the orientals exhibited; and leſt ſhame ſhould in ſome degree reſtrain them, they put on maſks, and ſet it at defiance; they go to *Italy* to learn ſ——y; they appear in public with their drabs by their ſides; they are the firſt and moſt extenſive vio-

[a] *Ubb. Emm.* 11. 204.

lators of the laws themselves have made; they are the destroyers of the constitution, for by openly bribing electors and members, and by leading both clergy and laity into dissimulation and perjury, they destroy the virtue of the people, without which no constitution ever stood long. And after all this, they complain of the people's want of respect for them, and their disobedience to the laws.

Zaleucus made great use of the innate sense of shame in enforcing his laws and establishing virtuous practices. For instance, in order to repress extravagance in the ladies, he ordered, with severe penalty, that no woman should go out with more than one attendant, unless she was drunk; nor be a night from home, unless she was with a gallant; nor dress herself gorgeously, unless she was a prostitute by profession. He likewise forbid the men's dressing themselves in an effeminate manner, unless they were whoremongers and adulterers [a]. These were good contrivances in a country in which shame had an influence. But such regulations would answer no end in a country where gentlemen were not ashamed of being thought adulterers, nor ladies of being known for professed wh——s. Governments, therefore, which suffer the sense of shame to be lost in their people, lose the best handle for governing them by, and must thank themselves if they find them ungovernable.

O shame to debauched *Christians!* Such was the sanctity of manners of the ancient *Heathen* court of *Areopagus*, that the members of it were not allowed to enter a tavern. If they did, they were expelled without mercy [b].

No

---

[a] *Ubb. Emm.* II. 296.

[b] *Ant. Thys.* De Repub. Athen. 249.

No man could be an *Athenian* archon, or magistrate, unless his character and life could bear the strictest examination [a]. And to be of the high court of *Areopagus*, was an unquestionable testimonial [b]. Even in the degenerate times of the republic, when a few persons of indifferent characters got into that sacred society, it was observed, that they reformed their manners [c]. The court of *Areopagus* preserved the dignity of its character to the last, even under the dominion of tyrants, and after the *Athenian* liberty was gone [d]. The *Athenians* did not suffer any man of an infamous character for lewdness, impiety, cowardice, or debts, to vote in the εκκλησια, or assembly of the people [e].

When one of the *Athenian* thesmothetæ was out of his office, and was to be advanced to the court of *Areopagus*, proclamation was made, that any one might accuse him of any mal-administration he could prove against him, while in office. If it was only found, that he had been too niggardly in his manner of living, so slight an objection excluded him.

It was not to be wondered, that an areopagite was reverenced by the people. And it would be wonderful, if the members of one of our highest courts, (be sure I cannot mean the present) were esteemed by the people, while many of them openly profess to be as much beyond their inferiors in wickedness as in station.

The authors of the ANCIENT UNIVERSAL HISTORY, vol. viii. p. 2. ascribe the long continuance of the *Spartan* commonwealth to the virtue of the people.

At *Sparta*, the poets could not publish any thing without licence: and all immoral writings were prohibited.

'The liberty and other emoluments which were enjoyed at *Athens* drawing thither a great concourse of

 'people

[a] *Ubb. Emm.* DE REP. ATHEN. I. 27. [b] Ibid. 31.
[c] Ibid. 33. [d] Ibid. 36. Ibid. 50.

'people from other parts, *Solon* foresaw, that this would 'have bad consequences, if some means were not devised 'to make these people industrious; he therefore esta-'blished a law, that a son should be released from all 'obligation to maintain an aged father, in case that 'father had not bred him up to some trade. He vested 'the court of *Areopagus* with a power of examining 'how people lived, and of punishing idleness: he al-'lowed every man a right to prosecute another for that 'crime, and in case a person was convicted of it thrice, 'he suffered Atimia, *i. e.* infamy.

'*Herodotus* and *Diodorus Siculus* agree, that a law of 'of this kind was in use in *Egypt*. It is probable, 'therefore, that *Solon*, who was thoroughly acquainted 'with the learning of that nation, borrowed it from 'them, a practice for which the *Greeks* were famous, 'though at the same time they styled those nations bar-'barous from whom their own laws and policy were 'borrowed.—He enacted, that whoever refused to 'maintain his parents, or had wasted his paternal 'estate, should be infamous. It seems, *Solon* did not 'conceive that a man could be privately bad, and pub-'lickly good, that one who neglected his duty to his 'parents should preserve it to the state, or be frugal of 'his country's revenue who had spent his own [a].'

When the *Athenians* became corrupt, they grew irreligious, and assisted the *Phocæans* to plunder the temple of *Delphi*, though they could not confute the general opinion of *Apollo*'s being really a god [b]. So our governors laugh at the Christian religion, which they have never so fully considered, so as to be able to produce any good reasons against its credibility, or rather which they are so ignorant of, as not to know the most plausible objections against it.

'*Nec*

[a] ANT, UNIV. HIST. VI, 312. [b] Ibid. 511.

'*Nec numero Hispanos*, &c. We have neither conquered *Spain* by numbers, nor *Gaul* by martial power, nor *Carthage* by craft, nor *Greece* by art; but we have prevailed over all nations by our being wise enough to know, that all human affairs are directed by the Divine Providence[a].' So says *Cicero*. But *Cicero* was an ignorant heathen. Our modern Christian statesmen are wiser than to regard the doctrine of their own scripture, 'That righteousness exalteth a nation; and that sin is the reproach of a people.'

Aristotle thinks a government compounded of monarchy, aristocracy, and democracy, the best. I suppose he thought that form of government the best, which had the broadest foundation, as least likely to throw the power into the hands of one, or a few, which are proper tyrannies. For my part, what I have read and seen, convinces me, that the great danger to liberty arises from a court possessed of a large revenue, and united together into a compact junto under a tyrant, who either actively supports them in their conspiracy against the people, or passively permits them to screen their villanies under his name.

Aristotle blames the *Carthaginian* constitution, because they would not choose into a station of power the most virtuous and able man, unless he was likewise rich. This led, he thought, too much to aristocracy. A needy man, they pretended, could hardly be supposed to have a mind sufficiently vacant for attending to public concerns. But the philosopher observes, that then the business was, to find honest and able men, to put them in easy circumstances, and then give them the management of public affairs.

N 4 *Lycurgus*'s

[a] *Cic.* PRO RULLO.

Lycurgus's intention[a] was to limit within proper bounds the power of the commons; to keep up equality among the people, the best nurse of concord, and strength of republics; to accustom the *Spartans*, from their childhood, to obey law and just authority, to live temperately, to subdue inordinate desires, to bear labour, to be patient under hardships, to be ready to run hazards for their country, and to suffer death, rather than act a part unworthy of a *Spartan*.

Solon made idleness penal at *Athens*[b]. *Herodotus* and *Diodorus Siculus* say, the *Egyptians* had a law to the same purpose.

The *Castilians* obliged every man to live agreeably to his rank, that there might be no temptation to expence, and consequent dependency and corruption[c].

The *Athenians* publickly rewarded merit, as well as punished guilt. The honour of the προεδρια, or first seat at the public shows must have had great effects. We give seats in the house of peers, as well as in the playhouse, to the richest, not to the worthiest. Even learned degrees are given at our universities to men of quality, on account of their birth and fortune, in spite of the grossest ignorance. The *Athenians* punished ingratitude.

In the early ages of the *Roman* republic, no man openly canvassed for places of power and trust. In the degenerate times of *Cinna*, *Sylla*, *Cæsar*, and *Pompey*, this modest reserve was thrown off, and the open contentions for honours and employments ran high. In the early ages of *Rome*, men placed their notions of honour in living frugally and serving their country. In

---

[a] *Ubb. Emm.* DE REP. LACO . I. 217.

[b] *Plut. in Solon*, Την εξ Αρειȣ Παγȣ βȣλην, κ. [illegible]

[c] MOD. UNIV. HIS. XX. 387.

fit the degenerate times, it was honourable to live expensively on the ſpoils of their country.

Plato ſays[a], unleſs philoſophers undertake the government of ſtates, or ſtateſmen put on the character of philoſophers, ſo as that wiſdom and power may be in poſſeſſion of the ſame perſons, there will be no end to the diſtreſſes of mankind. Εαν μη ην δ' εγω, κ. τ. λ.

It is impoſſible, ſays *Plato*[b], that both riches and virtue ſhould be held in ſupreme eſtimation in a ſtate. One or the other will prevail; and according as one or the other prevails, the ſecurity or the ruin of the ſtate is confirmed.

It is hard for a ſtate to be ſecure, unleſs it be either made impoſſible, as in *Sparta*, for individuals to grow dangerouſly rich and powerful, or proviſion be made againſt the evil effects of overgrown riches and power in ſubjects. With this view the ancient republics ſubjected to baniſhment for a time, by the oſtraciſm, or petaliſm, thoſe citizens, whoſe overgrown riches and exceſſive popularity, ſeemed dangerous to manners or to liberty.

'Vice and ignorance are the only ſupport of tyranny, as virtue and knowledge are the only ſupport of freedom. Tell a wiſe man what kind of government is eſtabliſhed in any particular ſociety, and he will tell you what are the manners, and what the underſtandings of the members of that ſociety[c].' The court-ſycophant *Clarendon*, makes a matter of wonder, that the parliament's army was more orderly than the tyrant's. But the excellent Mrs. *Macaulay* ſhews, that it was to be expected, the better cauſe ſhould have the better defenders, and contrariwiſe[d].

Rouſſeau

[a] De Republ. v. in fine. [b] Ibid. viii.
[c] *Macaul.* iv. 182. [d] Ibid.

Rousseau endeavours to depreciate knowledge, as the cause of pride and other vices, which deform the species. But he is diametrically wrong. For it is not knowledge, but the want of knowledge, that produces pride. The most ignorant clown is not more modest than were *Socrates*, *Newton*, *Boerhaave*, *Hales*. Extensive knowledge naturally leads to a just sense of human weakness.

> In parts superior what advantage lies?
> Say (for you can) what is it to be wise?
> 'Tis but to know how little can be known,
> To see all others wants, and feel our own. POPE.

It might be of good use to take care, that enormous riches be discountenanced, and made an objection to the advancement of individuals.

If there were a *ne plus ultra*, beyond which individuals could not go, they would, after attaining the limited sum, turn their ambition into another channel. As it is, there remains no object of pursuit, but money, money, money, to the end of life.

'Whoever contrives to make a people very rich and 'great, lays the foundation of their misery and destruc-'tion.——No condition is durable, but such as is 'established in mediocrity [a].

The first decline of the *Spartan* commonwealth was caused by the introduction of riches in consequence of *Lysander*'s conquests [b]. The *Roman* virtue begun to decline from the time of *Lucullus*'s conquests in the East. The *Spartans* chose their ephori out of the meanest rank, if they could not find proper men in the higher [c]. 'Tis true, there was but little variety of ranks among the *Spartans*.

Tiberius

---

[a] *Fletcher*, p. 438.

[b] *Ubb. Emm.* I. 329.

[c] Ibid. I. 63.

Tiberius Gracchus propoſed the revival of the law, by which no perſon was permitted to poſſeſs more than 500 acres of land [a].

A very ſalutary law was propoſed by *Licinius* for preventing exorbitant riches [b].

Yet the ſame *Licinius* was afterwards fined for having 1000 acres of land, while the law limited him to 500. He had falſely given in half the land as belonging to his brother.

Exorbitant riches in the hands of individuals, while the public treaſures are exhauſted, like ſwelled legs with an emaciated body, are a ſymptom of decline in a ſtate.

Who can imagine, that *Craſſus* could, by juſtifiable means, amaſs the enormous ſum of 1,356,000 *l.* ſterling [c].

When *Curius Dentatus* was offered, for his great ſervice in conquering *Pyrrhus*, 50 acres of land, he refuſed it, ſaying, That a citizen, who cannot content himſelf with ſeven acres, is dangerous to the community [d]. *Cornelius Ruffenus*, who had been conſul and dictator, was ſtruck out of the liſt of ſenators for having in his houſe ten pounds weight of plate [e]. The *Roman* ambaſſadors were preſented by *Ptolemy* with a golden crown each. They declined his preſent, and ſet the crowns on the heads of the king's ſtatues. Which ſuperiority to riches gained the *Romans* great reſpect in *Egypt* [f].

Monteſquieu [g] thinks equality ought to be preſerved in a ſtate, by all poſſible means.

By

---

[a] Ant. Univ. Hist. xii. 403. [b] Ibid. 24.
[c] Ibid. xiii. 127. [d] Ibid. xii. 150. [e] Ibid. 151.
[f] Ibid. 152.
[g] L'Espr. des Loix, i. 74.

By our constitution, a part of a gentleman's estate may be taken from him for the advantage of a public road, and a value set upon the damage by jury. Yet that price may be much below what he would choose to take for the land; but private advantage must yield to public.

No subject in any country ought to be exorbitantly rich. It is a thing of ill example, and excites unbounded desires, which lay men open to corruption.

Would it be any great hardship, if there were a law, that no *British* subject should have above 10,000 *l.* a year? 'My opinion,' says the *Czarina* [a], 'inclines 'most to the *division* of property, as I esteem it my 'duty to wish, that every one should have a compe-'tency. The state will receive more benefit from se-'veral thousands of subjects, who enjoy a competency, 'than from a few hundreds immensely rich.'

Most men are ruined by growing rich. Here follows, however, an instance to the contrary, which I insert for the sake of the noble example and instruction it exhibits.

'In the year 1464, died *Cosmo de Medici*, who, 'though the private subject of a republic, had more 'riches than any king in *Europe*, and laid out more 'money in works of taste, magnificence, learning, and 'charity, than all the kings, princes, and states of that, 'the preceding, or the subsequent age; those of his 'own family excepted. The riches he was possessed 'of would appear incredible, did not the monuments of 'his magnificence still remain, and did not his con-'temporaries give us unquestionable testimonies both 'of them and his liberality. They were such that we 'are

[a] Instr. p. 174.

'are tempted to believe, that he and his family knew 'of some channels of commerce that have been lost, 'probably by the discovery of *America*, and the fre- 'quency of the *East Indian* commerce by sea, to which 'the *Europeans*, in his time, were almost strangers. He 'lent vast sums of money to the public, the payment 'of which he never required; and there scarcely was a 'citizen in *Florence* whom he did not at one time or 'other assist with money, without the smallest expec- 'tation of its being returned. His religious founda- 'tions were prodigious. Not contented with having 'founded so many religious edifices, he endowed them 'likewise, with rich furniture, magnificent altars, and 'chapels. His private buildings were equally sump- 'tuous. His palace in *Florence* exceeded that of any 'sovereign prince, in his time; and he had other pa- 'laces at *Coreggio*, *Fesole*, *Casaggivolo*, and *Febrio*. His 'munificence even reached *Jerusalem*, where he erected 'a noble hospital for distressed pilgrims.

'In those works of more than royal expence, he might 'have been equalled by men equally rich; but his de- 'portment and manner were unexampled. In his pri- 'vate conversation he was humble, unaffected, unas- 'suming. Every thing regarding his person was plain, 'modest, and nothing differing from the middling 'rank of people; thereby giving a proof of his virtue, 'and wisdom, because nothing is more dangerous in a 'commonwealth than pomp and parade. His ex- 'pences begot no envy, because laid out in embellish- 'ing his country, of which all his fellow-citizens par- 'took. *Cosmo*, with all that simplicity of life, had 'towering bold notions of his country's dignity and 'interest. His intelligence was beyond that of any 'prince of *Europe*, and there scarcely was a court where 'he did not entertain a private agent. His long continuance in power, *viz.* for thirty-one years, is a proof of his great abilities, as the modeſt uſe he made of his power is of his diſpoſition [a].'

'It is to little purpoſe, that we multiply ſyſtems, doctrines, and moral treatiſes. Till government ſhall connect honour and proſperity with virtue, and infamy and unhappineſs with vice, little will be effected. That country ſtands moſt in need of rewards and puniſhments, where patriotiſm is at the loweſt ebb [b].'

A wrong diſpoſition in a people may be corrected by playing contrary paſſions againſt one another. Are they proud and lazy, like the *Spaniards?* Let the government give honours to the induſtrious, and diſgrace the idle, &c. Are they (like the *French)* too much given to war? Let a *Fleury* encourage the arts of peace among them, attaching to thoſe arts all the honours and advantages, and withdrawing the people from a delight in the art of murder. Are they, like the *Engliſh*, degenerating from that love of liberty, which was the glory of their anceſtors, and ſinking into the ſordid love of riches and pleaſure? Let a patriot king inſiſt on laws and regulations for gradually aboliſhing places and penſions, and reſtoring the nation to the condition it was in, when bribery was impoſſible; and ſo on.

'I have often thought (ſays Lord *Bathurſt* in his LETTER to *Swift)* that if ten or a dozen patriots, who are rich enough to have ten diſhes every day for dinner, would invite their friends to only two or three, it might perhaps ſhame thoſe, who cannot afford two, from having conſtantly ten, and ſo it would

[a] MOD. UNIV. HIST. XXXVI. 302.

[b] LOND. MAG. July 1771, p. 347.

'would be in every other circumſtance of life. But 'luxury is our ruin.'

No nation ever was very corrupt under a long continued virtuous government, nor virtuous under a long continued vicious adminiſtration. Whether this country is, and has long been very corrupt, let the reader determine, after he has impartially conſidered the contents of theſe volumes.

He who formed the human mind, and who therefore muſt be the beſt judge of the proper means for influencing it, has ſhewn us, that he judges thoſe to be, the propoſing of rewards and puniſhments, the former to act upon the hopes, and the latter upon the fears of our ſpecies. And though it be true, that beings, who attach themſelves to a right courſe of action, and avoid the contrary, from motives of this kind, are leſs praiſeworthy than thoſe who love virtue and abhor vice for their own ſakes merely, yet is it equally certain, that in this early ſtate of moral diſcipline, no incentives more efficacious could have been found. What ſo likely to ſtartle a mad miſcreant, and ſtop him in his vicious career, as the denunciation of puniſhments both in this world and the next, thoſe puniſhments to be inflicted by a hand that is omnipotent and irreſiſtible. The diſintereſted love of virtue and hatred of vice muſt come afterwards.

As to moral character, mankind may be divided into three claſſes: 1. The meaner and more ſordid, who are a great part of the ſpecies, whoſe minds, or the earthy ſubſtance they have inſtead of minds, are capable of being drawn to decency *only* by the groſs allurement of *pecuniary* rewards; and of being deterred from open wickedneſs *only* by the fear of priſons, fines, and corporal puniſhments. 2. The next rank above theſe, are perſons

persons of a nobler character, who are capable of great and good actions, when attended with fame and glory. 3. The highest, or those few of our species, who are more angels than men, are they, who love virtue for its own sake, without glory, and even with infamy and suffering, and who abhor vice though attended with profit, and surrounded with the false glare of honours, titles, and preferments. It is *only* with the first and second of these classes, that the statesman can have any thing to do. Those of the third are infinitely above his arts, and want neither allurements to virtue nor determents from vice; as they find both in the happy dispositions of their own godlike minds.

'*Il est du plus grand interet*, &c. It is of supreme con-'sequence to the state, that through the wise providence 'of the government, the people of all ranks observe the 'rules of justice in their intercourse with one another. 'It is evident, that, if men accustomed themselves to do 'to others, as they might, in reason, expect others to 'do by them, either there would be no injury done, or 'every injury would be more than repaired, which 'would render life infinitely happier for all ranks, 'high and low, than we see it[a].'

By the laws of *Geneva*, the son of a person who died insolvent, is excluded from the magistracy, and even from a seat in the great council, unless he pays his father's debts[b].

'The true love of liberty, (says Mrs. *Macaulay*) 'is founded in virtue[c].' She therefore generously 'apologises for the seeming preciseness of manners, which appeared in the republican parliament, by

[a] *S. Pierre* Oeuvr. Polit. xi. 30.

[b] *Montesq.* L'Esprit des Loix, ii. 173.

[c] Hist. v. 386.

by urging in their favour, that they had ſincerely at heart the promoting of virtue and religion among the people.

Many uſeful bills were left depending when *Cromwell* diſſolved the parliament. As, for uniting *Scotland* and *England*. For county regiſters. For compelling able debtors to pay, and relieving inſolvents. For preſerving and increaſing timber. For regulating weights and meaſures. For amending and reducing into one, the laws againſt fornication and adultery[a]. For ſuppreſſing the deteſtable ſins of inceſt, adultery, and fornication[b]. For prohibiting cock-matches[c]. Againſt challenges and duels, and all provocations thereto. For contribution of one meal in the week for raiſing and arming forces againſt the tyrant. For puniſhing ſuch perſons as live at high rates, and have no viſible eſtate, profeſſion, or calling anſwerable. Againſt drinking healths[d], &c.

The oath in *Cromwell's* time runs thus, 'I *A. B.* do, 'in the preſence of Almighty God, promiſe and ſwear, '&c.' Much more ſolemn than the unmeaning oath we uſe[e]; which is worſe than uſeleſs; as unthinking people are in no degree awed by it; and damn themſelves before they are aware. The *Iriſh* form of an oath is very awful. The oath among the *Siberians* is a moſt terrible ſtring of imprecations; 'May the bear 'tear me to pieces in the wood; may the bread I eat 'ſtick in my throat, &c. if I do not ſpeak truth.' The *Tunguſians* in *Ruſſia* kill a dog, and burn his body, and imprecate on themſelves the ſame fate, &c[f].

 The

[a] Parl. Hist. xxi. 203.
[b] *Macaul.* Hist. v.
[c] Ibid.
[d] Parl. Hist. xx. 398.
[e] Ibid. xxi. 128.
[f] Mod. Univ. Hist. xxxv. 73.

The form of the oath at *Athens* was very terrible, consisting of dreadful imprecations; and at *Athens* a false witness was punished in the same manner as the accused would have been, if regularly convicted. 'To make an oath too cheap, by frequent practice, 'is to weaken the obligation of it, and destroy its 'efficacy[a].'

Themistocles did once say, that of a small city, he could make a great people. This he spoke from the right sense he had of his own abilities and skill. Governors and magistrates that are the reverse of him, and who rule weakly, can render a potent country in a short time poor, despised, and miserable. Such to whom government is entrusted, should endeavour to hinder the growth of all kind of vices, as intemperance and luxury: for luxury is the parent of want, and want begets in the minds of men disobedience and desire of change. To see that impiety be not countenanced, nor books scattered among the vulgar, which tend to the overthrow or weakening of the general notions of religion, should be no less their care. It is no less their duty to promote virtue, and to encourage merit of any kind, and to give it their helping hand: such as have been counted great and able statesmen in all countries have so done; and judged that to propagate what was good, and to suppress vice, was the most material part of government. They should discountenance immoralities of all sorts; they should see them exposed in public; they should cause the pulpits to declaim against them; they should make them a bar to preferment, and the laws should be all pointed against them[b].

If

[a] *Czar*. Instr. 96.

[b] *Daven*. II. 44.

'If philosophy will not suffice to bind the common 'people to their duty, what must be said of some mo-'dern politicians who shew no desire of setting up 'morality, and yet are pulling down revealed religion? 'Statesmen have been accused of being uncertain them-'selves in religious points; but, till lately they were 'never seen to countenance in others such a looseness; 'and till of late years it was never known a recom-'mendation to preferment. Would it any thing avail 'the public to have the settled opinions concerning 'divine matters quite altered by the law? If not, why 'do such as propose innovations in revealed religion, 'find so many open advocates, and those of the highest 'rank? How comes it to pass that the majority suffer 'themselves to be guided, and often with hard reins, 'by a small number? Can it be imagined this is 'brought about merely by a right disposition of power, 'whereby the weak come to hold the strong in their 'dominion? Or can it be thought that laws are suf-'ficient to subject the bodies of men to government, 'unless something else did constrain their conscience 'and their minds? It is hardly to be doubted but that 'if the common people are once induced to lay aside 'religion, they will quickly cast off all fear of their 'rulers. But such as object against revealed religion, 'as it is now transmitted to us, have they another 'scheme ready? When they have pulled down the 'old frame, can they set up a better in its room? 'Most certainly by their own lives, either in private, 'or in relation to the public, they seem very unfit 'apostles to propagate a new belief. When the com-'mon people all of a sudden become corrupt, and by 'quicker steps than was ever known; when they do 'not revere the laws; when there is no mutual justice 'among them; when they defraud the prince; when 'they prostitute their voices in elections, it may be 'certainly concluded that such a country is by the artifice of some, and the negligence of others, set loose 'in the principles of religion. Nothing therefore can 'more conduce to correcting the manners of a depraved 'people, than a due care of religious matters; a right 'devotion to God will beget patience in national calamities, 'submission to the laws, obedience to the 'prince, love to one another, and a hatred to faction; 'and it will produce in the minds of all the different 'ranks of men, true zeal and affection to their country's 'welfare[a]. The preventive remedy against such 'distempers is to be had from the precepts of morality, 'which writers upon all sorts of subjects should 'endeavour to inculcate. For the vices or virtues of 'a country influence very much in all its business; so 'that he who would propose methods, by which the 'affairs of a kingdom may be any ways bettered, should 'at the same time consider the predominant passions, 'the morals, temper, and inclinations of the people[b].'

'*C'est le sublime de la politique*, &c. It is the height 'of political sagacity to establish society on such principles, 'that it shall preserve itself, and shall continually 'tend to its own improvement. For this purpose 'it is necessary that each member in the governing 'part of such a society, shall find, that he gets 'more profit or honour by consulting the common interest, 'than he could by attending only to his own '*private* advantage.

'From this maxim, that the most powerful motive 'for setting mankind to work, is, duly rewarding abilities 'and virtues, may be deduced, and explained all 'the causes of the rise and fall of states, and a probable

[a] *Daven.* II. 46.

[b] Ibid. II. 76.

'bable conjecture of their future fate, and on what 'side their decline will begin. I invite my philoso-'phical successors to pursue this thought, and to apply 'this maxim to the ancient states, which have perished, 'and on whose ruins the foundation of new ones has 'been laid[a].'

'Let any man, who has knowledge enough for it, 'first compare the natural state of *Great Britain*, and 'of the United Provinces, and then their artificial state 'together; that is, let him consider minutely the ad-'vantages we have by the situation, extent, and na-'ture of our island, over the inhabitants of a few salt 'marshes gained on the sea, and hardly defended from 'it; and after that, let him consider how nearly these 'provinces have raised themselves to an equality of 'wealth and power with the kingdom of *Great Britain*. 'From whence arises the difference of improvement? 'It arises plainly from hence: the *Dutch* have been, 'from the foundation of their commonwealth, a nation 'of patriots and merchants. The spirit of that peo-'ple has not been diverted from these two objects; the 'defence of their liberty, and the improvement of their 'trade and commerce, which have been carried on by 'them, with uninterrupted and unslackened applica-'tion, industry, order, and œconomy. In *Great Bri-'tain*, the case has not been the same in either re-'spects[b].'

On the necessity of attention to the manners of the people, the following protest against the gin-act, 1742, is excellent.

'Because the act of the 9th of his present Majesty, 'to prevent the excessive drinking of spirituous liquors, 'which is by this bill to be repealed, declares, that the

[a] *S. Pierre*, VI. 51.

[b] *Bolingbr.* ID. PATR. KING, 187.

'drinking of spirituous liquors, or strong waters, is 'become very common, especially amongst the people 'of inferior ranks, the constant and excessive use 'whereof tends greatly to the destruction of their 'healths, rendering them unfit for useful labour and 'business, debauching their morals, and inciting them 'to perpetrate all manner of vice; and the ill conse-'quences of the excessive use of such liquors, are not 'confined to the present generation, but extend to fu-'ture ages, and tend to the devastation and ruin of 'this kingdom. We therefore apprehend, that if an 'act designed to remedy such indisputable mischiefs, 'was not found adequate to its salutary intention, the 'wisdom of the legislature ought to have examined its 'imperfections, and supplied its defects, and not have 'rescinded it by a law, authorising the manifold ca-'lamities it was calculated to prevent. 2. Because 'the refusing to admit the most eminent physicians to 'give their opinions of the fatal consequences of these 'poisonous liquors, may be construed without doors, 'as a resolution of this house to suppress all authentick 'information of the pernicious effects of the health 'and morals of mankind, which will necessarily flow 'from the unrestrained licentiousness permitted by this 'bill. 3. Because, as it is the inherent duty of every 'legislature to be watchful in protecting the lives, and 'preserving the morals of the people, so the availing 'itself of their vices, debaucheries, and consequential 'miseries to the destruction of millions, is a manifest 'inversion of the fundamental principles of natural 'polity, and contrary to these social emoluments, 'by which government alone is instituted. 4. Because 'the opulence and power of a nation depend upon the 'numbers, vigour, and industry of its people; and its 'liberty and happiness on their temperance and mora-

'lity;

'lity; to all which this bill threatens destruction by 'authorizing fifty thousand houses, the number ad-'mitted in the debate, to retail a poison, which by uni-'versal experience is known to debilitate the strong, 'and destroy the weak; to extinguish industry, and to 'inflame those intoxicated by its malignant efficacy, to 'perpetrate the most heinous crimes: for what con-'fusion and calamities may not be expected, when 'near a twentieth part of the houses in the kingdom 'shall be converted into seminaries of drunkenness and 'profligacy, authorized and protected by the legislative 'powers? And as we conceive the contributions to 'be paid by these infamous recesses, and the money 'to be raised by this destructive project, are considera-'tions highly unworthy the attention of parliament, 'when compared with the extensive evils from thence 'arising, so are we of opinion, that if the real exi-'gences of the public required raising the immense 'sums this year granted, they could by no means pal-'liate the having recourse to a supply founded on the 'indulgence of debauchery, the encouragement of 'crimes, and the destruction of the human race[a].'

Let us hear the lord *Hervey* on the same subject. 'In the time of the late ministry, it has been observed 'that drunkenness was become a vice almost universal 'among the common people; and that as the liquor 'which they generally drank, was such, that they could 'destroy their reason by a small quantity, and at a small 'expence; the consequence of general drunkenness was 'general idleness: since no man would work any longer 'than was necessary to lay him asleep, for the remain-'ing part of the day. They remarked likewise that 'the liquor, which they generally drank, was to the

 'last

[a] Deb. Peers, viii. 479.

'last degree pernicious to health, and destructive of 'that corporeal vigour, by which the business of life is 'to be carried on; and a law was therefore made, by 'which it was intended that this species of debauchery, 'so peculiarly fatal, should be prevented. Against 'the end of this law, no man has hitherto made the 'least objection; no one hardened to signalize himself 'as an open advocate for vice, or attempted to prove, 'that drunkenness was not injurious to society, and 'contrary to the true ends of human being. The en- 'couragement of wickedness of this shameful kind, 'wickedness equally contemptible and hateful, was re- 'served for the present ministry, who are now about to 'supply those funds which they have exhausted by 'idle projects, and romantic expeditions, at the ex- 'pence of health and virtue, who have discovered a 'method of recruiting armies by the destruction of 'their fellow subjects, and while they boast themselves 'the asserters of liberty, are endeavouring to enslave 'us by the introduction of these vices, which in all 'countries, and in every age, have made way for de- 'spotic power [a].'

Manners, religion, and education are articles in *Richlieu's* Polit. Testam. which shews that he thought them a part of the concern of government. Our ministers would laugh in any body's face, who proposed to them any regulation upon any of these subjects.

The *Czarina* desires her grandees to prepare the people for the reception of new laws [b]. Our grandees (the reader sees I do not mean the present) would be the most improper set of men in the nation, to be employed

[a] Deb. Peers, viii. 270.

[b] *Czar.* Instr., p. 80.

employed in preparing the people for receiving a ſet of new and better laws. Themſelves the great violators of all laws divine and human, they would be more likely to teach the people to be lawleſs, than more regular in their behaviour.

My worthy friend Mr. Profeſſor *Ferguſon*, of *Edinburgh*, thus deſcribes the character and manner of life of men in higher ſtations, who are void of public ſpirit[a].

'Men of buſineſs and of induſtry in the inferior 'ſtations of life retain their occupations, and are ſecured by a kind of neceſſity in the poſſeſſion of thoſe 'habits on which they rely for their quiet, and for the 'moderate enjoyments of life. But the higher orders 'of men, if they relinquiſh the ſtate, if they ceaſe to 'poſſeſs that courage and elevation of mind, and to 'exerciſe thoſe talents which are employed in its defence and its government, are, in reality, by the 'ſeeming advantages of their ſtation, become the refuſe 'of that ſociety of which they once were the ornament; 'and from being the moſt reſpectable, and the moſt 'happy of its members, are become the moſt wretched 'and corrupt. In their approach to this condition, 'and in the abſence of every manly occupation, they 'feel a diſſatisfaction and languor which they cannot 'explain. They pine in the midſt of apparent enjoyments; or by the variety and caprice of their different purſuits and amuſements, exhibit a ſtate of agitation, which, like the diſquiet of ſickneſs, is not a 'proof of enjoyment or pleaſure, but of ſuffering and 'pain. The care of his buildings, his equipage, or 'his table, is choſen by one; literary amuſement, or 'ſome frivolous ſtudy, by another. The ſports of the 'country, and the diverſions of the town; the gaming 'table,

[a] *Ferg.* Civ. Soc. p. 399.

'table, dogs, horſes, and wine, are employed to fill 'up the blank of a liſtleſs and unprofitable life. 'Theſe different occupations differ from each other in 'reſpect to their dignity, and their innocence: but 'none of them are the ſchools from which men are 'brought to ſuſtain the tottering fortune of nations; 'they are equally avocations from what ought to be 'the principal purſuit of man, the good of mankind. 'They ſpeak of human purſuits as if the whole diffi-'culty were to find ſomething to do. They fix on 'ſome frivolous occupation, as if there was nothing 'that deſerved to be done. They conſider what tends 'to the good of their fellow-creatures as a diſadvantage 'to themſelves. They fly from every ſcene on which 'any efforts of vigour are required, or in which they 'might be allured to perform any ſervice to their 'country. We miſapply our compaſſion in pitying 'the poor; it were much more juſtly applied to the 'rich, who become the firſt victims of that wretched 'inſignificance, into which the members of every cor-'rupted ſtate, by the tendency of their weakneſſes and 'their vices, are in haſte to plunge themſelves.'

The perverſeneſs of ſtateſmen, in almoſt all ages and countries, with reſpect to this part of their duty, is very unfortunate for mankind. Governments have it not in their power to do their ſubjects the leaſt ſervice as to their religious belief and mode of worſhip. On the contrary, whenever the civil magiſtrate interpoſes his authority in matter of religion, otherwiſe than in keeping the *peace* amongſt *all* religious parties, you may trace every ſtep he has taken by the miſchievous effects his interpoſition has produced (of which more elſe-where), at the ſame time, that he has it in his power to do inexpreſſible ſervice to the people under his care, by a ſtrict attention to their manners and behaviour.

A king,

A king, a ſtateſman, or a magiſtrate, who does not know this, is very improperly ſituated in the high ſtation he fills; yet all hiſtory exhibits proofs of their miſconduct in this reſpect. They have perpetually haraſſed themſelves and their people about matters of belief, and forms of worſhip, and have neglected the moſt important duty of their function, the regulating of the moral and political principles and manners of the people.

The reaſon of this wrong-headed conduct is very ſhameful for our rulers, viz. becauſe by joining forces with thoſe of the prieſthood, and labouring for the eſtabliſhment of what they are pleaſed to call the true church, the true faith, &c. (which are different in almoſt every different country) they open to themſelves a direct path to enſlaving the people; whereas by guiding them into right, moral, and political principles and manners, they might enable them to judge ſoundly of the conduct of thoſe in power, and inſpire them with a noble ſpirit of reſiſtance to tyranny, the moſt formidable of all diſpoſitions to the greateſt part of ſtateſmen.

At the ſame time that our rulers ſhew great zeal for the true church, that is, a great deſire to keep up the ſacerdotal power, that the prieſthood may in return keep up theirs, we ſee them make no heſitation to declare their diſbelief of all religion. Chriſtianity, according to them, is a fiction; but yet the church of *England* is the only true chriſtian church. The inferior people ſeeing thoſe of higher ſtations ranging themſelves on the ſide of infidelity, are very much hurt in their manners. But chriſtianity, for any thing the greateſt part of our nobility and gentry know, may be either true or falſe. They do not know the ſtrongeſt objections, having never given themſelves time to examine

amine the ſubject; ſo that their belief or diſbelief are of very little conſequence to the people; but the declaration of their diſbelief ſhews very little regard to the good of their country.

Whether it be agreeable to ſound policy for the rulers of countries to throw contempt upon the religion of their countries, let the excellent *Montague*[a] decide. 'The Romans founded their ſyſtem of policy at the 'very origin of their ſtate upon that beſt and wiſeſt 'principle, the fear of the Gods, [what we ſhould 'call] a firm belief of a divine ſuperintending providence, and a future ſtate of rewards and puniſhments. 'Their children were trained up in this belief from 'tender infancy, which took root and grew up with 'them by the influence of an excellent education, 'where they had the benefit of example as well as precept. Hence we read of no heathen nation in the 'world where both the public and private duties of 'religion were ſo ſtrictly adhered to, and ſo ſcrupulouſly 'obſerved, as amongſt the *Romans*. They imputed 'their good or bad ſucceſs to their obſervance of theſe 'duties, and they received public proſperities or public calamities, as bleſſings conferred, or puniſhments 'inflicted, by their Gods. Their hiſtorians hardly 'ever give us an account of any defeat received by that 'people, which they do not aſcribe to the omiſſion or 'contempt of ſome religious ceremony by their Generals. For though the ceremonies there mentioned 'juſtly appear to us inſtances of the moſt abſurd and 'moſt extravagant ſuperſtition, yet as they were eſteemed eſſential acts of religion by the *Romans*, they 'muſt conſequently carry all the force of religious 'principle. We neither exceeded (ſays *Cicero*, ſpeak- 'ing

[a] *Mountag.* Ant. Republ. p. 294.

'ing of his countrymen) the *Spaniards* in number, nor 'did we excel the *Gauls* in strength of body, nor the '*Carthaginians* in craft, nor the *Greeks* in arts or sci-'ences. But we have indisputably surpassed all the 'nations in the universe in piety and attachment to reli-'gion, and in the only point which can be called true 'wisdom, a thorough conviction that all things here 'below are directed and governed by Divine Provi-'dence. To this principle alone *Cicero* wisely attri-'butes the grandeur and good fortune of his country. 'For what man is there, says he, who is convinced of 'the existence of the Gods, but must be convinced at 'the same time, that our mighty empire owes its ori-'gin, increase, and its preservation, to the protecting 'care of their Divine Providence. A plain proof, 'that these continued to be the real sentiments of the 'wiser *Romans*, even in the corrupt times of *Cicero*. 'From this principle proceeded that respect for, and 'submission to their laws, and that temperance, mode-'ration, and contempt for wealth, which are the best 'defence against the encroachments of injustice and 'oppression. Hence too arose that inextinguishable 'love for their country, which, next to the Gods, 'they looked upon as the chief object of veneration. 'This they carried to such a height of enthusiasm as 'to make every human tie of social love, natural affec-'tion, and self-preservation, give way to this duty to 'their dearer country. Because they not only loved 'their country as their common mother, but revered 'it as a place which was dear to their Gods; which 'they had destined to give laws to the rest of the uni-'verse, and consequently favoured with their peculiar 'care and protection. Hence proceeded that obstinate 'and undaunted courage, that insuperable contempt of 'danger, and death itself, in defence of their country,

'which

'which complete the idea of the *Roman* character, as 'it is drawn by historians in the virtuous ages of the 'republic. As long as the manners of the *Romans* 'were regulated by this first great principle of religion, 'they were free and invincible. But the atheistical 'doctrine of *Epicurus*, which insinuated itself at *Rome* 'under the respectable name of philosophy, after their 'acquaintance with the *Greeks*, undermined and de-'stroyed this ruling principle. I allow, that luxury, 'by corrupting manners, had weakened this principle; 'and prepared the *Romans* for the reception of atheism, 'which is the never-failing attendant of luxury. But 'as long as this principle remained, it controuled 'manners, and checked the progress of humanity in 'proportion to its influence. But when the introduc-'tion of atheism had destroyed this principle, the great 'bar to corruption was removed, and the passions at 'once let loose to run their full career, without check 'or controul. The introduction, therefore, of the 'atheistical tenets, attributed to *Epicurus*, was the 'real cause of that rapid depravity of the *Roman* man-'ners, which has never been satisfactorily accounted 'for either by *Salust*, or any other historian.'

The same author, in his 308th page, writes as follows on the same subject:

'*Polybius* firmly believed the existence of a Deity, and 'the interposition of a divine superintending Provi-'dence, though he was an enemy to superstition. Yet 'when he observed the good effects produced amongst 'the *Romans* by their religion, though carried even to 'the highest possible degree of superstition, and the 'remarkable influence it had upon their manners in 'private life, as well as upon their public counsels, 'he concludes it to be the result of a wise and con-'summate policy in the ancient legislators. He, there-'fore,

4

'fore, very justly censures those as wrong-headed and 'wretchedly bungling politicians, who at that time 'endeavoured to eradicate the fear of an after reckon-'ing, and the terrors of a hell, out of the minds of a 'people. Yet how few years ago did we see this mi-'serably mistaken policy prevail in our own country, 'during the whole administration of some late power-'engrossing ministers. Compelled at all events to se-'cure a majority in parliament, to support themselves 'against the efforts of opposition, they found the 'greatest obstacle to their schemes arise from those 'principles of religion, which yet remained amongst 'the people. For though a great number of the elec-'tors were not at all averse to the bribe, yet their con-'sciences were too tender to digest perjury. To re-'move this troublesome test at elections, which is one 'of the bulwarks of our constitution, would be imprac-'ticable. To weaken or destroy those principles, 'upon which the oath was founded, and from which it 'derived its force and obligation, would equally an-'swer the purpose, and destroy all publick virtue at 'the same time. The bloody and deep-felt effects of 'that hypocrisy which prevailed in the time of *Crom-'well*, had driven great numbers of the sufferers into 'the contrary extreme. When, therefore, so great a 'part of the nation was already prejudiced against 'whatever carried the appearance of a stricter piety, it 'is no wonder that shallow superficial reasoners, who 'have not logick enough to distinguish between the use 'and abuse of a thing, should readily embrace those 'atheistical tenets which were imported, and took root, 'in the voluptuous and thoughtless reign of *Charles* II. 'But that solid learning which revived after the Resto-'ration, easily baffled the efforts of open and avowed 'atheism, which from that time has taken shelter

'under

'under the lefs obnoxious name of deifm. For the 'principles of modern deifm, when ftript of that dif-'guife which has been artfully thrown over them to 'deceive them who hate the fatigue of thinking, and 'are ever ready to admit any conclufion in argument 'which is agreeable to their paffions, without exami-'ning the premifes, are in reality the fame with thofe 'of *Epicurus*, as tranfmitted to us by *Lucretius*. The 'influence, therefore, which they had upon the man-'ners of the *Greeks* and *Romans* will readily account 'for thofe effects which we experience from them in 'our own country, where they fo fatally prevail. To 'patronize and propagate thefe principles, was the beft 'expedient which the narrow, felfifh policy, of thofe 'minifters could fuggeft; for their greateft extent of 'genius never reached higher than a fertility in tempo-'rary fhifts and expedients, to ftave off the evil day of 'national account, which they fo much dreaded. 'They were fenfible that the wealth and luxury, 'which are the general effects of an extenfive trade, in 'a ftate of profound peace, had already greatly hurt 'the morals of the people, and fmoothed the way for 'their grand fyftem of corruption. Far from checking 'this licentious fpirit of luxury and diffipation, they 'left it to its full and natural effects upon the manners, 'whilft, in order to corrupt the principles of the peo-'ple, they retained at the public expence a venal fet 'of the moft fhamelefs mifcreants that ever abufed the 'liberty of the prefs, or infulted the religion of their 'country. To the adminiftration of fuch minifters, 'which may juftly be termed the grand æra of corrup-'tion, we owe that fatal fyftem of bribery, which has 'fo greatly affected the morals of the electors in almoft 'every borough in the kingdom. To that too we may 'juftly attribute the prefent contempt and difregard of 'the sacred obligation of an oath, which is the strongest 'bond of society, and the best security and support of 'civil government. I have now, I hope, satisfactorily 'accounted for that rapid and unexampled degeneracy 'of the *Romans*, which brought on the total subversion 'of that mighty republic. The cause of this sudden 'and violent change of the *Roman* manners has been 'just hinted at by the sagacious *Montesquieu*, but to 'my great surprize has not been duly attended to by 'any one historian I have yet met with. I have shewed 'too, how the same cause has been working the same 'effects in our own nation, as it invariably will in 'every country where those fatally destructive principles 'are admitted. As the real end of all history is in-'struction, I have held up a just portrait of the *Roman* 'manners, in the times immediately preceding the loss 'of their liberty, to the inspection of my countrymen, 'that they may guard in time against these calamities 'which will be the inevitable consequence of the like 'degeneracy.'

Unhappily the most simple, the easiest, yet the wisest laws, that wait only for the nod of the legislator, to diffuse through nations, wealth, power, and felicity; laws which would be regarded by future generations with eternal gratitude, are either unknown, or rejected. A restless, and trifling spirit, the timid prudence of the present moment, or a distrust and aversion to the most useful novelties, possess the minds of those who are impowered to regulate the actions of mankind.

Do magistrates and governors consider how they increase the difficulty of their own task by neglecting the necessary attention to manners, till it be too late? When the manners of a people once deviate from the standard of rectitude, it is impossible to foresee how far they will ramble into the wilds of irregularity and vice.

Who could imagine it poſſible ever to bring a whole people, once the patterns of virtue, humanity, delicacy, to ſuch a degree of infernality, as to be capable of exerciſing cruelty on beautiful and innocent young virgins, on whom one would think it was impoſſible for a *male* of the human ſpecies, even of the age of fourſcore, to look with any other eye than of love? Yet the *Turkiſh* hiſtory is full of inſtances of ſuch helliſh barbarities.

Thoſe ſtateſmen are inexcuſable, in whoſe time any good cuſtom is ſuffered to go into deſuetude, or any ſalutary law to loſe its efficiency. For it is very eaſy to keep up a good cuſtom once eſtabliſhed, and very difficult to get rid even of a bad one, as appears from the difficulty of bringing about reformations of all kinds, whether in civil or religious matters. The power of cuſtom has kept up for ages in the Eaſt, and keeps up ſtill, the horrid practice of burning wives with their deceaſed huſbands. One would imagine, that either women would give over marrying, or give over the ambition of ſuffering the moſt cruel of all deaths, if their huſbands happen to die firſt. Inſtead of which, thoſe wives of the deceaſed, who are not adjudged worthy to be burned alive, think themſelves very unhappy[a]. A *Tartar* conqueror ordered the *Chineſe*, on pain of death, to cut off their hair. Many thouſands choſe rather to loſe their heads[b]. *Peter* the Great found it infinitely difficult to prevail with his *Ruſſians* to part with their beards. To gain his point, he

[a] Mod. Univ. Hist. vi. 280. [b] Ibid. viii. 480.

he was obliged to order his soldiery to cut off, any how, every beard they saw.

The people at *Cape Komorin*, in *India*, are barbarous enough; yet there is among them such a sense of honour, that if a traveller, under the protection of one of the centinels on the roads is murdered, while in his care, he will not survive the murdered person. And, if one of those guards violates his trust, his wife, or son, will be his executioner. How strongly must a sense of fidelity be impressed upon the minds of these heathens, that even conjugal affection, or filial duty, is not sufficient to restrain from punishing the violator of it! In *England*, very few wives or sons would put to death a husband, or father, though they knew him to be guilty of the most unheard-of villany[a].

The public robbers in that country will not hurt children, nor those who are with them. Therefore children are the best guard for travellers in those roads, where there are no centinels. This is again another wonderful effect of manners among a barbarous people[b].

The *London* mob will not suffer in boxing the least foul play; as, for instance, two to fall upon one. Yet this very mob will set upon the house, or person, of an obnoxious minister, five thousand against one, and would, in their fury, tear him to pieces, without thinking of the foul play.

Queen *Margaret*, after the defeat of the *Lancaster* party, escaping with her son, is attacked by robbers; flies into a thick wood; sees one of them coming toward her with his sword drawn; she runs to him, and begs his protection. The ruffian, inspired with a sud-

[a] Mod. Univ. Hist. vi. 556. [b] Ibid.

den sentiment of humanity and honour, preserves them, till they escape to *France*[a].

Degenerate manners in the people are a severe reflexion on the government for the time being. In the days of *Will. Conq.* there was no robbing. In his predecessor's every wood was a nest of banditti[b].

We know that *Henry* II. was a weak Prince; accordingly an extreme licentiousness prevailed in *London* in his time. Bands of citizens, to the number of 100, took to housebreaking, robbing, and murdering; forced their way into houses through the very walls[c]. Their numbers and rank were such, that they grew at last too big to be punished[d].

In *Alfred*'s days the internal police of the kingdom, and the manners of the people, were in so good a state, that a golden bracelet might have been hung upon a hedge, and nobody would have touched it. Is it not the fault of our kings, parliaments, ministers, &c. that in our enlightened times, instead of improving, we have lost this noble police, and those virtuous manners? Yet our kings, parliaments, ministers, &c. are always putting us in mind of the respect with which we ought to treat those, who have neglected our manners, overthrown our police, corrupted our honesty, taught us to laugh at all love of our country, plunged us in debt, lengthened our parliaments, loaded us with an infinite multitude of placemen and pensioners, &c.

'The insolence of the common people at this time '[viz. *A. D.* 1737] was in a great measure owing to 'the discredit which some of the magistrates had fallen 'into. Most of the acting justices being men in needy 'cir-

[a] *Hume*, II. 391.

[b] *Rap.* I. 177.

[c] *Hume*, Hist. I. 326.

[d] Ibid. 332.

'circumstances, sought to mend their fortunes by making a trade of their duty, which was no secret to the 'commonalty.' Statesmen are wont to excuse their own laziness and negligence of the manners of the people, by alledging, that it is impossible to draw them to obedience. It is in part true, that the subjects are naturally prejudiced against laws made by governors, who shew plainly, that they have somewhat else in view than the good of the people. Let governors act the part of kind parents, and subjects will quickly assume that of dutiful children.

In *China*, the police resembles that of King *Alfred*. Communities are answerable for offences committed within their respective authorities [a]. And when gross crimes are committed, the magistrates of the district in which they happened are severely punished and incapacitated, and the whole community disgraced [b]. In the Mogol's country, the emperor's spies and officers are answerable for all irregularities in the people.

Gaming, and extravagance in dress, were prohibited under *Edward* IV [c]. One of the fashions of those times, for its silliness, seems almost incredible, *viz.* of long, small-pointed shoes, like skates, so slender, that they were obliged to support the points of them with silver chains, or silk laces fastened to their knees.

Drunkenness, swearing, and obscenity in conversation, were the fashionable vices of the times of *Charles* II. They were introduced by the court, as the much more odious ones of cant and hypocrisy were by *Cromwell*. This shews how much is in the power of the great.

'Her Majesty's pleasure is, that you do not keep 'with you notorious persons, either for life or beha-

 'viour,

[a] Mod. Univ. Hist. viii. 153. [b] Ibid. 1, -.
[c] Parl. Hist. ii. 370.

'viour, desperate debtors, pettifogging solicitors, who 'set dissension between man and man[a].' *Elizabeth's* speech at the opening of her last parliament.

The King, in his speech *A. D.* 1751, recommends means for putting a stop to robbery and violence about the metropolis, owing to irreligion, idleness, gaming, and extravagance[b].

'The extreme misery brought on the *French* nation '[by the contest between the Dukes of *Orleans* and '*Burgundy* in the time of *Charles* VI.] were owing 'to nothing but the corruption of their manners, 'which having, on one hand, introduced a luxury 'unknown to former times, excited a passion for wealth 'and power, which quickly stifled all principle. In-'stead of seeking to break off their party-disputes, 'they aimed only at deceiving one another, and kept 'faith no longer than they thought it their interest to 'keep it[c].'

Atheism prevailed in *Italy*, says *Voltaire*[d], in consequence of wickedness. For many superficial people argued, after *Lucretius*, in whose times the *Romans* were very debauched, that if there were a God, he would not suffer mankind to be so wicked. And if atheism was a consequence of corrupt manners, there can be no doubt but it was a cause of immorality, as tending to weaken the effect which the apprehension of a future judgment naturally produces.

The Kings and Queens of *Britain*, at their coronation, promise, among other things, to 'maintain, to 'the

---

[a] PARL. HIST. IV. 427.

[b] *Alm.* DEB. COM. V. 3.

[c] MOD. UNIV. HIST. XXIII. 521.

[d] ESS. SUR L'HIST. III. 136.

'the utmost of their power, the laws of God[a].' If any King, or Queen, keeps in a station of dignity and power any person, or number of persons, who have been public and notorious violators of the laws of God, and who never have publicly declared their repentance or intended reformation, I affirm, that such King, or Queen, have broke their coronation oath; for that to employ in important stations such characters, is the diametrical contrary of 'maintaining to their utmost 'power the laws of God;' is indeed the most effectual means our crowned heads can use for overthrowing the laws of God, excepting one, *viz.* Their shewing a bad example in their own persons.

The commons addressed the King, *A. D.* 1698, against profaneness and immorality, and particularly request him, that all vice, profaneness, and irreligion, may be discouraged in those who have the honour to be employed near his royal person, and in all commanders by sea and land[b].

An able legislator, or administrator, knows how to gain his great and good purposes by the proper application of every passion, every disposition, custom, prejudice, virtue, vice, folly, in human nature.

If you propose to our modern ministers to encourage industry and good behaviour by rewards, they will answer, They have not the necessary funds. Yet they can find wherewith to reward those who do their dirty work for them. They can buy boroughs, maintain an useless army of soldiery, another of tax-gatherers, and a third of placemen and pensioners.

The town of *Zbarras* was besieged, *A. D.* 1675, by the *Turks*. The garrison mutinied against the gover-

---

[a] *Blackst.* COMM. I. 235.

[b] DEB. COM. III. 82.

nor, becaufe he would not yield the place, when he knew he could hold it out. They threw him over the walls. The *Turkifh* general takes the town, and punifhes the mutineers with the gallies and death. 'You have deprived me, fays he, of the honour of 'conquering a hero; but you fhall not of the fatif-'faction of punifhing cowards[a].' The manners of that people, as to courage and military difcipline, muft have been neglected.

To prevent crimes, to fuperfede the neceffity of punifhment, and to make adminiftration eafy, let the governors convince the people that it is their good they feek, and not the filling of their own pockets. This they may do at any time, and they have one certain method of gaining this point, *viz.* ferving their country *gratis.* Then let them give orders for the education of the youth, and regulating the morals of the people; then will parents, relations, the clergy, the magiftracy, and inhabitants of diftricts, emulate one another in their obedience to commands fo falutary given out by perfons of fuch difinterefted characters. But our ftatefmen pretend a fort of neceffity for a certain competent quantity of art and craft, or if you choofe plain *Englifh*, of knavery. This doctrine, however, is wholly erroneous. Don *Alonzo* V. always acted fairly and openly. He did not underftand intrigues or reafons of ftate, or the *arcana imperii.* Yet he was fo efteemed, that 60 different authors wrote his hiftory.

The founders of the ancient republic of *Venice,* if we may believe the hiftorians, would not admit to citizenfhip any but men of the moft exemplary morals[b].

No

[a] Mod. Univ. Hist. xxxiv. 234.
[b] Ibid. xxvii. 12.

No man ought to be employed in any place of power or trust, who is known to have been immoral or wicked, and is not known to be penitent and reformed. Virtue ought to be above all other considerations at all times, and on all occasions. Besides the danger that a man void of principle runs in betraying his trust, and bringing affairs into confusion, the evil *example* of placing a bad man in an honourable station, tends to damp all desire of keeping up a character. And what can be imagined more ruinous to a state, than to kill emulation in the people—the noblest of all emulation, the emulation of being virtuous?

Officers of justice were established in *Galicia* by *Ferdinand* and *Isabella*, where things were gone into terrible disorder during the interregnum. The whole country was full of strong castles, inhabited by a set of despotic chiefs of clans. The commissioners, however, behaved with such firmness, that 1500 of those chiefs, who had committed actions which they could not answer, fled the country. *Ferdinand* and *Isabella* pursued the same scheme throughout *Spain*, which restored peace, and brought back many who had preferred exile to the tyranny of the chiefs [a]. Magistracy will always be too strong for licentiousness, where magistrates are wise, just, and, from consciousness of rectitude of intention, fearless.

The people of *Benin* in *Africa* are humane, civilised, so charitable, that they have no beggars among them, and keep up so good a police, that they have no idle people. At the same time the *Anfikans*, in the same country, are barbarous cannibals, who go to war merely to get captives to eat, whose flesh is regularly sold in the shambles. They never bury their dead relations,

[a] Mod. Univ. Hist. xxi. 163.

lations, but eat them. Mothers eat their new-born children; and if a family grows numerous, they kill the fattest for food[a]. What can make such a difference between the manners of these two nations, but different management in their government?

All savages are not cruel, but most are. Is humanity then the natural growth of the human heart? Or, is it that men will be cruel, if they be not led by civilisation to better habits? 'The dark places of the 'earth are full of the habitations of cruelty,' says Scripture[b]. The *American* savages are more devils than men, delight in cruelty and blood, as if the great murderer Satan[c] had been let loose among them, and ruled in them. Their ignorance and idolatry are brutish. Some worshipped red rags, all adored beasts, serpents, *&c.* They go to war about nothing, and then torture their captives in the most wanton manner, as if they fought only for the pleasure of getting so many of their fellow-creatures into their power to glut their infernality: for they did not always eat them. If they had, they might have pretended they went to war to get a belly-full; though even then there was no occasion to put their captives to more torture than we do our sheep and bullocks. There is a wonderful similarity between the *American* savages and those of the *East Indies*, though at so great a distance, in putting to death the wives and attendants of their great men when they die, and often to the number of 100 at once[d].

The ancient *Peruvians*, before the *Incas*, were the most brutish of all barbarians. They wandered about like beasts, dwelt in caves and woods, knew no towns or

---

[a] Mod. Univ. Hist. xvi. 350, 363.

[b] Psal. lxxiv. 20.

[c] John viii. 44.

[d] Mod. Univ. Hist. xl. 255.

or ſocieties, or government; human fleſh their higheſt luxury; no cultivation of lands. Their captives they tied to trees, cut into ſlices, and ate the living fleſh; the ſcreams of their tortures were the ſweeteſt muſic to their tormentors. Women wetted their nipples in the hot blood, to give their infants a reliſh for it. They copulated like bullocks in the open air, the firſt man with the firſt woman; brothers with ſiſters, fathers with daughters, the moſt libidinous women were the moſt eſteemed. Sodomy, beſtiality, ſorcery, poiſoning, were common among them. This is the character given of the ancient *Peruvians* by *Garcilaſſo de la Vega*, whoſe mother was a *Peruvian*. Yet theſe ſavages had a notion of gods and ſpirits [b].

It was a ſilly fancy of *Peter* the Great, to compel the *Ruſſians* to ſhave their beards. What matter whether a ſet of brave and free men have the chins of men or of women. Shaving is no part of civiliſation [c]. The ancient patriarchs, with beards down to their girdles, were men of better manners and principles, than many of our modern nations with chins ſcraped to the quick. 'It is bad policy to attempt to alter that by 'law, which ſhould be altered by cuſtom [d],' ſays the Czarina.

Adultery, blaſphemy, ſtriking or curſing a parent, and perjury in matters of life and death, in *New England*, are capital [e].

Great care is taken in *New England* of the morals of the *Indians*, and particularly to prevent drunkenneſs. In Old *England*, the government gains by the drunkenneſs of the people [f].

The

---

[b] Mod. Univ. Hist. xxxix. 4.

[c] Ibid. xliii. 540.

[d] Instr. 81.

[e] Mod. Univ. Hist. xxxix. 343.

[f] Ibid.

The timidity, or laziness, if not somewhat worse, of magistrates and governments, are a great hindrance to reformation of manners. The constables of *London* and *Westminster* do effectually keep the streets clear of carts, coaches, *&c.* in parliament-time, so that the members do actually go, without stop or interruption, every day to the house. Yet it is pretended, that there is no possibility of keeping the streets clear of lewd women; which is a very heinous evil under the sun. For there is a close connexion between the virtues and between the vices; and a modest youth, once deprived of delicacy with respect to chastity, will soon become daring and hardened with respect to others.

A single genius changes the face and state of a whole country, as *Gustavus Adolphus* of *Sweden*, and *Peter* the Great of *Russia*.

The great difference we see between the behaviour of the sagacious people called Quakers, and all others; the difference between *English*, *Scotch*, *Irish*, *West Indian*, *French*, *Spanish*, *Heathen*, *Mahometan*, *Christian*, *Papish*, *Protestant* manners and characters, *&c.* the regular and permanent difference we see between the manners of all these divisions of mankind, shews, beyond doubt, that the principles and habits of the people are very much in the power of able statesmen.

In the beginning of Queen *Anne*'s reign, an act was passed for giving liberty to magistrates to take up idle people for the army [a].

In pressing time, a neighbourhood is often cleared of idle and disorderly persons by an information's being sent them, and their securing such persons for the service. There might be a stated press-gang at all times to seize all idle and disorderly persons, who have been

[a] *Burn.* IV. 54.

been three times complained of before a magistrate, and to set them to work during a certain time, for the benefit of great trading, or manufacturing companies, &c. The profit of their work would be a temptation to put the law in execution. The fleet might be manned in this manner. I say nothing of the army, because a free people ought to have no army, but the militia, or the whole people.

By 5 and 6 *Edw.* VI. no person was to keep an alehouse without finding sureties for the observance of decency in his house[a]. I should be glad to know what would, in our times, be reckoned indecency in an alehouse, tavern, masquerading-house, &c. Perhaps sodomy or murder. We know that gaming, raking, cheating, swearing, blasphemy, drunkenness, obscene talk, adultery, and incest, are not reckoned indecencies, but are the common and regular amusements of such places.

By 1 *Jam.* I. cap. 9. it is penal to suffer any persons sitting and tippling in alehouses and inns, longer than the time necessary for refreshment[b]. Made perpetual by 21 of the same reign, cap. 7. In our times the innumerable multitude of alehouses, taverns, masquerading-houses, &c. is not restrained, because the debauching and depopulating the land, the enfeebling, the sickness, the death, and damnation of the people, are the great supports of the civil list.

The common people were suffered by our worthy ministers, *Walpole* and the *Pelhams*, to poison themselves with spirituous liquors, many thousands every year, for many succeeding years, in spite of innumerable authentic proofs laid before them of the frightful effects of dram-drinking. At last, *A. D.* 1760, a prohibition was

---

[a] STAT. AT LARGE, II. 76. [b] Ibid. 341.

was laid on the diſtillery, and afterwards it was reſolved in parliament, 'that the raiſing the price of ſpirituous 'liquors [by the ſtop of the diſtillery,] was a principal 'cauſe of a diminution of the conſumption of them, 'and had greatly contributed to the health, ſobriety, 'and induſtry, of the common people. That in order 'to continue the high price, a large additional duty be 'laid on them, to be drawn back on exportation [a].' There were many petitions preſented to the commons againſt taking off the prohibition, once particularly, from the city of *London*, becauſe it had proved ſo ſalutary. And many who conſidered corrupt parliaments as capable of any thing, ſcrupled not to ſay, the laying on of a high duty, on pretence of the people's good, was neither more nor leſs than a villanous impoſition on the common ſenſe of mankind, and was in reality giving the wretched people a licence to poiſon their bodies and damn their ſouls, for the good of the revenue.

9 *George* II, was the firſt act licenſing the retail of ſpirituous liquors [b]. The biſhop of *Worceſter* calls this act raiſing money for the ſupply of government, by what coſt the people their lives and their ſouls [c]. A thorough-paced ſtateſman will raiſe money from any thing, however hurtful to the people.

The debauchery of the people, as above obſerved, is ſuppoſed to ſupport the revenue. Therefore the boundleſs multitude of ale-houſes is not reſtrained. But this is a ſhort-ſighted kind of politics. For drunkenneſs, eſpecially in ſpirituous liquors, enfeebles the people, defeats population, ſhortens life, cuts off multitudes in infancy,

---

[a] LOND. MAG. *Sept.* 1760.

[b] STAT. AT LARGE, VII. 73.

[c] LETT. TO L. MAYOR.

infancy, lessens the quantity of labour, and hurts the revenue much more than it benefits it.

The act 9 *Anne*, cap. xiv. [a] for the better preventing of excessive and deceitful gaming, would effectually root that vice out of the nation, if the sober part of the subjects would associate against it, and keep one another in countenance in informing, prosecuting, &c. And the case is the same with respect to other epidemical vices.

By 1 *Edw.* VI. cap. 3. a person loitering idle three days, might be taken up by any body, and carried before two justices, marked with a hot iron, and enslaved for two years, to the person who apprehended him, &c. Expired and repealed [b]. And see 3 and 4 of the same reign, cap. 16 [c].

By 39 *Eliz.* cap. 4, rogues and vagabonds, besides other punishments, might be condemned to the gallies [d].

It is a monstrous absurdity in the *English* law, that the person injured by a thief or a cheat, is obliged to bear the expence and trouble of prosecuting the thief or cheat, and recovers no damages, or however, is a loser upon the whole. We pay taxes on pretence of being protected by government. But government protects us so well, that we are obliged to pay for protection besides our taxes. This inconvenience, and the extreme severity of our punishments in some cases, deter people of gentle natures from prosecuting offenders, which gives courage to the licentiousness of manners, and impunity to crimes.

The care of the manners of the people may be said to be the very business and calling of the clergy, in

[a] Stat. at Large, xiv. 352. [b] Ibid. ii. 4.
[c] Ibid. 53. [d] Ibid. ii. 298.

in such manner, that if they neglect it, it is no matter what they attend to. The errors, deficiencies, and abuses in the clergy of established churches merit a very copious display in these collections. And very copious is the quantity of materials I have, in the course of my reading, collected on this subject. At present I shall only observe, that what the clergy bestow their *principal attention* upon, is, comparatively of the *least service* for the important purpose of improving the manners of the people; I mean preaching. In the New Testament we read much of the importance of the apostles as heralds by divine commission, proclaiming the good message. That is the true meaning of the *Greek* phrase, which we translate preaching the gospel. But every body must see the difference between the importance of publishing to the world the amazing history of Christ, which history was either unknown to, or misunderstood by those to whom the heavenly heralds proclaimed it, and our explaining and inculcating a doctrine or a precept of a religion, of which we have the beautiful and simple code in our hands, and have been brought up in the belief of it. The business of the apostles was the same with that of missionaries sent from *Europe* to convert the heathens to christianity. The function of the modern clergy of *Europe* must be supposed to be different from this, as the state of the people of *Europe* is different from that of the heathens in *Asia*, *Africa*, and *America*. The clergy of *England* ought, therefore to apply themselves to teaching in more ways than one. They ought not to think they have discharged the duty of their function, when they have *read* over a velvet cushion a learned and elegant discourse on some point in theology or in morals: a true and faithful pastor will consider it as the principal part of his duty to be intimately acquainted with every

indi-

individual of his flock, to obtain and keep the firſt and higheſt place in the eſteem of every inhabitant of his pariſh, in ſuch manner, that the advice of their faithful, laborious, and diſintereſted ſpiritual guide ſhall, upon all occaſions, be acceptable to them. In all which there is no other difficulty, than the difficulty of ſhewing his people, that he is more deſirous of being ſerviceable to them, than of improving his income, of obtaining a fatter living, or a plurality, and for that purpoſe currying favour with thoſe who have livings in their gift, by plunging into party-quarrels, and doing dirty work at elections, &c.

A benevolent diſpoſition revolts againſt every diſcouragement to the exerciſe of the godlike virtue of charity. But truth is truth, and it muſt be acknowledged, that the profuſion of our charities is hurtful to the manners of our people. Even in this rich country, the number of thoſe who have it not in their power, without ſtrict care, conſtant labour, and ſevere parſimony, to ſave any thing for old age, is very great. All that policy is ſound, which tends to improve and increaſe induſtry and frugality amongtheworking people; and all that œconomy is hurtful, which tends to produce in the poor people a contrary ſpirit, and which occaſions their becoming more burdenſome to their richer fellow-ſubjects, than is abſolutely neceſſary; becauſe this lays an additional burden upon all our exports, and hurts our trade at foreign markets, upon which all depends. Let our innumerable and exorbitant public charities be conſidered in this light. If the poor are led by them to look upon induſtry and frugality as unneceſſary, they will neither be induſtrious nor frugal; and the conſequence will be, that they and their children will come upon the pariſh, inſtead of being maintained by labour and induſtry.

Besides the general hurtful consequences arising from the excessive number of our public charities, our manner of conducting them, and of admitting individuals to the benefit of them, are obnoxious to various censures, too numerous to be particularly specified here. Were the admission of individuals to the benefit of our charities put upon a proper foot, our charities might be of great benefit in improving (instead of hurting, as they do at present) the manners of the people. Did magistrates keep an attentive eye upon the behaviour of individuals, and were they to keep a register of the complaints made against the idle and debauched, the register to be inspected upon every individual's applying for the benefit of a public charity, that it might appear, whether he had lived a life of labour and frugality, or brought himself to want by his own fault. Did an individual among the lower people know, that he should be provided for in his old age, not in the present promiscuous way, but according to his behaviour through life; we should see him more attentive to his conduct, lest the justice's book, upon his applying for relief in his old age, or in case of an accident, should rise in judgment against him, and exclude him from the best provision.

'Hospitals abound, says Lord *Bacon*[a], and beggars 'abound never a whit the less.' This was written *A. D.* 1618.

A native of *Holland* is hardly ever seen begging in *Holland*.

The excellent *Montesquieu* thinks hospitals hurtful to industry; and that the best charity to the poor is to set them to work. He commends *Henry* VIII for dissolving the religious houses, which maintained multitudes in idleness, not only of those who resided in them,

[a] Lett. 234.

them, but of pretended poor, who resorted to them. At *Rome*, he says, the number of hospitals is the cause that every body is in easy circumstances, but the industrious, the land-holders, and traders; because they must maintain the hospitals.

Judge *Blackstone* condemns the present management of the poor [a].

A. D. 1760 a committee, appointed to inquire into the state of the poor, reported to the house of commons their resolutions, *viz.* That the present method of providing for the poor in the parochial way, is unequal and burdensome to parishes, and distressful to the poor. That giving money to poor people out of the parish-workhouse, to prevent their claiming a settlement, is an abuse. That the employing of the poor will be of great advantage to the public. That the placing of the poor in county-workhouses, under the direction of chosen trustees, will answer all purposes better than parish-workhouses. That this will improve waste lands, will put an end to expensive law-suits about settlements, will render the intricate laws relating to the settlement of the poor useless, &c. These wise resolutions produced no new regulation. For the parliament was prorogued in the mean time [b].

Besides what might be done by a government setting itself in earnest to correct and form the manners, it is certain that the morals and principles of all ranks, high and low, might be improved in the same way, that natural knowledge has been improved. If a set of gentlemen of respectable characters were to form a society, like the Royal Society, to meet statedly at *London*, to be wholly unconnected with government and with

[a] COMM. I. 362.

[b] LONDON MAG. *May* 1760, p. 238.

magiſtracy, to publiſh from time to time tranſactions analagous to thoſe of the Royal Society, I mean, moral diſcourſes, obſervations, reaſonings, examples from hiſtory and the beſt political writers, ancient and modern in all languages, with ſtrictures upon the manners of the times, ſatires upon the indecencies and crimes of eminent individuals, without names, &c. and if the correſpondent members of this ſociety were to uſe their endeavours in their reſpective countries to promote decency of behaviour, and agree to withdraw from, and diſgrace perſons of unexemplary characters. If, I ſay, a numerous and reſpectable ſet of gentlemen were to form themſelves into ſuch an *Areopagus*, there is no doubt, but they might give a very advantageous turn to the manners of the people of this nation, though they be ſo far gone in debauchery and corruption. The members muſt be balloted in, and any of them miſbehaving, be turned out in the ſame manner. It would damp the boldneſs of a debauched lord, to ſee his picture drawn by this ſociety of voluntary and uninfluenced cenſors, and held forth to the view of the nation in its true colours, and ſtriking likeneſs.

——— Abaſh'd the devil ſtood,
And felt how awful goodneſs is, and ſaw
Virtue in her own ſhape how lovely. MILT.

And on the contrary, it would excite men to a laudable emulation, to ſee amiable and reſpectable characters ſet in a bright and ſhining light before the public by the pen of a man of prime genius employed by the ſociety. Every man would be afraid of being ſtigmatized by a ſet of judges ſo unbiaſſed and ſo venerable. They might extend their cenſure and their approbation to authors and their works, eſpecially thoſe which were likely to affect the general character. The cenſure or praiſe of ſuch a ſociety would be more awful to writers, than that of a bookſeller's hireling, or a bookſeller himſelf

himself in the shape of a *Reviewer*. The society, by drawing into their circle all the men of *genius*, but the openly abandoned, and professedly negligent of the safety of their country, might form a party much too powerful for the defenders of debauchery and corruption. For virtue supported by abilities, will always be too hard for vice and stupidity. And men of parts, acting upon principle, will keep together, when weak and worthless men will quarrel and divide. A numerous set of virtuous and able men associated, and corresponding together, and all independent in temper and circumstances, would be a formidable check on wicked ministers and corrupt parliaments. See the account given in the MODERN UNIVERSAL HISTORY, XXXIV. 135, of the commonwealth of *Babina*, a society erected in *Poland* upon this foot, and with this view, which proved highly serviceable, and was encouraged by kings and emperors.

And let it be recollected, what effects were produced by the humorous romance of *Don Quixotte*, by the silly song of *Lillibullero*, and the like, which occasioned a person's saying, that if he had the making of the ballads in a country, who would might make the laws.

'It is an incontestible truth, that the virtues of the 'citizens constitute the most happy dispositions that can 'be desired by a just and wise government. This then 'affords a certain index from which the nation may judge 'of the intention of those who govern. If they endeavour 'to render the great and the common people virtuous, 'their views are pure and upright; and it is certain that 'their sight is fixed alone on the great end of govern'ment, the happiness and glory of the nation. But if 'they spread a corruption of manners, a love of luxury, 'effeminacy, the rage of licentious passions, and excite 'the great to engage in ruinous expences, the people 'ought to take care of these corrupters; for they endeavour to purchase slaves, in order to rule over them in an arbitrary manner[a].'

Though it must be owned that our liberties have made a small acquisition by the late demolition of general warrants, and seizure of papers; yet there is, and will be great reason to complain, so long as the riot-act is kept in force.

The first sketch of the riot-act was made in the time of *Edward* VI. and is thought by *Burnet* too severe[b].

Soldiers armed with firelocks are particularly improper for quelling riots. There is a necessary jealousy between them and the people; so that their encounter is likely to widen, not close the breach. They are the slaves of the court: the people, therefore, naturally conclude, that whenever they are employed, tyranny is going forward. The soldiers being all dressed alike, it is impossible to distinguish which of them is guilty of any violence against the people; this indeed, there is reason to suppose, the court cares little about, but to us it is an object. Musquets are not certain to hit the *guilty* persons in a riot; but may destroy the *innocent* in their own houses, or passing about their lawful business.

At *Rome* it was not lawful to enter forcibly a citizen's house, even to carry him to justice for a crime[c].

Charlemagne, the son of *Pepin* of *France*, always endeavoured to quiet seditions, and oppositions, by gentle means, before he made use of the sword.

The lord chief justice *Holt*, hearing of a mob, went among the people, and telling the soldiers, who were come

---

[a] *Vattel's* LAW OF NATIONS, quoted LOND. MAG. *Sept*, 1760, p. 456.

[b] PARL. HIST. III. 248.

[c] *Montesq.* L'ESPRIT DES LOIX, III. 202.

come to disperse them, that he would have every man of the party hanged, if one person was killed (all are principals who are present at a murder), quelled the mob himself[a].

When *Henry* IV. of *France* took *Paris*, which was in rebellion against him, there were two or three citizens killed. The king was extremely concerned that any lives should be lost, and said, he would rather have given 50,000 crowns, that posterity might read that *Paris* was taken by *Henry* IV. without blood. We have long complained, but in vain, that the military are called in to quell every trifling riot, where the peace officers would have done the business as effectually, and with more safety. We have seen the men of blood, the pretended keepers of the peace, but real butchers of the innocent, some reprieved, others thanked, for destroying their countrymen.

The riot-act was made with a view merely temporary, and therefore ought to have been repealed, when the occasion of making it was at an end. It is too cruel and bloody. A peaceable subject may chance to be wedged in the middle of a mob, so that he cannot extricate himself at the reading of the riot-act. The man may be lame; he may be overtaken with liquor; he may not even know, that the riot-act has been read, if the mob around him was noisy, if he was at a distance from the place, or if he was hard of hearing. Is the unhappy man to be seized, imprisoned like a felon, tried, and put to an infamous death, only because he was so unfortunate, as to get himself entangled in a mob? So says the riot-act. Yet we know, all good government is founded in paternal principles. But what should we think of that father,

 who

[a] Life of Lord Chief Justice Holt:

who ſhould murder his ſon, becauſe he would not go out of the room when ordered? Diſobedience in children or ſubjects is highly culpable: but cruelty and injuſtice in parents, or governors, in puniſhing diſobedience, is infamous. The intention, in making penal laws, ought to be, to prevent a greater evil by a leſs. Is the riot-act conſtructed upon this principle? I happen to offend the mob. Two or three hundred idle fellows aſſemble, and break my windows. Twenty ſhillings will repair the damage. No, ſays the riot-act. A magiſtrate ſhall ſend for the ſtanding army. They ſhall ſeize all they can lay hold on, after reading the riot-act. Thoſe they ſeize ſhall be hanged. And if, in apprehending the offenders, any one, or more, are killed, it ſhall not be murder. See the Act. This laſt clauſe may be ſaid to be, like *Draco's* laws, written in blood. For it naturally ſuggeſts to a cowardly magiſtrate (cowards are generally cruel), that the readieſt way to diſperſe the mob is, to order the ſoldiers to fire upon them. This is indeed a groſs abuſe of the intention of the law. For, abſurd and ill framed as it is, the intention of it was quite different from this. The meaning of the law is, that all perſons, ſoldiers as well as others, ſhould aſſiſt the civil magiſtrate in quelling riots. And, leſt the magiſtrate ſhould be intimidated in the diſcharge of this part of his duty, he, and all who are aiding to him, ſhould be indemnified from proſecution, on account of any perſon's being unavoidably killed in the ſcuffle. The riot-act, bloody as it is, was not ſo bloodily intentioned, as to mean, that whenever a diſturbance happens in the middle of a great town, which (ſuch is the well-known good-nature and good underſtanding of the people of *England)* may almoſt always be quieted by a few civil words from any man, who is in favour with them; immediately

mediately a band of ruffian ſoldiers ſhall be brought to fire in at windows, and murder women and children. This was not, I ſay, in any degree, the intention of the riot-act. But it is ſo ill contrived, that it is very eaſily abuſed to this cruel purpoſe. There ought to have been an expreſs prohibition of fire arms in the hands of thoſe who were to aſſiſt the civil magiſtrate, with capital puniſhment of any perſon on the ſide of the inſurgents, who ſhould uſe thoſe dreadful inſtruments of deſtruction. At *Conſtantinople*, the *Janizaries* are armed only with clubs. Fire-arms are not the proper implements for quelling the unruly diſpoſitions of our own children. They are very proper indeed, if our ſcheme be to murder them, and thin the land. Nor ought the ſoldiery to be, on any account, called in on ſuch occaſion. The verieſt court-ſycophant in the nation does not pretend, that a ſtanding army, numerous enough to conquer the world, is kept up in profound peace, merely for the purpoſe of keeping the people quiet. This he knows to be too groſs to paſs; becauſe he knows, that it is but very lately that we had a ſtanding army; that in *Henry* VIIth's time the yeomen of the guards were the whole regular force under the king's command, except in war time. No; he pretends, that the neceſſity of a ſtanding army ariſes wholly from the practice of the other crowned heads of *Europe*; and that, becauſe they who live on a vaſt continent together, and are liable to be attacked at any time by their neighbours, muſt keep up a military force for their defence, therefore we, who are ſurrounded by a ſea, and a fleet equal to all the naval force of *Europe*, muſt keep up a ſtanding army, as numerous as that of *Alexander* the Great. Let this be for a moment, admitted (though nothing can well be imagined more palpably abſurd) does it not follow,

that

that to call in the ſtanding army, with their murderous fire-arms, to keep the peace within the realm, is a groſs miſapplication of them? If the army can at any time quell an inſurrection of the people, why may they not quell the ſpirit of liberty in the people? And then a complete tyranny is eſtabliſhed. For every government will be tyrannical, if they dare. Had the riot-act been made before the Revolution, we had probably never ſeen that glorious event.

The intention of the riot-act being, to ſeize, and bring to regular trial by jury (ſee the Act), nothing can be more abſurd (beſides the cruelty of it) than the application of fire-arms for quelling mobs; becauſe fire-arms do not ſeize people, but murder them; a net, a rope, a ſhepherd's crook would be natural inſtruments for ſeizing, or apprehending.

The under-ſheriff of *Dublin*, *A. D.* 1738, was brought in guilty of murder for ordering a file of muſqueteers to fire upon a mob, and killing one man. He abſconded; fled to *England*; was outlawed; died for want in a ditch in *Marybone-fields* [a].

Sir *Stephen Theodore Janſſen*, when ſheriff of *London*, kept the peace at executions, and on other occaſions, when the populace were expected to be unruly, without any military force. He raiſed a body of 1000 men, armed, and ſome of them mounted on horſeback. Others, on like occaſions, have called in the ſoldiery, and ſhed innocent blood.

Is it no grievance, (ſays Sir *J. Hinde Cotton* in the debate on the repeal of the ſeptennial act, *A. D.* 1734 [b]) that a little dirty juſtice of the peace, the meaneſt and vileſt tool a miniſter can make uſe of, a tool who, perhaps, ſubſiſts by his being in the commiſſion; and who may

a LOND. CHRON. N°. 1786.

b DEB. COM. VIII. 179.

may be turned out of that ſubſiſtance whenever the miniſter pleaſes; is this I ſay, no grievance that ſuch a tool ſhould have it in his power, by reading a proclamation, to put perhaps 20 or 30 of the beſt ſubjects in *England* to immediate death, without any trial or form of law?

In the year 1747, an act paſſed for trying the rebels (not according to ancient cuſtom in the county, where they committed the offence, but) before ſuch commiſſioners, and in ſuch county as the king ſhould appoint. In conſequence of the riot-act, four perſons were executed in *Saliſbury* court, who would otherwiſe have been only puniſhed with fine and priſon. And a jury in *Southwark*, which had acquitted two gentlemen, were diſmiſſed, and another impanelled [a].

Lord *Bacon* ſays, what chiefly kept the peace in his times, when riots were apprehended, was drawing up and muſtering the trained bands, giving charge to the lord mayor, aldermen, juſtices, &c. and ſtrengthening the commiſſioners of the peace with new clauſes of lieutenancy [b].

'There is (ſays lord *Bathurſt* [c],) a very great difference between a magiſtrate's being aſſiſted by the poſſe of the county, and his having a body of regular troops always at command. In the firſt caſe, he muſt in all his meaſures purſue juſtice and equity, he muſt even ſtudy the humours and inclinations, and court the affections of the people; becauſe upon them only he can depend for the execution of his orders as a magiſtrate, and even for his ſafety and protection as a private man; but when a civil magiſtrate knows that he has a large body of regular

' well

[a] Use and Abuse of Parl. i. 334.

[b] L. *Bac.* Lett. 202.

[c] Deb. Lords, v. 152.

'well disciplined troops at command, he despises both 'the inclinations and the interest of the people; he 'considers nothing but the inclinations and the interest of the soldiers, and as these soldiers are quite 'distinct from the people, as they do not feel the oppressions of the people, and are subject to such arbitrary laws and severe punishments, they will generally assist and protect him in the most unjust and 'oppressive measures; nay, as the interests of the soldiers are always distinct from, and sometimes opposite to the interests of the people, a civil magistrate, 'not otherwise oppressive in his nature, is sometimes 'obliged to oppress the people, in order to humour 'and please the army. To imagine, my lords, that we 'shall always be under a civil government as long as 'our army is under the direction of the civil magistrate, is to me something surprising. In *France*, in '*Spain*, and many other countries, which have long 'been under an arbitrary and military government, 'they have the outward appearance of a civil government; even in *Turkey*, they have laws, they have 'lawyers, they have civil magistrates, and in all cases 'of a domestic nature, their services are under the 'direction of the civil magistrates; but, my lords, we 'know, that in all such countries, the law, the 'lawyers, and the civil magistrates, speak as they are 'commanded, by those who have the command of the 'army. Their lawyers have often occasion to make 'the same speech that one of our judges made to *Michael Pole*, earl of *Suffolk*, in *Richard* the IId's reign, 'who, upon signing it as his opinion, that the king 'was above the laws, said,——If I had not done this, 'my lord, I should have been killed by you; and now 'I have done it, I well deserve to be hanged for treason against the nobles of the land. I am afraid, 'my 'my lords, some of our civil magistrates, at least those 'of an inferior degree, begin to put too great confi- 'dence in their having a military force at their com- 'mand, and therefore make a little too free with the 'lower sort of people, or at least do not take pro- 'per measures for reconciling the people, in a good- 'natured and peaceable manner, to the laws of their 'country: a man who has power, is but too seldom at 'the pains to use argument.'

In the riot-act[a], there is no mention of military, nor of firing; but if any person happens to be killed in the apprehending, or endeavouring to apprehend him, it shall not be murder, &c.

'The liberty of firing at random, says a speaker in 'the house of peers, upon any multitude of his ma- 'jesty's subjects, is a liberty which ought to be most 'cautiously granted, and never made use of, but in 'cases of the most absolute necessity; and in this way 'of thinking, I am supported by the whole tenor of 'the laws of *England*. It is now three or four hun- 'dred years since fire-arms first became in use among 'us; yet the law has never suffered them to be made 'use of by the common officers of justice. Pikes, 'halberts, battle-axes, and such like, are the only 'weapons that can be made use of according to law, 'by such officers; and the reason is extremely plain, 'because, with such weapons they can seldom or ever 'hurt, much less kill any but such as are really op- 'posing or assaulting them; whereas if you put fire 'arms into their hands, and allow them to make the 'proper use of such arms, they may as probably hurt 'or kill the innocent as the guilty; nay in cities and 'towns, where such tumults generally happen, they 'may

[a] Stat. at Large, iv. 600.

'may kill people ſitting in their own houſes, or looking innocently over their windows, which all perſons are apt to do, but eſpecially women and children, when they hear any hubbub or noiſe in the ſtreets; and which was really in the affair now before us; for one woman was killed in her maſter's houſe, by her being unfortunately, but innocently, at the window when the ſoldiers fired [a].'

'There are two ſorts of mobs, or aſſemblies of the people; one is when a multitude of people aſſembles together upon any lawful or innocent occaſion, and afterwards happen to become riotous; and the other is when a multitude of people aſſembles together with a deſign to commit ſome unlawful or wicked action. With reſpect to the former, the moſt gentle meaſures ought to be made uſe of for diſperſing them, becauſe many innocent perſons being inveigled into the crowd, it may be ſome time before they can poſſibly get away; but with reſpect to the latter, as all that are aſſembled together upon ſuch an occaſion muſt be ſome way guilty, therefore more rough and violent meaſures may be made uſe of for diſperſing them, and for preventing the miſchief they intended. But in both theſe caſes the law is now certain and indiſputable. Your lordſhips all know that by a late ſtatute, which is in force in *Scotland* as well as *England*, the power of the civil magiſtrate, in the caſe of any mob, or riotous aſſembly, is fully and diſtinctly regulated; yet even by that law, which I have often heard complained of, as a law not tolerable in a free country, there is no expreſs power given to the magiſtrate or his aſſiſtants, to make uſe of fire-arms; ſo cautious was the legiſlature, even at that time, when

[a] Deb. Peers, v. 172.

'when tumults were more frequent and more dangerous than they are at present, of giving a legal authority for the making use of such weapons. After reading the proclamation, and after giving the mob an hour's time to disperse themselves, and to depart to their habitations, or lawful business, the peace-officers may then, by that law, seize or disperse them who shall afterwards continue unlawfully assembled; and if any person, by resisting them, shall happen to be killed, maimed, or hurt, the peace-officers and their assistants are indemnified; but I doubt much if a magistrate would be indemnified, even by this law, should he take the short way of dispersing a mob, by ordering his assistants to fire among them, and should thereby kill any person who had committed no overt act of resistance [a].'

'A law was made for preventing or quelling riots and tumults within the city of *Edinburgh*; for which purpose the magistrates of that city are enabled, with the King's allowance, to raise soldiers on pay, to use haquebuts, and all other arms, when they shall think expedient; and if any person resisting the said magistrates in the quelling of any riot, shall be hurt or slain, the magistrates and their assistants are indemnified; provided such hurt or killing was with long weapons, and not by shooting haquebuts or the like. I need not acquaint your lordships, that haquebut was the name then used in that country, and formerly in this, for fire-arms; that by long weapons was meant halberts, battle-axes, and such weapons as are commonly used by all assistants to officers of justice in that part of the island, as well as this. Thus your lordships see, that killing with any sort of fire-arms was expresly excepted out of that law [b].'

Upon

[a] Deb. Peers, v. 173. [b] Ibid. 174.

Upon occaſion of the debate about *Porteous*'s affair, the Duke of *Argyle* propoſed, that the Judges ſhould deliver their opinions upon the following queſtions relating to the above act, viz. ‘ 1. If an execution ſhould ‘ be performed in *Stocks-Market*, where a guard of the ‘ regular troops ſhould be drawn up by lawful com- ‘ mand to prevent a reſcue of the criminal, and ſhould ‘ ſeveral ſtones, thrown from among the crowd, light ‘ among them, by ſome of which ſeveral ſoldiers ſhould ‘ be bruiſed and wounded; would ſuch a guard be ‘ guilty of a crime, if, by firing among the crowd, ‘ they ſhould kill ſeveral perſons? And if guilty of a ‘ crime, what crime would it be? 2. Upon occaſion ‘ of a riot in or near a town where a regiment is quar- ‘ tered, ſhould the Sheriff of the County order the ‘ commanding officer to aſſemble the regiment, and ‘ march to his aſſiſtance againſt the rioters, is ſuch ‘ officer obliged to obey, or may obey? And what ‘ penalty is there, if he ſhould refuſe? 3. If a detach- ‘ ment of the army is ordered to prevent a number of ‘ people from pulling down of houſes, or committing ‘ any other illegal action, and that the commanding ‘ officer of ſuch detachment has orders to repel force ‘ by force, can ſuch detachment lawfully make uſe of ‘ force by firing, unleſs they are attacked by the riot- ‘ ers? 4. In caſe rioters ſhould be pulling down houſes, ‘ or doing any other miſchief in one part of the town, ‘ and a detachment of the army ſhould be ordered, in ‘ aid of the civil magiſtrate, to march thither to diſ- ‘ perſe them, and a number of people ſhould aſſemble, ‘ and ſtop up the paſſages through which ſuch detach- ‘ ment muſt neceſſarily paſs, whether ſuch detachment ‘ may uſe force to diſperſe the people ſo aſſembled, in 'order to pass that way, without being first attacked 'by them[a].'

When the three justices, *Blackerby*, *Howard*, and *Lediard*, were rebuked by the Speaker, *A. D.* 1741, for bringing a party of soldiers, on pretence of quelling a riot at the poll for *Westminster*, he asked them as follows:

'Has any real necessity been shewn for it? There 'might be fears, there might be some danger; but did 'you try the strength of the law to dispel these fears, 'and remove that danger? Did you make use of these 'powers the law has entrusted you with, as civil ma-'gistrates, for the preservation of the public peace? 'No.—You deserted all that; and wantonly, I hope 'inadvertently, resorted to that force the most unna-'tural of all others in all respects to that cause and 'business you were then attending, and for the free-'dom of which every Briton ought to be ready almost 'to suffer any thing[b].'

'The riot-act, says the author of Use and Abuse 'of Parliaments[c], which passed likewise this ses-'sion, no doubt the distempers of these times made 'necessary; but then surely it ought either to 'have been temporary, or should have been long 'since repealed. For while that yoke is upon our 'necks, though we are at liberty to preach resistance, 'we have little or no power to practise it; under 'whatever grievances labouring, or by whatever pro-'vocations compelled. A circumstance which, I fear, 'these in power are but too well acquainted with.'

'Sir, I declare upon my honour (says Mr. *Pulteney*, 'in the debate on the repeal of the septennial bill,

---

[a] DEB. PEERS, v. 179.

[b] DEB. COM. XIII. 105. [c] I. 201.

'A. D. 1734 a) that of all the actions I ever did in 'my life, there is not one I more heartily and sincerely 'repent of, than my voting for the passing of that law '[the riot-act]. I believe I am as little suspected of 'disaffection to his Majesty, or his family, as any man 'in the kingdom. It was my too great zeal for his 'illustrious family, that transported me to give that 'vote for which I am now heartily grieved. But even 'then I never imagined it was to remain a law for 'ever. No, Sir! This government is founded upon 'resistance; it was the principle of resistance that 'brought about the Revolution, which cannot be justi-'fied upon any other principle. Is then passive obedi-'ence and non-resistance to be established by a perpe-'tual law, by a law the most scarce and the most arbi-'trary of any in *England*, and that under a government 'which owes its very being to resistance? The Hon. 'Gentleman who first mentioned it, said very right; 'it is a scandal it should remain in our statute-books; 'and I will say, they are no friends to his Majesty, or 'to his government, who desire it should: for it de-'stroys that principle upon which is founded one of his 'best titles to the crown. While this remains a law, 'we cannot well be called a free people; a little Jus-'tice of the Peace, assisted perhaps by a serjeant and a 'parcel of hirelings, may almost at any time have the 'lives of twenty gentlemen of the best families in *Eng-'land* in his power.'

'I shall never be for sacrificing the liberties of the 'people, says a Speaker in the House of Peers, in 'order to prevent their engaging in any riotous pro-'ceedings; because I am sure it may be done by a 'much more gentle and less expensive method. A 'wise

a DEB. COM. VIII. 202.

'wise and a prudent conduct, and a constant pursuit 'of upright and just measures, will establish the autho-'rity as well as the power of the government; and 'where authority is joined with power, the people will 'never be tumultuous; but I must observe, and I do 'it without a design of offending any person, that ever 'since I came into the world, I never saw an admini-'stration that had, in my opinion, so much power, 'or so little authority. I hope some methods will be 'taken for establishing among the people in general that 'respect and esteem, which they ought to have for 'their governors, and which every administration 'ought to endeavour, as much as possible, to acquire. 'I hope proper methods will be taken for restoring to 'the laws of this kingdom their ancient authority; 'for if that is not done, if the Lord Chief Justice's 'warrant is not of itself of so much authority, as that 'it may be executed by his tipstaff in any county of '*England*, without any other assistance than what is 'provided by the law, it cannot be said that we are 'governed by law, or by the civil magistrate: If re-'gular troops should once become necessary for execu-'ting the laws upon every occasion, it could not then 'be said, that we were governed by the civil power, 'but by the military sword, which is a sort of govern-'ment I am sure none of your Lordships would desire 'ever to see established in this kingdom[a].'

What Lord *Carteret* said in the House of Peers, *A. D.* 1737, on occasion of the affair of *Porteous*, is very just.

'The people seldom or ever assemble in any riotous 'or tumultuous manner unless when they are op-'pressed, or at least imagine they are oppressed. If the

 'people

[a] DEB. PEERS, v. 142.

'people should be mistaken, and imagine they are oppressed when they are not, it is the duty of the next magistrate to endeavour first to correct their mistake by fair means and just reasoning. In common humanity he is obliged to take this method, before he has recourse to such methods as may bring death and destruction upon a great number of his fellow-countrymen, and this method will generally prevail where they have not met with any real oppression: But when this happens to be the case, it cannot be expected they will give ear to their oppressor, nor can the severest laws, nor the most rigorous execution of those laws, always prevent the people's becoming tumultuous; you may shoot them, you may hang them, but, till the oppression is removed or alleviated, they will never be quiet, till the greatest part of them are destroyed [a].

The court cant, in support of the practice of calling the soldiery to quell riots, is, That the soldiery are the king's subjects, as well as other men; and all subjects are obliged to assist the magistrate in case of need. But why must the *soldiery*, rather than any other subjects, be sent for from an hundred miles distance, to quell a disturbance, If it be not that the soldiery are more formidable to the people than any other subjects? Is it not therefore manifest, that every argument for calling in the military is a two-edged one? The more fit the military are for quelling riots, the more fit they likewise must be for quelling the spirit of liberty, and enslaving the people. If disciplined troops be necessary, it is not necessary that those troops be the hirelings of the court, enslaved for life.

The law means, even when it punishes, not revenge,

[a] Deb. Peers, v. 138.

venge, but example. The magistrate is not to mix his passions with the execution of justice; nor is he to enforce the execution of the best laws at all hazards. He is not to fire a city in order to force a nest of thieves out of their lurking holes. Violence on the part of government tends to irritate, not to quiet, the minds of the people. Better fifty were punished legally, than five massacred. Musquet-balls against brick-bats are an unequal match, and cowardly on the part of government. If the train-bands, town-guards, peace-officers, and *posse comitatus* be not sufficient, let the laws concerning them be mended. But let not an army, the bond-slaves of a corrupt court, find, that they have the people under their command, lest they first subdue the people, and then, like *Cromwell*'s men, turn upon their own masters.

The way to prevent mobs (every government shews its sagacity more by prevention than by punishment) is, to keep up a good police, to take care that the people be employed and maintained, and that they be well principled, which requires punishing an idle, or incendiary priesthood (as those in *Sacheverel*'s time) and making them, and the community where disorders are committed, answerable, according to King *Alfred*'s institution; and by a mild and fatherly government's taking care that the people have no just ground of complaint.

By 13 *Henry* IV. it is enacted, that in case of a riot, the Sheriff may come with the *posse comitatus*, if need be, (not with a regiment of soldiers) and arrest the disturbers of the peace, as was ordained by two statutes of *Richard* II. The Sheriff and two Justices are to present the guilty, and they are to be punished (as upon the presentment of twelve jurors) at the discretion of King and Council. But the accused may

 'traverse,

traverse, and the cause may be tried before the King's Bench. If the accused do not appear, they are to be held guilty. Sheriffs and Justices neglecting to quell riots to be punished [a].

The learned Judge *Blackstone* reckons the riot-act among the causes of a great accession of power to the court since the Revolution [b].

CHAP. IX.

Of the Liberty of Speech and Writing on Political Subjects.

IN an inquiry into public abuses no one will wonder to find punishment inflicted by government upon complainers, reckoned as an abuse; for it certainly is one of the most atrocious abuses, that a free subject should be restrained in his inquiries into the conduct of those who undertake to manage his affairs; I mean the administrators of government: for all such are undertakers, and are answerable for what they undertake: but if it be dangerous and penal to inquire into their conduct, the state may be ruined by their blunders, or by their villanies, beyond the possibility of redress.

There seems to be somewhat unnatural in attempting to lay a restraint on those who would criticise the conduct of men who undertake to do other people's business. It is an offence, if we remark on the decision of a court of law, on the proceedings of either house of parliament, or of the administration; all whose proceedings we are immediately concerned in. At the same

a STAT. AT LARGE, I. 448.

b COMM. IV. 434.

same time, if a man builds a house for himself, marries a wife for himself, or writes a book, by which the public gets more than the author, it is no offence to make very severe and unjust remarks.

Are Judges, Juries, Counsellors, Members of the House of Commons, Peers, Secretaries of State, or Kings, infallible? Or are they short-sighted, and perhaps interested, mortals?

In a petition to parliament, a bill in chancery, and proceedings at law, libellous words are not punishable; because freedom of speech and writing are indispensably necessary to the carrying on of business. But it may be said, there is no necessity for a private writer to be indulged the liberty of attacking the conduct of those who take upon themselves to govern the state. The answer is easy, viz. That all history shews the necessity, in order to the preservation of liberty, of every subject's having a watchful eye on the conduct of Kings, Ministers, and Parliament, and of every subject's being not only secured, but encouraged in alarming his fellow-subjects on occasion of every attempt upon public liberty, and that private, independent subjects *only* are like to give faithful warning of such attempts; their betters (as to rank and fortune) being more likely to conceal, than detect the abuses committed by those in power. If, therefore, private writers are to be intimidated in shewing their fidelity to their country, the principal security of liberty is taken away.

Punishing libels public or private is foolish, because it does not answer the end, and because the end is a bad one, if it could be answered.

The Attorney General *De Grey* confessed in the House of Commons, *A. D.* 1770[a], 'that his power of

[a] Alm. Deb. Com. ix. 22.

'of filing informations *ex officio* is an odious power, 'and that it does not answer the purpose intended; 'for that he had not been able to bring any libeller to 'justice.' Mr. *Pownal* shewed that power to be illegal and unconstitutional; for that, according to law, no *Englishman* is to be brought upon his trial, but by presentment of his country; a few particular cases excepted.

When the lawyers say a libel is criminal, though *true*, they mean, because it is, according to them, a breach of the peace, and tends to excite revenge. They allow, that the *falsehood* of the charge is an aggravation [a], and that, therefore, the person libelled has no right to damages, if the charges laid against him be *true*. But by this rule it should seem, that the *truth* of the libel should take away all its criminality. For if I have no right to damages, I have no pretence to seek revenge. Therefore to libel me for what I cannot affirm myself to be innocent of, is no breach of the peace, as it does not naturally tend to excite revenge, but rather ingenuous shame and reformation.

Let us hear on this subject the excellent Lord *Chesterfield*, on the bill for licensing the stage, *A. D.* 1737.

'In public, as well as private life, the only way to 'prevent being ridiculed or censured, is to avoid all 'ridiculous or wicked measures, and to pursue such 'only as are virtuous and worthy. The people never 'endeavour to ridicule those they love and esteem, nor 'will they suffer them to be ridiculed. If any one at'tempts it, their ridicule returns upon the author; he 'makes himself only the object of public hatred and 'contempt. The actions or behaviour of a private 'man

[a] *Blackstone*, IV. 150.

'man may pass unobserved, and consequently unap-'plauded and uncensured; but the actions of these in 'high stations, can neither pass without notice nor 'without censure or applause; and therefore an admi-'nistration without esteem, without authority, among 'the people, let their power be ever so great or ever so 'arbitrary, will be ridiculed: the severest edicts, the 'most terrible punishments cannot prevent it. If any 'man, therefore, thinks he has been censured, if any 'man thinks he has been ridiculed, upon any of our 'public theatres, let him examine his actions he will 'find the cause, let him alter his conduct he will find 'a remedy. As no man is perfect, as no man is infal-'lible, the greatest may err, the most circumspect may 'be guilty of some piece of ridiculous behaviour. It 'is not licentiousness, it is an useful liberty always 'indulged the stage in a free country, that some great 'men may there meet with a just reproof, which none 'of their friends will be free enough, or rather faithful 'enough to give them. Of this we have a famous in-'stance in the *Roman* history. The great *Pompey*, 'after the many victories he had obtained, and the great 'conquests he had made, had certainly a good title to 'the esteem of the people of *Rome*. Yet that great 'man, by some error in his conduct, became an object 'of general dislike; and therefore in the representation 'of an old play, when *Diphilus* the actor came to re-'peat these words, *Nostrâ miseriâ tu es magnus*, the 'audience immediately applied them to *Pompey*, who 'at that time was as well known by the name of *Mag-'nus* as by the name *Pompey*, and were so highly 'pleased with the satire, that, as *Cicero* tells us, they 'made the actor repeat the words one hundred times 'over. An account of this was immediately sent to '*Pompey*, who, instead of resenting it as an injury,

'was

'was ſo wiſe as to take it for a juſt reproof. He examined his conduct, he altered his meaſures, he regained by degrees the eſteem of the people, and then he neither feared the wit, nor felt the ſatire of the ſtage. This is an example which ought to be followed by great men in all countries[a].'

Even the cruel *Tiberius*, when in good humour, could ſay, 'In a free ſtate, the mind and the tongue ought to be free.' *Titus* defied any one to ſcandalize him. *Trajan* publiſhed abſolute liberty of ſpeech and writing. *Conſtantine*, when he was told that ſome ill-diſpoſed perſons had battered his head and face, meaning thoſe of his ſtatue, felt himſelf all about thoſe parts, and told his courtiers, he found nothing amiſs; deſiring that they would take no trouble about finding out the violators of the ſtatue.

Mr. *Gordon*[b] allows the maxim, that a libel is not the leſs a libel for being true. But this holds, he ſays, only in reſpect of *private* characters; and it is quite otherwiſe, when the crimes of men affect the *public*. We are to take care of the public ſafety at all adventures. And the loſs of an individual's, or a whole miniſtry's *political* characters, ought to be deſpiſed, when put in competition with the fate of a kingdom. Therefore no free ſubject ought to be under the leaſt reſtraint in reſpect to accuſing the greateſt, ſo long as his accuſation ſtrikes only at the *political* conduct of the accuſed: his private we have no right to meddle with, but in ſo far as a known vicious private character indicates an unfitneſs for public power or truſt. But it may be ſaid, this is a grievous hardſhip on thoſe who undertake the adminiſtration of a nation; that they

[a] Deb. Peers, v. 214.
[b] *Cato*'s Let. i. 246.

they are to run the hazard of being thus publicly accuſed of corruption, embezzlement, and other political crimes, without having it in their power to puniſh their ſlanderers. To this I anſwer, It is no hardſhip at all, but the unavoidable inconvenience attendant upon a high ſtation, which he who diſlikes muſt avoid, and keep himſelf private. *Cato* was forty times tried. But we do not think the worſe of *Cato* for this. If a ſtateſman is liable to be falſly accuſed, let him comfort himſelf by recollecting, that he is well paid. An enſign is liable to be killed in war; and he has but 3*s.* 6*d.* a day. If a ſtateſman has deſignedly behaved amiſs, he ought to be puniſhed with the utmoſt ſeverity; becauſe the injury he has done, is unboundedly extenſive. If he has injured the public through weakneſs, and without wicked intention, he is ſtill puniſhable; becauſe he ought not to have thruſt himſelf into a ſtation for which he was unfit. But, indeed, theſe caſes are ſo rare (want of *honeſty* being the general cauſe of mal-adminiſtration), that it is ſcarce worth while to touch upon them. If a ſtateſman is falſly accuſed, he has only to clear his character, and he appears in a fairer light than before. He muſt not inſiſt on puniſhing his accuſer: for the public ſecurity requires, that there be no danger in accuſing thoſe who undertake the adminiſtration of national affairs. The puniſhment of political ſatyriſts gains credit to their writings, nor do unjuſt governments reap any fruit from ſuch ſeverities, but inſults to themſelves, and honour to thoſe whom they proſecute.

A libel is in fact (criminally ſpeaking) a *non entity*, *i. e.* there is no ſuch offence as ſcandal. For if the puniſhment was taken away, the whole of the evil would be taken away, becauſe nobody would regard ſcandal; but people would believe every perſon's character

racter to be what they knew it. The old philosopher said all in a sentence, 'Live so that nobody shall believe your maligners.'

Filing informations by rule of court on motion of counsel, tends to set aside the old constitutional method of indictment and presentment by jury. But informations filed *ex officio* by the Attorney General, are not more consistent with libels than letters of cachet.

A. D. 1765, a motion was made in the house of commons, 'That general warrants for apprehending 'the authors of seditious or treasonable libels, and for 'seizing their papers, are not warranted by law, though 'they have been customary.' Nothing done in the matter. The house was too tender of the power of the court to make a resolution so favourable to the liberty of the subject.

General warrants are not a whit more reconcilable to liberty, than the *French* king's *Lettres de Cachet*. A general warrant lays half the people of a town at the mercy of a set of ruffian officers, let loose upon them by a secretary of state, who assumes over the persons and papers of the most innocent a power which a *British* king dares not assume, and delegates it to the dregs of the people; in consequence of which the most delicate secrets of families may be divulged; a greater distress to the innocent than the loss of liberty, or in some cases even of life.

Mr. *Pitt* issued out two general warrants, but neither on account of libels. One was, to stop certain dangerous persons going to *France*, and the other, for seizing a supposed spy, both in time of war [a].

The Duke of *Newcastle* issued innumerable warrants on frivolous occasions, as libels on the ministry, *&c.*

In

[a] *Alm.* DEB. COM. VI. 270.

In all cafes of danger to the main, there ought to be a regular and legal fufpenfion by parliament of the *Habeas Corpus* act, as is ufual in times of rebellion; which (fuppofing parliament incorrupt) would fecure the ftate, and at the fame time fave the liberty of the fubject inviolate. If it be objected, that it is not worth while to have the *Habeus Corpus* act fufpended by parliament for the fake of apprehending a fingle incendiary; be it anfwered, that then it is certainly not worth while on that account to iffue an illegal, unconftitutional general warrant, to the violation of the fubject's liberty, as often as a capricious fecretary of ftate fhall think proper.

In the arguments againft the privy-council's arbitrary power of committing to prifon by an anonymous member, *A. D.* 1681, he quotes laws for reftraining this power as old as 9 *Henry* III. 5 *Edw.* III. c. 9. 25 *Edw.* III. c. 4. 28 *Edw.* III. c. 3. 37 *Edw.* III. c. 18. 38 *Edw.* III. c. 9. and 42 *Edw.* III. c. 3. Befides *Magna Charta*, *Habeas Corpus*, bill of right, petition of right, &c. which ordain, that no man fhall be imprifoned, or ftripped, or diftrained, or outlawed, or condemned, or corporally punifhed, but by prefentment and trial by his peers, &c. That informers, who deceive the king into unjuft commitments, fhall be bound over to profecute, and be anfwerable for damages by fuffering the punifhment they defigned to bring on the innocent, or be obliged to fatisfy the injured. But all thefe have been violated by the privy-council's fending for gentlemen from very diftant parts, to their great vexation, and imprifoning arbitrarily, without other authority or proceeding than order of privy-council, and no redrefs or punifhment inflicted on the falfe informer, according to 37 *Edw.* III. c. 18 [a].

Shippen

[a] Deb. Com. II. 140.

Shippen makes a ſpeech againſt the ſuſpenſion of the *Habeas Corpus* act. Over-ruled [a]. The king did certainly make no bad uſe of his power. And in a time of open rebellion, it ſeems neceſſary that there be ſuch a power ſomewhere. But I think it would be better in the hands of a committee of the houſe of commons, who ſhould always ſit; but this ſuppoſes an independent houſe of commons.

A. D. 1766, Sir *W. Meredith* moved the houſe of commons, that it might be reſolved, That general warrants and ſeizure of papers are violations of the rights of the ſubject. Inſtead of which, almoſt the direct contrary was reſolved [b]. Yet it ſeems manifeſt, that nothing can be imagined more inconſiſtent with freedom (to ſay nothing of the *right* which every free ſubject has to ſpeak and write of public affairs), than putting a diſcretionary power into the hands of a ſet of low-bred, unprincipled, and beggarly officers or meſſengers, who may be *expected* to abuſe their power, and are incapable of anſwering the damages of ſeizing the perſons and papers of the innocent inſtead of the guilty. No man ought to be hindered ſaying or writing what he pleaſes on the conduct of thoſe who undertake the management of national affairs, in which all are concerned, and therefore have a right to inquire, and to publiſh their ſuſpicions concerning them. For if you puniſh the *ſlanderer*, you deter the *fair inquirer*. But even ſuppoſing *real* and juſtly puniſhable guilt, no ſubject is to be moleſted but on well-grounded ſuſpicion declared upon oath. Suppoſe the coroner's jury, upon a perſon found dead with marks of violence, brings in their verdict 'wilful murder againſt perſons unknown;'

a DEB. COM. VI. 60.

b LOND. MAG. *Aug.* 1766. p. 396.

'known;' we are not immediately to let loose a set of ruffian officers to seize and imprison the persons, rummage and expose the most secret papers, and carry off the bank-notes they find in the bureaus of the next twenty housekeepers. No; nor have our secretaries of state ever proceeded in this manner on such occasions. They have only broke loose upon the liberty of the subject when their maleadministrations have been exposed. Nor is this unnatural for such a sort of men. But what shall we think of a house of commons (once the constant and faithful guardians of our liberty, once our never-failing protectors against regal and ministerial encroachments), who refused to declare the lawless proceedings of secretaries of state unwarrantable, and supported their tyranny over the people, till a more faithful expounder of the law[a] wrenched it out of their hands?

The same year, 1766, a motion was made—but in vain—for abolishing the custom of the attorney general's *ex-officio*-informations, as oppressive to the subject, because that officer cannot be called to account for the damages suffered by innocent persons informed against by him.

It has been pretended, that it is impossible to administer government without general warrants. But this is a mistake. For all that is necessary, even when treasonable designs are suspected to be carrying on, is watchfulness in magistrates and officers to find out the guilty persons, who, when found or reasonably suspected, are to be apprehended by a special warrant from a magistrate, who is supposed to be a person of such fortune, as to be responsible for whatever damage an innocent person may suffer, if unjustly apprehended. and

[a] Lord *Camden*.

and imprisoned. Whereas to trust this power in the hands of a set of brutal and beggarly officers, is needlesly putting the safety of the best subjects in the power of the lowest of the people, unless the person who grants the general warrant be answerable for the behaviour of his officers, which is laying *him* at their mercy. If this be disputed, let it be considered, that supposing a set of persons taken up by general warrant, if they cannot be convicted, they must be set at liberty, whether guilty or innocent. And if they, or any of them, proves to be guilty, there must have been ways and means of fastening upon him sufficient suspicions to justify the issuing out a *special* warrant against him; else we must suppose the whole set taken at random, and the guilty afterwards found among them by chance. To issue a warrant for apprehending all persons who shall be found in the actual commission of punishable actions, may be at some times necessary; and this necessity does, in no respect, defend general warrants; because the confining of a warrant to those who are taken in circumstances of guilt, makes it a special warrant, and secures the innocent, (which is all that is wanted) from trouble.

To seize all the papers indiscriminately of the supposed writer of an accusation against a statesman, probably a just accusation (for there is little danger of accusing a statesman undeservedly), is treating the friend of his country, and detector of villany, worse than we treat a thief or a highwayman. For we seize nothing of what we find in the possession of such people, but what is likely to have been unfairly come by. But the truth is, neither thief nor murderer, is so much the object of a statesman's vengeance, as the man who detects and exposes ministerial rapacity.

In the pleadings for *Almon* againſt a writ of attachment, it was obſerved, that in proſecuting by attachment 'the court exerciſes the peculiar and diſtinct 'provinces of party, judge, evidence, and jury [a].'

It was, among other things, argued in defence of him againſt a writ of attachment, that Lord *M*—— had ſeveral methods of doing himſelf juſtice without this unconſtitutional one; he was a member of a moſt illuſtrious body, who would never ſuffer the ſlighteſt reflection on the character of any of their members to paſs unnoticed or uncenſured; that as a peer of the realm, he was entitled to his action of *ſcandalum magnatum*, wherein he need not fear but that a jury would give him a proper ſatisfaction for any injury he ſhould prove to them he had received.

Let us obſerve how differently different men have behaved in reſpect to liberty of ſpeech, and writing on political ſubjects.

Timoleon, when he was adviſed to puniſh one who had ſcandalized him, anſwered, 'So far from puniſhing 'on ſuch occaſions, I declare to you, that it has long 'been my prayer to the gods, that *Syracuſe* might be ſo 'free, that any man might ſay what he pleaſed of every 'perſon [b].'

Domitian encouraged the informers as much as *Titus* diſcouraged them [c].

Conſtantine puniſhed the *delatores*, or informers, with death [d].

Theodoſius repealed the laws againſt ſeditious words. 'If,' ſays he, 'ſuch words proceed from levity, they 'are

[a] Lond. Mag. *June* 1765, p. 310.

[b] *Corn. Nep.* Vit. Timol.

[c] Ant. Univ. Hist. xv. 54. [d] Ibid. 563.

'are to be despised; if from folly, to be pitied; if from 'malice, to be forgiven." [I suppose, because the malicious are sufficiently punished, by leaving them to their malice, and because the more injurious the offender, the more humanity, and the more christian spirit appears in forgiving him [a].]

Augustus used to say, *in liberâ civitate*, &c. 'In a 'free state, the tongues of the subjects ought to be free.'

The Abbé *de Thou* compliments *Henry* IV. of *France*, that his subjects might speak, as well as think, freely. *Tacitus* celebrates the Emperor *Trajan* on the same account.

Caligula rejected an information of a pretended conspiracy against his life, saying, 'I am not conscious to 'myself of any action that can deserve the hatred of 'any man, therefore I have no ears for informers [b]. Happy for himself and *Rome*, had he kept in this way of thinking! How pitiful the case of a prince or a statesman listening after railers and scribblers! How glorious that of the prince or statesman, whose rectitude of conduct enables them to rise superior to the malignancy of the envious and seditious!

Titus never shewed severity, but against informers [c]. If libellers attacked him unjustly, he held them more pitiable than blamable (because they made themselves odious); if they accused him justly, nothing could be more unjust than to punish them.

Mild means for this purpose are much preferable to severities. The intriguing *Spanish* ambassador *Gondomar* bribed even the ladies, to keep up such discourse at their routs as suited his purposes. Omits a present to Lady *Jacobs*. She resented it, and instead of returning

[a] Ant. Univ. Hist. xvi. 440. [b] Ibid. xiv. 266.
[c] Ibid. xv. 42.

ing his ſalute from her window, only gaped at him ſeveral times. He ſends to know her meaning. She anſwered, 'She had a mouth to ſtop, as well as other 'ladies [a].'

The *Czarina* [b] ſays, 'Great care ought to be taken 'in the examination of libels, how we extend the crime 'beyond a miſdemeanour ſubject to the police of a 'town or place, which is inferior to a crime; repre-'ſenting to ourſelves the danger of debaſing the human 'mind by reſtraint and oppreſſion, which can be pro-'ductive of nothing but ignorance, and muſt cramp 'and depreſs the riſing efforts of genius.'

Burnet makes no heſitation about the neceſſity of the government's having power to confine ſuſpected perſons in times of danger; but not of ſecurity [c]. It was propoſed by the lords, to make ſome limitations for ſeizing perſons, *A. D.* 1690. But it was rejected by the commons, and they thought it was better to leave the whole to parliament, that they might indemnify violations of *Magna Charta*, when they thought the miniſtry juſtifiable in ſeizing and confining ſuſpected perſons.

On occaſion of *Plunket*'s conſpiracy, *A. D.* 1723, ſeveral lords proteſted on paſſing the bill of attainder againſt him, for the following reaſons, which expreſs a noble ſpirit of liberty, and an amiable tenderneſs for the ſafety of accuſed ſubjects.

'1. Becauſe bills of this nature, as we conceive, 'ought not to paſs but in caſe of evident neceſſity, when 'the preſervation of the ſtate plainly requires it, which 'we take to be very far from the preſent caſe; the con-'ſpiracy having been detected ſo long ſince, and the

a *Rapin*, II. 200.

b *Czar*. INSTR. p. 186.

c *Burn*. HIST. OWN TIMES, III. 141.

'person accused seeming to us very inconsiderable in all 'respects, and who, from the many gross untruths it 'now appears he has written to his correspondents 'abroad, must appear to have been an impostor and de-'ceiver even to his own party. 2. Proceedings of this 'kind, tending to convict and punish, are in the nature, 'though not form, judicial, and do let the commons, 'in effect, into an equal share with the lords in judi-'cature, which the lords ought to be very jealous of 'doing, since the power of judicature is the greatest 'distinguishing power the lords have; and there will 'be little reason to hope, that if bills of this nature are 'given way to by the lords, the commons will ever 'bring up impeachments, or make themselves accusers 'only when they can act as judges. 3. This bill, in 'our opinion, differs materially from the precedents 'cited for it; as in the case of Sir *John Fenwick*, 'tis 'plain, by the preamble of that bill, that the ground 'most relied on to justify proceeding against him in 'that manner was, that there had been two legal wit-'nesses proving the high treason against him, that a 'bill was found against him on their evidence, and se-'veral times appointed him for a legal trial thereon, in 'the ordinary course, which he procured to be put off, 'by undertaking to discover, till one of the evidences 'withdrew; so that it was solely his fault that he had 'not a legal trial by jury; all which circumstances, 'not being in the present case, we take it they are not 'at all to be compared to one another. 4. As to the 'acts which passed to detain *Counter* and others con-'cerned in the conspiracy to assassinate the late King '*William*, of glorious memory, we conceive these acts 'were not in their nature bills of attainder, as this is; 'but purely to enable the crown to keep them in prison 'notwithstanding the laws of liberty; whereas this is a

'bill

'bill to inflict pains and penalties, and does import a 'conviction and sentence on the prisoner, not only to 'lose his liberty, but also his lands and tenements, 'goods and chattels, of which he having none, as we 'believe, we cannot apprehend why it was inserted, 'and this bill not drawn on the plan of *Counter*'s, &c. 'unless it was to make a precedent for such forfeitures 'in cases of bills which may hereafter be brought, to 'convict persons who have great estates, upon evidence 'which does not come up to what the law in being re- 'quires. 5. If there be a defect of legal evidence to 'prove this man guilty of high-treason, such defect 'always was, and, we think, bills of this nature 'brought to supply original defects in evidence do 'receive countenance, they may become familiar, and 'then many an innocent person may be reached by 'them, since 'tis hard to be distinguished, whether that 'defect proceeds from the cunning and artifice, or from 'the innocence of the party. 6. This proceeding by 'bill, does not only, in our opinion, tend to lay aside 'the judicial power of the lords, but even the use of 'juries; which distinguishes this nation from all its neigh- 'bours, and is of the highest value to all who rightly 'understand the security and other benefits arising 'from it; and whatever tends to alter or weaken that 'great privilege, we think, is an alteration in our 'constitution for the worse, though it be done by act 'of parliament; and if it may be supposed, that any of 'our fundamental laws were set aside by act of parlia- 'ment, the nation, we apprehend, would not be at 'all the more comforted from that consideration, that 'the parliament did it. 7. It is the essence of natural 'justice, as we think, but is most surely the law of the 'realm, that no person should be tried more than once 'for the same crime, or twice put in peril of losing his 'life, liberty, or estate; and though we acquiesce in 'the opinion of all the judges, that if this bill should 'pass into a law, *Plunket* cannot be again prosecuted 'for the crimes contained in the preamble of the bill, 'yet it is certain, that if a bill of this kind should hap-'pen to be rejected by either house of parliament, or by 'the king, the person accused might be attacked again 'and again in like manner, in any subsequent session 'of parliament, or indeed for the same offence, notwith-'standing that either house of parliament should have 'found him innocent, and not passed the bill for that 'reason; and we conceive it a very great exception to 'this course of proceeding, that a subject may be 'condemned and punished, but not acquitted by it.

'8. We think it appears in all our history, that the 'passing bills of attainder as this, we think, in its na-'ture, is, (except, as before is said, in cases of absolute 'and clear necessity) have proved so many blemishes to 'the reigns in which they passed; and therefore we 'thought it our duty in time, and before the passing 'this bill as a precedent, to give our advice and votes 'against the passing it, being very unwilling that any 'thing should pass which, in our opinions, would in 'the least derogate from the glory of this reign.

'9. We apprehended it to be more for the interest and 'security of his Majesty's government, that bills of 'this nature should not pass than that they should, 'since persons who think at all, cannot but observe, 'that in this case, some things have been received as 'evidence, which would not have been received in any 'court of judicature; that precedents of this kind are 'naturally growing, as we think, this goes beyond any 'other which has happened since the Revolution, and 'if from such like observations they shall infer, as we 'cannot but do, that the liberty and prosperity of the

'subject

'subject becomes, by such examples, in any degree more 'precarious than they were before, it may cause an 'abatement of zeal for a government founded on the 'Revolution, which cannot, as we think, be compen-'sated by any of the good consequences which are 'hoped for by those who approve this bill[a].'

A. D. 1640, the Earl of *Warwick* and Lord *Brook* were apprehended, and their papers seized, on suspicion of rebellious designs, by warrants from the secretaries of state. They complained of breach of privilege, which it was not, because the supposed crime is not covered by privilege. The warrant was declared illegal; and the proceeding a breach of privilege, because the two lords were in parliament. Satisfaction was made to them, and the clerk of the council brought on his knees before the lords, and afterwards committed to prison.

A. D. 1680, the Lord Chief Justice *Scraggs*'s general warrants for seizing libels, books, pamphlets, &c. were declared by the house of commons arbitrary and illegal, and he was impeached.

A. D. 1692, complaint was made by Lord *Marlborough* and others, of a breach of privilege, they being committed to the Tower, without information upon *oath*, and bail refused, in time of privilege. On this occasion, a bill was proposed to indemnify secretaries of state for such committments in treasonable cases, and to limit their powers by law. But that incorrupt house of commons would only resolve, that such powers being illegal, secretaries of state should exercise them at their own peril, to be condemned or justified according to the case[b].

 One

[a] Deb. Peers, iii. 280.

[b] *Alm.* Deb. Com. vi, 282.

One *Spence*, was taken up at *London*, *A. D.* 1684, on suspicion of being concerned in a plot against *Charles* II. He was sent to *Scotland* to be examined. There he was required to take an oath to answer all questions that should be put to him. 'This,' says *Burnet*, 'was done in 'direct contradiction to an express law against obliging 'men to swear, that they will answer *super inquirendis*.' The poor wretch was struck in the boots, he was kept from sleep nine days and nights, and afterwards put to the torture of the thumbkins, till he fainted away[a]. See also the horrible cruelties inflicted, about the same time, on *Baillie* and others[b].

Three peers and the bishop of *London*, publickly opposed *James*'s dispensing with the test for papists[c].

Even under *James* II, the judicious part of the house of commons proposed to demand redress of grievances, before they granted supplies[d].

Mr. *Cooke*, a member, was sent to the Tower for saying, 'We are *Englishmen*. We are not to be threat'ened.' He was an *Englishman*. But what were they who sent him to the Tower for such a speech?

A. D. 1728, a bill was brought into the house of commons, to prohibit lending money to foreign princes, &c. with a clause, that the attorney-general be impowered by an *English* bill in the court of exchequer, to compel the effectual discovery on oath of any such loans, and that in default of answer to such bill, the court shall decree a limited sum against the defendant refusing to answer. This was like examining by interrogatories.

Walpole said, the same strictness was observed before, in prohibiting commerce with the *Ostend* Company. But

[a] *Burn.* HIST. OWN TIMES, II. 252. [b] Ibid.
[c] Ibid. 356. [d] Ibid. 358.

But Sir *J. Barnard* ſaid, the liberties of *Engliſhmen* were weightier than any arbitrary precedent.

A. D. 1690, when the ſubſcriptions of ſeveral lords were forged to certain treaſonable papers, which was a direct attempt on the very lives of thoſe noblemen, the offenders, though clearly convicted, were only puniſhed with whipping and the pillory, which, to the reproach of our conſtitution, is the only puniſhment our law has yet provided for ſuch practices [a].

Some lords proteſted, *A. D.* 1692, againſt ſubjecting the preſs to the 'arbitrary will of a mercenary, and perhaps ignorant, licenſer,' to the checking of learning, the damage of literary property, and encouragement of monopolies [b].

Many printers were indicted for ſcandalous and ſeditious libels, *A. D.* 1681. The juries brought them off by not finding the writings malicious or ſeditious, and returned for verdict *ignoramus* [c]. They did not bring in for their verdict 'Guilty of printing and publiſhing only,' or, 'Guilty of what has no guilt in it,' which we have lately ſeen done by a learned jury.

In the reign of *George* I, was induſtriouſly ſpread into many parts of the kingdom, ſoon after his acceſſion, a pamphlet, intitled, *Engliſh Advice to the Freeholders of Great Britain.* Government offered 1000l. for diſcovering the author, and 500 l. for the printer. In vain it was ſuppoſed to have been written by *Atterbury.* Anſwers were publiſhed; which was wiſer than ſetting a price on the author and printer [d].

A. D. 1770, it was matter of much ſpeculation, that a bookſeller ſhould be puniſhed for his ſervant's ſelling a book

[a] *Burn.* HIST. OWN TIMES, III. 141.

[b] DEB. PEERS, I. 419.

[c] *Burn.* HIST. OWN TIMES, II. 136.

[d] *Tind.* CONTIN. I. 414.

a book which was brought into his ſhop, while he was out of town, and though proof was offered, that the bookſeller diſallowed the ſelling of the book [a]. The bookſeller was put to 140 l. expence, and obliged to find bail to the value of 800 l.

Theſe ſeverities upon private perſons, who write and ſpeak freely of miniſterial conduct, would, by an incorrupt parliament be immediately reſtrained, and the ſubjects be ſet at liberty to remark as they pleaſed, upon the conduct of thoſe who undertook the management of their affairs; but while miniſters have a ſcheme of iniquity to carry on, it is not to be wondered that they endeavour, by all manner of ſeverities, to drive away thoſe who come with prying eyes to inquire into their proceedings.

[a] *Alm.* Deb. Com, ix. 74.

CON-

CONCLUSION.

Addreſſed to the independent Part of the People of GREAT-BRITAIN, IRELAND, and the COLONIES.

My dear Countrymen and Fellow-ſubjects,

I HAVE in theſe volumes laid before you a faithful and a dreadful account of what is, or is likely ſoon to be, the condition of public affairs in this great empire. I have expoſed to your view ſome of the capital abuſes and grievances, which are ſinking you into ſlavery and deſtruction. I have ſhewn you, that as things go on, there will ſoon be very little left of the *Britiſh* conſtitution, beſides the name and the outward form. I have ſhewn you, that the houſe of repreſentatives, upon which all depends, has loſt its efficiency, and, inſtead of being (as it ought) a check upon regal and miniſterial tyranny, is in the way to be ſoon a mere outwork of the court, a *French* parliament to regiſter the royal edicts, a *Roman* ſenate in the imperial times, to give the appearance of regular and free government; but in truth, to accompliſh the villanous ſchemes of a profligate junto, the natural conſequences and unavoidable effects of inadequate repreſentation, ſeptennial parliaments, and placemen in the houſe. All which ſhews the abſolute neceſſity of regulating repreſentation, of reſtoring our parliaments to their primitive annual period, and of diſqualifying dependents on the court from voting in the houſe of commons.

I am

I am miftaken, if there be not many perfons of confequence in the ftate, who, by reading thefe collections, will fee the condition of public affairs to be much more diforderly than they could have imagined. For my own part, though I have long been accuftomed to look upon my country with fear and anxiety, I own frankly, that till I faw the abufes and the dangers difplayed in *one view*, I did not fee things in the horrid light I now do. Nor can I expect the readers of thefe volumes to fee them in the fame light, becaufe thefe volumes do not contain all the abufes I have collected, though they contain enough to put out of all doubt the neceffity of redrefs; as a prudent perfon, if he obferved one of his out-houfes on fire, would extinguifh it in all hafte, though he did not think his dwelling houfe in immediate hazard. I wifh we could fay, it is only an outwork that is in danger. The main body of the building, the parliament itfelf, on which all depends, is in a ruinous condition. Accordingly, I have not in the foregoing part of this work amufed you, my good countrymen, with a fet of frivolous or trifling remarks upon grievances which, though removed, would ftill leave others remaining, to the great diftrefs and difadvantage of the fubjects. The grievances I have pointed out, are fuch as all difinterefted men muft allow to be real; and fuch as, if redreffed, would infure the redrefs of all other grievances of inferior confequence; which is more than can be faid of many of thofe that have been pointed out in our late petitions and remonftrances. Concerning them wife and good men, and true friends to liberty, have differed; but no wife and good man, or true friend to liberty, can doubt, whether *England* can be fafe with a corrupt parliament, and the various other diforders and abufes

above

above pointed out, remaining unredressed and uncorrected.

Nor have I, my good countrymen, advised you to repose your confidence in one set of men rather than another. I have not told you, that the *Rockingham* party can save you any more than the *Bedford* party. I have not advised you to put your trust in Lord *Bute* rather than Lord *Chatham*. The truth is, that any set of ministers must misconduct the affairs of the nation, so long as the nation itself is upon a bad footing. And it is equally true, that an incorrupt parliament will make any ministry upright.

'The wisdom of these latter times in princes' affairs, 'is rather fine deliveries, and shiftings of dangers and 'mischiefs when they are near, than solid or grounded 'courses to keep them aloof [a].'

Have I, my good countrymen, imposed upon you in the least article? Can you seriously bring yourselves even to doubt, whether the grievances I have pointed out, be really such? Do you sincerely believe it possible to go on in the track we are now in? Is there a shadow of consistency between the present state of our public affairs, and liberty, safety, peace, or the *British* constitution? While the enemies of your liberties are active and vigilant to seize every opportunity for increasing their own emoluments, and their own power, and you are timid and thoughtless of your own safety, will your public grievances redress themselves? Will corruption and venality die away of course, or will they spread wider and wider, and take still deeper root, till at last it will become impossible to eradicate them? Look into the *Roman* history, and see how corruption in the people, and tyranny in the emperors, went

[a] *Bac.* ESSAYS.

went on increasing from *Augustus* to *Didius*, who fairly bought the empire, when it was put up to sale. Look back but a little way into your own history. It is but 86 years since the Revolution, a very short period, a lifetime! Yet we have not been able, or have not been willing, to keep up, for this short time, the constitution then settled, because indeed it was so imperfectly established at that time, and because we have been almost ever since in the hands of a set of foreign kings, and of flagitious ministers, which last have traitorously abused your easy generosity, and have, by introducing corruption, in great measure undone what was done by expelling the *Stuarts*. The standing army, the number of placemen in the house, the extension of excise-laws, and various other abuses, have crept on still increasing, till at last they are settled into a part of the constitution, and what formerly produced severe remonstrances, and violent debates in parliament, pass now unquestioned, and without debate or division.

Some unthinking, or interested, or timid people among us, insist, that there is no need of any reformation; that all is safe and secure; whilst others of a more dejected disposition allege, that all is gone past recovery; that reformation is chimerical and impossible; and that we have nothing left, but to sink as quietly as we can into ruin, bankruptcy, slavery, and whatever else we have brought upon ourselves. These opinions cannot both be right, because they are diametrically opposite; but they may, and I hope are, both wrong.

It is the cant of the court. 'Representation has 'always been inadequate; parliaments have long been 'septennial; place-men have sat long in the house.' So king *John* told his barons, 'The privileges granted 'by *Henry* I. have been long lost; you have been long 'in 'in a state of very imperfect liberty.' So at the Revolution the *Jacobites* might have said, 'The *Stuart* government has been long established. Why should 'the house of *Orange* be brought in, &c.?' This way of arguing is all heels uppermost. The longer grievances have continued, the more reason for redressing them.

Ministers think themselves in duty bound to their utmost to persuade you, my good countrymen, that all is safe. Yet it is strange, that they should think you so very easy of belief, that they should put into certain speeches assertions so very liable to contradiction. 'I can have no other interest, than to reign in 'the hearts of a free and happy people *.' That a particular prince may *actually* have, upon the whole, no interest different from that of his subjects, may be affirmed; but to say, he *can* have no other, or, 'that 'it is not *possible*, he should think himself interested in 'pursuing measures hurtful to his subjects;' is asserting what all history confutes. If there were a natural impossibility in the prince's gaining by the subject's loss, (as it is impossible, for instance, the king of *Bantam* should be advantaged by *Britain*'s being too heavily taxed) this might have been affirmed. But will any man say, it *can* be no more advantage to one of our kings, than to the king of *Bantam*, that the civil list revenue be double? If this cannot be said, neither can it be said, that our kings '*can* have no other 'interest, than to reign in the hearts of a free and 'happy people.'

Again, in the same spirit. 'The support of our constitution is our common duty and interest. By that 'standard I would wish my people to try all public 'principles

* Speech, *A. D.* 1771, *Alm. Deb. Com.* ix. 308.

'principles and professions.' Excellent! If it were but well founded. But what is our constitution? *Ans.* Government by king, lords, and commons. Do we enjoy the spirit and efficiency of this constitution? The king does no evil. But does not the *court* influence the greatest part of our elections? Do not many of the lords extend their power beyond their own house? Can the house of commons be called even the shadow of a representation of the property of the people? Are septennial parliaments the constitution? Is a house of commons filled with placemen and pensioners the constitution? Is the *ministry's* assuming in parliament the power and place of king, lords, and commons, the constitution? Will any man deny, that this has of late years been too much the state of things? Is not then a ministry's recommending the support of our constitution, while our constitution is almost annihilated, a solemn mockery? Is there any means for supporting the constitution, besides restoring it to its true spirit and efficiency by shortening parliaments, by making representation adequate, by incapacitating placemen and pensioners, &c. Ought not these salutary reformations to have been the burden of this speech, of every speech, and not recommendations to the members to lull the people in their several countries into a fatal security, which the speeches call submission to government, and supporting the constitution? Does not this shew you, my good countrymen, what hands you are in?

Compare the lullaby strain of this speech, with the complaints in the petition of the livery of *London* to the king, in the year 1769, two years before the date of the above speech. The speech represents all as safe and secure. But the speech is penned by those whose interest it is to have you believe that all is well. The petition

petition comes from the independent, unbiassed people, who *feel*, that all is not well.

The chief complaints in it are, that the ministry had invaded the right of trial by jury; had made use of the illegal courses of general warrants, and seizure of papers; had evaded the *habeas corpus* act; had punished [*Bingley*] without trial, conviction, or sentence; had used the military, where the peace-officers were sufficient, and had murdered the subjects, whom they ought only to have apprehended; had screened murderers convict of their own party; had established unjust and arbitrary taxes in the colonies; had procured the rejection from a seat in parliament, of a member no way unqualified by law, and the reception of one not chosen by a majority of the electors; had procured the payment of pretended deficiencies in the civil list without examination; had rewarded, instead of punishing, the public defaulter of unaccounted millions, &c. Heavy grievances all! But these were not the worst. What they should have dwelt upon, was, inadequate representation, septennial parliaments, ministerial influence in parliament, &c. Can it then be said, my good countrymen, that all is safe, and there is no need of any reformation?

Mr. *Page*, member for *Chichester*, in his very judicious farewell to his constituents, says, 'the *British* 'constitution is going to ruin faster than perhaps ap'pears to the common eye[a].'

Again, it is said, by the lullers, 'what probability 'that 800 men of property should enslave their coun'try?'

Who would have thought that the *Roman* senate, men of great property, would join the triumviri, whose

[a] LOND. CHRON. *October* 2, 1767.

whose visible design was to enslave their country? Who would have thought, that, when *Julius* was cut off, and a door again opened for the restoration of liberty, the men of property would not all join the party of *Brutus* and *Cassius*? Who would have thought, that, when the men of property saw the army of *Brutus* and *Cassius* equal to that of the tyrant at *Philippi*, they should not all, as one man, repair to the standard of liberty?

The destroyers of the virtue and liberty of the *Romans*, brought that once virtuous and free people to think the imperial form of government necessary. A corrupt government in *England* may bring the people to wish to be rid of parliaments.

'The crown of *Denmark* was elective, and subject 'to a senate. In one day, it was, without any visi-'ble force, changed into hereditary, and absolute, no 'rebellion, nor convulsion of state following[a].' So soon may a nation lose its liberties. This was mentioned to *Charles* II. by his courtiers, when they encouraged him to make himself absolute[b].

The crown of *Sweden* was formerly elective, with narrow powers and prerogatives. Nobles and clergy, encroaching and tyrannical, used to decide their quarrels by private wars; which produced continual scenes of confusion and cruelty. *Gustavus Ericson* being successful against the tyrannical *Danes*, who lorded it over *Sweden* and other countries, gains the affections of the *Swedes*. They enlarge his privileges, to render him more powerful against the *Danes*. They give him church lands, and humble the tyrannical clergy. The reformation prevailing in *Sweden*, *Gustavus* takes the opportunity of demolishing the Roman catholics,

[a] *Burn.* Hist. own Times, I. 377.

[b] Ibid.

catholics, on pretence of favouring *Luther*. *Gustavus* thus becomes absolute, and the crown of *Sweden* hereditary. Afterwards the crown was reduced again. After that, the senate was abolished by *Charles* IX. who becomes one of the most absolute princes of *Europe*, in consequence of a pretended misbehaviour of the senate. Thus the *Swedish* monarchs were once limited and elected; then absolute, and hereditary; then limited again; then absolute again; then limited after the tyrant *Charles* IX. and then absolute in the time of *Charles* XII. and then limited again, and now totally enslaved. For *Eleonora Ulrica*, upon *Charles* XIIth's death, offered the states of *Sweden* conditions, if they would elect her, and set aside the duke of *Holstein*, the more lineal heir. They elected and limited her effectually. But the people are enslaved still to the nobles, and the nation to the sovereign [a]. So unsteady and fluctuating has the political barometer of *Sweden* been; and so variable and so precarious a thing is liberty. Have you not then, my good countrymen, reason to be jealous of your liberties?

I cannot help considering judge *Blackstone* as one of the many among us, who endeavour to lull us asleep in this time of danger. I own I do not understand his ideas of free government.

'Wherever, says he [b], the law expresses its distrust 'of abuse of power, it always vests a superior coercive 'authority in some other hand to correct it; the very 'notion of which destroys the idea of sovereignty. If, 'therefore, for example, the two houses of parliament, 'or either of them, had avowedly a right to animadvert 'on the king, or each other, or if the king had a right 'to animadvert on either of the houses, that branch of 'the

[a] Mod. Univ. Hist. xxxiii. 10, 13, 14.

[b] Com. i. 244.

'the legislature so subject to animadversion, would instantly cease to be part of the supreme power; the balance of the constitution would be overturned; and that branch or branches, in which this jurisdiction resided, would be completely sovereign. The supposition of *law* therefore is, that neither the king, nor either house of parliament (collectively taken) is capable of doing any wrong; since in such cases the law feels itself incapable of furnishing any adequate remedy. For which reason all oppressions, which may happen to spring from any branch of the sovereign power, must necessarily be out of the reach of any *stated rule*, or *express legal* provision; but if ever they unfortunately happen, the prudence of the times must provide new remedies upon new emergencies.'

Here the learned judge tells us, that, because neither can the king exercise an arbitrary restraining power over either of the houses of parliament, nor either or both houses of parliament over the king,——therefore what?——Therefore 'the supposition of *law* is, that none of the three branches of the legislature can do wrong, because the law feels itself incapable of furnishing an adequate remedy.' If the law, or the lawyers, suppose, that none of the three branches of the legislature is capable of doing wrong, for that they are supreme, and whatever the supreme power establishes must of course be right, as none can say to the supreme power, what dost thou? yet history shews, that king, lords, and commons, have often (as was to be expected from the weakness of human nature) done very wrong things. And though the law 'feels itself incapable of furnishing any adequate remedy;' does it therefore follow, that there is no adequate remedy? The judge says, the prudence of future times must find new remedies upon new emergencies; and afterwards

afterwards adds, that we have a precedent in the Revolution of 1688, to shew what may be done, if a king runs away, as *James* II. did. Insinuating, that, if we had not such a precedent, we should not know how to proceed in such a case; and says expressly, that 'so 'far as this precedent leads, and no farther, we may *now* 'be allowed to lay down the *law* of redress against public 'oppression.' Yet he says, p. 245. that 'necessity and the 'safety of the whole, may require the exertion of those 'inherent (though latent) powers of society, which no 'climate, no time, no constitution, no contract, can 'ever destroy, or diminish.' For my part, I cannot see the use of all this hesitating, and mincing the matter. Why may we not say at once, that without any urgency of distress, without any provocation by oppression of government, and though the safety of the whole should not appear to be in any immediate danger, if the people of a country think they should be, in any respect, happier under republican government, than monarchical, or under monarchical than republican, and find, that they can bring about a change of government, without greater inconveniencies than the future advantages are likely to balance; why may we not say, that they have a sovereign, absolute, and uncontrolable right to change or new-model their government as they please? The authority of government, in short, is only superior to a minority of the people. The majority of the people are, rightfully, superior to it. Wherever a government assumes to itself a power of opposing the sense of the majority of the people, it declares itself a proper and formal tyranny in the fullest, strongest, and most correct sense of the word. I must therefore beg leave to submit to the public, whether the learned judge is not clearly erroneous in his meaning, as well as his words, when he ſays, p. 251, that ‘ na-‘ tional diſtreſs alone can juſtify eccentrical remedies ‘ applied by the people.’ I think I may ſafely defy all the world to prove, that there is any neceſſity of any diſtreſs, or of any reaſon aſſigned for a people's altering, at any time, the whole plan of government, that has been eſtabliſhed in their country for a thouſand years; beſides their will and pleaſure. I am not ſpeaking of the *prudence* of ſuch a ſtep; nor do I juſtify a people's propoſing to alter their conſtitution, if ſuch alteration is likely to be followed by worſe evils, than it is likely to redreſs; nor have I any thing to ſay concerning the difficulty of obtaining the real ſenſe of the majority of a great nation. But I aſſert, that, ſaving the laws of prudence, and of morality, the people's mere abſolute, ſovereign will and pleaſure, is a ſufficient reaſon for their making any alteration in their form of government. The truth is therefore, that the learned judge has placed the ſovereignty wrong, viz. in the government; whereas it ſhould have been in the people, next, and immediately under God. For the people give to their governors all the rightful power they have. But no body ever heard of the governors giving power to the people. If the teachers of the exploded doctrine of the divine right of kings, had taught the divine right of the people, they had ſtated that point in a juſt and proper manner.

The more impudent part of our court-men, if you expreſs anxiety about the ſtate of public liberty, will aſk you, Whether you think the miniſtry are a ſet of *Turks*, who want to introduce at once the bamboo, and the bow-ſtring, or a ſet of cannibals who want to eat all the friends of liberty? Hear the excellent lord *Strange* on the *gradual* and imperceptible, and therefore more formidable progress of tyranny in countries once free [a].

'Whilst arbitrary power is in its infancy, and creeping up by degrees to man's estate, no doubt it will, it *must*, refrain from acts of violence and compulsion. It will by bribery gain the consent of these it has not as yet got strength enough to compel; but when it is by bribery grown up to its full strength and vigour, even bribery itself will be neglected, and whoever then opposes its views will be ruined, either by open violence, or false informations, and cooked up prosecutions. I shall grant, Sir, that if the question were put in plain and direct terms, no man, or at least very few, would agree to give up their property in their estates for the sake of a much greater estate or pension depending upon the will of an arbitrary sovereign. But such a question never was, nor ever will be, put by those who aim at arbitrary power. They always find specious pretences for some new powers, or some little increase of power, and then another new power, or another little increase of power, till at last their power becomes by degrees uncontrolable; and men of corrupt hearts, are by mercenary motives prevented from considering or foreseeing the consequences of the new or additional powers they grant. It is, I think, highly probable, that *Julius Cæsar* had laid the scheme of enslaving his country, before he obtained the province of *Transalpine Gaul*. For this purpose he rightly judged, that it was necessary to get a great army under his command, and by his continuance in success in that command, to render that army more attached to him than the laws and liberties of their country. For

[a] DEB. COMM. XIV. 41.

obtaining that command, and for continuing in it, he knew he must depend upon the votes of his fellow-citizens. If he had told his fellow-citizens, that he wanted from them such an army as might enable him to oppress the liberties of his country, they would certainly have refused it. Notwithstanding the avarice, luxury, and selfishness then prevailing amongst them, he could not by all his bribery have got them to agree to such a direct question. He therefore at first proposed to them to give him the command of *Cisalpine Gaul*, with *Illyria* annexed, which by bribery, and by having insinuated himself into great favour with the people, he obtained; and by the same means he got the *Transalpine Gaul* added to it. This gave him the command of a great army, and the people being blinded by his largesses and his successes, they continued him in that command, till he made his army so absolutely his own, that it established him in arbitrary power, and so effectually destroyed the liberties of the people, that they could never again be restored; for the short interval between his death and the establishment of his successor, *Augustus Cæsar*, was no free or regular government, but a continued series of usurpation, murder, and civil war. If the people of *Rome*, Sir, had foreseen the consequences of their favours to *Julius Cæsar*, they would certainly have refused granting him so many; but they were so blinded by their corruption, that they did not consider the consequences. This destroyed irrecoverably that glorious republic, and this will destroy every republic, where any one man has wealth or power enough to corrupt a great number of the people.'

It is the common cant of the court-sycophants, 'The army has never yet enslaved you. The laws, which

'which you thought ſo dangerous when firſt enacted, 'have not ruined you. What do you fear from the 'government?' &c.

Now though we were to own that we are not yet ruined; though we ſhould go ſo far as to hope againſt hope, that the national debt, for inſtance, inſtead of going on increaſing, will, by ſome unknown means, be reduced; though we ſhould grant the poſſibility of corruption's falling into diſgrace, inſtead of its ſpreading wider and wider, as it has done in all the ſtates where it has to a great degree prevailed; granting all this, and more, muſt we therefore ſay we are in a ſtate of ſafety? The army is compoſed of *Engliſhmen*; the magiſtrates and peace-officers are *Engliſhmen*. There is a native generoſity in the hearts of ninety-nine in every hundred *Engliſhmen*, of the middling and lower ranks of life, which prevents their making a violent or unjuſtifiable uſe of power. But are we therefore obliged to traitorous miniſters, who bribe worthleſs parliaments to keep up armies, and enact laws, which our good-nature only prevents our applying to miſchievous purpoſes againſt one another? What ſhould we think of thoſe parents who gave their children leave to beat one another? Should we juſtify the parents becauſe the children, being of gentle tempers, had made no bad uſe of their liberty? Should we not every day, and every hour, expect to hear of ſome bad conſequence of ſuch management?

Suppoſe the *people* to have had as little humanity as their *governors*, what havock would not have been made by the ſmuggling act, the game acts, the intolerant acts, &c.!

The *French* King had an army, and conſequently power to compel the parliament of *Paris* to regiſter his edicts, long before he actually attempted it. When he he did attempt it, he found he could do it. Now he has swept the parliament themselves away. Who can tell what a daring and flagitious ministry in *England*, with the advantages now in their hands, could effectuate to the prejudice of liberty, and what they may effectuate very suddenly?

Is this state of dependence upon the generosity of the individuals, who fill the throne and the seats round it, who compose the army, the magistracy, *&c.* fit for this great empire to continue in? Will the *British* people be contented to lie at mercy?

'Some persons, says lord *Bolingbroke*, are often calling 'upon and defying people to instance any one article of 'liberty, or security for liberty, which we once had, and 'do not still hold and enjoy. I desire leave to ask them, 'whether long parliaments are the same thing as having 'frequent elections?—Is the circumstance of having 'almost 200 members of the house of commons vested 'with offices or places under the crown, the same 'thing as having a law that would have excluded all 'persons who hold places from sitting there?—Is an 'army of above 17,000 men at the expence of 850,000 *l.* '*per Annum*, for the service of *Great Britain*, the same 'thing as an army of 7000 men at the expence of '350,000 *l. per Annum* for *England*; and I will suppose there might be about 3000 men more for *Scotland*?—Is the riot act, which establishes passive obedience and non-resistance by a law even in cases of 'the utmost extremity, the same thing as leaving the 'people at liberty to redress themselves, when they are 'grievously oppressed, and thereby oblige the prince in 'some measure to depend on their affections[a]?'

'Upon

[a] *Bolingbr.* POLIT. TRACTS, 295.

'Upon a moderate computation (says Mr. *Hume*[a]), 'there are near three millions at the disposal of the 'crown. The civil list amounts to near a million; 'the collection of all taxes to another million; and 'the employments in the army and navy, together with 'ecclesiastical preferments, to above a third million. 'An enormous sum, and what may fairly be computed 'to be more than a thirtieth part of the whole income 'and labour of the kingdom. When we add to this 'immense property the increasing luxury of the nation, 'our proneness to corruption, together with the great 'power and prerogatives of the crown, and the com-'mand of such numerous military forces, there is no 'one but must despair of being able, without extraor-'dinary efforts, to support our free government much 'longer under all these disadvantages.'

Judge *Blackstone* says[b], 'The constitution of *England* 'had arrived to its full vigour, and the true balance 'between liberty and prerogative was happily esta-'blished by law in the reign of *Charles* II.' And that 'the people had as large a portion of real liberty as is 'consistent with a state of society, and sufficient power 'residing in their own hands, to assert and preserve 'that liberty, if invaded by the royal prerogative,' is evident, he thinks, from the people's effectually resist-ing *James* II. in his attempts to enslave them, and oblig-ing him to quit his enterprise and his throne together. Now we know, that since the days of *James* II. a great deal has been pretended to be done for *enlarging* and *strengthening* liberty, and enabling the people to assert and preserve it. Judge *Blackstone* fills two large pages with only the heads of what has been done since the Revolution

---

[a] *Hume*, I. 86.

[b] *Blackst.* COMM. IV. 432.

Revolution for the advantage of public liberty, and of private justice; as the bill of rights; the toleration-act; the act of settlement; the union of the two kingdoms; the confirming and exemplifying the doctrine of resistance; establishing the authority of the laws, and maintenance of the constitution above the royal prerogative; overthrowing the sovereign's dispensing power; religious toleration [which however is still miserably defective] exclusion of many placemen from the house of commons [another improvement likewise very defective], and many others. So that in our times, the people ought to have much more power of redress in their own hands, than they had in those days. How is it then, that it is so common to hear the condition of our country given up as desperate? Are we in a worse situation than in the days of *James* II.?

If we be more corrupt than in the days of *James* II. if the court has more to give, and the members of the house of commons are more ready to receive, than in those days; and if, besides, we have more to fear from the army than our fathers before the Revolution, we are in a worse situation for resisting tyranny than they were, and are only in a more eligible state, in as much as the character of the princes of the house of *Hanover* is less formidable to liberty than that of the *Stuarts*. This, then, is the slender thread upon which the freedom of the once illustrious *British* empire is suspended. Our liberties lie at the footstool of the throne, but our kings and ministers have hitherto been either too timid or too good to seize them.

Even the learned commentator himself, who shews no disposition to find fault without reason, finishes his encomium on the improvements which law and liberty have gained since the Revolution, with the alarming words which follow: 'Though these provisions have

 'nominally,

'nominally, and, in appearance, reduced the strength 'of the executive power to a much lower ebb, than in 'the preceding period; if, on the other hand, we 'throw into the opposite scale (what perhaps the immo-'derate reduction of the ancient prerogative may have 'rendered in some degree necessary) the vast acquisition 'of force arising from the riot-act, and the annual ex-'pedience of a standing army; and the vast acquisition 'of personal attachment, arising from the magnitude 'of the national debt, and the manner of levying those 'yearly millions that are appropriated to pay the in-'terest; we shall find that the crown has gradually and 'imperceptibly gained almost as much in influence as it 'has apparently lost in prerogative [a].'

Upon this paragraph I cannot help making a few strictures. What may the learned judge mean by the *immoderate* reduction of the ancient prerogative? Have not the *people* power to fix the prerogative of their kings where they please? Is that immoderate, or in any respect wrong, which pleases the people? If a king thinks his prerogative too much retrenched by his people, has he any thing to do but decline the crown, and leave it to one who will accept it with such limitations as shall please the people, who have a right to be pleased?

Again, when the learned judge was summing up the disadvantages to liberty, which have arisen since the Revolution, how could he miss taking notice of the greatest, viz. The total loss of the parliament's efficiency (the present always excepted) for resisting court influence, and obtaining for the people whatever laws and regulations they may think necessary for their safety?

The

[a] *Blackst.* COMM. I. 334, 5, 6. 412, 13, 16.

The difference between the condition of the *British* empire with an independent parliament, and with a parliament influenced, not to say *enslaved*, by a designing court, is so great, that it may be said to be the whole. The former to be, humanly speaking, absolute safety, and the latter certain ruin. How then could our learned commentator overlook the mountain, and fix his eye upon a set of molehills?

The court-sycophants, whose business it is to lull us asleep, are wont to sooth us by telling us, that no harm is yet come of the army, or the excise, or parliamentary corruption. Were this true, which is far from being the case, it would be nothing to the purpose; for so it might have been said at the beginning of almost every tyranny. No people ever, from free, became absolute slaves in one day, but the *Danes*.

Some among us are ever magnifying the great advantages we gained by the Revolution; thereby insinuating, that we do not want any farther improvements upon public liberty.

So our bishops, and other high-church-men, are always celebrating the great advantages which religion gained by the Reformation, in order to damp our pursuit of what (as has lately been made fully to appear) we still want to set us upon a foot tolerably favourable to truth, and liberty of conscience.

But without disparagement to the great and undeniable advantages we gained by the expulsion of the *Stuarts*, it must be owned, that the Revolution was but an imperfect redress of grievances.

Let us hear Lord *Perceval* on the subject:

'The Revolution,' says he in the House of Commons, *A. D.* 1744, 'was brought about so suddenly, 'and in such a manner, that it is rather a wonder, that

'we

'we gained what we did, than that we gained no more. 'The Prince of *Orange* was in effect our King the 'moment that he landed; backed with a great army, 'supported by men who, having called him in, could 'not quarrel with him without ruining themselves. 'It was too late to make terms with a Prince who was 'already possessed of the regal power, and who plainly 'shewed, that though he desired to be ruled by law, 'he still intended that the law should not bear much 'harder upon the crown during his reign, than it had 'done in former times[a].'

Whilst some false brethren among us sooth us to repose by telling us all is well, others on the contrary affect, as above observed, to conclude all endeavours vain for recovering a state so far gone as the *British* in luxury and corruption. Thus we find a pretence, of one kind or another, for deserting our country.

States, they cry, have their old age, decay, and death, as individuals. And when the fatal hour is come, the efforts of the physician, and of the patriot, prove equally ineffectual.

We know, that the health and life of the individual are limited within the boundaries of seventy or eighty years; that a few, a very few, exceed those limits; and that no individual since the deluge has reached two hundred. But the durations of states regulate by no laws of nature; nor can my inestimable friend Dr. *Price* construct any tables of the physical probabilities of the continuance of kingdoms or commonwealths. His sagacity can reach no farther than to affirm, that any country will continue free, while it deserves to be free, and contrariwise.

The

[a] *Alm.* DEB. COM. I. 273.

The affairs of nations ſeldom continue long in the ſame condition. When tyranny goes beyond a certain pitch, it ſometimes draws upon itſelf the united vengeance of the people, which cruſhes it. When liberty degenerates into lawleſs corruption of manners, a nation becomes the prey of the ambition and tyranny either of an overgrown ſubject, or of a foreign invader. This unſteadineſs of human affairs is cauſed either by a conſtitution originally deficient, and ill-balanced, or by a deviation from the intent and ſpirit of a conſtitution originally good.

Mr. *Hume* is of opinion, that the *Britiſh* conſtitution muſt come to an exit; and thinks it is more to be deſired, that it ſhould end in abſolute monarchy, than in ſuch a republican ſcheme as that ſet up by *Cromwell*, which he thinks the beſt we have to expect in caſe of a diſſolution of the preſent [a].

The conſtitution of the Republic of *Venice* is repreſented by ſome hiſtorians as having continued free, with very little variation, excepting ſome of the improving ſort, theſe thirteen hundred years. Others differ with reſpect to the period.

The means which have kept the *Venetians* ſo long free, in ſpite of ambition within, and the attacks of potent neighbours, are alleged by hiſtorians to be, 1. Their attachment to the original principles on which the Republic was eſtabliſhed. 2. Their wiſdom in keeping clear of quarrels among other States. 3. The ſenators being obliged to riſe gradually through all ſtations, ſo that they never come to the management ignorant of buſineſs. 4. The impoſſibility of coming to power in any indirect manner. 5. The total excluſion of prieſts from all ſtations of power and truſt. 6. The

[a] Eſs. I. 89.

6. The judicious distribution of the public revenues, and impossibility of embezzling them. 7. Punishing strictly, but always according to clear and explicit laws, excepting in the case of information of treason against the state, on which occasion they break through law, justice, and humanity. 8. The dreadful danger of the least attempt toward a change in the state. 9. Punishing capitally every degree of corruption; even the ambassadors from foreign countries being obliged to give a strict account of all monies, or presents, received by them. 10. Profound secrecy of all the Republic's measures, and severe punishments inflicted on the betrayers. 11. The strict limitation of the doge, senate, and all persons in power, so that they can do nothing, but what is warranted by law and constitution. 12. Voting by ballot. 13. Above all, their invariable plan of education, which plants at the bottom of every *Venetian* heart, from the highest to the lowest, an insuperable love of their country [a].

The Abbé *S. Pierre* thinks, the opinion, That states, like individuals, are naturally perishable, and that the *greatness* of a state naturally brings on its ruin, is a vulgar error. The permanency of states depends, he thinks, on their original good constitution, and subsequent faithful administration [b]. To which I will add, that most depends on an original sound constitution, securing effectually the exclusion of corruption. For, as to administration, most kings will be tyrants, and the greatest part of ministers corruptors, if the people will suffer them.

The excellent *Davenant* (ii. 294.) writes on this subject as follows:

 'Men,

[a] Mod. Univ. Hist. xxvii. 5.

[b] Oeuvr. Polit. ix. 12.

'Men, when they are worn out with diseases, aged, 'crazy, and when besides they have the *mala stamina* '*vitæ*, may be patched up for awhile, but they cannot 'hold out long; for life, though it is shortened by ir-'regularities, is not to be extended by any care beyond 'such a period. But it is not so with the body po-'litic; by wisdom and conduct that is to be made 'long lived, if not immortal; its distempers are to be 'cured, nay its very youth is to be renewed, and a 'mixed government grows young and healthy again, 'whenever it returns to the principles upon which it 'was first founded.'

'So great, says Mr. *Hume*, is the force of laws, and of 'particular forms of government, and so little dependence 'have they on the humours and tempers of men, that 'consequences almost as general and certain may be de-'duced from them, on most occasions, as any which 'the mathematical sciences afford us[a].' And again, 'Legislators ought not to trust the future government 'of a state entirely to chance; but ought to provide a 'system of laws to regulate the administration of public 'affairs to the latest posterity. Effects will always 'correspond to causes; and wise regulations in a com-'monwealth are the most valuable legacy that can be 'left to future ages. In the smallest court, or office, 'the stated forms and methods in which business must 'be conducted, are found to be a considerable check 'on the natural depravity of mankind: Why should 'not the case be the same in public affairs? Can we 'ascribe the stability of the *Venetian* government, 'through so many ages, to any thing but its form? 'And is it not easy to point out those defects in the 'original constitution, which produced the tumults in '*Athens*

[a] *Hume*, POLIT. ESS. IV. p. 27.

2

'*Athens* and *Rome*, and ended in the ruin of those 'Republics[a]?'

Whilst a people continue capable of liberty, the period of their ruin will never approach.

It is therefore more melancholy to see public virtue lost in a people, where the people, as in *England*, have power in government, than to see a tyrant on the throne, with the people's liberties under his feet. He may reform. He may die. The fury of a brave and incensed people may rise, like a whirlwind, and scatter him and his enslaving crew like chaff. But the manners of ten millions, when they come to be so degenerate as to invite slavery, are not easily to be corrected, and if not corrected—my blood freezes at the thought of what must follow.

Nothing can be imagined more dastardly than the disposition of those men who despair of their country. They make me think, I see a graceless son, after supporting a little while the languid head of his sick mother, toss her back upon the bed, and cry, 'she will 'die, and why then should I give myself any trouble 'about her?'

Very different was the spirit of young *Scipio*.

After the battle of *Cannæ*, which proved so fatal to *Rome*, when several young officers in his presence talked of the state of affairs as desperate, and seemed inclinable to give all up, and abandon *Italy*, that young hero drew his sword, and solemnly vowing never to forsake his country, forced all the others, by threats of immediate death, in case of refusal, to enter into the same solemn engagement.

When the great and good *Scaurus* was, by the contests between *Cæpio* and *Mallius*, betrayed into the hands

---

[a] *Hume*, POLIT. ESS. IV. 37.

hands of the *Gauls*; and saw one hundred-and-twenty-thousand *Romans* cut in pieces, with the Consul's two sons, he did not even then despair of his country. Being consulted by the *Gauls* about a descent into *Italy*, which they were then meditating, he advised them against it, telling them, that they would find the *Romans* invincible, though they had lately been, through an unhappy difference among their commanders, unfortunate. His bold answer so provoked one of the *Gaulish* generals, that the barbarian run at him, and stabbed him on the spot[a].

Plutarch says, *Cato*'s virtue would have saved *Rome*, if the gods had not decreed her fall. The truth of the matter is, the gods never decree that a state shall be enslaved, so long as there remains in it a competent number of *Catos* to preserve its liberties; one is not sufficient. For, as Mr. *Addison* says,

> ——What can *Cato* do
> Against a world, a base degenerate world,
> Which courts the yoke, and bows the neck to *Cæsar*?

In *Sully*'s Memoirs we find that *Henry* IV. of *France* turned his whole application to every thing that might be useful, or even convenient to his kingdom, without suffering things that happened out of it to pass unobserved by him, as soon as he had put an end to the civil wars of *France*, and had concluded a peace with *Spain* at *Vercins*. Is there a man, either prince or subject, who can read, without the most elevated and the most tender sentiments, the language he held to *Sully* at this time, when he thought himself dying of a great illness he had at *Monceaux*? 'My friend,' said he, 'I have no fear of death. You who have seen me expose 'my life so often when I might so easily have kept out 'of

[a] Ant. Univ. Hist. Vol. xii. p. 499.

'of danger, know this better than any man. But I 'must confess that I am unwilling to die, before I 'have raised this kingdom to the splendour I have pro-'posed to myself; and before I have shewn my people 'that I love them like my children, by discharging 'them from a part of the taxes that have been laid on 'them, and by governing them with gentleness.'

'The state of *France* (says *Bolingbroke* on the passage) 'was then even worse than the state of *Great Britain* is 'now: the debts as heavy, many of the provinces en-'tirely exhausted, and none of them in a condition of 'bearing any new imposition. The standing revenues 'brought into the king's coffers no more than thirty 'millions, though an hundred and fifty millions were 'raised on the people; so great were the abuses of that 'government in raising of money: and they were not 'less in the dispensation of it. The whole scheme of 'the administration was a scheme of fraud, and all who 'served cheated the public from the highest offices down 'to the lowest; from the commissioners of the treasury 'down to the under farmers and the under treasurers. '*Sully* beheld this state of things when he came to have 'the sole superintendency of affairs with horror. He 'was ready to despair; but he did not despair. Zeal 'for his master, zeal for his country, and this very 'state seemingly so desperate, animated his endeavours; 'and the noblest thought that ever entered into the 'mind of a minister took possession of his. He resolved 'to make, and he made the reformation of abuses, the 'reduction of expences, and frugal management, a 'sinking fund for the payment of national debts, and 'the sufficient fund for all the great things he intended 'to do without overcharging the people. He succeeded 'in all. The people were immediately eased, trade 'revived, the king's coffers were filled, a maritime 'power was created, and every thing necessary was 'prepared to put the nation in a condition of executing great designs, whenever great conjunctures should 'offer themselves. Such was the effect of twelve years 'of wise and honest administration.'

John Duke of *Braganza* was the most unlikely man in the world to produce a revolution. Gentle, meek, peaceable, fond of pleasure and company. But he was esteemed and trusted by the nobles; of which he was the most considerable, and related to the family who were competitors against *Philip* for the crown of *Portugal*. And the people (whose patience is only not boundless) were irritated beyond all pitch by the wanton tyranny of their *Spanish* masters, who seemed to intend by all possible means to enrage, and force them, if any cruelty would force them, to shake off the yoke[a]. The unanimity was so great, when once the people found a proper person to head them, that the whole business was done in a day. The shops in *Lisbon* were shut in the morning; but they were opened again in the afternoon. The Duke of *Braganza* was crowned king of *Portugal*, and the people declared free from the *Spanish* yoke; and the Spaniards, knowing, that there were then in *Portugal* 210,000 fighting men, did not attempt to dethrone their deliverer again[b].

The reformations made in the corrupt city of *Rome* by *Vespasian*, shew that governments, if they were in earnest, could do great things even in a corrupt state[c].

Andros was a tyrannical governor of *New England*. The people attempted to get rid of him. *James* II. liked tyrants, therefore refused the repeated requests of Sir *William*

---

[a] Mod. Univ. Hist. xxii. 280. [b] Ibid. 282.
[c] Ant. Univ. Hist. xv. 23.

William Phipps against *Andros*. At last the principal men of *Boston* got a report spread at the north end of the town of *Boston*, that the people at the south end were in arms, and the same at the south end that those of the north were risen. *Andros*'s creatures were immediately secured in jail. The governor flies to the east. The leading men send him a letter, desiring him to resign immediately, else they could not answer for the consequences. He takes their advice. The principal inhabitants call a general assembly, and, without consent of the governor, resumed their charter, which King *William* confirms. Thus the Revolution of *Old England* was attended with one in *New England*[a].

Farther, in favour of the proposed restoration, and against despairing of our country, please to observe, my good countrymen, that every tyranny is founded in wickedness; that it has in itself the seeds of its own destruction, and the curse of heaven hanging over it; and that it wants only a shock from the heavy hand of the people, to bring it down in ruins on the heads of its supporters.

Mr. *Sandys*, in his speech in favour of a place bill, *A.D.* 1739, observes, 'that a good bill, or motion, 'once proposed in parliament, and entered on the 'journals, can never die, unless our constitution be ab'solutely and irrecoverably destroyed; but will, by its 'own merits, at last force its way through the houses[b].'

Lord Keeper *Finch* says, Neither *Romans*, *Saxons*, *Danes* nor *Normans*, who conquered the land of *England*, could conquer its laws or constitution[c].

I would therefore hope, even if need were, against hope, that, though it will soon, it is not yet too late, to

a Mod. Univ. Hist. xxxix. 310.

b Deb. Com. xi. 202.

c Parl. Hist. ix. 59.

to retrieve all, and to set things on a foot as much surer than what the Revolution left them upon, as the Revolution-settlement exceeded the times of *James* II.

There are lengths, which our kings and ministers would be afraid to go; which shews, that they stand in some fear of the people. They would not venture upon authorising a massacre, nor upon setting up edicts for laws, nor upon taxing the subjects without authority of parliament; though they have come mighty near to such proceedings.

Whenever any reformation or improvement is proposed, the answer of some is, 'This is not a proper 'time.' It was not a proper time to disband the army, while there was a Pretender to the throne; nor is it a proper time now that there is none. It was not proper in war, nor is it now proper in peace, though our kings, that is our ministers, tell us in their speeches, that the peace will be lasting. It was not a proper time to abolish articles, subscriptions, and test-acts, when bigotry to those absurdities prevailed, and the cry, 'that the church was in danger,' was in the mouths of the clergy, and priest-led part of the laity. Nor is it now a proper time, when no body, besides the half-popish part of the bishops and clergy, care one farthing about such matters.

The courtiers pretend, that it is dangerous to alter any thing. *Quietum non movere*, they say, is a good maxim. Did they observe this rule, when they bethought themselves of enraging the colonists, by taxing them, without giving them representation? When they extended the excise laws? When they laid restraints upon marriage and population?

Antiquity is no plea. If a thing is bad, the longer it has done harm the worse, and the sooner abolished

the

the better. Establishment by law is no plea. They who make laws can repeal them [a].

Our modern court-sycophants are many years too late in applying their maxims of *Quietum non movere, nolumus mutari leges Angliæ*, and the like. These rules are good, while a kingdom or commonwealth stands firm upon its original foundation. But when the constitution is unhinged, when the first principles on which a state was established, are annihilated, when the only security of the people's liberties is turned against the people, to insist, that nothing shall be altered, is to insist, that whatever is gone into disorder, shall remain in disorder. The time to urge those maxims was, when the first disorders were introduced, when bribes, places, and pensions were first given to members of parliament.

Montesquieu observes, that it was constitutional among the ancient *Cretans* to correct the abuses which crept into their government, by the people's rising in arms, and forcing their corrupt magistrates to resign. The *Polish* constitution admits the same kind of remedy. But such a cure seems worse than the disease. He says, the ancient *Cretans* were so strongly tinctured with love for their country, that they were thereby restrained from carrying redress too far [b].

The Prince of *Orange* was not King of *England*, when he ordered letters to be written to the protestant lords, spiritual and temporal, to meet him in parliament, and to counties, cities, and towns to send members. There never were seventy-six citizens to represent *London*, but in the convention-parliament. Yet did that parliament, so irregular in its construction, bring

[a] Parl. Hist. ix. 367.

[b] L'Esprit des Loix, i. 190.

bring about for us the greatest thing that ever was done for this island, I mean the Revolution. Let no man, therefore, object to a salutary proposal, that is new, unusual, or unheard of.

Machiavel says, that to render a commonwealth long lived, it is necessary to correct it often, and reduce it towards its first principles, which is to be done by punishments and examples. If the wild proceedings of rash and giddy ministers are now and then looked into and animadverted upon, it creates fear and a reverence to the laws; and in great men strong examples of clean hands, self-denial, personal temperance, and care of the public treasure, do awaken the virtue of others, and revive these seeds of goodness which lie hid in the hearts of most people, and would spring out, but that they are choked up for a time by avarice and ambition [a].

'Those commonwealths have been most durable, 'which have oftenest reformed, and re-composed them-'selves according to their first institution: for by this 'means they repair the breaches, and counter-work the 'natural effects of time [b].'

It was enacted in the time of *Henry* VII. that in case of a revolution in the kingdom, no man should be questioned for his loyalty to the king for the time being [c]. This shews, that the people of those days had no idea of such a stubborn immutability as we often hear of in our times, admitting no reformation of any thing, however universally allowed to be wrong.

To restore what is, through lapse of time, degenerated, is not altering the constitution.

To

---

[a] *Daven.* II. 72.

[b] *Pym*'s Speech in Parl. 4 *Car.* I. *A. D.* 1628: Parl. Hist. VIII. 173.

[c] *Hume*, Hist. Stuarts, II. 151.

To alter the *British* constitution would be, to change the form of government from king, lords, and commons, into somewhat else, as a republic. So the constitution was wholly changed under *Edward* I. by the barons, who oblige the king to give them and the bishops a commission to elect twelve persons, whose power should be supreme in legislation and administration [a]. This was throwing out all the three estates at once.

To propose to restore parliaments to their original period of one year; to attempt to obtain a more adequate representation, and the effectual exclusion of placemen from the house of commons, is certainly not proposing to alter the constitution, because it is not proposing to abolish either king, lords, or commons; but to preserve and re-establish them, on their original and proper foot.

It is the common cry of the friends of arbitrary power, A prince is in duty bound to deliver down to his posterity the prerogative undiminished, as it was delivered to him by his ancestors. No. It is the duty of a prince to consult at all adventures, the greatest good of his people, his *children*; and if the diminution of his prerogative will increase the happiness of his people, the superfluous power of one is certainly to yield to the happiness of millions. Some men of slavish principles affect a mighty anxiety about the danger of innovations. To depart, they say, from the ancient constitution, is opening a door for endless faction and dissension. Not, if the majority of the society are for the reformation proposed. Nor has any power on earth a right to hinder the majority of a people from making, in their form of government, what innovations they please.

It

[a] *Hume*, Hist. ii. 130.

It is the constant speech of the court dependents, when mention is made of redressing any thing, that by lapse of time is got into disorder, 'The king is bound by his coronation oath, not to alter any thing,' &c. But, in one particular, if not more, the oath itself speaks a contrary language. For the king promises, that he will 'preserve to the bishops all their rights and 'privileges which do, or *shall* by law appertain to them.' So that if it should happen, that some future parlia-liament should be wiser than any of the past, and should think three thousand pounds a year might be better bestowed than upon a bishop, and should legally strike off two of the three, the king will then be obliged to preserve to him only one thousand a year.

One of the questions put to *Edward* II. at his coronation was, Sir, Will you govern according to the laws and customs, '*quas vulgus elegerit*,' in the old *French*, *les loyes et customes les quieles la communaute aura eslu*, and this was the form after him. *Prynne* thinks *elegerit* and *aura eslu*, are in sense as well as sound, the future tense, and that therefore the kings promised to govern according to the laws and customs established, and *to be* established. But *Brady* thinks *elegerit*, and *aura eslu* are to be understood as *elegit*, and *a eslu*; which is strange grammar [a].

Sidney englishes *quas vulgus elegerit*, such laws as the people *shall* propose [b].

By the treaty of *Troyes* after the battle of *Azincourt*, which was regularly ratified and confirmed, and no opposition made to it either by *England* or *France*, the two kingdoms were for ever unrepealably united under *Henry* V. Where is now the unrepealable union between *England* and *France*?

Some

a *Brady*, 1. Gloss. 36.

b Dis. Gov. 458.

Some of our ancient kings ſwore, at their coronation, that they would '*abrogate* and diſannul all evil laws 'and wrongful *cuſtoms*, and make, keep, and ſincerely 'maintain thoſe that were good and laudable.' The archbiſhop charged the king in God's behalf, 'Not to 'preſume to take upon him this dignity, unleſs he re-'ſolved to keep inviolably the vows and oaths he had 'then made;' about the end of the 12th century[a].

Oaths were heaped on oaths to bind the nobility of *England*, never to violate any of the conſtitutions of *Richard* II[b]. Where are his conſtitutions now? He and his conſtitutions were ſent a packing a very ſhort time after they were eſtabliſhed by theſe oaths.

An act 11 and 21 *Richard* II. unrepealable by any future parliament. Such acts, ſays Biſhop *Williams*, are *felò de ſe*, becauſe no parliament can preclude the power of a future[c].

The excluſion bill was a greater change than the reſtoration of independency to parliament. So was the reformation from popery, the diſſolution under *Henry* VIII, the changes under and after *Charles* I; the Revolution in 1688, &c. But our forefathers had more ſpirit than we[d].

Magna Charta ſays, '*Diſtringent et gravabunt nos*,' &c. The barons complaining, and failing of redreſs, ſhall lawfully diſtreſs and aggrieve the king all manner of ways, as by taking his caſtles, lands, poſſeſſions, &c. till redreſs is granted. After the Reſtoration comes the corporation-act, and declares all reſiſtance unlawful. The ſame doctrine is preached in the act of attainder, and militia-acts. Not thirty years after this comes

a *Rap.* I. 245.

b PARL. HIST. I. 520. DEB. COMM. I. 435.

c Ibid. IX. 354.

comes the Revolution, and abolishes the whole system of passive obedience and non-resistance; sends the whole royal family a packing, and brings in the house of *Nassau*. The liberty of the press was taken away 13 *Car*. II. The liberty of petitioning was abolished the same year; and then the corporation charters taken away. All these were restored by the bill of rights. In short, as Mr. *Hume* says [a], the history of *England* is little else than a history of reversals, every age overthrowing what was done by the former.

That author therefore [b] thinks, there was somewhat peculiarly absurd in one clause of the test, which was framed under *Charles* II. and required swearing, that they would not alter the government either in church or state; since all human institutions, being imperfect, must, from time to time, want amendments; and amendments are alterations.

How did the *Newcastle* ministry twenty years ago, rage against the salutary remonstrances of the friends of mankind on the destructive cheapness of gin. The duty, they said, (which amounted to the hideous sum of near four hundred thousand pounds) was appropriated as part of ways and means. Experience shews us, that the nation can subsist, though the people do not now, as in those times, destroy themselves, by thousands and myriads, with that liquid fire.

Great things are often brought about very easily, as the deliverance of *Athens* from the thirty tyrants by *Thrasybulus*, of the *Sicyonians* by *Aratus*, and of *England* at the Revolution, all with hardly the loss of a drop of blood.

Philip II.'s ordering Count *Egmont* to be beheaded at *Brussells*, *A. D.* 1568, enraged the people of the Low Countries

[a] Hist. ii. 264.

[b] Hist. Stuarts, ii. 243.

Countries to madneſs, and determined them never to ſubmit more to the *Spaniſh* yoke, ſays *Strada*[a].

It is not eaſy to underſtand how ſo clear-headed a man as judge *Blackſtone* ſhould write, that the union muſt be diſſolved, before any reformation can be made either in the church of *England* or *Scotland*, becauſe the king has ſworn to maintain both churches. Is it poſſible, that the judge ſhould imagine, a coronation-oath binds a king to maintain any eſtabliſhment whatever, *at all adventures*, even though it be found, by conſent of the *people*, neceſſary, or convenient, to aboliſh it? A coronation-oath only binds a king not to alter any thing fundamental, of his *own authority*, and contrary to the will of the people. And it ſeems inconceivable, that the learned and able judge ſhould imagine, that the meaning of a coronation-oath is, to fix upon the people all the preſent eſtabliſhments, however inconvenient the change of circumſtances in after-times may render them; and to make all improvements and reformations impoſſible. Suppoſe every king, from the conqueſt to our times, to have underſtood his coronation-oath in this ſenſe. We muſt have been now no forwarder in political improvements, than we were 700 years ago. It is waſting words to expoſe ſuch abſurdity.

'It is really pleaſant,' ſays Lord *Sandys*, 'to hear ſome 'lords talk of innovations in our conſtitution. For God's 'ſake my lords what are the laws we paſs yearly? Is not 'every public law an innovation in our conſtitution? Do 'we not thereby add to, allow, or abridge ſome of the 'powers or prerogatives of the crown? If we had not 'made many laws for the purpoſe, could it be ſaid we 'ſhould now have any liberty left? Criminals are every 'day

a *Pap*. 11. 82.

'day inventing new crimes, or new methods for evading 'the laws that have been made for punishing or pre-'venting them, which obliges us almost every year to 'pass new laws against them: by these the power of the 'crown is generally enlarged. Ministers again are al-'most always contriving new methods for extending the 'prerogatives of the crown, to the oppression of the peo-'ple, which obliges us to be often contriving new laws 'for restraining them: by these the power of the crown 'I shall grant is lessened. What then? Is not our 'government a limited monarchy? Is not the power 'of the crown limited by our constitutions and laws? 'If by experience it be found that the power of the 'crown is not in some cases sufficiently limited by the 'laws in being, must not we, ought we not, to con-'trive new laws for that purpose? Some lords may, if 'they please, call this an encroachment upon the prero-'gatives of the crown: I shall not fall out with them 'about the term, because I think the prerogative may, 'and ought to be, restrained as often as experience 'convinces us that it is turned to a wrong use[a].'

The horror which some among us have against what they call an innovation, resembles that of the ancient *Poles*, when their king *Stephen* having conquered *Livonia*, a part of the *Russian* empire, proposed to new model the government of the country, and among other particulars, thought to change an accustomed punishment of whipping with rods, till the blood came, for one more humane. The wretched peasants threw themselves at his feet, and begged, that nothing might be altered; for that innovations are dangerous[b].

Men of timid natures are startled at every proposed alteration, however likely to be of advantage. Lord *Nottingham*,

---

[a] Lord *Sandys*, 1742. DEB. PEERS, VIII. 519.

Mod. Univ. Hist. xxxv. 261.

Nottingham, when the union was in agitation, boggled at the change of ſtyle from *England* to *Great Britain*, alleging, that it was ſuch an innovation as would totally ſubvert all the laws of *England*. He therefore moved, that the opinion of the judges ſhould be aſked. They very ſenſibly anſwered, that they did not ſee how a *word* ſhould alter, or hurt the conſtitution, whoſe laws muſt remain the ſame after the union, as before [a]. Lord *Nottingham* concluded, however, that the union muſt utterly ruin all .

Lord *Haverſham* was againſt the union becauſe of the diverſity of religion, laws, and government between the two kingdoms. The united kingdom of *Britain*, he ſaid, would be like *Nebuchadnezzar*'s image, part iron, part clay [c].

So wiſe a man as *Cicero* ridiculed *Cæſar* for propoſing to reform the calendar [d].

It is chiefly weakneſs, or lazineſs, that puts princes and ſtateſmen upon declining to redreſs what is amiſs, on pretence of its being impracticable. If *Lycurgus* could perſuade the *Spartans* to give up their property, and agree to his levelling ſcheme, what can be called impoſſible to an able and willing prince, or ſtateſman?

That illuſtrious legiſlator altered the whole national character of the *Spartans*. Why might not a genius in politics do the ſame in *England?* It will perhaps be anſwered, *Sparta* was but a county, compared with *England*. Let us then ſee a county of *England* (the county of *Middleſex*, for inſtance, which is but a ſmall one) as much reformed as *Sparta* was by *Lycurgus*. Have we no perſon in the proper ſtation public-ſpirited enough to make the attempt? Printing, good roads,

 and

a Deb. Peers, ii. 169. b Ibid. 176. c Ibid. 170.
c Ant. Univ. Hist. xiii. 257.

and post-chaises make it as easy to communicate any thing to the whole people of *England*, as formerly to those of *Sparta*.

All schemes are not romantic, which are called so, when first started. For all improvements are objected to at first. How many rebuffs did *Columbus* meet with, in his attempt to discover *America*? Men, therefore, of courage and perseverance are of inestimable consequence to mankind. How few would have gone through what he did? And how meanly was he rewarded for doing mankind so prodigious a service! *America* ought to have been called after him; not after *Americus Vesputius*; for the latter went out six years after the former.

'Whatever is, (says *Pope*) is right.' Whatever is law, is just. Whatever is creed, is true. Whatever is in the state, is constitutional.

The worldly ecclesiastic cries, 'no innovations (reformations he means, and reformations he dreads) in the church. They will produce disturbances.' He is pretty sure of this fact: for he intends to produce disturbance by opposing every salutary proposal. Yet we know, that christianity was an innovation upon heathenism, and the protestant religion upon popery. The reformers of states and churches, the deliverers of mankind from tyranny and bigotry, the friends of human nature, the prime benefactors of our world, thought it worth while to risk a temporary disturbance for a lasting advantage.

There is as much difference between proper liberty, and anarchy, as between the state of things at *Athens* or *Rome*, in the best times of those republics, and that which *Wat Tyler* and *Jack Straw*, intended to have introduced into *England* [a]; which was a total demolition

[a] *Brady*, III. 349.

tion of all subordination, and all rule; so that every man was to be detached from every man, and all legislation, and all obedience, at an end. *Wat* and *Jack* carried their scheme of liberty and equality to an extravagant pitch on one side, and the exorbitant power of one, or a few, which we commonly see in monarchical governments, carries government and subordination beyond pitch on the other. The legislative and executive power diffused among several hands, in such a manner, as to keep up a proper balance, and sufficient restraint on every person possessed of power, that he may not be able (for, such is the nature of man, he will certainly be willing) to carry it on to tyranny;——this only can be called just government, safe for the people, and sufficient for the rulers. And surely, it is pity, my good countrymen, that mere inactivity and timidity should deprive you of this great advantage.

It is the common cry of the courtiers, look back to the times of *Henry* VIII. and his bloody daughter, *Mary*; and be thankful for the liberty you enjoy. But the friends of liberty ought to call upon the people, to look back to those days of darkness and cruelty, that they may learn to dread slavery more than death, and to keep a watchful eye upon the first approaches toward it.

'One rash law, says Mr. *Gordon* [b], may overturn 'our country and constitution at once, and cancel all 'law and property for ever.'

Rome (says the author of GRAND. ET DECAD. DES ROM. p. 99.) was so constituted, that it had in itself the means of correcting its own abuses. The *Carthaginians* perished, because they could not bear the hand

X 2 of

[b] *Cato*'s LETTERS, III. 291.

of even *Hannibal* himself to reform them. The *Athenians* sunk, because their errors were so pleasing to them, that they could not find in their hearts to quit them. The *Italian* republics can only boast the long continuance of their errors. They have neither strength nor liberty. The government of *England* (says he) is such, that there is a set of examiners [the parliament] who are always attentive to abuses, and the mistakes they fall into are seldom of any continuance, and are often useful. [This would be the happy case of *England*, were our parliaments uncorrupt.]

I hope therefore, my good countrymen, you will not let yourselves be discouraged from using the proper means for restoring the constitution, by such frivolous objections as these; and that you will remember, that restoration is not alteration, and that antiquity is a reason for removing abuses, not for keeping them up.

As, on one hand, it is absolutely necessary, that a due subordination be kept up in states and kingdoms, that the people be willing to regulate their conduct according to the laws, which themselves, or their uninfluenced representatives have framed; so on the other, nothing can be conceived more base and despicable, than a voluntary submission to slavery. To stand in fear of a worm like myself! What can be imagined more dastardly and spiritless? Were indeed an archangel, or other being of a superior nature, to require of us implicit obedience to all his dictates, it might be said, there is somewhat decently modest and suitable to our inferior station, in our yielding to so great, so wise, and so good a master. But when we consider the character of most kings, and most ministers; when we view them and their actions in the light in which they stand in the faithful page of history, their flatterers and their slanderers alike silent, it is then that we are filled with indignation

indignation at the dastardly spirits, who sat still, and suffered a handful of men of contemptible abilities and odious characters, to gain so shameful an ascendancy over them.

Let us, my good countrymen, act a more manly part, and avoid the disgrace, which we see come upon those, who support, or submit, to the impotency of a set of tyrants, whose power owes its existence to the cowardice, or the corruption of the people.

Tyrants, says *Aristotle*[a], do what they can to debase the spirit of the subjects. For no mean-spirited man rises against tyranny, or promotes redress of grievances. Εϛι δε ὡς ειπειν, κ. τ. λ.

Octavius makes a feint to resign his power. Is prevented by the worthless senators, who had rendered themselves so obnoxious to the people, that they dreaded the loss of his protection against their injured country[b].

Cowardice became common in the latter times of the *Romans* when the spirit of liberty was gone. Defeats and losses were the consequence. *Domitian*, the emperor, agreed to pay the obscure *Dacians* a tribute, to prevent their attacking the empire[c].

It is probable, that if the *Romans* had been, by means of printing, then unknown, accustomed to read the history of the free and heroic times of their own country, they would not have suffered their precious liberties to have been wrested from them, or would have been animated by the example of their illustrious ancestors, to rise and recover them. Instead of which, the execrable senators passed an edict, exempting *Augustus* from all submission to the laws of his country[d].

---

[a] Polit. v. 11.

[b] Ant. Univ. Hist. xiii. 486. [c] Ibid. xix. 493.

[d] Ibid. xiii. 496.

'A melancholy consideration it is, that, from the 'very nature of things, arbitrary and despotic forms 'of government tend to perpetuate themselves by 'enervating the mind; whereas free forms of government, if not carefully watched over and cherished, 'tend to destroy themselves by introducing riches, 'luxury, vice, a want of due subordination, and in 'consequence a general corruption of manners [a].'

Nations lose their liberties, because a single tyrant, at the head of a compacted body of slaves, acts against an innumerable, divided, incoherent, jarring multitude.

Does not this shew the necessity of dividing power, and not trusting too great a force, or too much influence, in one or a few hands?

Surely the people ought to have at least as good a chance for preserving their liberties, as the leviathans of power for robbing them of them.

Have mankind constituted their governments upon this obvious principle? Have they not, on the contrary, voluntarily, and with their eyes (if eyes they had) open, thrown all the advantage against themselves into the hands of kings and priests? Even when the friends of liberty have gained considerable advantages, how easily do they lose those advantages? Such is the laziness and timidity of the species.

'Thus a confederacy [the protestant] lately so powerful as to shake the imperial throne, fell to pieces, 'and was dissolved in the space of a few weeks [b].'

Mr. *Clem. Coke*, in the time of *Charles* I. said in the house, 'It was better for the subjects to die by the 'hands of a foreign enemy, than to suffer at home [c].'

There

[a] *King*'s Ess. Engl. Const. 193.

[b] *Robertson*'s Charles V. iii. 108.

[c] Whitel. Mem. 3.

There is undoubtedly somewhat very abject in a people's suffering themselves to be cheated out of their liberties by a handful of the most worthless men in the country, a few ministers. A foreign power may invade a state with a superior force, which will oblige the latter to yield, and no disgrace to their courage or conduct. But a nation has almost every natural advantage against its own court; many millions against a few hundreds. And yet we see that the hundreds always prevail against the millions. The reason is, generally, that the court is a junto closely compacted, and acting in concert,

(——— Devil with devil damn'd
Firm concord holds.————) MILT.

while the people are a rope of sand. So that instead of exclaiming on the 'danger of embarrassing government, and the necessity of strengthening the hands of government, &c.' the eternal cant of the tools of power, the friends of mankind will advise the strengthening the hands of the *people*, as all history, and every day's experience shews us, that government is too strong for the people.

The people can never be too jealous of their liberties. Power is of an elastic nature, ever extending itself and encroaching on the liberties of the subjects. And it has accordingly, in most ages and nations, overwhelmed them. The *inertia* of the people is the opportunity of the government. And the people have ever been too inactive in their own defence; which is incomparably the more dangerous error of the two. For if the people secure the power in their own hands, their dethroning a king, oversetting a government, or even massacring a court, with all its connexions (though such scenes revolt humanity) these are only temporary horrors, thunderstorms which soon clear off;

off; and the people restore the serenity of a better state of things. Whereas tyranny is a permanent evil, distressing and debasing the human species from generation to generation, and deluging the world in a never ebbing sea of blood.

It is difficult to rouse the people to an apprehension of danger. And if, headed by a spirit of an unusual boldness, they do rise like a whirlwind, and sweep away the combination against their liberties; they often, by trusting power too far or too long in the hands of their deliverers, give them the hint to erect themselves, like *Cromwell* and others, into tyrants, and to rivet on the unhappy people the very fetters they had just before knocked off. But desperate diseases require desperate remedies.

A vote of credit given a king of *Spain*, suggested to him, with the help of the d——l, the inspirer of all such thoughts, that he had no occasion to depend on the cortes, or parliaments, for supplies. This ruined the *Spanish* liberties.

As every instance of timidity which has given tyranny an opportunity of seizing the liberties of a people, reflects disgrace on that people, so every instance of resistance to unjust domination shines in history with a distinguished lustre.

The ancient *Argives*, like the *Romans*, irritated by their tyrants, expelled them, and changed their form of government into republican [a].

'The ancient *Corinthians* were always admirers of 'liberty, and enemies to tyrants. They waged many 'wars, not through desire of power, nor for the sake 'of plunder, but in defence of the liberties of *Greece*. 'Therefore the *Sicilians*, when under the tyranny of '*Dionysius*,

[a] *Ubb. Emm.* 11. 76.

'Dionysius, and in fear of the Carthaginians, chose to 'apply to the Corinthians rather than any other people. 'And when Dionysius was expelled from Syracuse, and 'banished to Corinth, and when Timoleon had successfully terminated the war, and restored liberty, the 'Syracusans extolled to the skies the Corinthians, their 'glorious deliverers. And those praises were heightened afterwards when Timoleon, a second time, drove 'out the Carthaginians, and restored liberty to the other 'cities as well as to Syracuse[a].'

'Arminius (says Tacitus[b]), aspiring to dominion 'over his country (Germany), and encroaching upon 'her liberty, raised civil wars with various success, 'and, at last, was privately cut off by his own relations, though he had delivered Germany, and had successfully resisted the Roman invasions, at a time when 'Rome was in the zenith of her power.' Those brave savages would have no master, not even an illustrious or a gentle one.

Statilius and *Favonius* thought slavery preferable to civil war about liberty[c]. A way of thinking very different from *Salust*'s, who, speaking of liberty, uses these words, *Quam nemo bonus nisi cum vitâ amisit.*

Brutus declared he would never be a slave to the mildest master[d]. The point is not merely, Whether the people are actually groaning under oppression, and expiring by hundreds in a day in the hands of the tormentors; but whether the free constitution is safe. If that is unhinged, if the mounds are thrown down which stood between the people and power, no one can say how soon oppression may rush in upon them like a deluge.

---

[a] *Ubb. Emm.* II. 110.

[b] ANNAL. lib. II cap. 88.

[c] ANT. UNIV. HIST. XIII. 273.

[d] Ibid. 311.

deluge. Of that great patron of liberty, the Antient Universal Historians write as follows:

'Thus fell *Brutus*, in the 43d year of his age, and 'with him fell the liberty of *Rome*, and of the *Roman* 'people. He was a man in whom the malice of his 'enemies could discern no fault, in whom the virtues 'of humanity were eminent; in whom a constant, 'firm, and inviolable attachment to the public good, 'formed the principal and most distinguishable part of 'his character, and the uninterrupted business of his 'life ever in view, ever pursued from the inherent 'equity of his mind; for he was, as his historian well 'observes, by nature exactly framed for virtue, with- 'out one breach of that never to be omitted distinction 'of *fas* and *nefas*, right and wrong. And here it may 'not be altogether foreign to our purpose, to illustrate 'this transcendent rectitude of his mind, by instancing 'his refusal, contrary to the opinion of *Cicero* and his 'other friends, to employ the arts of oratory in gild- 'ing over the fairest cause, when after the death of '*Cæsar* he addressed himself to the *Roman* people. It 'cannot be supposed that *Brutus*, who had long been 'famed for eloquence, could be ignorant of speaking 'to the passions of men, an art too successfully made 'use of by *Antony* on the same occasion. Such, then, 'was the integrity of *Brutus*'s mind, that he could not 'stoop to employ any indecent means even in the pur- 'suit of virtue. The death of *Cæsar* was undoubtedly 'justifiable under the government which then prevailed 'in *Rome*, notwithstanding all the dirt that has been 'thrown at this transaction by the mean and groveling 'abettors of arbitrary power. We may see what the '*Romans*, and *Tully* the least adventurous of men, 'thought of this action by a passage in one of his let- 'ters to his friend *Atticus*, bemoaning the misfortunes

'of

'of the times, when he says, But notwithstanding the 'cloud that hangs over us, I console myself in the 'ides of *March*. Our heroes have done every thing 'within their power, and with a resolution by which 'they have acquired immortal glory. Nor was the 'putting the destroyer of their constitution and liber- 'ties to death, by violent hands, without precedent in 'the *Roman* history. And as to the method they made 'choice of, it appears adequate to the dignity of the 'action; for who more proper to compass such an 'event, than a number of senators distinguished by 'their attachment to liberty? Or what place could be 'more justly fixed on for the tyrant of *Rome* to expire 'in, than that dictatorial chair which he possessed in 'violation of the laws of his country? We often see 'the love of one's country the bent and inclination of 'very different men, influenced either by passion, acri- 'mony of temper, vanity, resentment, a lust of power, 'or any other inducement; nor were all those who 'joined in that glorious cause, altogether free from 'such suspicions; for an uniform, steady, constant 'attachment to the public good, was to be met with 'in *Brutus* alone. Men generally differ from them- 'selves as much as from one another; *Brutus* was al- 'ways the same. If we have dwelt too long in con- 'sidering the virtues of this great man, the mighty 'excellence of his character, and his inviolable at- 'tachment to the public cause, may plead our excuse. 'We are not only indebted to history for the enlarge- 'ment of our minds, but likewise for the improvement 'of our moral virtues; and to an *Englishman*, the fore- 'most of the rank is the pursuit of liberty. Who then 'more properly can become the object of our contem- 'plation than *Brutus*, the genius of liberty[a]?'

The

[a] Ant. Univ. Hist. xiii. 408.

The *Swiss* fought 60 battles against the *Austrians* for liberty [a].

Every country of small extent, says *Voltaire* [b], that is poor, and governed by good laws, will continue free, if once enfranchised. I should rather say, 'Every 'country that is once free, will continue free so long 'as it continues virtuous and incorrupt.'

'*Quinimo asseverare verissime*, &c. We can posi-'tively assert, that *Holland* and *Zealand* have not, in the 'space of 800 years, been subdued by any force, in-'ternal or external. In which it is to be doubted, 'whether any kingdom or commonwealth can be com-'pared with us, unless *Venice* may be excepted [c].'

'I am an old man, upwards of eighty, and have 'seen more difficult times than these, even the *French* 'at our gates; but, by the blessing of God, on our 'firmness and resolution we have hitherto preserved 'our own state.—If at last we are overpowered, let us 'lay our cities under water, betake ourselves to our 'ships, and sail to the *East Indies*, and let those who 'see our country laid waste say, There lived a people 'who chose to lose their country rather than their 'liberties [d].' Words of old *Corverin* in the assembly of burgomasters, *A. D.* 1712.

The emperor *Henry*, *A. D.* 1110, offended with the *Bolognese* for the resistance they had made, built a citadel to bridle them. Countess *Matilda* animated them to demolish it. *Henry*, far from resenting, honoured them for their brave spirit, and gave them a charter of immunities [e].

The

[a] *Volt.* Ess. sur l'Hist. ii. 59. [b] Ibid.

[c] Decr. of the States establishing their Lib.

[d] *Tind.* Contin. i. 275.

[e] Mod. Univ. Hist. xxxvii. 5.

The people of the republic of *Sienna* in *Italy* fled from their native country, when taken by *Cosmo*, general to *Charles* V. *A. D.* 1555, not because they had then lost their liberties; but because they feared they should lose them. They went and settled at *Monte Alcino*, and other places [a].

The first funeral oration is said to have been spoken over *Du Guesclin*, who dethroned *Peter* the cruel of *France* [b].

Clovis, king of the *Franks*, going to give the archbishop of *Rheims* a piece of plate, taken among the plunder, was prevented by a common soldier, who hewed it in pieces with his battle-axe, and divided it equally, not allowing the king the prerogative of dividing in an arbitrary manner. Nor was the man punished for it, though the king found an occasion against him afterwards. A plain proof of great liberty among the *Franks*. See likewise the *Aragonian* manner of electing their kings [c].

An elegant writer observes, that the '*Florentines* ' made the same figure in the 14th century in *Italy*, as ' the *Athenians* had done in *Greece*. The fine arts appeared in no part of *Europe* but amongst them; and ' they were by far the most respected people in *Italy*. ' Their civil dissensions, however unhappy, increased ' their courage, and added to their experience. In ' matters of religion, though they professed themselves ' votaries to the see of *Rome*, they exercised the independency that became a free people, and were, perhaps, the most void of superstition of any we read of ' in history. When the *Pope* touched upon the string ' of sovereignty over them, they acted with the same ' spirit

[a] *Robertson*'s CH. V. III. 318.

[b] *Volt*. Ess. SUR L'HIST. II. 142.

[c] *Rap*. I. PREF. IV.

'spirit against him as they had done against the emperors and their own tyrants; and what is most incredible in that bigotted age, his fulminations and interdicts served but to increase their unanimity in despising them, while in other countries they were dethroning princes, and subverting constitutions. Next to this the great character of the *Florentines* consisted in the good faith with which they fulfilled all their engagements, and in their passion for freeing all the other states of *Italy* from tyranny. The *Florentines* always took the lead amongst the states of *Italy*; but it ought to be mentioned, to their honour, that we have not upon record any act of unprovoked oppression, that they were guilty of, towards their neighbours; nor do we know one instance of their infringing the terms upon which any people came into their alliance, or under their protection[a].'

Florence in a manner supported the liberty of *Tuscany*. She paid immense subsidies. Kept armies on foot. And yet her citizens out-vied all *Europe*, in the splendor and elegance of their equipages, in their manner of living, in their buildings, and public exhibitions, in which they imitated the *Trojan* games, so finely described by *Virgil*, and common amongst the *Romans*, who were the patterns of the *Florentine* policy, both in peace and war; but with this advantage in favour of the latter, that they were a commercial state[b].

Florence was, at that time, at a very high pitch of happiness and prosperity. Her people were rich, powerful, united, and flourishing in learning, arts, and sciences; all this prosperity was owing to the wisdom and virtue of a private citizen, *Lorenzo de Medici*. The tranquillity of this country was such, that it afforded no events

---

[a] Mod. Univ. Hist. xxxvi. 151. [b] Ibid. 175.

events proper for history to record, unless we mention the encouragement given to men of learning, who filled the country with writings, and works, that will ever be the admiration of mankind. *Lorenzo* resembled his illustrious predecessors in their public and private virtues, but exceeded them in personal accomplishments. He had a turn for military affairs, though peace was his darling object. Compositions are still extant, that prove him to have been both a poet and a critic. He was a good judge of architecture, which in his time was commonly combined with painting; and of music. He founded the university of *Pisa*, to which he brought the most learned and ingenious men in *Italy*. He is said to have been more amorous than was consistent with the strict practice of virtue; and like other great men of antiquity, unbent his more serious hours with juvenile recreations. To amuse his busy pragmatical countrymen, and to render *Florence* more populous, he exhibited justs, tournaments, plays, and other diversions, which reconciled them, in a great measure, to that aristocracy of which they were so naturally jealous.

Upon his death, all the *Italian* states and princes sent compliments of condolance by their ambassadors to *Florence*[a].

The *Florentines* were, at last, split into a thousand factions about resettling their form of government. They seemed to look back with surprise and horror at their situation, under the family of the *Medici*; they did not consider the advantages brought to their country, as an equivalent for the interruption which they had given to the power of the people. They had preserved the forms of the constitution, but had deprived them of the substance.

Soderini

[a] Mod. Univ. Hist. xxxvi. 341.

Soderini proposed, that all the magistrates, should be chosen by an assembly, who were legally qualified to partake of the government. This method, he thought, would be an incentive for citizens, to aspire to publick offices, by virtue and merit. As to extraordinary powers, and matters of high importance, he proposed the people should chuse a separate magistracy for that purpose, who were to deliberate independently of them. He thought that on those two points depended the true form of popular government.

The madness of a *Dominican* frier set at nought all their wisdom; his name was *Savanarola*, he was perpetually haranguing from the pulpit, but from his enthusiasm the foundations of a noble constitution was laid, by placing the legislative power in the hands of citizens, legally qualified for posts in government, who were to dispose of the executive power, as they saw proper [a].

In the year 1766, a terrible insurrection was made in *Jamaica* by the negroes, upon the same principle as the bravest people of ancient or modern times have struggled for recovery of their liberties. They killed many of their tyrants, who never have been used to hesitate about killing them. They were however immediately suppressed, and those who were taken (I can scarce hold my pen to write it) ‘ were burnt alive, says ‘ the account, on a slow fire, beginning at their feet ‘ and burning upwards,’ while those hardy creatures, like so many *Scævolas*, smiled with disdain at their tormentors, and triumphantly called to the spirits of their ancestors, that they should quickly join them [b].

I ask any human being, who has in him any thing human, whether all the yellow dirt of this world is an

---

[a] Mod. Univ. Hist. xxxvi. 356.
[b] Lond. Mag. 1767, p. 258.

an object of consequence, enough for men——for *Englishmen*——to turn themselves thus into fiends of hell; and to break loose upon their fellow-creatures with such infernal fury, for doing what no people in the world are more ready to do than themselves, I mean, resisting tyranny.

A. D. 1730, the brave *Corsicans*, galled by the cruel yoke of the tyrannical *Genoese*, rose in arms, and published a manifesto, importing, that their intention was only to assert their liberty [a].

No revolution, says *Voltaire* [b], was ever brought about with so little trouble and bloodshed, as that of *Sweden*, when *Christiern* received from a single unarmed magistrate, *Mans*, the order to quit the throne, and abdicated immediately. But he had made himself thoroughly odious to the people by his cruelty, of which one example shall be given *instar omnium*, viz. his ordering the mother and sister of the great and good *Gustavus*, in revenge for his endeavours to rescue his country, to be put in two different sacks, and thrown into the sea.

The human mind (*Buchanan* [c] says) has something sublime and generous implanted in it by nature, which impels it to resist unjust power. The *Scots*, he says, never failed to restrain, or punish their kings for maladministration. *Baliol*, particularly, was dethroned for giving up his kingdom to the *English*. The *Scots*, he says, bound their kings to the observance of the laws and customs by a very strict coronation-oath. He labours to shew, that the apostolical directions to the christians, concerning submission to kings and magistrates, are no argument against resisting tyrants; but a caution to the professors of the new religion, that

 they

a Contin. Rapin, viii. 80.

b Volt. Ess. sur l'Hist. iii. 18.

c De jure regni, &c.

they muſt not think themſelves exempted thereby from the duty of peaceable ſubjects;' and he ſhews, that what is ſaid in honour of the ſupreme magiſtrate, as appointed of God, and bearing the ſword for puniſhing the wicked, &c. does not relate to the infamous *Roman* tyrants of thoſe times; but to the office, abſtracted from him who bore it. He mentions the divine order, 2 CHRON. xviii. 19. for killing king *Achab*, as a proof that ſcripture does not require abſolute ſubmiſſion to tyrants; and obſerves, that if the ſlaves of power ſhould argue from one ſet of texts, that tyrants are never to be reſiſted, they muſt, to be uniform, allow that other paſſages authorize the diſpatching of wicked princes. And he inſiſts, that, as in holy writ, there are general orders for cutting off all irreclaimably wicked perſons, without any exception in favour of kings; it muſt follow, that tyrants are, in obedience to ſcripture authority, to be cut off. He approves of the putting to death of *James* III. of *Scotland*; for his cruelty and wickedneſs, and of the regulations made for ſecuring thoſe, who deſtroyed him, and mentions, that twelve, or more of the Scottiſh kings, were condemned to perpetual priſon, or baniſhment, or death, for their crimes.

It is an unſurmountable argument againſt ſlavery, that nature, in every human being, revolts againſt it, when it comes to touch himſelf. We wonder to read of daſtardly people, and crafty prieſts, ſtanding up for the divine right of tyrants, as if they forgot, that by and by themſelves may come to be ſufferers. But the partiſans of tyranny keep always a mental reſervation in their own favour. They are for enſlaving all mankind, and intend that themſelves ſhall be little tyrants under the great one. Even among the eccleſiaſtics, the zealous trumpeters of paſſive obedience in all ages and countries,

countries, whenever those clumsy kings, who had not sense enough to keep to the fundamental maxim, That the king and the priest are to play the game into one anothers hands, or those few, very few noble minded princes, who have been above the meanness of both king-craft and priest-craft, have broken in upon what churchmen call their sacred prerogative, and proposed to put them, either as to taxes or incomes, nearly upon a foot with the laity, we always find, that slavery is a very terrible affair; kings, who use freedom with their sacred order, are tyrants; and heaven is appealed to in vindication of their quarrel. Of this the reader will see instances in these collections.

There is always a somewhat, where human nature, even in the most feeble spirits, vindicates to itself its unalienable right. The following private anecdote, told me by one who knew the parties concerned, illustrates this.

In the mad times of *Sacheverel*, when many seemed willing to go all lengths in obedience to authority, a man of sense took some pains to give a lady, a friend of his, juster notions than she had of the limits of obedience. 'Suppose,' says he, 'Madam, that the king 'should seize, by a *quo warranto*, your husband's estate, 'and make him, and yourself, and children, beggars; 'would you think resistance unlawful?' 'I should 'have much cause of complaint,' says the lady; 'but,' (raising her pretty eyes to heaven) 'we must not resist 'the Lord's anointed.' 'But, Madam, I will put a 'harder case still. Suppose the king should force your 'ladyship into his bed, don't you think your husband 'might lawfully promote an association for extirpating 'such a brutish *Tarquin?*' The lady, with down-cast eyes, and a countenance covered with a rosy blush, answered: 'The case you now put, Sir, is undoubtedly 'harder than the former. But, as the whole sin should 'be the king's, and kings are answerable to God only, 'I do not think, my husband could lawfully do any 'thing toward vindicating his honour by violence.' The gentleman knowing, that the lady was, as all the votaries of passive obedience, staunch for the established church, and bitter, if a lady can be bitter, against the dissenters, resolved to put to her one question farther, which he did as follows: 'Give me leave, Madam,' says he, 'to ask you once more; Suppose the king should 'order your ladyship to go to meeting?' 'What,' (says she, rising in a lovely passion, which enlivened every feature, with eyes sparkling, lips quivering, and bosom heaving) 'me to a wicked schismatical presbyterian 'meeting!' (These opprobrious words she had learned from the parson of the parish.) 'I would kill him,' (says she, clenching her little, weak, soft hand, which made the gentleman hope he should have the pleasure of a box on the ear, of which however he was disappointed) 'if I were to die for it, sooner than he should 'make me enter the door of a conventicle.'

If a weak delicate woman could be thus roused in defence of what she called her religious liberty, surely a man ought to suffer emasculation as soon as to yield himself a voluntary slave.

Hardly any people ever were so sordid, as not to shew some love of liberty. Even the *Polish* peasants, *A. D.* 1620, oppressed by their tyrannical lords, fled to the *Ukraine*, where there was more freedom [a].

However indifferent about the welfare of his country a man may be in his heart, it seems strange, that any man should fairly *declare* himself so. For he who owns himself unconcerned about the liberty and happiness of so

[a] Mod. Univ. Hist. xxxiv. 198.

so many millions of his fellow-creatures, (many of whom are persons of amiable characters, and connected with himself by the most endearing ties,) declares himself an unfeeling, sordid, selfish brute, hardened against natural affection, and incapable of every generous, every tender, and virtuous attachment. One would think, instead of making such a character a man's boast, there should not any where be found a human being, who should not be enraged at the imputation of such baseness of disposition.

Here let it be observed, at what a frightful rate of velocity we degenerate. 'The *love* of our *country*, or '*public spirit*, (says Mr. *Gordon*[a],) is a phrase in *every* '*body's mouth*, but it is talked of without being felt.' Mr. *Gordon* wrote this, *A. D.* 1721. So miserably are we sunk in half a century, that scarce any body now *mentions* love of country for any other purpose than to turn it to *ridicule*.

'Whatever character we may have,' says Mr. Alderman *Heathcote*, in his speech in the house, *A. D.* 1744, 'or whatever character we may deserve among foreigners, I hope we shall always take care to preserve 'the character of being a brave and a free people. 'Foreign slaves may think as highly as they please, Sir, 'of the steadiness of their public councils; but among 'such, I hope, we shall always be deemed a turbulent 'and unsteady people. This character must always 'necessarily attend a free government; because in all 'such governments, there have been, there will always 'be, some minister, or some set of ministers, forming 'schemes for overturning the liberties of the people, 'and establishing themselves in arbitrary power. Such 'men are generally at first the idols of the people, and 'before their latent designs come to be discovered, they

[a] *Cato*'s Lett. ii. 11.

'generally prevail with the people to enter into such 'measures, or to make such regulations as may contribute to the success of their designs. But if the people 'are wise enough, and sufficiently jealous of their liberties, as the people of this country, thank God! have 'always hitherto been, they never fail to discover these 'designs before they are ripe for execution. As soon as 'they have made this discovery, they begin to see the 'evil tendency of the measures or regulations they have 'been led into, and of course they must alter the former 'and repeal the latter. This therefore which foreign 'slaves, as most of the people around us, impute to a turbulency or unsteadiness in our temper, is nothing but 'the natural effect of the freedom of our government; 'and whilst the cause lasts, which I hope it will always 'do, the effect must continue the same.'

And will you, my good countrymen, will the brave and generous-spirited *English*, so soon after the expulsion of popery and slavery, will you submit to be enslaved by a handful of your fellow-subjects? You, who have so often made the mighty monarchs of *France* and *Spain* tremble on their thrones, and so lately have made *Europe* stand aghast, are you not ashamed to shew yourselves afraid of a *Harley*, a *Walpole*, a *Pelham*, a *Bute*, a *North?* For either you were afraid of them, or you suffered yourselves to be deceived by them, which is almost as shameful; or you would, before now, have demanded, and obtained, either by petition or by force, the correction of the ruinous abuses I have, in these volumes, pointed out.

Besides the general reluctance in the people against commotions or alterations in public affairs, occasioned by their timidity, indolence, and want of public spirit; there are certain bodies of men in the nation, who think

think themselves particularly interested in opposing all such proceedings, viz. the proprietors of stocks, the placemen, pensioners, expectants, and other dependants on the court, the established clergy, the army, and the inhabitants of the rotten boroughs, who now make a rich harvest, every seven years, by sending up a majority of the house of commons.

Whenever opposition is made to an apparently wise reformation, let the people look that corruption be not at the bottom. When the Mareschal *d' Humieres* had over-run the *Netherlands*, and *Holland* appeared to be in the utmost danger from the arms of *France*, the villanous magistrates of *Amsterdam*, *Leyden*, *Delft*, &c. bribed (as by intercepted letters appeared) with French money, still opposed the raising of an armament, fearing, as they pretended, to trust the Prince of *Orange* with an army. The Prince, from despair, and fear of utter ruin to his country, attempted to obtain authority for raising an army by a plurality of voices, whereas by the constitution unanimity is absolutely necessary. This proposal had almost lost the Prince his whole popularity. His enemies alleged, that, from motives of ambition, he meant to overthrow the constitution of his country. Shortly after this, he intercepted letters from *D' Avaux*, the French ambassador, to the king his master, with accounts of money disbursed by him in corrupting those patriotic magistrates, so jealous of the Prince of *Orange*'s ambition. This turned the tide in favour of the Prince and his proposed armament against *France*. In the same manner, my good countrymen, whenever you observe men expressing great fear lest the redress of undoubted and ruinous grievances should produce fatal consequences; look, whether those cautious patriots are not

not already, or do not expect to be gainers by present measures and present men. If you find this to be the case, let every word those gentlemen say against measures for redress, go for nothing. They are interested.

If it be urged, that those who now depend on places will be undone by the proposed reformation, it may be answered, That it is easy to provide in a moderate way for the necessitous; and that the others may drink port instead of claret. The dependents on the court, though very numerous, much too numerous, are but a handful, compared with the great multitude, who have neither hopes nor fears from the ministry. In the year 1714, most of the merchants and monied men were for the *Hanover* succession, and against the Jacobites; because they thought their property would be most likely to be safe under protestant kings. In our times, we see many of the monied men against their country's good. Our men of property in the public funds, oppose whatever can be offered for restoring independency to parliament, which alone can give hope of getting our finances put into order. If you go to altering any thing, they cry, it will produce disturbance, and then public credit may suffer. But will public credit be safe, if you do not alter any thing? Such men as *Price*, and *Hume*, and *Grenville*, who have heads for calculation, will tell you, that in the way we have hitherto conducted our money-matters, there is the highest probability of a national bankruptcy. And the excellent *Price*, particularly, tells you, that it is not yet too late to save the nation. But he tells you, at the same time, that nothing will save it but the faithful application of a fund for diminishing the debts and taxes. And every body knows, that nothing will make

make a ministry faithful, but the fear of an independent parliament. Yet our men of property in the funds are afraid of proposals for rendering our parliaments independent. This is literally *ne moriare mori*. It is resolving to sit still, till the house tumbles in ruins upon our heads, because being old and crazy, we are afraid of propping it up.

It is true, that many of those whose property is chiefly in the funds, are disposed to put the negative on all proposals for alterations even for the better. They are apprehensive, that in the concussion of reformations and restorations, public credit may be affected, by which they may come to be losers.

Were public credit upon a sure foundation at present, it might be pretended that it is prudent to avoid what may be likely to shake it. If a patient is in a fair way toward recovery, there is no occasion to disturb his slumbers, for the sake of his taking medicines. But if he is in a lethargy, it would be strange practice to let him sleep on. Can any man of common understanding look upon our public funds as in a state of safety, while the nation, with all that belongs to it, lies at the mercy of a profligate court, and in the power of a set of blundering ministers, who are pursuing measures, the natural tendency of which is, To prejudice trade, and consequently to lessen the national income, on which public credit depends? No certainly. On the contrary, the only means for securing public credit, are, first, to associate for its support, as was done on occasion of the rebellion in 1745, (this ought not to be put off one day,) and then to associate for such redress of grievances, and such a restoration of the constitution, especially respecting the house of commons, as will of course put public credit and every thing else, upon a very

very different foot from the present. In forming a national association, it will not be amiss to make a proviso, that all public creditors who join the association, shall have certain preferences, and other advantages, not to be allowed to those who decline.

The established clergy in every country, are generally the greatest enemies to all kinds of reformations, as they are generally the most narrow-minded and most worthless * set of men in every country. Fortunately for the present times, the wings of clerical power and influence are pretty close trimmed; so that I do not think their opposition to the proposed reformations could be of any great consequence, more of the people being inclined to despise than to follow them blindly.

The most formidable opposition to the proposed redress

* The opposition lately shewn by the clergy of *England* to an enlargement of religious liberty proves, that this maxim is equally just, when applied to the clergy of this, as of other countries. In the course of my reading, in order to make the collection, of which I have published a part, I could not help setting down as many proofs of this observation, as would make two volumes in octavo. Had our clergy behaved themselves as they ought on the late occacasion, I should have had thoughts of mercy toward them, and probably should have suppressed what I had collected to their disadvantage. But as they have lately shewn themselves enemies to religious liberty, I think it is every honest man's duty to do all he can to detect and defeat their mischief. At the same time that I am thus severe on the body of the established clergy of this and other countries, I own with pleasure, that I have been happy in the friendship of many excellent men of that order, who really believed what they subscribed and professed, which was the case of my most venerable parent, whose memory will ever be sacred with me.

dress of grievances may be apprehended likely to come from the standing army, the great instrument of slavery, without which no people ever were enslaved. But even this formidable difficulty does not appear unsurmountable; of which in the sequel.

A tyrant, says *Aristotle* [a], cannot be overthrown, but by agreement among the people. Therefore all tyrants [whether kings, grandees, or ministers,] labour to keep up dissensions and parties among the people. Ου καταλυεται γαρ, κ. τ. λ. *Aristotle* [b] thinks the most precarious species of tyranny is that which is supported by a few, as being particularly exposed to the envy of the people, and liable to contests among themselves. Και τοι πασων, κ. τ. λ. A corrupt parliamentary government is a sort of oligarchy, and if we will take *Aristotle*'s word, not so formidable as some other kinds of tyranny.

I wish it may not be found, that the wickedness of some and the folly of others among us, have produced a ground of opposition and party-spirit of a peculiar kind, the effects of which may disturb our measures for procuring redress.

It is an old and vulgar error, That opposition and party are necessary in a free state. It is true, that when the government is of the common character of governments, that is, a junto of artful and pushing grandees, who have thrust themselves into the management, in order to enrich themselves and their families; it is very necessary that there should be a party to detect and expose their schemes and machinations against the country. But this is only saying, that one evil is necessary to balance another evil. Nobody ever thought an opposition

---

[a] Polit. v. 11.

[b] Ibid. v. 12.

opposition necessary in a private family, where the heads have nothing but the good of the family in view. Sound politics therefore direct, not to set up one party against another, the one to battle against the other; but to take away the fewel of parties, the emolumentary invitations to the fatal and mischievous strife, in which every victory is a loss to the country.

'It is amazing, says *Schoock*[a], that though history 'shews so many kingdoms and commonwealths ruined 'by civil discord, yet we see, in many countries, a 'set of men, blinded by pride and ambition, forcing 'their country upon this fatal rack; and the people 'still as thoughtless of the danger, as if there were no 'warnings of it upon record.

'We treasure up money, and lay in store of provi- 'sions; we build walls and fortifications, and form 'magazines of arms against our enemies; and we neg- 'lect what is at all times in our power, and is incom- 'parably more useful for our defence, viz. the arts, by 'which, as history teaches, we may secure the state. 'From history we should learn, that *Cyrus*, called in 'by the *Carians* to quell a civil broil, enslaved that 'country; that the *Romans* took the same advantage 'of subjecting to their yoke the states of *Greece*; many 'others involved in domestic quarrels, which that 'ambitious people artfully fomented; that the aristo- 'cracy of the *Rhegians* in this manner lost their liber- 'ties; that the *Seleucians*, while they agreed among 'themselves, despised the *Parthians*, but when discord 'prevailed among them they were ruined; that the 'ancient *Britons*, calling in the *Saxons* to assist them 'against their neighbours the *Picts* and *Scots*, were 'oppressed

[a] Resp. Achæor. p. 79.

'oppressed by their auxiliaries[a].' '*In commune non consulunt, &c.* They do not consult the common interest. It is seldom that two or three states will assemble to repulse the general danger. Thus while they resist singly, they are all conquered[b]. *Cæsar* had not made so easy a conquest of *Gaul*, had not that country been torn with intestine divisions[c].' 'Civil discords, says *Livy*, have been, and will be, more ruinous to states and kingdoms than foreign war, pestilence, and all the calamities which the wrath of heaven sends down upon mankind.' '*Nulla quamvis minima, &c.* No nation (says *Vegetius*) however inconsiderable, can be totally overthrown by its enemies, unless it be divided within itself. But intestine divisions arm one party against the other, and disqualify both for opposing the common enemy[d].'

A writer in the *London Magazine*, *July* 1762, p. 377, treats this subject as follows:

'Attempts have been made to excite jealousy and ill-will between one part of the nation and another. The northern part of the kingdom has been represented as less worthy of the royal countenance and protection than the southern. People, whose dwelling is parted from ours only by a wall or a rivulet, are mentioned as a different species; and every one who happens to be born on the farther side, is stigmatized as being destitute of honesty and parts, incapable of public service, and unworthy of public confidence: but the same difference might with the 'same

[a] Resp. Achæor. p. 80.

[b] *Tacit.* in Agric.

[c] *Cæs.* Bell. Gall. lib. i. pass.

[d] *Schoock.* Resp. Achæor. 78.

'same reason be made between a native of *Lancashire* 'and one of *Kent*, as between a native of *York* and of '*Edinburgh*. And a man might with as much propri-'ety reject the advice of a physician, because he lives 'in another parish, as a prince the service of an honest 'and able subject, because he was born in a particular 'county. It is indeed the characteristic of a wise and 'good prince to avail himself of integrity and parts 'wherever they happen to be found, without any re-'gard to external circumstances, least of all to the 'particular spot of his dominions where they were 'produced. These who labour to spirit up intestine 'broils and divisions, at a time when our utmost united 'strength is necessary to support us against the united 'force of foreign and intestine enemies, cannot surely 'be considered as the friends of their country; for it 'is impossible to give a stronger proof that their interest 'is not that of the public.'

'Eating oatmeal, scratching for the itch, lousiness, 'and beggary, are what an *English* porter would very 'readily apply to a *Scotch* nobleman of the most inde-'pendent fortune. Even this hackneyed and vulgar 'abuse, which one would expect to hear only in gin-'shops and alehouses, was for years the standing topic 'of wit and raillery in a political paper, professing to 'handle the most important concerns of the state; and 'the *Scots* had the good fortune to hear themselves re-'proached every day for beggary. Every vice and bad 'quality, which could render the *Scotch* people the 'object of hatred and abhorrence to the human race 'itself, and to *Englishmen* in particular, was imputed, 'and boldly charged to them. In short, the very 'name of *Scot* was made a term synonimous to every 'thing that was rascally and dishonourable in charac-

'ter, excepting only that of coward. Why this imputation among innumerable others equally false and ridiculous, was always carefully avoided, I can only see one good reason, and that was, the writer's regard for his own personal safety. He knew that this charge was the only one he could make which might be directly, and in point confuted, by sending him a challenge. Amidst all his folly he was wise enough not to give every *Scotchman*, who bore the appearance of a gentleman so very fair a pretence, which he suspected many would gladly lay hold on to call him out, and, if he refused a meeting, to use him according to the rules established among men of honour[a].'

Lord *Chatham* shews a nobler way of thinking; who, in the debate on the Stamp-act, spoke as follows: 'I have no local attachments. It is indifferent to me, whether a man was rocked in his cradle on this side of the *Tweed*, or on that. I sought for merit, wherever it was to be found. It is my boast, that I was the first minister that looked for it; and I found it in the mountains of the north. I called it forth, and drew it into your service. A hardy race of men! men, who, when left by your jealousy, became a prey to the artifices of your enemies, and had gone nigh to overturn the state in the war before the last. These men were, in the last war, brought to combat on your side. They served with fidelity, as they fought with valour; and conquered for you in every part of the world. Detested be the national reflexions against them! They are unjust, groundless, illiberal, unmanly. When I ceased to serve his Majesty

'as

[a] Lond. Mag. 1768, p. 309.

'as a Minister, it was not the country of the man by 'which I was moved; but that the *man* of the country 'wanted wisdom, and held sentiments incompatible 'with liberty, &c.'

The minds of the railers against our northern brethren are so narrow, that they can take in but half this little island. A generous spirit, according to our elegant poet, embraces all human kind.

Our times have, I suppose, exhibited the first instance of persons setting up for patriots upon the avowed principle of making one half of their country enemies to the other half. All patriots before those who published a series of writings intitled *The North Briton*, which very title was intended to make *North Britain* odious to *South Britain*, have contented themselves with making a tyrant, or his tools, odious to the people; but never thought of teaching the people to hate the people.

This jealousy, industriously fomented by certain partisans, shews itself in various ways, and, among others, in an affectation of calling the *British* parliament the *English* parliament, as was usual and proper before the union; but ridiculous, so long as the union subsists. This attachment to the terms *England* and *English*, in preference to *Britain* and *British*, is peculiarly absurd in men, who profess themselves admirers of liberty; because we received the name of *England* from the *Angles*, or *Anglo-Saxons*, who conquered us, in exchange for the name we were known by, when free, and before the *Romans* set foot on our island.

The *South Britons* ought not to be too narrow-hearted to their northern brethren. Time was when

5 the

the *English*, flying from the oppressions of *William the Conqueror*, received protection in *Scotland*[a].

'It is held by true politicians (says Sir *R. Steele* in 'his speech *A. D.* 1719, against a bill for altering the '*Scotch* Peerage) a most dangerous thing to give the 'meanest of the people just cause of provocation, much 'more to enrage men of spirit with downright inju- 'ries[b].' And afterwards, 'We may flatter ourselves 'that property is always the source of power; but 'property, like all other possessions, has its effects ac- 'cording to the talents and abilities of the owner. 'And as it is allowed that courage and learning are 'very common qualities in that nation, it seems not 'very advisable to provoke the greatest, and, for 'ought we know, the best men among them.'

'The direct tendency of libels is the breach of the 'public peace, by stirring up the objects of them to 'revenge, and perhaps to bloodshed[c].' But the wicked man scattereth fire-brands, arrows and death, and sayeth, Am I not in sport[d].

The *Sicilian* vespers are a sufficient warning against fomenting national quarrels. In that massacre eight thousand *French* were butchered in one night in *Sicily*. The head of the conspiracy was *Procida*, whose wife had been debauched by a *Frenchman*. The bloody project was kept secret three years, and its execution hastened by the rudeness of a *Frenchman* to a *Sicilian* bride. The *Sicilians* massacred several of their own country-women, because they had married *Frenchmen*; and

[a] *Hume*, Hist. i. 175.

[b] Deb. Com. vi. 206.

[c] *Blackst.* iv. 150.

[d] Prov. xxvi. 18.

and dashed out the brains of many infants, the issue of those marriages [a].

One would suspect that they who set up, and keep up, the division between the two kingdoms, must have a warm side to *France*. For the union between the two kingdoms, which some among us seem desirous to be dissolved, was one of the severest blows *France* has ever suffered, as being the effectual shutting of the back door, by which she annoyed *England* the most fatally.

It is remarkable that in *Charles*'s time, the patriotic parliament blame the papists and bishops for sowing divisions between *Scotland* and *England* [b]. In our times the patriots are the sowers of divisions. And it is to be observed, that in those times the *nation* appeared in defence of *Scotland*, and threw the blame upon the incendiaries. In the late squabble we have not seen such a spirit of justice exerted by any *national* act, though all men of sense and breeding have execrated the railers in private conversation. This neglect ought to be made up, in order to heal the breach, and pave the way for unanimity, without which it will be impossible to procure redress of grievances.

'An incendiary (says *Whitelock*, in his speech at a 'consultation concerning danger apprehended from '*Cromwell*, *A. D.* 1644) is one that raiseth the fire of 'contention in a state. Whether *Cromwell* be such an 'incendiary between the two kingdoms [*England* and '*Scotland*] cannot be known, but by proofs of his 'words, or actions, tending to the kindling of this 'fire

---

[a] Mod. Univ. Hist. 147.

[b] Parl. Hist. x. 51.

'fire of contention between the two nations, and 'raising differences between us [a].''

'Surely (says Mr. *Maynard* [b]) he who kindles the 'coals of contention between our *brethren* of *Scotland* 'and us, [this was long before the union] is an incen-'diary, and to be punished as it is agreed on by both 'kingdoms.'

No wise and public-spirited citizen of this great and growing empire will think of disgracing any part of it; but, on the contrary, of improving all. But our portentous times have produced ministers who have laboured to alienate our colonies; and patriots, who have sought popularity by acting the part of incendiaries. If we do not gain sufficiently by our colonies, let us encourage, not oppress them. If our northern brethren have not such high notions of liberty as we have (what nation ever had?) let us improve their conceptions; not enrage their minds by illiberal reflections. We shall find a corrupt court but too hard for us, if we even keep ourselves ever so well united. How much more, if we become a chaos of jarring and furious factions?

Do we not look back with horror on the times, when we were at enmity with *Scotland*, *Wales*, and *France*, or when we were sheathing our swords in one another's bosoms, the father massacring the son, and the son the father, in the cursed contest between the roses? What *Englishman* would wish to see those dreadful times return?

There was a shameful riot against foreigners *A. D.* 1517. The complaint against them was, that there were such numbers of them employed as artificers, that the *English* could get no work. But it is probable

 (says

[a] *Whitel.* MEM. 112. [b] Ibid.

(says Mr. *Anderson*[a]) that the true cause of complaint was, their working cheaper, and being more industrious than our own people, who trusted to their exclusive privilege.

The first and chief article against *Lauderdale* was, that he had 'contrived and endeavoured to raise jealousies and misunderstandings between your majesty's 'kingdoms of *England* and *Scotland*, whereby hostilities 'might have ensued and may arise, if not prevented[b].' 1679.

An article against *Radcliffe* was, that he and *Strafford* directly conspired to stir up enmity and hostility between his majesty's subjects of *Ireland* and of *Scotland*[c].

'If I should but touch upon the usage we [the 'Scots] continually meet with from this nation [*England*] I should not be believed, if all *Europe* were 'not sufficiently informed of their hatred to all strangers, and inveterate malignity against the *Scots*. I 'know very well, that men of gravity and good breeding among you [the *English*] are not guilty of scurrilous reflections upon any nation. But when we are 'to consider the case in question, we must have a regard to the general temper and disposition of the 'people[d].'

When *James* I. came into *England*, it was alleged, that he too partially encouraged the *Scots*, who came with him, by giving them places and pensions; and that many of them established themselves in *England* by rich matches. This excited the jealousy of the *English*, and not without some appearance of reason, because

---

[a] Hist. Com. i. 348.

[b] Deb. Com. i. 354.

[c] Parl. Hist. ix. 193.

[d] Fletcher, p. 372.

because *Scotland* was then a foreign country to *England*. But it would be as absurd, in our times, to object to our united northern brethren's coming to the southern part of the island, as for the people of *Sussex* to complain of some *Surry* men coming to settle among them, to earn, and spend money, and to raise families among them. The people of *North-Britain* have, indeed, great reason to complain of the continual emigration of the flower of their youth, which thins and impoverishes their part of the island. And if the northern parts lose, the southern must certainly gain: and the greatest of all gains to a country is people.

'If what King *James* I. had given the *English* had 'been as carefully examined as what was given the '*Scots*, it would have been found ten times more, by 'the confession of the historians themselves; but herein 'was not seen the same inconvenience.' And *Weldon* tells us, that 'Lord *Salisbury* used to make the *Scots* 'buy books of fee-farms of perhaps one hundred 'pounds a year, and would compound with them for 'one thousand pounds, which they agreed to, because 'they were sure to have them passed without any con- 'troul or charge. Then would *Salisbury* fill up these 'books with such prime land, as should be worth ten 'or twenty thousand pounds, which, as treasurer, he 'might easily do, and so enriched himself infinitely, 'and cast the envy on the *Scots*, in whose names these 'books appeared, and are still on record to all posterity[a].' The consequence was, that the commons resolved, *A. D.* 1614, to pray the king especially to prevent future settlement of the *Scots* in *England*, the very contrary of what a due attention to their own interest would have taught them to request[b]. By such

 arts

[a] RAP. II. 186. [b] Ibid.

arts as these, it is easy to make any set of people odious.

'If *Scotland* pays to *England* a balance of a million 'yearly, I insist upon it, that country is more valuable 'to *England* than any colony in her possession, besides 'the other advantages I have specified. Therefore they 'are no friends either to *England* or to truth, who 'affect to depreciate the northern part of the united 'kingdom[a].'

Sir *Christopher Pigot* was severely handled by the commons in the time of *James* I. for speaking scandalously of the *Scotch* nation in the debates about the union. He was committed to the Tower, and expelled the house. He begs to be released on account of his health. He was set at liberty; but no more received into the house[b]. 'No *Scotchman* will speak 'dishonourably of *England* in the *Scotch* parliament,' said *James* I. on this occasion[c]. *James* told the parliament he understood, there was a great jealousy among the commons, that the *Scots* would have all the lucrative places; while, on the contrary, the *Scots* thought the union would prove a grievous degradation from being an ancient independent monarchy (three hundred years before the christian æra, according to some authors) down to a set of remote, disembodied, neglected counties, an appendage to the *English* dominion. He tells them, he wonders they should not be proud that the empire, of which they were subjects, should comprehend a great many different nations, *England*, *Scotland*, *Wales*, *Ireland*, *America*, &c. He mentions the happiness which had already been produced by the union of the crowns only. That the bordering counties

---

[a] *Smollet, quoted* LOND. MAG. *July* 1771, p. 370.

[b] PARL. HIST. v. 179, 181. [c] Ibid. 200.

ties of *Cumberland*, *Northumberland*, and *Westmoreland*, which used, for many ages, to be a scene of blood and devastation, were now in peace. He asks them, if they wish the former disorderly state of things renewed, or for ever abolished[a]? If we had nothing of *James* I. but these thoughts on the union, we should say, he was a very judicious prince.

'The happy union of *Scotland* with *England*, hath 'ever since the accomplishment of it flourished in inter'changeable blessings, plenty, and mutual love and 'friendship; but of late, by what fatal disasters and 'dark underminings we are divided and severed into '*Scotch* and *English* armies, let their well-composed 'preambles speak for me, which I wish were printed 'as an excellent emblem of brotherly love, which dis'covers who has wounded us both, and how each 'should strive to help the other in distress, seeing their 'and our religion and laws lie both at stake together, 'Think of it what you will, your subsistence is ours; 'we live or die, rise or fall together. Let us then find 'out the *boute-feu* of this prelatical war, and make 'them pay the shot for their labour, who no doubt 'long for nothing more than that we should break 'with them who worship the same God and serve the 'same master with us[b].' Sir *John Wray*'s speech on the demands of the *Scots*, *A. D.* 1640. See other speeches shewing a great desire of unity between the two nations[c].

On this let us hear lord *Bolingbroke*[d]:

'King *James* Ist's design of uniting the two king'doms of *England* and *Scotland* failed. It was too

[a] Parl. Hist. v. 194, 199.
[b] Ibid. ix. 204. [c] Ibid.
[d] *Bolingbr.* Rem. Hist. Eng. 255.

'great an undertaking for so bad a workman. We 'must think that the general arguments against it were 'grounded on prejudice, or false and narrow notions. 'But there were other reasons drawn from the jealou-'sies of that time, and from the conduct of the king, 'who had beforehand declared all the *post nati*, or per-'sons born since his accession to the *English* throne, 'naturalized in the two kingdoms; and these were 'without doubt the true reasons which prevailed against 'the union.'

March 1645, a formal complaint was sent from the *Scotch* parliament to that of *England*, of accusations written by one *Wright*, tending to divide the two kingdoms, and desiring that he may be found out and punished [a]. The parliament of *England* orders inquiry to be made after this incendiary. Another letter was sent from the *Scotch* commissioners to the house of peers to the same purpose [b]. The *Scots* might justly have made such a demand not long ago. 'Resolved, That the book 'intituled, SOME PAPERS OF THE COMMISSIONERS 'OF SCOTLAND, &c. doth contain matter false and 'scandalous, and the lords and commons do order that 'it be burnt by the hands of the hangman, and do de-'clare, that the author thereof is an incendiary between 'the two kingdoms of *England* and *Scotland* [c].'

The *Scotch* army came into *England* in defence of the cause of liberty, against great promises made them by the king, at the time when his party was uppermost in the winter season; they continued in the field night and day skirmishing with the enemy, who possessed all the forts and places of lodgment, pursued the king's army to *York*, joined the parliament's forces, and beat prince

---

[a] PARL. HIST. XIV. 273. [b] Ibid. 303.
[c] Ibid. 318.

prince *Rupert*; took *York*, took *Newcastle* by storm, blocked up *Carlisle*, sent part back to *Scotland* to oppose the *Irish* and disaffected *Scots*. They were ill fed and ill paid in *England*. A month's pay promised *January* 4, not received till *April*[a]. Parliament shews great anxiety about the *Scotch* army's advancing southward, and sends letters about it to the *Scotch* commissioners, which shews how much they depend upon it. They send two members of the house of commons with the letter signed by the Speaker, full of acknowledgments of past services[b].—'The *Scotch* army, by 'whom the northern counties were reduced and kept 'in obedience.' The *Scotch* army gains advantages in *Herefordshire*, for which a jewel, value 500*l.* was voted to general *Lesley*[c]. Commissioners repeatedly sent to the *Scotch* parliament, full of the great importance of a good understanding between the two nations.—'The 'common soldiers begin to be sick with eating of fruit.' Letter from the *Scotch* army to parliament from *Herefordshire*[d]. Subsisted on pease, apples, and what they found on the ground[e]. They were fourteen months in arrears[f]. Parliament always acknowledges, but pleads poverty. A remonstrance afterwards from the *Scots* to parliament says, they must perish or disband; not being paid, nor allowed to have free quarters, nor any means of subsistance. That the *English* parliament sent for them, and starved them when they came. The *Scotch* army lying in the northern parts, undoubtedly kept the king from going into *Scotland*, by which he might have gained a great advantage. When the *Scots* came into *England*, the parliament had nothing in the north parts but *Berwick*; soon after *Sunderland* was

---

[a] Parl. Hist. xiii. 474. [b] Ibid. 496.
[c] Ibid. xiv. 28. [d] Ibid. 36. [e] Ibid. [f] Ibid. 46.

was taken and garrisoned for the parliament. Then the army under the earl of *Newcastle* was driven into *York*, and the north cleared of the king's party. The town of *Hartlepool* and castle of *Stockton* were taken and garrisoned for parliament. The *Scotch* had likewise their share in the defeat of *Rupert* at *Long Marston*. They stormed *Newcastle*, took *Tinmouth*. All this they did in a manner *gratis*; for they had neither pay nor maintenance, nor clothes, to defend them from the injuries of the weather. The *Scots*, in *November* 1645, were in garrison in *Carlisle*, *Newcastle*, *Tinmouth*, *Hartlepool*, *Stockton*, *Warkworth*, and *Thirleston*. Parliament insisted on their evacuating those places immediately, without their pay; which they promise to make good to them [a]. In one of their remonstrances to parliament, they beg to have clothes to cover their nakedness [b]. Parliament publishes a declaration, in which they excuse themselves as well as they can, saying, they had done every thing in their power for paying and entertaining the *Scotch* army.

We find in the PARL. HIST. XV. 59. a remonstrance from the *Scotch* commissioners, vindicating their nation, and offering to withdraw their army. They complain of many calumnies and execrable aspersions cast upon the kingdom of *Scotland*, in pamphlets, expecting from the justice of the honourable house that they would of themselves vindicate the *Scots*, as the *Scots* had them. Accordingly the lords afterwards made a resolution, that the *Scots* at *Newcastle* had behaved in every respect properly, and with perfect fidelity to *England*. That they (the lords) are resolved to use all means that may clearly evidence to the world their good affections to that kingdom, and care to preserve inviolably the happy

---

[a] PARL. HIST. XIV. 130. [b] Ibid. 132.

happy union. Resolved, that all devisers or printers of any scandalous pamphlets or papers that shall, from this day, be printed against the kingdom of *Scotland*, or their army in *England*, shall be punished in a parliamentary way according to their demerits. A committee appointed for managing all matters concerning the peace and union of the two kingdoms.

The following are the words of the freemen and citizens of *London*, in their petition to parliament, *A. D.* 1646:

'We cannot but with sorrowful and perplexed 'hearts, resent the devilish devices of malignant, fac-'tious, and seditious spirits, who make it their daily 'practice, and would rejoice in it as their master-piece, 'if they could once effect to divide these kingdoms of '*England* and *Scotland* so firmly conjoined by a blessed, 'and we hope, everlasting union [a].' They request that by the 'justice of parliament, condign punishment 'may be inflicted upon such firebrands, the greatest 'enemies to the church and state;' with more to the same purpose.

We have likewise a petition of the mayor, aldermen, and commons of *London*, to the lords, desiring that jealousies against the *Scots* may be abolished, to whom they acknowledge great obligations for coming so readily, when at peace, to the help of *England*, at so unseasonable a time of the year, when *England* was so weak, and to whose interposition the success against the king was greatly owing, and how necessary for future happiness to keep the amity between the two kingdoms.

'We are confident that a curse from heaven shall 'be upon those persons, who, for their own ends and 'interests,

[a] Parl. Hist. xv. 232.

'interests, coloured with specious pretences, apply 'themselves to sow discord between brethren, to make 'divisive motions, and to create and increase differences 'between the kingdoms.' *Scotch* committee at *London* to parliament, *June* 16th, 1646 .

'The kingdom stands involved in many engage-'ments and debts both to their brethren of *Scotland*, '(who, like true christian brethren, came to our aid 'against the common enemy) as also to a multitude of 'officers.' Petition of the lord mayor, aldermen, &c. of *London*, to the lords, *July* 1647 . And afterwards one of the articles of their petition is, 'that by just 'and good means, the correspondence with our bre-'thren of *Scotland* may, according to the national co-'venant, be maintained and preserved .' 'When this 'kingdom [*England*] was in difficulties, if the king-'dom of *Scotland* had not willingly, yea, cheerfully 'sacrificed their peace to concur with this kingdom, 'your lordships all know what might have been the 'danger: therefore let us hold fast that union which 'is so happily established between us, and let nothing 'make us again two, who are so many ways one, all 'of one language, in one island, all under one king, 'one in religion, yea in covenant, so that in effect we 'differ in nothing but in name, as brethren do, which 'I wish were also removed, that we might be altoge-'ther one, if the two kingdoms shall think fit. For 'I dare say, not the greatest kingdom upon earth can 'prejudice both, so much as one of them may the 'other.' Marquis of *Argyle*'s speech at a committee of both houses [d].

In the famous protestation, *A. D.* 1641, all the members of both houses solemnly swear to keep up the union

[a] PARL. HIST. XIV. 418.
[b] Ibid. XVI. 53.
[c] Ibid. 57.
[d] Ibid. XIV. 464.

union among the three kingdoms of *England*, *Scotland*, and *Ireland*, and this before the union of the two kingdoms of *Britain*. [In those days, people understood the importance of union.] The commons wanted the lords to agree to a bill for the general taking the protestation. The lords reject the bill, though they thought it right for both houses to take the protestation [a]. The commons conclude that this was done by the influence of the popish members and bishops. They resolve that no person refusing it, is fit to be in any place of trust. Order this resolution to be sent by the members to their several counties, cities, and boroughs, and to be printed and published.

This king expected parliament to support him against the *Scotch* army at *Newcastle*. 'But it was the leading 'men of the party against the king that encouraged the '*Scotch* army to enter *England*, and this party was so 'superior in parliament, that few of the king's friends 'durst open their mouths to support his interest. It 'was this *Scotch* invasion that compelled the king to 'call a parliament, and enabled the parliament to break 'all the king's measures, and oblige him to suffer a 'redress of grievances. In a word, it was solely by 'means of the *Scots* that the parliament had it in their 'power to restore the government to its ancient and 'natural state. They (parliament) would have acted 'against their own interest, and directly contrary to 'the end they proposed, if they had supplied the king 'with means to drive the *Scots* out of the kingdom. 'Accordingly they took not one step tending to that 'purpose. On the contrary, it evidently appeared 'that they considered the *Scots* as brethren, who having the same interest as the *English*, were come to 'assist them, and act in concert with them [b].' The

English

---

[a] PARL. HIST. IX. 503.

[b] *Rap.* II. 365.

English ought never to have forgot this. Sir *William Widrington* member for *Northumberland*, happening to call the *Scotch* army rebels, would have been sent to the *Tower* if he had not retracted, and promised never more to offend in like manner. Parliament (instead of opposing the *Scots*) voted them 300,000 *l.* in reward for their brotherly assistance, and prolonged the treaty with them till the triennial bill was passed, and more of the grievances redressed, 1641, the very contrary of the tyrant's hopes, and a treaty was made with the *Scots* for securing and restoring their liberties [a].

'Had the *Scots* been as *tame* as the *English*, for ought 'that appears, *Charles* I. might have avoided calling a 'parliament as long as he lived [b].'

The approach of the *Scotch* army was the cause of the king's calling a parliament; and their presence kept the king in awe. 'We cannot do without the *Scots*,' said *Strode* in the house [c].

'We, the lords and commons assembled, in the 'parliament of *England*, considering with what wisdom 'and public affection our brethren of the kingdom of '*Scotland* did concur with the endeavours of this par'liament, in procuring and establishing a firm peace 'and amity between the two nations, and how loving'ly they have since invited us to a nearer and higher 'degree of union,—— cannot doubt but they will with 'as much forwardness and affection, concur with us 'in settling peace in this kingdom, and preserving it 'in their own, that so we may mutually reap the be'nefit of that amity and alliance so happily made, and 'strongly confirmed between the two nations, &c.

'Wherefore

---

[a] *Rap.* II. 365.

[b] HIST. ESS. ENGL. CONST. p. 101.

[c] *Hume*, HIST. STUARTS, I. 252.

'Wherefore we have thought good to make known to 'our brethren, &c.' Parliament's declaration to the *Scots*, *November* 1642. The *Scots* in those days, when the spirit of liberty ran highest, were always called by the parliament, our brethren; not as now, the slavish, beggarly, itchy, thieving *Scots*[a].

'By the assistance of the *Scotch* nation, reality was 'given to those schemes of government, which had 'long been the ardent wish of the generous part of the '*English*[b].'

It is certain that *Scotland* began the solemn league against the tyranny of *Charles*, and that *England* and *Ireland* came into it after[c].

The solemn league and covenant, *A. D.* 1638, was occasioned by the king's attempt to introduce the liturgy in *Scotland*; it contained an engagement to support religion, as it was established in 1580; all, *Scotland*, but the court, subscribed it[d]. The malcontents were reckoned 1000 to one. The *Scots* shewed twice the spirit the *English* shewed against the king's innovations. They brought him to make proposals. Not being content with the proposals, they protest publickly against his declaration, in which they positively insist on a general assembly and parliament, that they were not guilty, as pretended by the king of any unlawful combination or rebellion; that the king, did not disallow nor discharge any of the innovations complained of, &c. They tell the commissioner that if the king refuses to call a general assembly, they will call one themselves[e]. They reject eleven propositions from the king.

---

a Parl. Hist. xii. 31.

b *Macaul.* Hist. v. 384.

c Parl. Hist. xvi. 18.

d *Rap.* ii. 303.

e Ibid. 305.

king. He reduces them to two. They reject them. An assembly is called. The commissioner orders them to break up. They sit by their own authority. It is therefore unjust to blame them as if their whole motive for resisting the king had been the support of presbyterianism. They meant liberty as much as the *English* did. It was as much a point with them not to receive the liturgy, when forced upon them, as with the *English* not to receive popery. It was the very wantonness of tyranny to impose the liturgy upon them, because they could do without it. They made almost twenty acts directly opposite to the king's intention [a]. Among others, an act condemning the clergy's holding civil offices, as of justices, &c. and sitting and voting in parliament. They boldly annulled (says *Rapin*) things established by parliament.

The king raises an army in *England* to suppress the *Scots*. Pretends (in order to prevail with the *English* to go to war against the *Scots*) that the *Scots* were going to invade *England*. And the deluded king-ridden *English* rise at the call of the tyrant, to crush the spirit of liberty in their brave brethren of *Scotland*. The *Scots* publish papers in *England*, calling on the *English* to bestir themselves against the tyranny, instead of taking part with it. And they order their forces not to approach within ten miles of the borders, which, overthrows the king's pretence of their intending an invasion. The *Scots* intimidated suddenly, send to the king in his camp, offering proposals of peace, which, however, make the king's pretences of the rebellious spirit of the *Scots*, and their intended invasion, appear very ridiculous [b]. A peace is patched up, on very precarious terms [c]. A new assembly. They make

[a] *Rap.* 307. [b] Ibid. II. 309. [c] Ibid. 311.

make several acts directly opposite to the king's intentions. A parliament. They do the same, 1639. Thus the wings of prerogative were very close cut in *Scotland*; which demonstrates that the *Scots* valued civil liberty as well as religious. See the titles of those free acts[a]. The king accordingly prorogues them suddenly. They protest against the prorogation. The king published his pretence for breaking the late peace with the *Scots*. The real reason was, their opposition to his tyranny. The king makes a mighty noise about a letter said to have been sent to the *French* king, by the malcontents for his assistance[b].

Among other things, the popular leaders were encouraged by the example of the *Scotch*, 'whose encroachments had totally subverted monarchy[c].' All this ought to give our northern brethren great honour in the estimation of the friends of *liberty*. Instead of which we have seen some, whose pretences to that character have been very loud, setting themselves at the head of the disparagers of that people; how consistently, let themselves explain, if they can.

Charles I. lost all his power in *Scotland*, long before his authority in *England* was annihilated. 'The *Scots* 'now considered themselves as a republic, and made 'no account of the authority of their prince,' says Mr. *Hume* .

It is true, Mrs. *Macaulay* insists, that the *Scots*, by their interposition in the time of *Charles* I. meant chiefly the establishment of presbyterianism. So Mr. *Hume* thinks, the *English*, in their struggle for liberty, meant chiefly religious liberty[e].

 Whatever

---

[a] *Rap.* 312. [b] Ibid. 314.
[c] *Hume*, HIST. STUARTS, I. 292. [d] Ibid. I. 291.
[e] Ibid. I. 254.

Whatever our modern patriots may think, it is certain, that our wise anceſtors in all ages had thought the union between the two kingdoms a matter of great advantage for *England*.

The union of the two kingdoms was propoſed ſo long ago, as *Edward* Iſt's laſt parliament at *Carliſle*. *A. D.* 1307[a].

The union between the kingdoms was attempted by *Henry* VIII. by *Edward* VI. though *England* had lately conquered a great part of *Scotland*. Repeatedly by *James* I. in whoſe time ſeveral articles were agreed on. No mention of it under *Charles* I. He wanted rather to conquer both kingdoms, than unite them. There was a ſtrong confederacy between the kingdoms during the civil wars. After the battle of *Worceſter*, commiſſioners were appointed by parliament. All *Scotland* was then for the union. *Cromwell's* turning out the parliament, prevented its eſtabliſhment. *Cromwell's* ſcheme for a general parliament of the three kingdoms was in fact an union; and *Cromwell*, *April* 12th, 1654, publiſhed an ordinance for uniting *England* and *Scotland*, by which wards, ſervices, and ſlaviſh tenures were taken away. They were reſtored at the reſtoration, to the great damage of the country. Under *Charles* II. the *Scotch* make overtures towards union. Difficulties were ſtarted by lawyers, particularly that the conſtitution would be altered, and that it was treaſon to attempt altering the conſtitution by 8 *Jac.* VI. Thus the *Scotch* firſt moved this treaty, and firſt broke it off. Under *James* II. nothing was done. The times too buſy, and too turbulent for union. *William* afterwards recommended it; but it could not be brought about till

[a] PARL. HIST. I. 146.

till Queen *Anne*'s time. And now ſome patriots want to have it broken again. It was thought neceſſary to aboliſh the *Scotch* parliament, becauſe two parliaments would be always battling it, and the *Scots* would demoliſh the union whenever they pleaſed, and the intention was, 'a laſting and incorporating union, 'that ſhould put an end to all *diſtinctions*, and unite 'all intereſts.' Queen *Anne* was ſo earneſt about it, that ſhe went twice to the meeting of the committee, to ſee how they went on, and to preſs the execution. 'An union of the two kingdoms has been long wiſhed 'for, being ſo neceſſary for eſtabliſhing the laſting peace, 'happineſs and proſperity of both nations.' Commiſſioners words. Queen's anſwer. 'I ſhall always look 'upon it as a particular happineſs if the union, which 'will be ſo great a ſecurity to both kingdoms, can be 'accompliſhed in my reign[a].'

I believe moſt impartial men have blamed the conduct of *England* in the affair of the *Darien* colony, and think we owe the *Scots* a good turn toward making up for our ill uſage of them on that occaſion, I do not ſay, the *injury* we did them, becauſe I write with *healing* views.

The queſtion was put concerning the *Darien* colony, in the houſe of peers, *A. D.* 1698. Several lords proteſted againſt ſevere proceedings, becauſe there was not time enough to judge of the merits of the cauſe. The houſe, however, addreſſed the king againſt it, becauſe it was likely to be hurtful to the *Engliſh* plantation-trade, and to break the good correſpondence between *Spain* and *England*. [Therefore *England* was to do an unjuſt thing.] They acknowledged, that the caſe of the *Scots* was pitiable; for that they muſt be great loſers by being

[a] *Tind.* CONTIN. I. 734, 739, 740, 741.

ing disappointed of the advantage they proposed, and by the loss of the great sum they had laid out. They wish [kind souls!] that the *Scots* may desist, because they will only be greater losers in the end. They put the king in mind, that there had been a former address to him, which shewed the sense of the nation. [The nation did not certainly approve of the *Scotch* nation's becoming considerable in commerce. Neither did the *Dutch* approve of the *English* settlement at *Amboyna*.] This address, however, was carried by only four or five votes; and sixteen lords protested against it, and the commons refused to concur with it. The king very humanely took notice, in his answer, of the hardship to which the *Scots* were to be reduced by this opposition from *England*, and of the clashing of interests, which would probably continue, while the two kingdoms remained separate, and again recommends to them the union. Steps were accordingly taken toward it; but nothing done effectually[a].

Queen *Anne*, in her first speech, 'had renewed the 'motion made by the late king, for the union of both 'kingdoms. Many of those who seemed now (*A. D.* '1702,) to have the greatest share of her favour and 'confidence, opposed it with much heat, and not 'without indecent reflections on the *Scotch* nation. Yet 'it was carried by a great majority, that the queen 'should be empowered to name commissioners for 'treating of an union. It was so visibly the interest 'of *England*, and of the present government, to shut 'the back door against the practices of *France*, and the 'attempts of the pretended prince of *Wales*, that the 'opposition made to this first step towards an union, 'and the indecent scorn, with which *Seymour* and 'others treated the *Scots*, were clear indications, that 'the

[a] DEB. PEERS, II. 8.

'the posts they were brought into, had not changed 'their tempers; but that, instead of healing matters, 'they intended to irritate them farther by their re-'proachful speeches. The bill went through both 'houses, notwithstanding the rough treatment it met 'with at first.'

'It is with the greatest satisfaction, that I have given 'my assent to a bill for uniting *England* and *Scotland* 'into one kingdom. I consider this union as a matter 'of the greatest importance to the wealth, strength, 'and safety of the whole island, and at the same time 'as a work of so much difficulty and nicety in its own 'nature, that, till now, all attempts, which have been 'made toward it in the course of above a hundred 'years, have proved ineffectual, and therefore I make 'no doubt, but it will be remembered, and spoken of 'hereafter to the honour of those who have been in-'strumental in bringing it to such a happy conclusion. 'I desire and expect from all my subjects of both na-'tions, that from henceforth they act with all possible 'respect and kindness to one another; that so it may 'appear to all the world, they have hearts disposed to 'become one people. This will be a great pleasure 'to me, and will make us all quickly sensible of the 'good effect of this union [a].'

The lords and commons answer, 'That they thank 'her Majesty for her gracious approbation of the share 'they had in bringing the treaty of union between the 'two kingdoms to a happy conclusion; a work which '(after so many fruitless endeavours) seems designed by 'Providence to add new lustre to the glories of her ma-'jesty's reign [b].' And see another speech and answer, to the same purpose [c].

 In

[a] Queen *Anne's* SPEECH TO PARL. *A. D.* 1706.

[b] DEB. COM. IV. 59. [c] Ibid. 70, 72, 73.

In the year 1714, a virulent pamphlet was complained of in the house of peers, exclaiming against the union as very advantageous to *Scotland*, and the contrary to *England*. The printer was taken into custody of the black rod. Said, he had the MS. from *Barber's*, printer of the Gazette and Votes of the Commons. *Barber* would answer no questions tending to strengthen the charge against himself. Lord *Oxford* was suspected for the author. A peer [anonymous] said, They had nothing to do with the printer or publisher; but that it highly imported the house to find the author, in order to do justice to the *Scotch* nation. *Barber* and *Morphew* were thereupon enlarged from the custody of the black rod. The house of peers address the Queen, and observe, 'That the pamphlet was highly dishonourable and 'scandalous to her subjects of *Scotland*,' &c. They take notice, that the Queen had often 'been pleased to 'declare from the throne, that the union of the two 'kingdoms is the peculiar happiness of her reign.' They humbly request the Queen to publish her royal proclamation, with reward and promise of pardon to accomplices, in order to the discovering of the author. This was accordingly done, and a reward of 300 l. proposed [a].

Small, member for *Gloucester*, obliged to ask pardon of the house, for reflecting on the *Scotch* nation, *A. D.* 1716, just after the rebellion [b]. Our incendiary writers reflect on them immediately after a glorious war, which, (if Lord *Chatham* is to be believed,) we could not have carried on without them [c].

There has been a great outcry made by some, about the supposed mischief which has been the con-

[a] DEB. PEERS, II. 404.

[b] *Tind.* CONTIN. I. 495.

[c] Ibid.

consequence of the union. 'North Britain sends (they 'observe,) sixty-one members to both houses. They 'are particularly obnoxious to court-influence. They 'are, therefore, a dead weight on every vote for liberty 'and the public good,' &c. But suppose it were true, that all the members for *North Britain* have always voted on the court-side, (the contrary of which may be easily seen by turning over the debates,) what are 61 to 800? The *Scotch* members are but a thirteenth part of the whole legislature. Let the *English* members on all occasions vote for their country's good, and leave the *Scotch* to stand by the court alone. This will more effectually expose them, than writing ten thousand incendiary papers against them. And if I live to see all the *English* members of both houses, without exception, vote for those restorations of the constitution, which are necessary for its preservation, (viz. annual parliaments, with exclusion by rotation, &c.) while all the *Scotch* members unite in opposing those salutary measures, and are not reproved by their constituents; I will give up the *North Britons* for a nation of slaves, and will be the first to propose that they be deprived of all share in the legislature of the united kingdoms. But, so long as I observe some *Scotch* members, as well as some *English*, voting against the interest of their country, I cannot, in conscience, single out the former as alone guilty; nor can I look upon those who are thus grossly partial, in any other light than that of a set of shameless and determined mischief-makers.

The Earl of *Findlater* laid the *Scotch* grievances before the house of peers, *A. D.* 1713, viz. Their being deprived, since the union, of a privy-council. The laws of *England*, in cases of treason, extended to *Scotland*.

land. *Scotch* peers, made *British* peers, not allowed to sit in the house of peers, as *Englishmen* made peers. The malt-tax, which fell very unequally upon *Scotland*, because *Scotch* malt was not worth a third part of the price of *English*, and yet was to pay the same tax. Besides, it was said to be a violation of the XIVth article of union. He moves, that, as the effects of the union had not answered expectation, it might be dissolved again. The Duke of *Argyle* seconds him. They were opposed by Lord *North* and *Grey*, and others. Lord *Oxford* said, he did not see how the union could be dissolved, because the *Scotch* parliament which had made it with the *English*, was now no more. Lord *Nottingham* answered, that the *Scotch* parliament was included in the *British*; and that the *British* parliament could do any thing, but destroy the constitution. *Sunderland*, *Townshend*, and *Halifax*, were all for dissolving. Several *Scotch* lords said, If the union was not dissolved, their country would be the most miserable under heaven. Carried against dissolving by only four voices [a].

The Earl of *Rochester* thought the disgrace of the *Scotch* peers losing their birth-right after the union, and being reduced to representation by a few in the legislative assembly, instead of sitting of course, as the *English*, was so great, that he declared in the house of peers, he wondered they should ever submit to it [b].

'If *Scotland* [when united to *England*] sends fewer 'representatives to parliament than *England*, the former 'is enslaved to *England*,' says *Harrington*[c]. Therefore he was rather for having *England* and *Scotland* con- 'federated

[a] DEB. PEERS, II. 313. [b] Ibid. II. 174.

[c] *Harringt.* OCEANA, 518.

federated in the manner of the States of *Holland*, than united by an incorporating union.

'If *Scotland* be a gainer [by the union] in some 'particulars, we [of *England*] are infinitely recom-'pensed by the many advantages accruing to us upon the whole.' Lord *Halifax* on the union [a].

At the union, it was agreed, that *Scotland* should have 398,085 l. equivalent-money, in consideration of *England*'s being in debt, and partly to make up for the *Darian* loss. But Lord *Nottingham* justly observed, that the money would not come into the hands of the individuals who were the losers; but would be swallowed up by a few [b].

'We are now,' says Lord *Bolingbroke* [c], [since the union,] 'one nation under one government, and must 'therefore always have one common interest: the same 'friends, the same foes, the same principles of security 'and of danger. It is by consequence now in our 'power to take the entire advantage of our situation; 'an advantage which would make us ample amends for 'several which we want; and which some of our neigh-'bours possess; an advantage which constantly attended 'to, and wisely improved, would place the '*British* na-'tion in such circumstances of happiness and glory, as 'the greatest empires could never boast. Far from being 'alarmed at every motion on the continent; far from 'being oppressed for the support of foreign schemes; we 'might enjoy the securest peace and most unenvied 'plenty. Far from courting or purchasing the al-'liances of other nations, we might see them suing 'favours. Far from being hated or despised for involv-'ing ourselves in all the little wrangles of the conti-'nent,

[a] DEB. PEERS, II. 173. [b] Ibid.

[c] *Bolingbr.* REM. HIST. ENGL. 195.

'nent, we might be respected by all those who maintain the just balance of *Europe*, and be formidable to 'those alone who should endeavour to break it.'

Sir *Edward Coke* (no *Scotchman)* observes[a], how marvellous a conformity there was, not only in the religion and language of the two nations, but also in their ancient laws, the descent of the crown, their parliaments, their titles of nobility, their officers of state, and of justice, their writs, their customs, and even the language of their laws. So that in attacking the *Scots* we reflect on the *English*[b].

It is one of the articles of the union, (of which the *English* were more desirous than the *Scots)* that there shall be a communication of all rights and privileges between the subjects of both kingdoms, except where it is otherwise excepted. But there was no exception against any *Scotch* nobleman's being employed by the king. Yet they who set up and kept up the late clamour, openly avowed their dislike to a particular nobleman, merely because he was a *Scotchman*.

Montesquieu calls it an admirable contrivance of the *Tartars*, the conquerors of *China*, that they have incorporated *Chinese* and *Tartars* together, in their civil and military establishment. It unites, he says, the two nations, it keeps up a spirit and power in both, and one is not swallowed up by the other, &c.[c] Some far-sighted politicians among us, are against allowing our *united* brethren of *North Britain* the privileges, which *Montesquieu* thinks a victorious nation ought to grant a *conquered* people. He says[d], *England* was not arrived at her highest relative greatness, till the union.

'Exclusive

---

[a] 4 Inst. 345.

[b] *Blackst.* Comm. I. 95.

[c] L'Espr. des Loix, I. 235.

[d] Ibid. I. 125.

'Exclusive of other motives,' says the author of a LETTER TO LORD TEMPLE, p. 31, [for the union between *England* and *Scotland*,] 'we see present expe-'dience, and the like causes interfere. And the event 'having taken place, all measures for producing that 'likeness and cordiality, which is the strongest political 'band, should be pursued by every honest man; and to 'this we are warmly admonished by the example of '*Rome*, where the want of affection between the new 'and old citizens, threw the weight of the former into 'the scale of every corrupt party that arose in the state, 'and attached them not to their country, but to a *Ma-'rius*, a *Cinna*, a *Cæsar*.' The same author goes on to shew, that irritating the people of *North Britain* tends to make them either unserviceable friends or resolved enemies. He shews how hurtful their hostility has been, and may be again to *England*, by joining with *France*. He then touches, but in a humane and gentleman-like manner, upon the national failings of our northern brethren, (we are not ourselves without failings) who emerged into light, and knowledge, and liberal sentiment, later than *England*, and may therefore be supposed a little backwarder in political knowledge. 'As I write,' says he, 'without any design of lowering that brave and 'prudent people in the estimation of their neighbours, 'and my strictures being on their government, not on 'individuals, I hope I shall stand acquitted in endea-'vouring to remove prejudices against any systems 'which may promote that assimilation with *England*, 'for which I have contended. Let *Scotland* discern, 'acknowledge, and imitate, where *England* is confes-'sedly her superior. It derogates not from the merit 'of any single person to make the concession. For it 'is time, circumstances, and situation, that have con-

'ferred

'ferred the superiority. Let not *England* value her-'self too much upon this accidental superiority, nor 'despise her northern fellow-subjects for being inferior 'as a people, whilst, as individuals, they are incontest-'ibly their equals; and let them consider, that the less 'merit they allow the *Scotch*, the more it is to be ex-'pected, that they, as a brave and spirited nation, 'should insist on [a].'

To this natural principle of resistance to injury, ought, in common candour, to be ascribed the proceeding of the people of *North Britain*, in sending up addresses of a spirit and tendency contrary to those of the remonstrances presented by a vast multitude of the people of *England*. The *North Britons* are farther from being slaves in their disposition, than any people in the world, if those of *South Britain* be excepted; but they saw, or thought they saw, a very unjustifiable spirit of natienal prejudice, acting in many of those concerned in the remonstrances; and they thought themselves obliged to oppose them on this very account. And this is the only public step they have taken on the occasion; while the scatterers of firebrands, arrows, and death, whose unpatriotic and diabolical labour has been to divide the united kingdom, by reviving the long-buried animosity between those whom nature and interest direct to cultivate peace and unanimity; have been but too much countenanced by many unthinking and narrow-minded people on this side the *Tweed*. It must be confessed, that the late remonstrances were, to say the least, founded on a narrow bottom, and were in their tendency but frivolous. Had they been what they ought; had they proposed steps toward

[a] Ibid. p. 45.

toward the restoration of independency to parliament, which will effectually secure, and which only can secure the redress of all internal abuses in administration; had this been done, and had any community in *North*, or *South Britain*, addressed on the contrary side, I should not have hesitated to declare my opinion of such community to be, That they were traitors to their country, and the bribed slaves of a designing ministry.

Lord *Clarendon*, in his speech on *James* II.'s abdication, lays great stress on the bad consequences of the possibility of a rupture with *Scotland*. Which shews, that the people of *England* had, in those days, some regard for their northern brethren. 'I hope, Gentlemen, says he 'you will take into your consideration what is 'to become of the kingdom of *Scotland*, if they should 'differ from us in this point. Then will that king- 'dom be again divided from ours. You cannot but 'remember how much trouble it gave our ancestors, 'while it continued a divided kingdom. And if we 'should go out of the line, and invert the succession in 'any point, I fear you will find a disagreement there, and 'then very dangerous consequences may ensue[a].' It so happened, however, that the *Scots* were of the same mind with the *English* in this point. See '*Declaration* '*of the Estates of Scotland concerning the misgovernment of* 'James VII., *and filling up the throne with King* William '*and Queen* Mary[b],' in which all his irregular proceedings are condemned with as little reserve by the *Scots* as the *English*.

On occasion of *Porteous*'s affair, *A. D.* 1737, it was thought necessary to send for the *Scotch* judges. A long debate arose in the house of peers, about the honours

[a] DEB. COM. II. 241. [b] Ibid.

nours to be shewn them in the house. One lord, not named [a], insists on their being received in the same manner as the *English* judges, and placed on the woolsacks, &c. 'The *Scots*,' says he, p. 182, 'have a 'right to claim, that the same honours, the same re'spect, may be shewn by this house to the judges of '*Scotland* as are shewn to the judges of *England*, ex'cepting only, that a preference is to be allowed to the 'latter with respect to their ranks or degrees.' And afterwards, p. 183, 'This is the first time it has ever 'been thought necessary to ask the *Scotch* judges any 'questions; and if your lordships now oblige them to 'attend, I hope you will shew them the same honours, 'the same respect you would shew the judges of any of 'the courts of *Westminster-hall*, if they should be or'dered to attend for the like purpose.' And again, p. 184, 'The right now in dispute before your lord'ships, is not the right of a private man, nor is it a 'right of a private nature; it is the right of a whole 'people, it is the right of a nation once free and inde'pendent; and it is a right stipulated by one of the 'most public and most solemn contracts that was ever 'made; a contract, which, on our parts, we are oblig'ed to observe and fulfil with the greatest nicety, be'cause the people of *Scotland* trusted entirely to our 'honour for a faithful performance; a submitting to be 'governed by one and the same parliament, in which 'they knew we would always have a great majority, was 'really, in effect, submitting every thing to our honour; 'and I hope, they shall never have the least occasion to 'repent of the confidence they have reposed in us. 'For this reason, in all cases where the rights or the 'privileges of the people of *Scotland*, by virtue of the 'articles

[a] Deb. Lords, v. 180.

'articles of union, come to be questioned, I shall always have a strong bias in their favour, especially when the matter in question relates to a piece of ceremony. But in the present case I must think, there can be properly no question; for whether the judges of *Scotland* ought to be in this house as assistants to give their opinions upon such matters of law, as may arise in the course of our proceedings, in the same manner as the judges of *England* do, is a question, I think, determined not only by the articles of union, but by the very nature of the thing itself; because, while *Scotland* continues to be governed by laws different from *England*, it will be impossible for us to do our duty without such assistance. My lords, as nothing contributed more than the union between the two kingdoms, towards the securing the protestant succession in the present illustrious family, so there is nothing can contribute more to the preservation of that succession, than the rendering that union every day more firm and unalterable; which can no way be done more effectually than by cementing the people by an union in hearts and affections, as well as an union established by law. While we have such a majority in both houses of parliament, the people of *Scotland* will always find it impossible to break through, or dissolve the legal union which subsists between us; but if we should ever make use of that majority, which I hope we never shall, to break through, or encroach upon those articles, which have been stipulated between us, then the legal union will be of little force, it will only serve to make them desperate, and to run the risk even of their own perdition, in order to rid themselves of the yoke they groan under. They will be apt to ascribe to the present royal family all the ills they feel, or imagine

'they

'they feel; and if they should unanimously join in a 'contrary interest, we know they would be supported 'by a numerous party in this part of the island, as well 'as by a powerful party beyond seas; for which reason 'we ought to take all possible care, not to give them 'any just ground of complaint; we ought even to 'avoid a measure which may be made use of by the 'enemies of government for sowing discontent and 'disaffection in that part of the island.' And again, p. 186, 'As I am not of that country, [*Scotland*,] I 'have spoken with the more freedom in this debate, 'because I think I cannot be suspected of prejudice or 'partiality. If I have any, I confess it is upon that 'side, on which I think my own honour, and the ho-'nour of my country most deeply concerned, which I 'take to be in a most exact observance, not only of the 'words, but of the spirit and intention of the articles 'of union. We contracted together as nations quite 'independent of one another, and by the whole 'tenor of the contract it appears, that the subjects of 'both kingdoms are intitled to equal honours, privi-'leges, and advantages. We have no pretence to any 'pre-eminence, but only that those of any rank in *Eng-*'*land*, shall have precedence of those of the same rank in '*Scotland*. This they have always, since the union, 'allowed us, and I hope we shall never dispute con-'ferring upon any gentleman of rank in *Scotland* these 'marks of honour or respect, which are bestowed upon 'gentlemen of the same rank in *England*.'

Mr. *Hume* has remarked, that the hatred between *France* and *England*, subsists more on the part of the latter than the former. And I think it must be acknowledged, that in the quarrel between *England* and *Scotland*, the *English* have often, especially of late, shewn the greatest inveteracy of the two. A narrow-ness

ness against strangers is indeed the only national disposition we could wish altered in the *English*. It has sometimes happened that *England* has suffered by this narrowness. As in the case of the rupture between the two nations, when *Cromwell* was made general gainst the *Scots*. Had the *English* treated their northern brethren with the generosity they shew to one another, the war had never happened. A very short time before, there was the strictest amity possible between the two kingdoms. But that being interrupted, by unjustifiable conduct on the side of the *English*, (see the historians of those times) and war between the two kingdoms following, General *Fairfax* declined the command, fairly declaring that he thought the war against *Scotland* unjust. On this *Cromwell* (whose conscience was not so rigid as *Fairfax*'s) was employed. He was successful; gained honour; came into high power; and at last overset the glorious scheme of a republic, which, but for him, would probably have been established in this country.

But after all I have said with a view to suggest the necessity of correcting the narrowness of the *English* to strangers, and even to their northern brethren, let me add, That their *incorporating* the *Scots*, whom they had conquered at the battle of *Worcester*, and their giving them such advantageous terms at the union, notwithstanding their strong attachment at that time to what are called Tory principles, are proofs of great magnanimity in the people of *England*.

To pretend that a native of *North Britain* has not a right to hold the place of secretary of state, or any other of the great offices, would be to assert, that there ought to be a peculiar mark of disgrace put upon the northern inhabitants of the united island, to place them in a worse condition than those of *Ireland* or the Colonies; in short, to make them Helotes, slaves,

 hewers

hewers of wood, and drawers of water. If there be any reason for this disadvantageous distinction, it ought to be produced.

'If the *Scots* had a spark of spirit or of love of their 'country left, if they were worthy of being admitted 'to the honour of an union with this great and illus- 'trious nation, they ought, every man of them, to 'submit their throats to the sword of the *English*, ra- 'ther than suffer the oppression, the injustice, the in- 'dignity, the ingratitude of such a doctrine prevailing 'against them, that their country is held so infamous, 'so accursed of God and man, that it is not entitled 'to the same chance with the *English*, of a promiscuous 'election of its natives to civil and military posts [a].'

This silly narrowness has, in all times, been a prejudice and not an advantage. Time was when every little town insisted on monopolizing its own manufacture. *Bridport*, in the time of *Henry* VIII. petitioned and (such was the ignorance of the legislature) obtained an act prohibiting the making of ropes any where out of *Bridport*; and the towns of *Worcester*, *Evesham*, *Droitwich*, &c. the same for the woollen manufacture [b]. Has not *England* improved more since these restraints were removed, than while they took place?

Partiality for our own country, and contempt of others, arise from a disposition as thoroughly despicable as the same partiality in an individual in favour of himself. How much more magnanimous does the modesty of *Horace* appear, when he advises the *Roman* writers to study the *Greek* models, than if he had preferred those of his own country?

—Vos

[a] LOND. MAG. *October* 1774. p. 524.

[b] *Anders.* HIST. COM. I. 359, 363.

———Vos exemplaria Græca
Nocturnâ versate manu, versate diurnâ.

How graceful is *Cicero*'s (even the vain *Cicero*'s) acknowledgment of the superiority of the *Gauls* to his countrymen in bodily strength, of the *Carthaginians* in cunning, and of *Greece* in the arts? And when *Virgil* owns, that other countries may produce abler orators and artists than those of *Rome*,

Excudent alii sperantia, &c.

do we not esteem his candour much more than if he had set his country above all others? It is, in short, always to be concluded, that he who disparages other countries, is both conceited and ignorant. He overpraises his own country because it is his; and he despises other countries, because he does not know them. Accordingly national prejudice appears always strongest in the vulgar.

'*Operæ pretium foret*, &c. It would be worth while 'to recite the tragical proceedings which our national 'inhospitality of disposition, and our hatred and con'tempt of strangers, have produced, as well in the reigns 'of King *John*, *Henry*, *Edward* II. *Henry* VI. as 'lately, that we may hereafter extinguish this infamy, 'and now that we are enlightened with the beams of 'a better religion, we may behave ourselves with more 'humanity to strangers [a].'

'*Anglis ut plurimum*, &c. The *English* in general 'admire themselves, their national manners, genius, 'and courage, above all others. This disposition oc'casions such a bluntness in the behaviour of those of 'them who have not travelled, that, in speaking and 'writing, they disdain to use the common terms of 'politeness, as thinking them too slavish [b].'

B b 2 Even

[a] *Lambard*. De Morib. Angl. 107.

[b] *Johan. Barcl.* De Morib. Angl. 98.

2

Even the *Spaniards*, though famous for their narrow and suspicious temper, observing the depopulation of their country by the expulsion of the *Moors* and *Jews*, invited all foreign manufacturers and farmers of the Roman catholic religion to come and settle in *Spain*, offering them perpetual immunity from taxes [a].

The states of *Holland* and *West Friseland*, in their decree for establishing their liberty, after observing, that they have remained unsubdued either by internal or external force for 800 years, assert, that this is singly owing to a constant harmony among themselves.

By 4 *James* I. c. 1. the laws of hostility between *England* and *Scotland* are utterly repealed, 'seeing all 'enmity and hostility of former times between the two 'kingdoms and people is now happily taken away, and 'under the government of his Majesty, as under one pa-'rent and head, turned into brotherly friendship [b],' &c.

May it not be, with justice, affirmed, that though the *English*, 'take them for all in all, as *Hamlet* says, 'are such a people that we can no where look upon 'their like,' yet they would be improved by a little *French* politeness, a little *German* steadiness, a little *Dutch* frugality, and a little *Scotch* education? In other words, Are we not too rough in our manners, too impatient under adversity, too prone to luxury and pleasure, too much attached to money, and too negligent of the improvement of the mind?

Let us hear Lord *Lyttelton* [c] on the subject.

'*England* has secured by the union every public 'blessing which was before enjoyed by her, and has 'greatly augmented her strength. The martial spirit 'of

---

[a] *De Laet* HISP. DESCR. 105.

[b] STAT. AT LARGE, II. 397.

[c] Lord *Lyttelton*'s Works, p. 503.

'of the *Scots*, their hardy bodies, their acute and vi-'gorous minds, their industry, their activity, are now 'employed to the benefit of the whole island. He is 'now a bad *Scotchman* who is not a good *Englishman*, 'and he is a bad *Englishman* who is not a good *Scotch*-'*man*.' And 'To resist the union is to rebel against 'nature.——She has joined the two countries, has 'fenced them both with the sea against the invasion 'of all other nations; but has laid them entirely open 'the one to the other. Accursed be he who endea-'vours to divide them.——What God has joined, le 'no man put asunder [a].'

The justice of the late accusation against our northern brethren as if not sufficiently attached to liberty, will appear from the following paragraphs:

The president *Bradshaw*, before passing sentence on *Charles* I. observed, that many kings had been, for misgovernment, deposed and imprisoned by their subjects; and particularly that in *Scotland* of 109 kings, the greatest part were proceeded against, deposed, or imprisoned, particularly *Charles*'s grandmother [b].

Scotland had trial by juries of 9, 11, 13, 15, or more, men of known character, as early as *A. D.* 840 [c].

'*Scotland*, through all ages till the battle of *Wor*-'*cester*, maintained her independency against the force 'and fraud of the *English* and *French* monarchies [d].'

'I must take leave to put the representatives of this 'nation [*Scotland*] in mind, that no monarchy in *Eu*-'*rope* was, before the union of the crowns, more li-'mited,

[a] Lord *Lyttelton*'s Works, p. 504.

[b] *Whitelock*'s MEM. 368.

[c] King *Kenneth*'s LAWS. *Spelm.* CONCIL. I. 341.

[d] *Macaul.* HIST. V. 76.

'mited, nor any people more jealous of their liberties [a].'

'These principles [of arbitrary power] were first introduced among us [the *Scots*] after the union of the crowns, and the prerogative extended to the ruin of the constitution, chiefly by the prelatical party [b].'

No legate from the pope ever entered *Scotland* [c].

It is well known, that in the time of Queen *Elizabeth* the flame of liberty burnt very dim in *England*. Yet in those very times, 'the *Scotch* commissioners at *London* presented memorials, containing reasons for deposing their queen, and seconded their arguments with examples drawn from the *Scotch* history, the authority of laws, and the sentiments of the most famous divines. The lofty ideas which *Elizabeth* had entertained of the absolute indefeasible right of sovereigns, occasioned her being shocked at these republican topics [d].'

James I. complained sadly of the sauciness of his *Scotch* subjects, and expected to do what he pleased when he came to *England*. The *Scots* had murmured, and actually taken up arms, when the king or his ministers did not govern to their mind. They had dethroned his mother, and put him in her place, during her life: Therefore they considered him as dependent on them. *James* was infatuated with the notions of absolute power.

Their steady resistance against the foolish and tyrannical fancy of *James* I. and *Charles* I. of imposing upon them

---

[a] *Fletcher*'s speech in the *Scotch* parliament, *A. D.* 1703, p. 277. [b] Ibid. 278.

[c] Mod. Univ. Hist. xxv. 474.

[d] *Hume*, Hist. Tud: ii. 520.

them the liturgy, shews a spirit very far from slavish[a]. When the Marquis of *Hamilton*, by the king's orders, asked them what would satisfy them, they answered, Nothing but a parliament and general assembly, which they would call of their own authority, without waiting for the king's; and that they would as soon renounce their baptism, as the covenant[b]. I wish we saw such a spirit in *England* on a proper occasion. 'This was 'the fountain from whence our ensuing troubles did 'spring,' says *Whitelocke*[c]. So that the resistance, which in the end overthrew the tyranny of *Charles* I. took its rise in *Scotland*.

A *Scotch* gentleman, who came into *England* with king *James* I. observing how the *English* flattered him, said, Thir foulke wull spull a gude keeng.

There was more sense in the *Scots* pinning down *Charles* II. too much (if too much could be) at his arrival in that country, than in the *English* leaving him too much at large at the Restoration. Does not this shew that the *Scots* are not enemies to liberty more than the *English*?

The city of *Edinburgh* had from King *William* a grant of its guard of 300 men, 'on account of the 'laudable zeal they discovered, when religion and li-'berty were at stake[d].'

The people of *Scotland* shewed themselves friends to liberty in the year 1760[e]; elected a Peer last vacancy, *A. D.* 1770, in direct opposition to the court, which

 had,

---

[a] See *Whitel.* MEM. 25. [b] Ibid. 26. [c] Ibid. 27.

[d] DEB. PEERS, V. 205.

[e] See the *Edinburgh* instructions, and sense of the royal burghs, in favour of a militia in *Scotland*. LOND. MAG. *Apr.* 1760, p. 194.

had, as always, the modesty to interpose on that occasion[a].

If *James* I. and his son *Charles* I. and *James* II. had read *Buchanan*'s works, they might have lived and died in peace. There they would have learned, that kings are the protectors not masters of their kingdoms; that a kingdom is a stewardship, not an estate. That if princes were republicans, subjects would be royalists; and that the more authority princes challenge, the less free subjects will grant, and contrarywise.

What country has produced more strenuous advocates for liberty than *Buchanan* and *Fletcher?* Bishop *Burnet* was a very active promoter of the Revolution, as well as an able writer on the side of liberty. The late earl of *Stair* was turned out of all his employments by *Walpole*, on account of his free principles. The great duke of *Argyle* was a constant champion in parliament against all the enslaving measures of his times. And in the year 1741, 'the approaching session' (says *Tindal*[b]) 'being the last of the parliament, great 'efforts were made to have one returned which should 'be against the minister. Though these endeavours 'were general all over the kingdom, where the opposition had any interest, they were *most* prevalent in '*Scotland*, where the duke of *Argyle* exerted himself 'with extraordinary vigor——and soon acquired influence enough to procure a great majority of the '*Scotch* representatives against the court at the next 'election.'

The

[a] See Lord *Elibank*'s [a *Scotch* nobleman] Considerations on the present state of the Peerage in *Scotland*. Printed for *Cadell*, *A. D.* 1771, a piece which breathes as high a spirit of liberty as any in the *English* language.

[b] CONTIN. *Rap.* VIII. 471.

The earl of *Marchmont* was a constant opposer of *Walpole* and his corrupt measures.

And see the brave speeches of Messrs. *Erskine* and *Dundass* against the army[a].

To conclude this head, you may depend upon it, my good countrymen, that neither railing against the *Scots*, nor even breaking the union, nor massacring the whole inhabitants of *North Britain*, (for who can tell how far our incendiaries wish to carry their animosity) nor any popular cry against lord ——— or for Mr. ———, nor any other party-object, is of consequence enough to be named in a day with the restoration of independency to parliament. They who are for this indispensable measure are undoubted friends to *England*; they who are against it, no matter what banners they list under, they are more desirous of the emoluments of places and pensions, than studious of the good of their country. But to return;

It may be objected, that it will be difficult to find gentlemen properly qualified to send into parliament, when so many, must be new men every new parliament. To this may be answered, That if the possibility of bribing were taken away, which I have above shewn may be done, any man of common sense and common honesty may be a member; because his constituents may instruct him how to vote, and he will have no interest separate from that of his country, and the speaker, clerks, officers, &c. who may be permanent, will be masters of forms and the routine of business.

If it be said, the boroughs, which send in the majority of the house, cannot be deprived of a *right* they have enjoyed by so long *prescription*; which must for ever

[a] Deb. Com. ix. 69.

ever shut the door against all proposals of rendering parliamentary representation adequate; the answer is easy: The rotten boroughs obtained their right through the indirect views, or the caprice, of a set of crowned heads. General good is to be secured, though to the prejudice of unjust privilege. The more ancient the grievance, the more is redress wanted. If this objection be valid in this case, there can be no reformation, nor any new law or regulation made; for every new law brings prejudice to some individuals. See above, vol. I. p. 62, *et alibi*.

It is, and always has been, the cry of the defenders of present measures, 'What would you have? Is not 'every person free to do what he pleases? Would you 'possess a greater degree of liberty than that which all 'enjoy at present?' But may not this be said in a country, and at a period when the *constitution* of that country is overturned? For that will always be the case, where the genius of the government, though absolute, is *mild*. I doubt not, but the partisans of *Augustus* lulled the *Romans* to submission with such discourses as these; for the individuals were as free at *Rome* the very next year after the bloody proscription was at an end, as in *England* now. But would a *Brutus* or a *Cassius* have let themselves be deceived by such means into a submission to *Augustus*? No. They would have rewarded him for violating the *constitution* as they did *Julius*.

'*Pour la populace, &c.* As to the common people, 'it is never from a desire of attacking that they rise, 'but from impatience of suffering[a].'

The *inertia* and timidity of the people are the great difficulties in the way of every reformation. It is not statesmen

---

[a] MEM. *Sully* I. 272.

ſtateſmen nor clergymen that promote reformations either in the ſtate or the church; it lies upon the people, and it is very hard to drive the people to it. This is well known to all tyrants in church and ſtate; and their hope is that the people will not ſtir, till they be violently abuſed: and unfortunately it is then commonly too late. For the tyrant and his tools muſt have a conſiderable confidence in their own ſtrength, and the weakneſs of the cauſe of liberty, before they will venture on thoſe violences; and then there is but little hope of procuring a revolution.

'Far from being ready to protect the rights of others, 'every one muſt have ſeen his own many times flagrantly attacked, before he reſolves to defend them; 'and it is difficult to conceive how great an advantage 'government takes from that want of ſpirit to oppoſe 'its criminal attempts, and how much it concerns 'public liberty, that ſubjects be not too patient.

'When we peruſe attentively the hiſtory of deſpotiſm, we ſometimes behold with aſtoniſhment a handful of men keeping a whole nation in awe. That 'inconſiderate moderation of the people, that timidity, 'that fatal propenſity to ſeparate their common interests, are the true cauſes of this ſurprizing phænomenon. For what is the voice of the people, if every 'one is to continue ſilent [a]?'

Whatever excuſes or delays may be interpoſed by the intereſted, or the timid, one thing is indiſputably clear, viz. That, as above obſerved, if there be now difficulties in the way, thoſe difficulties will not be leſſened by time, but increaſed and multiplied. As a preſumptuous ſinner, by putting off repentance, renders his own reſtoration more and more difficult, ſo it is

[a] CHAINS OF SLAVERY, 74.

is with nations. Corruption and venality, if they be not rooted out, will increase more and more, and the power of the court will increase with them.

The principal difficulty in all such cases arises from the *inertia* of the people. Would all the independent people of *England* set themselves in earnest to begin and carry on the great work, what could prevent their success?

The excellent *Sidney* employs his whole 41st section in proving, that 'the people, for whom, and by whom 'the magistrate is created, can only judge whether he 'rightly performs his office, or not.'—'The people,' says he, p. 438, 'cannot be deprived of their natural 'rights upon a frivolous pretence to that which never 'was, nor ever can be. They who create magistracies, 'and give to them such name, form, and power as they 'think fit, do only know, whether the end for which 'they were created be performed or not. They who 'give a being to the power which had none, can only 'judge whether it be employed to their welfare, or 'turned to their ruin. They do not set up one or a 'few men, that they and their posterity may live in 'splendour and greatness, but that justice may be ad-'ministered, virtue established, and provision made for 'the public safety. No wise man will think this can 'be done, if those who set themselves to overthrow 'the law, are to be their own judges.' Again, p. 439, 'It is as easy for the people to judge whether 'their governors, who have introduced corruption, 'ought to be brought to order, and removed if they 'would not be reclaimed, or whether they should be 'suffered to ruin them and their posterity, as it is for 'me to judge whether I should put away my servant, if 'I knew he intended to poison or murder me, and had 'a certain facility of accomplishing his design; or 'whether

'whether I should continue him in my service till he 'had performed it. Nay the matter is so much the 'more plain on the side of the nation as the dispropor-'tion of merit between a whole people, and one or a 'few men intrusted with the power of governing them 'is greater than between a private man and his servant. 'This is so fully confirmed by the general consent of 'mankind, that we know no government that has not 'frequently either been altered in form, or reduced to 'its original purity, by changing the families or per-'sons who abused the power with which they had been 'intrusted. Those who have wanted wisdom and vir-'tue rightly and seasonably to perform this, have been 'soon destroyed.'

'It has been the general unhappiness of countries, 'in which corruption has prevailed, that the bad men 'are bold and enterprising, forward and active; where-'as such as keep their integrity, are unactive, cold, 'and lazy; contented with the barren praise of not 'being guilty themselves, they suffer others to invade 'so much power, as that they can do hurt, and do it 'safely, and in a nation debauched in principles, many 'parts of the state may be filled by persons of high 'knowledge and virtue; but their love and zeal for 'the public, and their vigilance for its safety, their 'prudence, foresight, and caution, shall be all rendered 'ineffectual by the over-ruling madness of others. 'The side which would tread in the path of honesty 'and wisdom, shall be overborn and shoved out of the 'way, by the crowd and strong faction of those who 'find their account in promoting disorder and mis-'government. Such as maintain their understanding 'in this general frenzy, shall be admired but not fol-'lowed; esteemed, but not consulted; heard, but not 'regarded. Mend things they cannot; if they will be 'quietly

'quietly wise and say nothing, they are endured; and 'if inactive, they are suffered; when their superior 'skill is forgiven and connived at, when such as have 'more than common endowments are allowed to sub-'sist and preserve themselves, though they cannot save 'their country, it is thought a sufficient favour; but 'all the while they shall be made uneasy; pursued with 'malicious whispers, blackened as disaffected, and 'made obnoxious to the people; till at last they are 'forced to retire, and let their brethren of the state ruin 'and betray the nation in quiet[a].'

There is nothing to be done, say worthless lazy statesmen, It is impossible to amend any thing either in the state or the church. With how much more reason might the great Czar *Peter* have excused himself from the glorious labours he undertook for the good of his vast dominion! 'These *Russians*,' he might have said, 'are grown inveterate in their errors and bad customs. What chance is there of drawing a set of unreasoning and bigotted savages from their old prejudices, to which they have been inseparably attached for an innumerable series of ages?'

See *Charles* I.'s proclamation against stirring new opinions[b]. Old errors were preferable to new truth.

'The political constitution of *Poland* has been the 'source of continual misfortunes. Yet the natives are 'attached to it to a degree of enthusiasm, and especially 'to those parts, which produce the greatest inconve-'niencies[c].'

Even such salutary regulations as the reformation of the Calendar, demolishing the city-gates, and new pav-ing

[a] *Daven.* II. 70.

[b] *Rym.* FOED. XVIII. 719.

[c] MOD. UNIV. HIST. XXXIV. 6.

ing the streets, improving the roads by setting up turnpikes, establishing county-workhouses, have been strenuously opposed by wrong-headed, or interested men.

A *French* gentleman, who resided some time in *England*, returning to his own country, among other remarks on the character of the *English*, observed, That they never redressed any nuisance, till some notable mischief consequent upon it, compelled them[a].

How can the people be too jealous of their liberties, when they know, that the best of kings and governments, are, to say the least, more solicitous about their own power than about the people's liberties; that the best kings and governments are unwilling to give up the power they find within their reach, however unjustly acquired by their predecessors; so that the evil done by a tyrannical government is seldom effectually excluded by a good one, while the good done by a just government is often overset by a succeeding tyranny.

I have shewn you, my dear countrymen, that it is in vain to think of going on in the way we are in, without timely redress; that we have nothing before our eyes, but the diminution of our trade, and consequently of the national income, which must produce a deficiency of that which ought to go to the payment of the dividends, after which may be expected to follow the despair and rage of thousands reduced to beggary, against those who shall be the supposed causes of this mischief; all which may lead on to insurrections of the people, to burning of houses, cutting of throats, and this horrible confusion may be expected to end, as those in *Denmark* did lately, in a general request to the reigning prince, to give the nation peace, by taking into his own

---

a DEB. LORDS, IV. 241.

own hands the whole power, which is now in king, lords, and commons, and making himself what the king of *Denmark* is now.

Why must slaves be chained; but because slavery is a state of such misery, that no person will continue in it, if he can extricate himself.

The *Spartan* helotes, the *Roman* slaves in the ergastula, the negroes in the *West Indies*, all have at times struggled for the recovery of their liberty. Shall it be said, that the *English* only are to be brought to bear slavery tamely?

'*Germany* and *Rome* continuing, the one in a state 'of liberty, the other of slavery, yield the most illustri'ous and evident proof of the consequences that attend 'those conditions. That great city, which from small 'beginnings in a free state, extended its empire so 'widely, that as *Livy* expresses himself, it laboured 'under its own greatness; that city, whose inhabitants 'whilst it was free, notwithstanding its continual wars, 'multiplied so fast, that it sent colonies into the re'motest parts of its far extended command; when re'duced to slavery, soon became depopulated, as did its 'provinces: though many means were tried to allure 'and compel the inhabitants to marry, yet they all 'proved ineffectual, and well they might, for who 'would exert his industry in acquiring a property, that 'was insecure, or get children, who could be certain of 'no other inheritance but slavery, and were sure of that? 'The strength of the empire was not only decayed in 'numbers, but more in spirit; for slavery debases the 'minds of men: and it fares with nations as with pri'vate persons; both by oppression grow stupid and de'cline, even as low as the brutal part of the creation, 'unless they have spirit enough to relieve themselves. 'And then the causes of their woe, as in justice they

'ought,

'ought, and ever will, meet with an ample retribution[a].'

The authors of the ANCIENT UNIVERSAL HISTORY thus describe the lamentable fall of the mighty *Roman* empire[b].

'Thus ended the greatest commonwealth, and at the same time began the greatest monarchy, that had ever been known, a monarchy which infinitely excelled in power, riches, extent, and continuance, all the monarchies and empires which had preceded it. It comprehended the greatest, and by far the best part of *Europe*, *Asia*, and *Africa*, being near four thousand miles in length, and about half as much in breadth. As to the yearly revenues of the empire, they have by a modest computation been reckoned to amount to forty millions of our money: but the *Romans* themselves now ran head-long into all manner of luxury and effeminacy. The people were become a mere mob; those who were wont to direct mighty wars, to raise and depose great kings, to bestow or take away potent empires, were so sunk and debauched, that if they had but bread and shews, their ambition went no higher. The nobility were indeed more polite than in former ages; but at the same time idle, venal, insensible of private virtue, utter strangers to public glory or disgrace, void of zeal for the welfare of their country, and solely intent on gaining the favour of the emperor, as knowing that certain wealth and preferment were the rewards of ready submission, acquiescence, and flattery. No wonder therefore they lost their liberty, without being ever again able to retrieve it.'

a *St. Amand*, PARL. HIST. 8.

b ANT. UNIV. HIST. XIII. 489.

Slaves lose all courage for war. When *Lucullus* was told how numerous *Tigranes*'s army was, 'No 'matter, says he, the lion never hesitates about the 'number of the sheep.' His army was but 14,000. *Agesilaus* invaded the *Persian* empire with 14,000 men, and drove all resistance before him. The little free state of *Athens* was always an overmatch for that vast enslaved empire. In the war between *Cyrus* and *Artaxerxes*, 13,000 *Greeks* routed 900,000 *Persians*. The same *Greeks*, reduced to 10,000, made good their retreat under the command of *Xenophon*, through a hostile country of 2300 miles.

The *Greeks* and *Romans*, because free, conquered the enslaved nations. The only formidable enemies the latter had were the free *Carthaginians*. With the liberties of the *Greeks* and *Romans* sunk their valour. What are now the descendants of those conquerors of the world?

Xerxes, with his world in arms, was defeated by a handful of *Greeks*, and fled with such rapidity, that he took only a month to perform the same journey homeward, in which he spent six from his setting out to his arrival in *Greece*.

The free trading city of *Tyre* cost *Alexander* the Great more trouble to conquer, than all *Asia*. And though he demolished it in such a manner, that he thought it could never more lift its head, in 19 years afterwards it was in a condition to stand a siege of 15 months by *Antigonus*.

Where liberty is restrained, commerce languishes. Compare old *Tyre*, *Carthage*, *England*, *Holland*, *Venice*, the free *Hanse towns*, with all other countries in which commerce has been attempted. The proud tyrants of *France* have never been able to establish an *East India* company, while those of *England* and *Holland* astonish the

the world, and overawe the greatest of the eastern empires[a].

All the best writers on trade labour to shew, that even in this free country trade is too much cramped by duties; and that it would be greatly for the general advantage, that the revenues were raised rather any other way.

Naval power cannot subsist without commerce, nor commerce without liberty. The naval force of the great but enslaved kingdoms of *France* and *Spain* is contemptible, while that of the little republic of *Holland* has long been formidable. In two months after their defeat in *Cromwell's* time, they fitted out a fleet of 140 men of war. Whereas the *Spaniards* have never recovered the loss of their armada in the days of queen *Elizabeth*.

France has almost every advantage above *England* towards thriving, yet *England* hitherto thrives better than *France*. *Holland* labours under every disadvantage, yet makes almost as good a figure as *England*. Were *England* as well governed as *Holland*, would not she be greatly superior to *Holland*? Were *France* governed as *Holland* is, would not she be still more superior to both *England* and *Holland* as to wealth and commerce? How foolish then the cry of the court-sycophants, 'Your thriving 'is a proof that you are well governed.' No: on the contrary, our not thriving in proportion to *Holland*, is a proof that we are not so well governed.

All the kingdoms of *Europe*, as the *Goths* and *Vandals* settled them, were free[b]; yet the most complete slavery grew out of the feudal tenures set up by them, with the design of securing themselves against foreign

enemies,

[a] See *Davenant*, *Gee*, *Child*, *Decker*, *Postlethwayt*, *Anderson*.
[b] *Robertson's* Hist. Ch. V. i. 13.

enemies, by giving lands to those who served in the wars, which gave landholders an opportunity of erecting themselves into despots, and destroyed all internal happiness. So naturally does slavery steal upon mankind, and so precarious is the hold they have of liberty.

Where liberty is lost, property there is none. In the enslaved parts of *Italy*, the people perish with hunger in the midst of plenty, because the fruits of the earth are not their own. In *France*, if a peasant has saved 5*l.* he must bury it in the ground, lest the fermier general, hearing of it, tax him accordingly.

In an enslaved country, there may be magnificence; but it is confined to the capital, the seat of the tyrant. All besides is poverty and desolation.

The authors of the Antient Universal History [a] describe as follows the horrors of slavery:

'These three tyrants, *Antony*, *Lepidus*, and *Octavianus*, went on adding daily to the number of the proscribed, till it amounted to 300 senators, and above 2000 knights. It is impossible to paint the horrors of this bloody proscription. By it every considerable man in *Rome*, who was disliked, or suspected by the triumvirate to disapprove their tyranny, who was rich, and had wherewithal to glut their avarice, was doomed to die. As it was death to conceal or help them, and ample rewards were given to such as discovered and killed them, many were betrayed and butchered by their slaves and freed men, many by their treacherous hosts and relations. Many fled to the wilderness, where they perished for want with their tender children. Nothing was to be seen but blood and slaughter; the streets were covered with dead bodies; the heads of the most illustrious senators were exposed upon

[a] Ant. Univ. Hist. xiii. 353.

'upon the rostra, and their bodies left unburied in the 'streets and fields, to be devoured by the dogs and 'ravenous birds. This looked like dooming *Rome* to 'perish at once. Many uncondemned persons perished 'in this confusion; some by malice or mistake, others 'for concealing or defending their friends. Several of 'the ancient historians seem to take pleasure in describ-'ing the horrors of this bloody and cruel proscription, 'which reduced the populous capital of the world al-'most to a wilderness. They produce many remark-'able and moving instances of the affection of wives 'for their husbands, and of the fidelity of slaves to-'wards their masters; but few, very few, as they own 'with great concern, of the love of children towards 'their parents. However, the dutiful behaviour of '*Oppius* may stand for many, who, like *Æneas*, carried 'his old and decrepit father on his shoulders to the 'sea-side, and escaped with him into *Sicily*. His piety 'was not long unrewarded; for on his return to *Rome*, 'after the triumvirs had put an end to the proscrip-'tion, he found the people so taken with that generous 'action, that all the tribes unanimously concurred in 'raising him to the ædileship; and because he wanted 'money to exhibit the usual sports, the artificers 'worked without wages; and the people not only 'taxed themselves to defray the necessary charges at-'tending such shows, but gave proofs of the esteem 'they had for so dutiful a son, by such contributions 'as amounted to twice the value of his paternal estate, 'which had been confiscated by the triumvirs. *Caius* '*Hosidius Geta* was likewise saved by his son, who 'spread a report, that his father had laid violent hands 'on himself, and to render the fact more credible, 'spent the poor remains of his fortune in performing 'his obsequies. By this means *Hosidius*, not being 'searched after, made his escape, but lost one of his 'eyes, which he had kept too long covered with a 'plaster, the better to disguise him. As for the bar-'barous impiety of those children, who by a strange 'apostasy from nature betrayed their own parents, it 'ought to be buried in oblivion. Nothing can reflect 'greater infamy on the memory of the triumvirs, than 'their countenancing such impious monsters. Several 'slaves chose rather to die on the rack, amidst the most 'exquisite torments, than discover the place where 'their masters lay concealed; others, not caring to 'outlive them, fell by their own hands upon their dead 'bodies. Many illustrious matrons gave remarkable 'proofs of their conjugal love in those times of cala-'mity, which ought not to be passed over in silence. 'The wife of *Q. Ligarius*, seeing her husband betrayed 'by one of his slaves, declared to the executioners, 'who cut off his head, that she had concealed him, 'and consequently ought, in virtue of the decree, to 'undergo the same fate. But they not hearkening to 'her, she appeared before the triumvirs themselves, 'upbraided them with their cruelty, owned she had 'concealed, in spite of their decree, her husband, and 'begged death of them as a favour. Being driven 'away by their officers, she shut herself up in her own 'house, and there, as she was determined not long to 'outlive her husband, starved herself to death. *Acilius* 'was betrayed by one of his slaves, and apprehended, 'but redeemed by his wife, who readily parted with 'all her jewels to save his life. *Apuleius Antistius* '*Antius*, *Q. Lucretius Vispallis*, *Titus Vinnius*, and many 'others, were saved by the ingenious contrivances of 'their wives, after they had given themselves up for 'lost. *Lucius*, the uncle of *Antony*, was saved by his 'sister *Julia*, in whose house he had taken refuge.

'Though

'Though the country, as well as the city, swarmed 'with informers and assassins, yet many illustrious citi-'zens found means to avoid the fury of the proscrip-'tion, and to get safe, either to *Brutus* in *Macedon*, or to '*Sextus Pompeius* in *Sicily*. The latter kept constantly a 'great number of small vessels hovering on the coasts 'of *Italy*, to receive such as made their escape, and 'treated them with great kindness and civility. As to '*Cicero*, he had not the good luck to escape, but fell a 'sacrifice to the implacable rage of *Antony*. The great 'reputation of that orator, the obligations which all 'men of learning owe to his memory, and the inimi-'table works he has left behind him, require of us a 'particular account of his death, and the most minute 'circumstances attending it. He was with his brother '*Quintus*, who was likewise proscribed, at his country 'house near *Tusculum*, when the first news were 'brought him of the proscription, which he no sooner 'heard, than he left *Tusculum* with his brother, taking 'his route towards *Austura*, or as some call it, *Stura*, 'another of his country-houses on the sea side, between 'the promontories of *Antium* and *Circæum*. There 'they both designed to take shipping, and endeavour 'to join *Brutus* in *Macedon*. They travelled together 'each in his litter, oppressed with sorrow, and often 'joining their litters on the road to condole each other. 'As they had in the first alarm and hurry forgot to 'take with them the necessary money to defray the ex-'pences of their voyage, it was agreed between them, 'that *Cicero* should make what haste he could to the 'sea side, and *Quintus* return home to provide neces-'saries. Then they embraced each other, and parted 'with reciprocal fear. *Quintus* returned to *Rome*, and 'got to his house undiscovered, where he thought him-'self safe, at least for a short time, since it had been

 'lately

'lately searched by the ministers of the triumvirs. But 'as in most houses there were as many informers as 'domestics, his return was immediately known, and 'the house of course was filled with soldiers and assas-'sins, who not being able to find him out, put his 'son to the torture, in order to make him declare 'where his father lay concealed. But filial affection 'was proof in the young *Roman* against the most ex-'quisite torments. However, the tender youth could 'not help sighing now and then, and groaning in the 'height of his pain. *Quintus* was not far off; and 'the reader may imagine, though we cannot express, 'how the heart of a tender father must have been af-'fected in hearing the sighs and groans of a son dying 'on the rack to save his life. He could not bear it; 'but quitting the place of his concealment, he pre-'sented himself to the assassins, begging them with a 'flood of tears to put him to death, and dismiss the 'innocent child, whose generous behaviour the trium-'virs themselves, if informed of the fact, would judge 'worthy of the highest encomiums and rewards. But 'those inhuman monsters, without being in the least 'affected with the tears either of the father or the son, 'answered, that they must both die, the father because 'he was proscribed, and the son, because, in defiance of the 'decree of the triumvirs, he had concealed his father. 'Then a new contest of tenderness arose between the 'father and the son who should die first: but this the 'assassins, destitute of all sense of humanity, and no 'way affected with such melting scenes, soon decided, 'by beheading them both at the same time. Though '*Quintus Cicero*'s wife was not perhaps without re-'proach, his death, it must be owned, was truly glo-'rious: as for that of his son, it has been, and ever 'will be, celebrated by the writers of all nations and

'ages

'ages as an instance of the most heroic affection, and 'filial duty. But to return to the elder brother, *Cicero* having reached *Austura*, and by good luck found 'a vessel there ready to weigh anchor, went on board 'with a design to pass over into *Macedon*, and join '*Brutus*. But either dreading the inconveniencies of 'such a voyage, or still depending on the friendship of '*Octavianus*, whom he had all along supported with 'his credit and eloquence, he soon changed his mind, 'and ordered the master of the ship to set him ashore at '*Circæum*, whence he took his route towards *Rome* by 'land. But after he had gone about two hundred furlongs 'he altered his resolution anew, and returned to sea, 'where he spent the night in a thousand melancholy 'and perplexing thoughts. One while he resolved to 'go privately into *Octavianus*'s house, and there kill 'himself upon the altar of his domestic gods, in order 'to bring upon him the wrath of those furies who 'were deemed the avengers of violated friendship. But 'the fear of being taken on the road, and the apprehension of the cruel treatment he expected, if taken, 'soon made him drop that resolution. Then falling 'into other thoughts equally perplexing, and wavering between the hopes he had in *Octavianus*'s friendship, and the fear of death, he at last suffered his domestics to convey him by sea to a country-house, 'which he had in the neighbourhood of *Caieta*; where 'he had not been long, when his domestics carried him 'again in a litter towards the sea-side. They were 'scarce gone, when a band of soldiers under the command of *Herennius* a centurion, and *Popilius Lænas* 'a military tribune, came to the house. *Cicero* had 'formerly undertaken the defence of *Popilius*, when 'he was under a prosecution for the murder of his 'own father, and by his triumphing eloquence, had 'got him absolved by those very judges, who a little 'before were ready to condemn him to a most cruel 'death. But the ungrateful wretch, unmindful of 'former obligations, and wholly intent on currying 'favour with *Antony*, had promised to find out *Cicero*, 'wherever he lay concealed, and bring him his head. He 'found the doors of his house shut, but breaking them 'open, and searching in vain every corner, he threatened 'to put all the slaves in the house to the torture, if 'they did not immediately declare where their master 'lay concealed. But the faithful slaves, without be- 'traying the least fear, answered with great constancy 'and resolution, that they knew not where he was. 'At length a young man, by name *Philologus*, who had 'been slave to *Quintus*, and afterwards enfranchised by 'him, and instructed by *Cicero* in the liberal arts and 'sciences, with all the tenderness of a father, disco- 'vered to the tribune, that *Cicero*'s domestics were 'then carrying him in a litter through the close and 'shady walks to the sea side. Upon this information '*Popilius*, with some of his men, hastened to the place 'where he was to come out, while *Herennius* with the 'rest followed the litter through the narrow paths. 'As soon as *Cicero* perceived *Herennius*, he commanded 'his servants to set down his litter, and stroking, ac- 'cording to his custom, his head with his left hand, 'he put out his head, and looked at the assassins with 'great intrepidity. This constancy, which they did 'not expect from him, his face disfigured and emaci- 'ciated with cares and troubles, his hair and beard ne- 'glected, and in disorder, &c. so affected the soldiers 'who attended *Herennius*, that they covered their eyes 'with their hands, while he cut off his head, and pur- 'suant to *Antony*'s directions his right hand, with 'which he had written the *Philippics*. With those tro-

'phies of their cruelty, *Herennius* and *Popilius* hastened 'back to *Rome*, and laid them before *Antony*, while 'he was holding an assembly of the people for the 'election of new magistrates. The cruel tyrant no 'sooner beheld them, than he cried out in a transport 'of joy, Now let there be an end of all proscriptions: 'live, *Romans*, live in safety; you have nothing more 'to fear. He took the head in his hand, and looked 'on it a long time with great satisfaction, smiling at 'a sight, which drew tears from all who were present. 'After he had satiated his cruel and revengeful temper 'with so dismal a spectacle, he sent, as we are told by 'several writers, the head of the orator to his wife. '*Fulvia* was naturally more cruel than the trium-'vir himself, and had born an implacable hatred to '*Cicero*, ever since the time of her first husband *P. Clo-*'*dius*, who was slain by *Milo*. That fury, after hav-'ing insulted the poor remains of her enemy with the 'most injurious reproaches, took that venerable head 'in her lap, and drawing out the tongue of the de-'ceased which had uttered many bitter invectives against 'both her husbands, pierced it several times with a 'golden bodkin which she wore in her hair. When '*Fulvia* had satiated her impotent rage, *Antony* ordered 'both the head and the hand to be set up on the ro-'stra, where *Rome* could not without horror behold the 'remains of a man who had so often triumphed in that 'very place, by the force and charms of his eloquence. 'Thus fell the greatest orator which *Italy*, or any other 'country, ever bred; a man, who, as *Cæsar* the dic-'tator used to say, had obtained a laurel as much above 'all triumphs, as it was more glorious to extend the 'bounds of the *Roman* learning than those of the *Ro-*'*man* empire. In his consulate, which was truly 'glorious, he discovered with wonderful sagacity the

'most

'most secret plots of the seditious *Catiline*, defeated 'his best concerted measures, and saved, we may say, '*Rome* from utter destruction; whence he was deser-'vedly honoured with the glorious title of The father 'of his country. The *Roman* people no doubt owed 'him much, and he took care to put them frequently 'in mind of their obligations; for he was quoting on 'all occasions, in and out of season, the nones of *De-'cember*, as *M. Brutus* observed in one of his letters 'to *Atticus*. He loved his country; but his zeal did 'not carry him so far as to make him sacrifice his pri-'vate interest to the public welfare. But after all, 'the intrepidity with which he offered himself to death, 'ought to make us in a manner overlook the timo-'rousness, pusillanimity, and irresolution, which he 'betrayed in most occurrences of his life. He died on 'the seventh of the ides of *December*, in the sixty-fourth 'year of his age, and was greatly lamented by all ranks 'of men. *Antony* himself made some sort of reparation 'to his memory; for, instead of rewarding the perfi-'dious *Philologus*, who betrayed his master and bene-'factor, he delivered him up to *Pompona* the widow of '*Quintus Cicero*, and sister of *Pomponius Atticus*, who 'after having glutted her impotent rage, and desire of 'revenge with the most exquisite torments cruelty it-'self could invent, obliged the miserable captive to cut 'off his own flesh by piece-meal, boil it, and eat it in 'her presence. But *Tiro Cicero*'s freeman has not so 'much as mentioned the treachery of *Philologus*, as we 'have observed above out of *Plutarch*. *Octavianus*, 'who shamefully sacrificed *Cicero* to his most cruel 'and bitter enemy, declared several years after, the 'esteem he had for him: for visiting one day his 'daughter's son, and finding him with a book of *Ci-'cero*'s in his hand, the boy for fear endeavoured to

'hide

'hide it under his gown; which *Octavianus* perceiving, 'took it from him, and turning over a great part of 'the book standing; gave it him again, saying, This, 'my child, was a learned man, and a lover of his coun- 'try.'

Such are the miseries, which the *Romans* brought upon themselves by not securing their liberties in time. And it is impossible to say what distresses any country may come into, which, through want of a due attention to the smallest inroads upon their liberties, suffer the floodgates to be once opened.

In our country, if a chimney-sweeper is murdered, especially with the sword of justice, all *England* is alarmed. In the imperial times of *Rome*, 500, or 5000 people were destroyed in a single insurrection of the army, or massacred by order of a hell-hound emperor, and no notice taken.

In the assembly of the states-general of *France*, *A. D.* 1614, the clergy (ever enemies to liberty, ever trumping up church-power) hallowed out for the reception of the council of *Trent*; and the *tiers-etat*, which answers to our commons, who are naturally, if not debauched by a corrupt and corrupting court, friendly to liberty, as knowing that their own happiness depends on it, opposed, as they, and all mankind ought to do, the enslaving schemes of the priesthood; and demanded a declaration against the pope's power over kingdoms, and against the assassinating of heretical kings. Neither obtained their demands. Many grand points were disputed; but nothing decided. The whole proved confused, turbulent, and ineffectual. There has no free assembly of the states-general of *France* met since that time. Then the benign and cheering beams of the sun of liberty set on that unhappy country, never more to rise. Since that time, a sullen gloom of darkness and

and despotism, from a terrible throne, has overshadowed that people, and a frowning tyrant, in one hand brandishing a bloody sword, and clanking a bundle of fetters with the other, chills their souls with slavish horror; damps all manly spirit, and kills all hope of emancipation. Accordingly our times have seen the only remaining appearance of a citadel, from whence a national effort for recovery of liberty could have originated, at one stroke of regal power reduced to nothing, by the total suppression of all the parliaments of *France*. Which final heart-stab to the constitution, the poor enslaved people have seen, and resented only by shrugging up their shoulders.

O *Britain!* See here the consequence of suffering power to pass from the hands of the people into those of kings and ministers; and remember, a corrupt and enslaved parliament is in no degree a more effectual check upon the power of kings and courts, than no parliament.

'Victory is more especially founded upon courage, 'and courage upon liberty, which grows not without 'a root planted in the policy or foundation of the go- 'vernment [a].

The richest soil in *Europe*, *Italy*, is full of beggars; among the *Grisons*, the poorest people in *Europe*, there are no beggars [b]. The balliage of *Lugane* is 'the 'worst country, the least productive, the most exposed 'to cold, and the least capable of trade of all *Italy*, and 'yet is the best peopled. If ever this country is 'brought under a yoke like that which the rest of '*Italy* bears, it will soon be abandoned, for nothing 'draws so many people to live in so bad a soil, when 'they

[a] *Harringt*. OCCEANA, p. 289.

[b] *Burn*. TRAV. p. 97.

'they are in sight of the best soil in *Europe*, but the 'easiness of the government [a].'

Italy shews, in a very striking light, the advantage of free government. The subjects in all the *Italian* republics are thriving and happy. Those under the pope, the dukes of *Tuscany*, *Florence*, *&c.* wretched beggars.

Lucca, to mention no others at present, is a remarkable instance of the happy effects of liberty. The whole dominion is but thirty miles round, yet contains, besides the city, 150 villages, 120,000 inhabitants, and all the soil cultivated to the utmost [b]. Government, a gonfalonier, or standard-bearer, whose power is like that of the doge of *Venice*, and nine counsellors, whose power is only for two months, (and those two months they were in some troublesome times obliged to live all together in the town-hall, without even going to their own houses [c],) chosen out of 240 nobles, and they changed every two years.

The city of *Fez* in *Africa* has the strange privilege of being allowed to yield to any enemy, who shall get within half a mile of its walls. Every king, at his coronation, confirms this privilege. So dastardly does slavery make a people [d].

Many of the *Chinese* nobility, on the decisive sea-fight between the *Chinese* and *Tartars*, in which 100,000 of the former were killed, *A. D.* 1279, would not submit to the *Tartar* government, though they might have enjoyed all their honours and advantages. They preferred, like *Cato*, or *Brutus*, an honourable death to shameful servitude [e].

Asia

---

[a] *Burn.* TRAV. 108.

[b] MOD. UNIV. HIST. XXXVI. 6.

[c] Ibid. 36.

[d] Ibid. XVIII. 132.

[e] Ibid. VIII. 467.

Asia has greater riches than *Europe*. But slavery makes that vast quarter of the world despicable, compared with our little spot of *Europe*.

The slave trade produces, among the *Africans* infinite cruelty, deceit, and oppression. Parents sell their children; creditors their debtors by families at a time; false accusers the unjustly condemned; savas, or lords, whoever offends them [a].

While the *Spaniards* were masters of *Portugal*, they oppressed it much in the same manner as the *Egyptians* the *Israelites*, or the *Spartans* the *Helotes*. Since the *Portuguese* became independent, they have grown rich, flourishing, and ungrateful [b].

'It is constantly (said a member in Queen *Elizabeth*'s time) in the mouths of us all, that our lands, goods, and laws, are at our prince's disposal [c].'

The *English* seem hardly to have deserved the name in the time of *Philip* and *Mary*, so abject and slavish they were, beyond most other nations of *Europe*. *Caseley*, a member, was put in custody of the serjeant at arms, only for shewing some anxiety, lest the queen, from her necessitous circumstances, should alienate the crown from the lawful heir [d].

In *Britain*, an industrious subject has the best chance for thriving, because the country is the freest. In the *Mogul*'s dominions, the worst, because the country is the most effectually enslaved [e].

'*Liber homo*, &c. The title of freemen was formerly confined chiefly to the nobility and gentry, who were descended of free ancestors. Far the greatest part of the common people was formerly restrained under some species of slavery, so that they were not masters

[a] Mod. Univ. Hist. xvi. 195. [b] Ibid. xliii. 382.
[c] *Hume*, Hist. Tud. ii. 640. [d] Ibid. ii. 398.
[e] Mod. Univ. Hist. vi. 301. *et pass.*

'masters of themselves[a].' To what a low degree of slavery must a people be reduced, who were obliged to give the first night of their brides to the lord of the manor, if he demanded it[b]?

What has been in *England* may be again. If liberty be on the decline, no one knows how low it may sink, and to what pitch of slavery and cruelty it may grow.

Martial law was the most horrible of all tyranny. By it any man was punishable without judge or jury, who became suspected to the lieutenant of a county, or his deputy, of treason, or of aiding or abetting treason. It was used by bloody *Mary* in defence of orthodoxy[c]. *Edward* (or rather his villanous ministers, for he was but a boy) granted a warrant for martial punishments, at a time when there was no rebellion apprehended, viz. *A. D.* 1552, and the judges were to act 'as should be thought by their discretions most 'necessary.' *Elizabeth* ordered the importation of bulls, indulgences, or even prohibited books, to be punished with martial law; and rioters and vagrants to be hanged upon the spot where taken; so that almost any body might hang any body, any how, or any where[d]. Imprisonment in those days was arbitrary at the pleasure of the privy council, or secretary of state, and the torture might be used upon the secretary of state's warrant: so that the government of *England* was, in the days of *Henry* VIII. *Mary*, *Elizabeth*, and *James* I. upon much the same arbitrary principles as that of *Turkey* is now. The crown had every power but that of laying on taxes; and the subject was not the less oppressed for the court's not having that power. *Elizabeth*'s arbitrary proceedings made up for this. She

 gave

a Spelm. *Gloss. voc. Liber homo.* b Ibid. *voc. Marchet.*
c *Hume*, Hist. Tud. II. 718. d Ibid. 719.

gave patents and monopolies, she extorted loans, she forced the people to buy off expensive offices, she demanded benevolences, she increased arbitrarily the duties upon goods, she obliged the sea-port towns to find a certain number of ships, and the counties a certain quota of men, clothed, armed, and sent to the place of their destination; she laid arbitrary embargoes upon merchandise, she demanded new-years gifts, she victualled her navy by purveyance, that is, her officers seized whatever they could of provisions, and paid what price they pleased; the crown enjoyed all rents during the minority of heirs and heiresses. The good lord *Burleigh* proposed to the queen an inquisitorial court for correcting all abuses, which court should profit her revenue more than her father's demolition of the monasteries did him, which court should proceed according to law, and to 'her absolute power, from whence 'law proceeded [a].' All these proceedings were unwarranted by authority of parliament; and the legislative authority of parliament was of no avail, because it might at any time be set aside by the dispensing power of the crown, and the royal proclamations had the force of laws. *Elizabeth* went so far as to prohibit the cultivation of woad, a very useful dyeing material, because she was possessed with a whim against the smell of that plant. She sent about her officers to break every sword, and trim every ruff they found, that were larger than she allowed, in the same manner as the Czar *Peter* ordered his men to shave by force, and with a blunt razor, all the old-fashioned beards they met [b]. *Peury* was hanged for some papers found in his pocket, which allowed the queen's absolute power, but did not assert it quite so strongly as the court desired. Yet all this

---

[a] *Hume*, HIST. TUD. II. 722. [b] Ibid.

this tremendous power did not prevent ſhocking miſrule among the people; for ſevere puniſhment hardens, inſtead of making ſubjects obedient. Two or three hundred criminals, or pretended criminals, were to be tried at the aſſizes in ſingle counties, and innumerable multitudes of vagabonds and ruffians filled the whole nation with rapine, terror, and confuſion. Theſe laſt particulars are a very conſiderable derogation from the praiſe of *Elizabeth*'s wiſdom as a ſoveraign[a].

See, in *Rymer*, 'a noate of all cauſes, which the moſt 'honourable courte of ſtarchamber doth from tyme to 'tyme heere and determyne, together with the manner 'and forme of the proceedings in the ſame cauſes, as well 'by proceſſe, as otherwayes[b];' according to which nothing could be more inconſiſtent with liberty, becauſe it excluded all trial by peers, and left the ſubject at the mercy of the perſons who compoſed it, viz. the great officers of the ſtate, the creatures of the court; the very perſons in the whole nation the leaſt fit to have ſuch power.

The court of ſtar-chamber, of which Mr. *Hume* ſays, he doubts whether there be ſo abſolute a tribunal in *Europe*, had unlimited power of fining, impriſoning, and inflicting corporal puniſhment for all manner of offences. Privy counſellors and judges were the members of it, who depended immediately upon the court. If the prince was preſent, he was ſole judge[c].

The high commiſſion court had power of puniſhing, as hereſy, any practice offenſive to the court.

When ſerjeant *Maynard*, almoſt ninety years old, went to compliment the prince of *Orange* on his arrival,

 'You

a *Hume*, Hist. Tud. II. 727.

b *Rym*. Foed. xviii. 192.

c Hist. Tud. II. 717.

'You have, I suppose, says the prince, outlived all 'the lawyers of your time.' The old gentleman answered, 'I have; and if your Highness had not come, 'I should have outlived the law itself[a].'

On the contrary, the advantage of liberty appears in a very striking light in the following narration:

'In the year 1708 happened an accident, the more 'disagreeable to the *Russians*, as *Peter* was at that time 'unprosperous in war. *Matueof*, his ambassador to the 'court of *London*, having obtained an audience of leave 'of queen *Anne*, was arrested for debt in the public 'street by two bailiffs, at the suit of some tradesmen, 'and obliged to give in bail. The plaintiffs asserted, 'that the laws of commerce were of a superior nature 'to the privileges of ambassadors; on the other hand, '*Matueof*, and all the other foreign ministers who 'espoused his cause, maintained that their persons ought 'to be sacred. *Peter*, by his letters to queen *Anne*, 'strongly insisted upon satisfaction; but she could not 'comply with his desire, because, by the laws of *England*, the creditors had a right to sue for their just 'demands, and there was no law to exempt foreign 'ministers from being arrested for debt. The murder 'of *Patkul*, the Czar's ambassador, who had been 'executed the preceding year, by order of *Charles* XII. 'was in some measure an encouragement to the people 'of *England* not to respect a character so grossly abused. 'The other foreign ministers residing then in *London* 'were obliged to be bound for *Matueof*, and all that 'the queen could do in favour of the Czar, was to 'prevail on the parliament to pass an act whereby it 'was no longer lawful to arrest an ambassador for debt. 'But after the battle of *Pultowa*, it became necessary 'to

[a] *Burn.* HIST. OWN TIMES, II: 550.

'to give a more public satisfaction to that prince. 'The queen, by a formal embassy, made an excuse 'for what had passed. Mr. *Whitworth*, who was 'pitched upon for this ceremony, opened his speech 'with the following words, Most high and most 'mighty Emperor. He told the Czar that the queen 'had imprisoned the persons who had presumed to arrest 'his ambassador, and that the delinquents had been 'rendered infamous. This was not true; but the ac-'knowledgment was sufficient; and the title of Em-'peror, which the queen had not given him before the 'battle of *Pultowa*, plainly shewed the degree of esti-'mation to which he was now raised in *Europe*. This 'title had been already granted him in *Holland*, not 'only by those who had been his fellow-workmen in 'the dock yards at *Sardam*, and seemed to interest 'themselves most in his glory, but even by the chief 'persons in the state, who unanimously styled him Em-'peror, and celebrated his victory with rejoicings in 'the presence of the *Swedish* minister. The Czar '(says the preface to lord *Whitworth*'s account of *Rus-'sia)* who had been absolute enough to civilize savages, 'had no idea, could conceive none, of the privileges 'of a nation civilized in the only rational manner by 'laws and liberties. He demanded immediate and se-'vere punishment on the offenders; he demanded it 'of a princess, whom he thought interested to assert the 'sacredness of the persons of monarchs even in their 'representatives; and he demanded it with threats of 'wrecking his vengeance on all *English* merchants, and 'subjects established in his dominions. In this light 'the menace was formidable; otherwise happily the 'rights of a whole people were more sacred here than 'the persons of foreign ministers. The Czar's memo-'rials urged the queen with the satisfaction which she 'herself had extorted, when only the boat and servants 'of the earl of *Manchester* had been insulted at *Venice*. 'That state had broken through their fundamental 'laws, to content the queen of *Great Britain*. How 'noble a picture of government, when a monarch that 'can force another nation to infringe its constitution, 'dare not violate his own. One may imagine with 'what difficulty our secretaries of state must have la-'boured through all the ambages of phrase in *English*, '*French*, *German*, and *Russian*, to explain to *Muscovite* 'ears and *Muscovite* understandings, the meaning of 'indictments, pleadings, precedents, juries, and ver-'dicts; and how impatiently *Peter* must have listened 'to promises of a hearing next term? With what asto-'nishment must he have beheld a great queen engaging 'to endeavour to prevail on her parliament to pass an 'act to prevent any such outrage for the future? What 'honour does it not reflect on the memory of that 'princess to own to an arbitrary emperor, that even to 'appease him she dared not to put the meanest of her 'subjects to death uncondemned by law. There are, 'says she, in one of her dispatches to him, insuperable 'difficulties with respect to the ancient and fundamen-'tal laws of the government of our people, which, we 'fear, do not permit so severe and rigorous a sentence 'to be given as your imperial majesty at first seemed to 'expect in this case. And we persuade ourself that 'your imperial majesty, who are a prince famous for 'clemency and exact justice, will not require us, who 'are the guardian and protectress of the laws, to inflict 'a punishment upon our subjects, which the law does 'not empower us to do. Words so venerable and 'heroic, that this broil ought to become history, and 'be exempted from the oblivion due to the silly squab-'bles of ambassadors and their privileges. If *Anne* de-

'served

'served praise for her conduct on this occasion, it 'reflects still greater glory on *Peter*, that this ferocious 'man had patience to listen to these details, and had 'moderation and justice enough to be persuaded by the 'reason of them [a].'

That the states of *Holland* are what they are in consequence of their being free, appears by the following:

'The duke of *Parma* succeeding to the government 'of the *Netherlands*, upon the death of *Don John* of '*Austria*, he began his government with the taking of 'the strong town of *Mastrecht* from the States, and 'next by his reducing the *Walloon* provinces of *Artois*, '*Hainault*, and *Walloon-Flanders*, by capitulation to 'the dominion of *Spain*. Hereupon, and for other 'reasons, the Prince of *Orange* duly considering the 'emulation amongst the great men, as well as that the 'difference of religion in the several provinces could 'hardly ever be reconciled; and being at the same time 'desirous to secure himself, and to establish, as far as 'possible, the protestant religion, he procured the 'states of *Guelderland*, *Holland*, *Zealand*, *Friesland*, 'and *Utrecht*, to meet at the last-named city in this 'year, 1579; when they mutually and solemnly 'stipulated to defend one another as one joint body, 'and with united consent to advise of peace, war, 'taxes, &c. and also to support liberty of conscience. 'And to complete the present number of seven pro'vinces now of the united *Netherlands*, *Overyssel*, and '*Groningen*, were soon after admitted into the union; 'an union which, in a few years, formed the most 'potent republic which the world had seen since that 'of old *Rome*; and of the greatest commerce and mari-

a MOD. UNIV. HIST. XXXV. 454.

'time power that (as a republic) ever was on earth
'For, that so small a state should between this year
'1579 and 1600, not only preserve its independency
'against the then mightiest potentate in *Europe*, but
'likewise get footing in *Flanders*, by mastering the
'strong and important towns of *Sluyce* and *Hulst*, &c.
'to ruin the trade of the most famous city of *Antwerp*;
'to conquer the strong forts of *Bergen-op-zoom*,
'*Breda*, and sundry other places on the *Mease* and
'*Rhine*, &c. also to attack and annoy so great a mo-
'narch in his own ports at home; and maugre all the
'vast expence of such great exploits, to grow rich and
'opulent as well as potent, will, perhaps, scarcely
'obtain an historical credit in another century; but
'with us it serves only to shew the immense effects of
'an universally extended commerce, an indefatigable
'industry, joined to an unparalleled parsimony and
'œconomy. Soon after this famous period, the indus-
'trious and parsimonious traders of these united pro-
'vinces pushed into a considerable share of that com-
'merce to several parts of *Europe*, which, till then,
'*England* had solely enjoyed. Yet the great and happy
'accession of the fugitive *Walloons* into *England* about
'the same time, whereby the old *English* drapery was
'so greatly improved, and sundry new and profitable
'manufactures introduced, did more than counter-
'balance the loss of some part of the *English* commerce
'to the said *Dutch* traders. Neverthelefs, the im-
'menseness of the fishery of these *Netherland* provinces,
'with which they about this time supplied the most
'part of the world, is almost incredible; and could
'only be described by so great a genius as Sir *Walter*
'*Raleigh*. Their *East India* trade soon after this time
'commenced, and, like all new trades, brought most
'profit in the beginning, frequently so far as twenty

'times the original outset. In brief, the *Hollanders* 'soon thrust themselves into every corner of the universe for new means of commerce, and for vending 'their vastly improved manufactures; whereby *Amsterdam* soon became (what it still is) the immense magazine or staple for almost all the commodities of the 'universe. Sundry, indeed, were the grounds or causes 'of so great a change in the condition of these *Netherland* provinces in about less than half a century: One 'very great one was what Sir *William Temple* observes, 'viz. "That the persecution for matters of religion in "*Germany* under *Charles* V." in *France* under *Hen.* II. 'and in *England* under Queen Mary, had forced great 'numbers of people out of all these countries, to 'shelter themselves in the several towns of the seventeen 'provinces, where the ancient liberties of the country, 'and the privileges of the cities, had been inviolate 'under so long a succession of princes, and gave protection to these oppressed strangers, who filled their 'cities with people and trade. But when the seven 'provinces had united, and began to defend themselves 'with success under the conduct of the Prince of '*Orange*, and the countenance of *England* and *France*, 'and when the persecution began to grow sharp on 'account of religion in the *Spanish Netherland* provinces, all the professors of the reformed religion, 'and haters of the *Spanish* dominion, retired into the 'strong cities of this new commonwealth, and gave 'the same date to the growth of trade there, and the 'decay of it at *Antwerp*. It would be too tedious to 'instance all the other causes of the said vast increase of 'the wealth and power of the united *Netherlands* in 'those early times, and afterwards: Such as, 1st, the 'long civil wars first in *France*, next in *Germany*, and 'lastly in *England*; which drove thither all that were

'perse-

'persecuted at home for their religion. 2. Moderation 'and toleration to all sorts of quiet and peaceable 'people, naturally produce wealth, confidence, and 'strength to such a country. 3. The natural strength 'of their country improved by their many sluices for 'overflowing it, and rendering it inaccessible to land 'armies. 4. The free constitution of their govern-'ment. 5. The bank of *Amsterdam's* safety, security 'and convenience for all men's property, &c.'[a]

Venice has preserved its liberty, says *Voltaire*[b], by being surrounded by the sea, and wisely governed. *Genoa* conquered *Venice* about the end of the fourteenth century; but *Genoa* sunk, and *Venice* rose. *Venice* has, he says, but one fault, viz. the want of a counterpoise to the power of the nobles, and encouragement to the plebeians. A commoner cannot rise in the state, as in ancient *Rome*, or in *England*. *Voltaire* therefore, I suppose, thinks *England* as safe as ancient *Rome*, which we know lost its liberties.

The *Swiss* keep the same unchanged character of simplicity, honesty, frugality, modesty, bravery. These are the virtues which preserve liberty. They have no corrupt and corrupting court, no blood-sucking placemen, no standing army, the ready instruments of tyranny, no ambition for conquest, no debauching commerce, no luxury, no citadels against invasions and against liberty. Their mountains are their fortifications, and every householder is a soldier, ready to fight for his country[c].

'Before the government of *Denmark* was made he-'reditary and absolute in the present royal family, by 'that fatal measure in 1660, the nobility and gentry 'lived

[a] *Anders.* Hist. Comm. i. 419.

[b] Ess. sur l'Hist. ii. 107.

[c] Ibid. 60.

'lived in great ſplendour and affluence. Now they are 'poor, and their number diminiſhed. Their eſtates 'will ſcarce pay the taxes. They are neceſſitated to 'grind their poor tenants. They often give up an 'eſtate to the king, rather than pay the taxes laid upon 'it. Sometimes the king will not have them; the tax 'is better; the beſt parts being obliged to make up the 'deficiencies which the worſt cannot. Very different 'from their condition, when they voluntarily contri-'buted to the public expence according to their abili-'ties. They now retire into obſcure and cheap places, 'unleſs when they can obtain court-places, of which 'there are but few, and of ſmall value. And many of 'them are given to foreigners, rather than natives; as 'the court thinks it can better depend on thoſe, whoſe 'fortunes it has raiſed, than on thoſe whom it has 'ruined. This policy likewiſe ſerved the purpoſe of a 'miniſtry, who wanted to break the ſpirit of the 'nobles. Therefore they give the court-employments 'chiefly to the meaneſt of the nobility, as the fitteſt in-'ſtruments for executing their tyrannical ſchemes. 'And when ſuch perſons grew rich by extortion upon 'the people, and clamours began to riſe, they ſtripped 'them of their ill-gotten wealth, reduced them to their 'former condition, and increaſed the revenue by the 'bargain, giving themſelves an air of patriotiſm in 'plundering the people by proxy. So the leviathans 'of power deceive and rob the ſubjects in almoſt all 'countries. The conſequence of this oppreſſion is, that 'the people of *Denmark*, finding it impoſſible to ſecure 'property, ſquander away their little gettings, as faſt as 'they gain them, and are irremediably poor. Oppreſ-'ſion and arbitrary ſway beget diſtruſt and doubts about 'the ſecurity of property; doubts beget profuſion, men 'chooſing to ſquander on their pleaſures what they

'apprehend

'apprehend may excite the rapaciousness of their superiors; and this profusion is the legitimate parent of 'that universal indolence, poverty, and despondency, 'which so strongly characterize the miserable inhabitants of *Denmark*. When Lord *Molesworth* resided in 'that country, the collectors of the poll-tax were obliged to accept of old feather-beds, brass and pewter 'pans, &c. instead of money, from the inhabitants of a 'town, which once raised 200,000 rixdollars for '*Christiern* IV, on twenty-four hours notice[a].'

In *Zealand* (says Lord *Molesworth*) the peasants are as absolute slaves as the negroes in *Jamaica*, and worse fed. They and their posterity are unalterably fixed to the land in which they were born; the landholders estimating their worth by their stock of boors. Yeomanry, the bulwark of happy *England*, is a state unheard-of in *Denmark*; instead of which the miserable drudges, after labouring hard to raise the king's taxes, must pay the overplus of the profits of the lands, and of their own toil, to the greedy and necessitous landlord. If any of them, by extraordinary labour or skill, improves his farm, he is immediately removed to a worse, and the improved spot let to another at an advanced rent.

The quartering and paying the king's troops (in all absolute dominions, vast armies are kept up,) are another grievance no less oppressive. The late experience of our own inn-keepers, and their complaints to parliment, *A. D.* 1758, may give us an idea of the condition of the *Danish* peasants, oppressed by those insolent inmates, who lord it over all wherever they have power[b]. The authors afterwards add to the oppression of the wretched boors, by obliging them to furnish the king, and every little insolent courtier, with horses and waggons

[a] Mod. Univ. Hist. xxxii. 13. [b] Ibid. 16.

waggons in their journies, in which they are beaten like cattle. In consequence of this misery, *Denmark*, once very populous, as appears from the swarms of the northern nations, which in former ages over-ran all *Europe*, is become thin of inhabitants; as poverty, oppression, and meagre diet do miserably check procreation, besides producing diseases, which shorten the lives of the few who are born [a]. All this the rich, and thriving, and free people of *England* may bring themselves to, if they please. It is only letting the court go on with their scheme of diffusing universal corruption through all ranks, and it will come of course.

The *Scots* and *Welch* climbed their churlish mountains, to escape from *Roman* chains, and there remained unconquered. The *Dutch* escaped to the stinking bogs of the Low Countries, to get free from the tyranny of *Spain*. The *Pennsylvanians* and *New-Englanders* abandoned the fruitful plains of their sweet native country, crossed the vast *Atlantic*, and pierced the haunts of savages and wild beasts, rather than submit to ecclesiastical tyranny. *Don Pelayo*, with all the brave spirits of *Spain*, betook themselves to the inhospitable rocks, and dreary dens of *Liebana*, to escape the *Moorish* fetters, and expelled the tyrants. The brave *Corsicans*, a handful of men, maintained, in our times, a stubborn and bloody war of some years continuance, against the haughty *Genoese*, and the mighty monarchy of *France*, the sworn enemy of the liberties of *Europe*.

In *Turkey* there is no written law; no parliament; no property; no rank, but that of serving the Grand Seignor. And the family of the emperor's first slave, or prime vizier, sinks into their former obscurity, the moment he is dispatched by the mutes, which is the common end of those ministers of state.

---

[a] Mod. Univ. Hist. xxxii. 16.

'The descendants of the heroes, philosophers, ora-'tors, and free citizens of *Greece*, are now slaves to the 'Grand *Turk*. The posterity of the *Scipios* and *Catos* of '*Rome* are now singing operas, in the shape of *Italian* 'eunuchs, on the *English* stage[a].' Whence this grievous fall? *Ans. Greece* and *Rome* have lost their liberties.

Reflect, my dear countrymen, on these instances of resistance to tyranny, which do so much honour to human nature, think of the glorious struggles of the ancient *Grecian* republics. Think of the resistance made by *Carthage*, by *Spain*, and other ancient free nations, to the unbounded ambition of the all-conquering *Romans*. Remember the heighth of glory to which freedom has raised so many people, which otherwise would have continued in obscurity. Think of the free States of *Holland*, of *Venice*, of *Malta*. Remember the riches and power of the free *Hans-towns*. But above all, reflect on the glorious figure your ancestors make in history.

Remember, O my friends, the laws, the rights,
The generous plan of freedom handed down
From age to age, by your renowned forefathers;
So dearly bought, the price of so much blood. ADDIS.

Shall it be said, that the history of *England* during the greatest part of the 17th century is filled with instances of resistance to the tyranny of kings, and that the following century exhibits little else than a series of shameful concessions to the encroachments of corrupt courts?

'Here is the natural limitation of the magistrate's 'authority; he ought not to take what no man ought 'to give; nor exact what no man ought to perform: 'all

[a] *Bolingbr.* POLIT. TRACTS, 270.

'all he has is given him, and these that gave it must 'judge of the application. In government there is no 'such relation as lord and slave, lawless will, and blind 'submission; nor ought to be amongst men: but the 'only relation is that of father and children, patron 'and client, protection and allegiance, benefaction and 'gratitude, mutual affection and mutual assistance[a].'

It is not bellowing out for liberty alone, that will keep a people free. *Poland* is a republic, and the 'people are passionately fond of liberty, yet live in a 'perpetual state of servitude to their own avarice, pro-'fusion, and necessities, whereby they are rendered the 'infamous pensioners of foreign states, the creatures of 'their own kings, or the hirelings of some faction[b].' The peasants are the most perfect slaves on earth. If one lord kills another's peasant, he is only obliged to make good the damage. They have no property. They have no possible means for becoming free; and have no redress against the most cruel and unjust usage of their lords[c]. We have seen this wretched people sunk, if possible, still lower in our times. Liberty seems indeed to be bidding mankind farewell, and, like *Astræa*, to be taking her flight from the earth. All *Europe* was once free. Now all *Europe* is enslaved, excepting what shadow of liberty is left in *England*, *Holland*, *Switzerland*, and a few republics in *Italy*. And such is the encroaching nature of power, and so great the inattention of mankind to their supreme worldly interest, that the states of *Europe*, which still boast themselves free, are like to be soon in the same condition with the others, which do not even pretend to possess any degree of liberty.

Pursuing

a *Cato's* LETT. II. 229.

b MOD. UNIV. HIST. XXXIV. 5.

c Ibid. 6.

Pursuing these gloomy ideas, I see,—how shall I write it?——I see my wretched country in the same condition as *France* is now. Instead of the rich and thriving farmers, who now fill, or who lately filled, the country with agriculture, yielding plenty for man and beast, I see the lands neglected, the villages and farms in ruins, with here and there a starveling in wooden shoes, driving his plough, consisting of an old goat, a hide-bound bullock, and an ass, value in all forty shillings. I see the once rich and populous cities of *England* in the same condition with those of *Spain*; whole streets lying in rubbish, and the grass peeping up between the stones in those which continue still inhabited. I see the harbours empty, the warehouses shut up, and the shop-keepers playing at draughts, for want of customers. I see our noble and spacious turnpike roads covered with thistles and other weeds, and scarce to be traced out. I see the studious men reading the *State of Britain*, the *Magazines*, the *Political Disquisitions*, and the histories of the 18th century, and execrating the stupidity of their fathers, who, in spite of the many faithful warnings given them, sat still, and suffered their country to be ruined by a set of wretches, whom they could have crushed. I see the country devoured by an army of 200,000 men. I see justice trodden under foot in the courts of justice. I see *Magna Charta*, the *Habeas Corpus* act, the bill of rights, and trial by jury, obsoleted, and royal edicts and arrets set up in their place. I see the once respectable land-owners, traders, and manufacturers of *England* sunk into contempt, and the placemen and military officers the only persons of consequence.

This is a fearful and horrid prospect. I wish it could be, upon sure grounds, alleged, that it is merely visionary. If all history be not fable and fiction, so far

from

from visionary, it is the very condition, my dear countrymen, into which you are sinking, and where you will soon be irrecoverably fixed, if you do not bestir yourselves and prevent it, while it is in your power to prevent it.

Be the consequences what they will, I thank Heaven, I have endeavoured to honour virtue and truth, and to detect and disgrace corruption and villany. I have unburdened my own conscience. I have delivered my own soul. I have sounded a loud and distinct alarm. I have endeavoured to raise the standard of liberty higher, and to unfurl it wider, than has been attempted by any private person before. Whether my well-meant attempt will prove effectual for rousing you from your long and dangerous lethargy, remains to be seen. Of what I have myself written, I say nothing; but surely I may affirm, that far the greatest part of the matter I have collected is highly deserving of the public attention. And I think hardly any person will pretend to publish on political subjects any thing more interesting, or to treat those subjects in any better, or indeed in any other manner, than is done by the illustrious writers and speakers, from whom I have made my collections.

'The nation will hold as long as our lives will hold,' is the heroic and patriotic way of speaking among some. But who told them how long the nation would hold? The *Danes* were free one day; slaves the next.

What mortal (who does not pretend to be master of the black art) will pretend to determine how long the *British* empire may last?

A country may lose its liberties in a very short time, though there were now a very high spirit of liberty appearing in it, which is far from being the case in *England*. In the minority of *Lewis* XIV. *A. D.* 1647, the parliaments and supreme courts of *France* continued sitting in spite of the king's order to dissolve them. On this *Mazarine* orders *Blancmenil* the first president, and the counsellor *Broussel*, to be arrested. All *Paris* rises. The streets are barricaded. The queen regent finds herself obliged to set the prisoners at liberty. *Mazarine* afterwards arrests others. The parliament persists in, and heightens its demands. *Mazarine* finds himself obliged to recall those he had banished. The court is forced to yield; to remove taxes, and to make a regulation, that persons, accused of state crimes, shall be tried according to law, not punished arbitrarily by order of the court. Many new lords were created, to strengthen the court-party. The insurrections of the people force the royal family to make their escape from the palace of the *Louvre*, at four in the morning, and fly to S. *Germains en Laye*. *Turenne* saves the young king and queen mother twice from being taken. *Mazarine* is declared, by the parliament of *Paris*, a public disturber of the peace, and enemy to their kingdom, a price set on his head, and all cardinals forbidden to be of the king's council. Other parliaments and provinces revolt. The mob force their way into the queen's apartments, and undraw the young king's curtains at midnight, to see whether he was safe, suspecting, that she had conveyed him away again. All *France* is in rebellion against an encroaching and tyrannical court.

Would any one in those times, when the flame of liberty blazed so high, have allowed it to be possible, by any management whatever, to quench it so effectually in five years, that *Lewis* XIV. with an army of only 1200 men, then but a youth, on his return from hunting, having been informed, that the parliament of *Paris* was met without his leave, went directly, booted and spurred as he was, and turned the members of of it out of the house; and no resistance made either at the time, or afterwards[a]?

The appearance of a spirit of liberty in a nation is no argument, that its liberties are absolutely safe. There was a great appearance of a spirit of liberty at *Rome* in *Sylla's* time. There was enough of the spirit of liberty in *Cæsar's* time, to lay the invader of liberty weltering in his own blood in the open senate-house. There was enough of the spirit of liberty, after his execution, to produce the battle of *Philippi*. Yet all considerate *Romans* saw the liberties of their country to be in danger, as early as the days of *Lucullus's* conquests in *Asia*.

The liberties of a country can only be safe in the difficulty of enslaving it. It is folly to trust to such securities, as, 'that the grandees know if the state is 'ruined, they must be ruined with it. The officers of 'the army will not promote slavery, because they are 'gentlemen of families, and will not enslave their own 'families. There is a great spirit of liberty still in the 'nation. We have a good king on the throne. We 'have good laws,' &c. If these securities had been sufficient, how many enslaved states in ancient and modern times had preserved their liberties!

A nation is then, and only then, secure against foreign invasion, when it has within itself, by means of a fleet, or of the people's being generally trained to arms, a greater force than any that can probably be brought against it; and when there is such a prevalency of public spirit, integrity, and contempt of riches, that the government are not likely to betray it to a foreign enemy. A nation is then, and only then, secure against the encroachments of its own government,

 when

[a] Mod. Univ. Hist. xxv. 36, 38, 40, 45, 51, 52, 64.

when there is no such prevalency of luxury and corruption, as to give reason to apprehend danger from the court, and when the people have in themselves a sufficiency of public spirit to prevent their being bought, and a sufficiency of force in their own hands, and ready for immediate exertion, to prevent their being violently crushed by a tyrannical court or nobility

As soon as any one of these barriers is removed, there remains nothing but the fearful expectation of the enslaving chain, that is to gall every free and stubborn neck.

'Men, says the excellent *Davenant*, do as industriously contrive fallacies to deceive themselves, when 'they have a mind to be deceived, as they study frauds 'whereby to deceive others, and if it leads to their 'ends, and gratifies their present ambition, they care 'not what they do, thinking it time enough to serve 'the public when they have served themselves; and in 'this view very many betray their trusts, comply, give 'up the people's right, and let fundamentals be invaded, 'flattering themselves, that when they are grown as 'great as they desire to be, it will be then time enough 'to make a stand and redeem the commonwealth. The 'same notion led *Pompey* to join with those who in-'tended to subvert the *Roman* liberties; but he found 'them too strong, and himself too weak, when he de-'sired to save his country. In the same manner, if 'there be any in this nation who desire to build their 'fortunes upon the public ruin, they ought to consi-'der that their great estates, high honours, and pre-'ferments, will avail them little, when the subversion 'of liberty has weakened and impoverished us so, as 'to make a way for the bringing in of a foreign 'power [a].'

People,

[a] *Daven.* II. 302.

People, who know human nature, do not expect from mankind much disinterested public spirit.

> Nec reperire licet multis e millibus unum
> Virtutem precium qui putet esse suum.
>
> SIL. ITAL.

But while the worthless and sordid affect to sneer at the anxiety of those who see farther than themselves; they would do well to consider, that to say, 'What care I for politics?' is to say, 'What care I for my liberty, my religion, my house, my lands, my ships, my commerce, my money in the funds, my wife, my children, my mistress, my bottle, my club, my plays, operas, masquerades, balls, pleasures, profits, honour, and life?' For on the safety of our country depends the safety of all we have; or hope to have in this world. A tyrannical government can deprive a man of every thing, but his soul. They cannot send him to hell; but they can do every thing short of that. They can, and do, make this world a hell. If our country comes to be enslaved, any one of these, or all of them, may come into danger. And, that this country may come to be enslaved, cannot seem improbable to any one, who knows, that this country, and almost all the countries in the world, have been enslaved; much less will it seem improbable to any person, who knows a little of history, and sees, that this country has upon it every symptom of a declining state, especially that most decisive one, of an universal decay of public spirit.

In most histories, different proceedings produce different catastrophes: but in the history of our parliamentary proceedings there is a corrupt sameness, which makes the perusal execrably stupid. A good motion made by the opposition; quashed by ministerial influence. An impudent demand made on the people, to fill the pockets of the minister's dependents, granted. A king's (that is, a minister's) speech trumping up the happiness of an enslaved, corrupt, and ruined nation; echoed back by the house, that is, by the minister's tools in the house; and so on to the end of the chapter. Whenever we read the motion, we know beforehand its fate. We peruse the arguments on both sides; we see on one side massy sterling sense; but we see it weighed up by massy sterling guineas. These are shocking symptoms of a tendency to ruin in a state. But lord *Bathurst* in his following letter to *Dean Swift*, goes still farther [a].

'I am convinced, says he, that our constitution is 'already gone, and we are idly struggling to maintain, 'what in truth has been long lost, like some fools 'here, with gout and palsies at fourscore years old, 'drinking the waters in hopes of health again. If 'this was not our case, and that the people are already 'in effect slaves, would it have been possible for the 'same minister who had projected the excise scheme '(before the heats it had occasioned in the nation were 'well laid) to have chosen a new parliament again exactly to his mind? And though perhaps not altogether so strong in numbers, yet as well disposed in 'general to his purposes as he could wish. His master, 'I doubt, is not so much beloved, as I could wish he 'was; the minister, I am sure, is as much hated and 'detested as ever man was, and yet I say a new parliament was chosen of the stamp that was desired, 'just after having failed in the most odious scheme that 'ever was projected. After this, what hopes can 'there ever possibly be of success? Unless it be from 'confusion, which God forbid I should live to see.

'In

[a] Lord *Bathurst* to Dean *Swift*, LOND. MAG. 1768, p. 114.

'In short the whole nation is so abandoned and corrupt, that the crown can never fail of a majority in both houses of parliament, he makes them all in one house, and he chuses above half in the other. Four and twenty bishops, and sixteen *Scotch* lords, is a terrible weight in one. Forty-five from one country, besides the West of *England*, and all the government boroughs is a dreadful number in the other. Were his majesty inclined to-morrow to declare his body coachman his first minister, it would do just as well, and the wheels of government would move as easily as they do with the sagacious driver, who now sits on the box. Parts and abilities are not in the least wanting to conduct affairs; the coachman knows how to feed his cattle, and the other feeds the beasts in his service, and this is all the skill that is necessary in either case. Are not these sufficient difficulties and discouragements, if there were no others, and would any man struggle against corruption, when he knows, that if he is ever near defeating it, those who make use of it, only double the dose, and carry all their points farther, and with a higher hand, than perhaps they at first intended.'

Some are of Lord *Bathurst's* opinion, that our liberties are already gone: others think them only in extreme danger. Whichsoever is the case, no friend to *England* will advise you, my good countrymen, to sit still. If your liberties are going, you ought to bestir yourselves for their preservation; if they are gone, for their recovery.

Let no free people deceive themselves by the false persuasion, that it must take up a long series of years to wear out their liberties, because it was the work of ages to establish their constitution. Great works require long time in finishing. A short space destroys them. A first rate ship of war is several years in building. She slips a plank, or founders at sea; is swallowed up in a moment. The great city of *London* was many ages in building; the conflagration in 1666, in four days reduced the work of ages to ruins.

Farther, Have you considered, my dear countrymen, that it is not in your option to preserve, or give up your liberties as you please, any more than your lives. Liberty, and life, are the rich gifts of all gracious Heaven. And you cannot think it lawful to spurn from you your Maker's godlike bounty, which he gave you in trust to be preserved, and enjoyed by you. Besides, if it were lawful for you to sell *yourselves* for nothing, you will certainly not pretend that you have power to enslave your *posterity* * for ever. I therefore charge you before Almighty God, and as you shall hereafter answer to him, to take care how you trifle in a matter of such awful importance. If you be not absolutely certain (which is impossible) that there is no account to be given hereafter, you run yourselves into the most dangerous condition that can be imagined, by making yourselves partakers of the guilt of those who are actively concerned in enslaving your country. In what light do we look upon him, who knows of a murder to be committed, and makes no attempt to prevent it?

He who pretends to exempt himself from all concern for his country, may as well reject all obligation to do his duty to God, to his neighbour, or himself. Yet every man knows, that he is obliged to perform these duties; and

* 'No people can alienate their posterity's immunities.' LOCKE.

and that he is obliged to obey the laws of his country, preferably to those of his parents, and in neglect of, and opposition to his own interest.

It is undoubtedly dangerous for the people to be employed in redressing grievances. It is not safe to teach them to unite, and to give them the means of knowing their own strength. When they go to redressing, they generally do great mischief, before they begin redressing. But this is the fault of those who resist them. They are generally in the right, as was the case at *Florence*, in the 14th century [a]. The tyranny of the eighth field deputies was intolerable, and the people were right in demanding the abolition of it; all that was wrong was the magistrates refusing the people redress, and the people's redressing themselves, in too violent a manner. Commotions of this kind, with all their terrible consequences, are almost always owing to the unreasonable difference made between princes, or nobles, and the people, by prerogative or privilege. The people may be brought, by inveterate tyranny, to bear patiently to see the most worthless part of mankind (for surely the great by mere birth, in all ages and countries, are commonly among the most worthless of mankind) set up above them, and themselves obliged to crouch. But sometimes the people grow uneasy under this. And if the people rouse to vengeance, woe to those who stand in their way. Let merit only be honoured with privilege and prerogative, and mankind will be contented. The wise ancients understood this, and therefore were very cautious of making differences. A crown of grass, or a couple of twigs, was the reward of the most heroic actions. 'I do not like that *Aristides* should be distinguished by 'the

[a] Mod. Univ. Hist. xxxvi. 149.

'the title of Just, any more than myself,' says the *Athenian*, and puts in his shell for banishing that great and good man. This indeed was the very design of the ostracism, viz. to prevent unreasonable inequalities, and the desire of power and pre-eminence, which always produces disturbance.

Nothing is much more formidable, than a popular insurrection. When 60,000 men, in the time of *Richard* II. assembled, and demanded redress of grievances, they made the king and nobles tremble. The government was glad to quiet them by any means; and granted them charters after charters [a]. There were many lives lost, and much mischief done on that occasion. All wise governments will carefully avoid irritating the people beyond measure. And all sound patriots will avoid rousing the people, if redress can be any other way obtained. Therefore I do not propose having recourse to force. What I propose is, to apply the power of the people, guided, limited, and directed by men of property, who are interested in the security of their country, and have no income, by place or pension, to indemnify them for bringing slavery and ruin upon their country——to apply this power (if found absolutely necessary) to prevent the application of the same power unrestrained, unlimited, and directed by mere caprice, or the spirit of party. Perhaps, when things come to a crisis, which most probably they will soon, our government may recollect themselves so far as to grant voluntarily, and with a good grace, that redress, to which the people have an undoubted right, and which they see the people resolute to have. I will, therefore, attempt to draw the sketch of such a plan for retrieving

[a] *Brady*, III. 346.

retrieving the nation, and restoring the constitution, as to me seems the most promising. Might the hand of an angel guide my pen, or rather an abler pen—— my country might yet be saved. Or might I have for a rostrum the highest of the *Peruvian Andes*; could I borrow the angelic trumpet, whose blast is to break the slumber of ten thousand years; and might I have for my audience the whole human race; on what subject could I address them, that would be more interesting to them, than warning them to preserve their liberty and their virtue?

But I need not have recourse to a mountain for a pulpit, nor to the angel's trumpet to swell my voice. If the still small voice of reason will not move you, all the terrors of mount *Sinai*, or of the day of judgment, will not produce the proper effect.

In the mean time, for our encouragement, that the spirit of liberty is not totally extinct in the people, we observe that some of the constituents have required their candidates to promise solemnly, that if elected, they would promote certain reformations, and the correction of various gross abuses.

It were to be wished that those who first drew up the terms of the engagements, had not overloaded their demands; but that they had confined themselves to one only article. I mean the endeavouring to get an independent parliament. An independent parliament would at all times secure the rights of the people, as has been shewn in the foregoing volumes. A candidate's refusing to promise his best endeavours in the house, if elected, for obtaining independent parliaments, would be an open declaration, that, in aspiring to a seat, his object was not the service of his country, but the gratifying his own ambitious or avaricious private views.

One

One set of readers will pretend to have found me inconsistent with myself. This writer, they will say, must either mean to shew us that we are in danger, and how to escape that danger, or his labour can be of no service. And yet in several parts of his work he magnifies the peril, from the army, as if a tyrannical prince or ministry could at any time, by its means, seize our liberties at theirpleasure. If this be true, how can this writer pretend to talk of our extricating ourselves? If this be true, the point is decided, the case is desperate, our liberties are gone; we have nothing left, but to bear patiently what we have brought upon ourselves. But do not you, my good countrymen, suffer yourselves to be duped by such quibbles as these. I have not absolutely pronounced upon the state of our liberties. It is the very point which remains to be determined. If a nation is in the condition in which we now see *France*; there can be no doubt concerning its liberties; they are *utterly* gone. And yet no wise man will say that they are *irretrievably* gone. On the contrary, if a nation were in the condition we now see *Holland*, or rather on a much better footing as to liberty than that commonwealth is now upon; we should consider the liberties of that state as in no immediate danger. But the condition of *England* is neither that of *France*, nor that of *Holland*, which renders it on the one hand highly improper to sit still unconcerned, as if all was well; or on the other, to give all up as if irretrievable and desperate.

And now——in the name of all that is holy—— let us consider whether a scheme may not be laid down for obtaining the necessary reformation of parliament.

Before all other things, there must be established a GRAND NATIONAL ASSOCIATION FOR RESTORING THE

THE CONSTITUTION. Into this must be invited all men of property, all friends to liberty, all able commanders, &c. There must be a copy of the ASSOCIATION for every parish, and a parochial committee to procure subscriptions from all persons whose names are in any tax-book, and who are willing to join the Association. And there must be a grand committee for every county in the three kingdoms, and in the colonies of *America*.

'The people at large, when they lose their constitutional guard, are like a rope of sand, easily divided asunder; and therefore when the acting parts of the constitution shall abuse their trust, and counteract the end for which they were established, there is no way of obtaining redress but by associating together, in order to form a new chain of union and strength in defence of their constitutional rights. But instead of uniting for their common interest, the people have suffered themselves to be divided and split into factions and parties to such a degree, that every man hath rose up in enmity against his neighbour; by which they have brought themselves under the fatal curse of a kingdom divided against itself, which cannot stand [a].'

By the readiness of the people to enter into the associations, it may be effectually determined, whether the majority are desirous of the proposed reformations. This, as has been observed before, is a matter of supreme consequence, for resistance to government, unless it be by a clear majority of the people, is rebellion. Therefore, with all due submission to the judgement of Bishop *Burnet* upon that point, the true criterion between rebellion and reformation consists not in

[a] HIST. ESS. ENGL. CONST. 151.

in the atrociousness of the abuses to be reformed, but in the concurrence of the people in desiring reformation. For whatever the majority desire, it is certainly lawful for them to have, unless they desire what is contrary to the laws of God.

Confederacies and associations have been usual in all countries, especially in *England*.

A confederacy of the nobility of *France* was formed against that weak and worthless prince *Lewis* XI. in which 500 were concerned; and their places of rendezvous were the most public, as the church of *Notre Dame*. At last they assembled an army of 100,000 men. Yet the king's party never found them out till they had got together a great force[a].

King *John* summoned the barons to pass the seas to him in *Normandy*, and assist him to quell his rebellious subjects. They refused, unless he would promise to restore and preserve their liberties. This was the first attempt toward an association for a plan of liberty, according to Mr. *Hume*[b].

Lord *Lyttelton* mentions an association in the time of *William* the Bastard, to defend that blessed saint, and all his territories, both within and without the realm[c].

The opposition in those days was between a solitary tyrant (for *John* could not command the army without the concurrence of the barons) and all *England*. In *Charles* Ist's time, the opposition was between a frantic bigotted king, and a brave and free parliament. In our times, the opposition is between a corrupt court, joined by an innumerable multitude of all ranks

a MOD. UNIV. HIST. XXIV. 53.

b *Hume*, HIST. I. 356.

c HIST. HEN. II. III. 85.

ranks and stations, bought with the public money, and the independent part of the nation.

The general association all over *England* for the defence of *Elizabeth*, *A. D.* 1586, and afterwards for that of *William* and *Mary*. Catholic leagues, protestant leagues, the *Hanseatic* association, the solemn league and covenant, and the non-importation association in *America*, &c. are all acts of the people at large [a].

Upon the lords throwing out the exclusion-bill, another was brought into the house of commons for an association for the support of the protestant religion, and exclusion of the duke of *York* [b]. They voted, that till the exclusion-bill should pass, no supplies ought to be granted the king; and lest he should raise money on credit, they threatened their vengeance on those who should lend the king on the credit of any tax. The sequel shewed how much the commons were in the right in all these proceedings; and of what consequence an uncorrupt house of commons is.

A grand national association against popery was proposed in the house of commons, *A. D.* 1680. A tyrannical government is an association with a vengeance. Why should not the people associate against it? Resolved, that it is the opinion of this house, that the house be moved that a bill be brought for an association of all his majesty's protestant subjects for the safety of his majesty's person, the defence of the protestant religion, and for preventing the duke of *York*, or any other papist, from succeeding to the crown [c].

A. D. 1744, the merchants of *London*, to the number of 520, associated themselves for the support of public

[a] ACT. REG. IV. 40.

[b] *Hume*, HIST. STUARTS, II. 329.

DEB. COM. II. 30.

public credit, and effectually supported it at a very perilous conjuncture[a]. The whole county of *York* was associated against the rebels, and several noblemen raised regiments at their own expence.

See the act for associating the kingdom in defence of king *William* III. *A. D.* 1696[b]. The court was glad to encourage such an association of the *people* in a time of danger. They did not then insist, as has been done since, that the people are annihilated, or absorbed into the parliament; that the voice of the people is no where to be heard but in parliament; that members of parliament are not responsible to their constituents, &c. The association was begun by the people, and parliament gave it sanction afterwards. Surely it is as necessary to associate for preserving the kingdom, as it was then for preserving the king. The associated 'engage to stand by and assist each other to the utmost 'of their power in support and defence of king *William*; 'and if his majesty comes to a violent or untimely 'death, they oblige themselves to stand by each other 'in revenging the same upon his enemies and their adherents,' &c. Put instead of a design by papists, 'against the life of the king;' a design by courtiers, 'against the life of the constitution;' and you have here a model for the association for restoring annual parliaments, adequate representation, and an unbribed house of commons.

The next question is, Who shall set himself at the head of this grand association?

In a monarchy, we know full well who ought to be at the head of all schemes for the general good. And would to God, the Father of his people would lay hold of such an opportunity of declaring himself a friend to inde-

[a] Contin. Rap. viii. 24.

[b] Stat. at Large, iii. 236.

independent parliaments! How glorious would the character of *Augustus* have appeared to all posterity, had he really intended what he only affected to intend; I mean the restoration of the republican government upon the fall of *Julius*, which he certainly had power to bring about, notwithstanding his pretences to the contrary? In the same manner, would not every worthy *British* bosom glow with affection, would not every angel in heaven tune his lyre to the praises of that monarch, who, shaking off and trampling under his feet the ministerial trammels, should dare to think for himself, and to speak for himself, should astonish both houses of parliament, and all *Europe*, by opening a new parliament, or a new session, with a speech composed by himself, in which he should condemn the long prevalence of corruption in the legislative assemblies, and should earnestly recommend to them the making and bringing in effectual bills for restoring annual parliaments, for making representation adequate, for exclusion by rotation, and for limiting the number of placemen and pensioners sitting in the house. But if our sovereign for that time being should judge such interposition improper, the great privileges of our nobility are to be the king's counsellors, the protectors of the constitution, and the people's example. Ought not therefore our independent nobility to take care that such a scheme be properly headed? But should our nobles think otherwise of this subject, and decline assuming to themselves a principal part in the conduct of this infinitely important, though not infinitely difficult, business, let the great, the rich, the independent city of *London* take the lead.

'The corporation of *London* has, since the Restoration, usually taken the lead in petitions to parliament for the alteration of any established law [a].'

a *Blackst.* Comment. iv. 147.

In the famous association signed by the illustrious Seven, for inviting over the prince of *Orange A. D.* 1688, it is observed, that the people were generally dissatisfied. The Seven lay great stress on this, as likely to be a support to the prince in his enterprize, if they (the people) could have 'such a protection to 'countenance their rising, as would secure them from 'being destroyed before they could get into a posture 'of defence.' They observed that the army was divided, the officers discontented, and the men strongly set against popery. And that the seamen were almost all against the king[a].

The objects of such a general association as I propose are, 1. The securing of public credit. 2. Obtaining the undoubted sense of the people, on the state of public affairs. 3. Presenting petitions, signed by a clear majority of the people of property, for the necessary acts of parliament. 4. To raise, and have in readiness, the strength of the nation, in order to influence government, and prevent mischief.

If any person is alarmed at the boldness of this paragraph, let him remember that it is less than what was done at the Revolution. For it was not certain, at that remarkable period, that the *majority* of the people were for the exclusion. Besides, the restoration I propose is a much less considerable alteration, though like to be of much greater public advantage, than the setting aside the whole royal family of the *Stuarts*. And let it be ever remembered, that rebellion is not merely opposition to government; if it were, then was the Revolution direct rebellion. The opposition of a minority to government, backed by a majority, is proper rebellion.

---

[a] *Dalr.* II. 228.

sion. The opposition of a majority of the people to an obstinate government is proper patriotism. You have therefore, my good countrymen, only to make it certain beyond all possibility of doubt, that you have the majority on your side. Whatever they choose is right.

Let the first business of the *London* association be, as I said, securing public credit; the next, for *petitioning*, exclusive of all views to any thing *farther*, and as taking for granted, that the petitions will be effectual. Let this example be followed by all the great cities, towns, counties, corporate bodies, and faculties throughout the island, and the same in *Ireland* and the colonies.

The people of *Ireland* extorted the passing of the bill for limiting the length of their parliaments, by assembling to the number of twenty thousand men, securing all the avenues to the parliament-house, and threatening vengeance on all the members, if the bill was not passed. But for this spirited behaviour, they had been jockeyed out of that salutary act [a].

A. D. 1588, the year of the Barricades, the *Parisians* rose, and drove out six thousand regular troops, chiefly *Swiss*, and defeated the king's guards [b].

A large mob, *A. D.* 1773, surrounded the palace at *Madrid*, and insisted, that the effects lately taken from some *Jesuits* should be restored to their relations. The guards were called to disperse them; but would not fire upon the people. The court was obliged to yield [c].

Ff 2 It

[a] Lond. Mag. 1768, p. 132.

[b] Mem. *Sully*, I. 267.

[c] Whitehall Even. Post, *March* 27, 1773.

It is always to be expected that, as *Sallust* says, men should act with more earnestness for the preservation of their all, than the partisans of tyranny for superfluous power.

In the decisive battle of *Marston Moor*, the tyrant's army and the parliament's were nearly equal, about fourteen thousand each. But of the former four thousand were killed, and fifteen hundred taken; of the latter only three hundred lost in all [a].

'Provocation will sometimes rouse valour, when a 'sense of honour will not. In the year 1746, when '*Botta*, the *Austrian* general, demanded a severe con-'tribution of the *Genoese*, they begun paying, and all 'went on quietly, though it was with the utmost dif-'ficulty that the second payment was made; but the '*Austrians* being possessed of a notion which was not 'groundless, that though the government of *Genoa* 'was exhausted, yet that many of their individuals 'were immensely rich, still advanced in their demands; 'and the senate took care that all the sums paid to the '*Austrians* should be carried with great parade to their 'quarters in full view of the people. This had the 'effect they secretly desired, which was to render mat-'ters ripe for a revolt, without their being openly con-'cerned in it; though some of the senators were bold 'enough to disguise themselves in *Plebeian* dresses, and 'mixing with the common people blew the flame of 'discontent, which, notwithstanding all the terror 'of the *Austrian* general and army, at last broke out. 'For the siege of *Antibes* being resolved upon, *Botta*, 'amongst other pieces of artillery, which he designed 'to be put on board the *British* fleet for carrying on 'that

[a] *Macaul.* IV. 119.

'that siege, ordered a large mortar, which happened 'to be overturned in the streets, and an *Austrian* officer 'endeavouring to oblige some of the inhabitants of '*Genoa* to assist in dragging it down to the harbour, 'they refused; and he striking one of them with his 'cane, a shower of stones from the rest obliged the '*Austrians* for that night to retire. Next day, when '*Botta* prepared to chastise the insurgents, he found 'them grown to a formidable head, and without en-'tering into the particulars of the insurrection, all the 'intrepidity and discipline of his troops could not with-'stand that spirit of liberty which once more animated 'these republicans, who for many years had been 'looked upon as degenerated, even to a proverb. Ac-'cording to *Bonamia* a *British* man of war had been 'sent thither by his *Sardinian* majesty to bring off for 'him part of the plunder; and we are told, that that 'monarch was by no means pleased with the indepen-'dent negociation which the *Austrians* had entered into 'with the *Genoese*. However that may be, it is cer-'tain, that *Botta* in his turn made application for 'some respite of hostilities. But the inhabitants of 'the neighbouring villages, seized with the same spirit 'as these of *Genoa*, had by this time taken arms, and 'poured into the city. The effect was, that the '*Austrian* regulars, notwithstanding some advantages 'they had gained at first, were drawn from one strong 'post to another, till *Botta* applied to the senate, and 'under pretence of the capitulation, demanding that 'they should unarm their soldiers, and join with him 'in suppressing the insurrection. The doge and senate 'of *Genoa*, upon this occasion, behaved with wonder-'ful address, and temporised so well, that they neither 'discouraged the insurgents, nor did they give *Botta* 'any just handle to accuse them of breach of faith. 'By this time the insurgents, by the help of some '*French* and *Spanish* officers, who were prisoners to the '*Austrians*, but had mingled themselves in disguises 'with the *Genoese*, were disciplined and rendered excel-'lent troops, and they had regularly fortified all the 'strong posts of the city; nor would they longer hear 'of any terms, but that the *Austrians* should evacuate 'the city, restore their artillery, and give them an 'acquittance of all further demands of any kind. 'Upon this *Botta*, after another desperate but fruitless 'attempt to recover possession of the city, found him-'self obliged to evacuate the same, which he did with 'great loss to himself, and satisfaction to the *Genoese*[a].'

Put no trust in any *living* man, or set of men, farther than you yourselves see. The dead have no design upon you. Therefore have I called them up to warn and alarm you. Pay no regard to what I have written, otherwise than as supported by fact and the judgment of your wise ancestors.

Members of parliament would hardly dare to reject the proposed reformation-bill, as knowing themselves not to be invulnerable, and remembering that they could not command a guard of 500 soldiers each at their country houses at all times.

Let the petitions be drawn up and presented in the most respectful and most unexceptionable way that is possible, so that the fault may all come upon government (if they reject the petitions) and none upon the people.

'Petitioning, in better English, is no more than re-'questing

[a] CONTIN. RAP. IX. 279.

'questing or requiring, and men require not favours 'but their due[a].'

If the government shew themselves so wise and so friendly to the people as to grant the petitions, all is safe and secure. For an honest parliament will make every body else honest, and all will go well.

A government which opposes and refuses the undoubted demands of the people, in such manner that the people come to be defeated of their desire, be the subject matter what it will, is no government, but a proper tyranny. Supposing the government to be really and *bonâ fide* persuaded that the demand of the people is unreasonable, in this or any other case, and would prove hurtful to them if granted, they are only to remonstrate against it; and if the people still insist upon it, the government ought to a man to resign, not to resist the supreme power, the majesty of the people. Whoever undertakes to manage any person's or any people's affairs in spite of the proprietors, is answerable for all consequences.

'Whenever the fundamentals of a free government 'are attacked, or any other schemes ruinous to the ge'neral interest of a nation are pursued, the best service 'that can be done to such a nation, and even to the 'prince, is to commence an early and vigorous oppo'sition to them; for the event will always shew, as 'we shall soon see in the present case, that those who 'form an opposition in this manner, are the truest 'friends to both, however they may be stigmatized at 'first with odious names, which belong more properly 'to those who throw the dirt at them. If the oppo'sition begin late, or be carried on more faintly

 'than

[a] MILT. EIKON, 109.

‘ than the exigency requires, the evil will grow; nay, ‘ it will grow the more by ſuch an oppoſition, till it ‘ becomes at length too inveterate for the ordinary ‘ methods of cure; and whenever that happens, when- ‘ ever uſurpations on national liberty are grown too ‘ ſtrong to be checked by theſe ordinary methods, the ‘ people are reduced to this alternative: they muſt ei- ‘ ther ſubmit to ſlavery and beggary, the worſt of all ‘ political evils, or they muſt endeavour to prevent the ‘ impending miſchief by open force and reſiſtance, ‘ which is an evil but one degree leſs eligible than the ‘ other. But when the oppoſition is begun early, and ‘ carried on vigorouſly, there is time to obtain redreſs ‘ of grievances, and put a ſtop to ſuch uſurpations by ‘ theſe gentle and ſafe methods which their conſtitu- ‘ tion hath provided; methods which may and have ‘ often proved fatal to wicked men, but can never prove ‘ fatal to the prince himſelf. He is never in danger ‘ but when theſe methods, which all arbitrary courts ‘ diſlike, are too long delayed. The moſt plauſible ob- ‘ jection to ſuch proceedings, and by which well-mean- ‘ ing men are frequently made the bubbles of theſe ‘ who have the worſt deſign, ariſes from a falſe notion ‘ of moderation. True political moderation conſiſts ‘ in not oppoſing the meaſures of government, except ‘ when great and national intereſts are at ſtake; and ‘ when that is the caſe, in oppoſing them with ſuch a ‘ degree of warmth as is adequate to the nature of the ‘ evil, to the circumſtances of danger attending it, and ‘ even to theſe of opportunity. To oppoſe upon any ‘ other foot, to oppoſe things which are not blame- ‘ worthy, or which are of no material conſequence to ‘ the national intereſt, with ſuch violence as may diſ- ‘ order the harmony of government, is certainly fac-

‘ tion;

'tion; but it is likewise faction, and faction of the 'worst kind, either not to oppose at all, or not to 'oppose in earnest when points of the greatest import-'ance to the nation are concerned[a].'

When an injured nation calls aloud for redress, and can have none from government, the people may be expected to do *themselves* justice, says *Shippen* on the South Sea affair.

'Parliament has declared it no resistance of magis-'trates to side with the just principles of law, nature, 'and nations. The soldier may lawfully hold the 'hands of that general, who turns his cannon against 'his own army; the seaman the hands of that pilot, 'who wilfully runs the ship on a rock.' So our brethren of *Scotland* argued, in the remonstrance of the army in *June* 1646[b].

'*Britain*, according to our present constitution, 'cannot be undone by parliaments; for there is some-'thing which a parliament cannot do. A parliament 'cannot annul the constitution; and whilst that is 'preserved, though our condition may be bad, it can-'not be irretrievably so. The legislative is a su-'preme, and may be called in one sense an absolute, 'but in none, an arbitrary power. It is limited to the 'public good of the society. It is a power that hath 'no other end but preservation, and therefore can 'never have a right to destroy, enslave, or designedly 'to impoverish the subjects; for the obligations of the 'law of nature cease not in society, &c.——If you 'therefore put so extravagant a case, as to suppose 'the two houses of parliament concurring to make at 'once

[a] *Bolingbr.* REM. HIST. ENG. 274.

[b] PARL. HIST. XV. 460.

'once a formal cession of their own rights and privi-'leges, and of those of the whole nation, to the crown, 'and ask who hath the right and the means to resist the 'supreme legislative power; I answer the whole nation 'hath the right, and a people who deserve to enjoy 'liberty will find the means. An attempt of this kind 'would break the bargain between the king and the 'nation, between the representative and collective body 'of the people, and would dissolve the constitution. 'From hence it follows, that the nation which hath a 'right to preserve this constitution, hath a right to 'resist an attempt that leaves no other means for pre-'serving it but those of resistance. From hence it fol-'lows, that if the constitution was actually dissolved, 'as it would be by such an attempt of the three estates, 'the people would return to their original, their na-'tural right, the right of restoring the same constitu-'tion, or of making a new one. No power on earth 'could claim any right of imposing a constitution up-'on them, and less than any that king, those lords, 'and those commons, who having been intrusted to 'preserve, had destroyed the former.——But to sup-'pose a case more within the bounds of possibility, 'though one would be tempted to think it as little 'within those of probability; let us suppose our par-'liaments in some future generation to grow so corrupt, 'and the crown so rich, that a pecuniary influence 'constantly prevailing over the majority, they should 'assemble for little else than to establish grievances in-'stead of redressing them; to approve the measures of 'the court without information; to engage their coun-'try in alliances, in treaties, in wars, without exami-'nation, and to give money without account, and al-'most without stint; the case would be deplorable. 'Our constitution itself would become our grievance

'whilst

'whilst this corruption prevailed; and if it prevailed 'long, our constitution could not last long; because 'this slow progress would lead to the destruction of it, 'as surely as the more concise method of giving it up 'at once. But in this case the constitution would help 'itself, and effectually too, unless the whole mass of 'the people was tainted, and the electors were become 'no honester than the elected. Much time would be 'required to beggar and enslave the nation in this 'manner. It could scarce be the work of one parlia-'ment, though parliaments should continue to be sep-'tennial. It could not be the work of a triennial par-'liament most certainly; and the people of *Great Bri-'tain* would have none to blame but themselves; be-'cause, as the constitution is a sure rule of action to 'those whom they chuse to act for them, so it is like-'wise a sure rule of judgment to them in the choice 'of their trustees, and particularly of such as have re-'presented them already. In short, nothing can de-'stroy the constitution of *Britain* but the people of '*Britain*; and whenever the people of *Britain* become 'so degenerate and base as to be induced by corruption '(for they are no longer in danger of being awed by 'prerogative) to chuse persons to represent them in 'parliament whom they have found by experience to be 'under an influence arising from private interest, de-'pendents on a court, and the creatures of a minister, 'or others who are unknown to the people that elect 'them, and bring no recommendation but that which 'they carry in their purses; then may the enemies of 'our constitution boast that they have got the better 'of it, and that it is no longer able to preserve itself, 'nor to defend liberty [a].'

Ten

---

[a] DISSERT. UPON PARTIES, 210.

Ten millions of people are not to sit still, and see a villanous junto overthrow their liberties. Formalities are then at an end. The question, in a season of such extremity, is not, who has a *right* to do this or that? Any man has a right to save his country. 'In such 'cases, says *Sidney*[a], every man is a magistrate, and 'he, who best knows the danger, and the means of 'preventing it, has the right of calling the senate or 'people to an assembly.' The people would, and certainly ought to follow him, as they did *Brutus* and *Valerius* against *Tarquin*, or *Horatius* and *Valerius* against the *Decemviri*. To wait for formalities, while our country lies bleeding, would be as foolish as the stiffness of the officers about *Philip* IV. of *Spain*, who let him catch a violent cold and fever, because the person whose place it was to help the king to his cloak was out of the way, in time of a storm of hail and rain, when he was a hunting.

'The law does not, neither can it, permit any private man, or set of men, to interfere forcibly in 'matters of such high importance, [the redress of public grievances] especially as it has established a sufficient power for these purposes in the high court of 'parliament. Neither does the constitution justify any 'private, or particular resistance for private or particular injuries; though in cases of national oppression, the nation has very justifiably risen as one man, 'to vindicate the original contract between the king 'and people[b].'

The *Spanish* grandees resisted *Charles* V. their sovereign, though he commanded an army of 40,000 men. Nor did he dare to shew resentment. *Nemo potest odio multorum resistere*[c].

[a] Disc. Gov. 421.

[b] *Blackst.* Com. iv. 82.

[c] *Robertson*'s Hist. Ch. V. ii. 430.

Wise nations have always insisted on redress of grievances, before they gave money. A free gift from the cortes of *Castile* to *Charles* V. without the previous conditions, occasioned *A. D.* 1530, a most furious insurrection [a]. On this occasion the society called the Junta, set up the lunatic queen *Joanna* against *Charles*, and shook his throne. The Junta remonstrates, requiring not only redress of disorders, but new regulations; among other particulars, against foreign troops, a foreign regent, or foreigners in employments; against free quarters for soldiers; against alienation of royal demesnes; against new erected places; for an adequate representation in the cortes, or parliaments; against court-influence in electing those representatives; a member's receiving for himself, or any of his family, any office, or pension, to be confiscation, or death; each community to pay a competent salary to its representative; the cortes to meet, whether summoned by the king, or not; the unequal privileges of the nobles to be abrogated; inquiry to be made into the disposal of the royal revenues, by the cortes, if the king does not order it in a certain time [b]. The same demands were made by the people in many of the other countries of *Europe*, in their struggles for liberty.

Parke, governor of *Antigua*, about the beginning of this century, provoked the people to such a pitch by his tyranny, lewdness with the wives of some of the principal men of the island, and other debaucheries, that they rise upon him, attack him in his own house, and murder him. Remarkable that when *Parke* seemed willing to give security for a change of conduct, the people would not quit their purpose, fearing that if the difference was made up again, he might have

[a] *Robertson*'s HIST. CH. V. II. 156. [b] Ibid. II. 106.

have interest to bring some of them to punishment, as was the case of *Charles* I.[a] People in power had better avoid driving things to such an extremity, as to render their destruction necessary, or seemingly so. When the people take redress into their own hands, woe to the tyrants.

'*Blackstone*'s cautions for the choice of able men, as 'so much power is lodged in the parliament, are most 'certainly obvious and just; but his quotations from '*Burleigh*, *Hale*, *Montesquieu*, and *Locke*, and his con- 'clusions therefrom, require a more close examination. '*Burleigh* said *England* could never be ruined by a par- 'liament. Sir *Matthew Hale*, The parliament being 'the highest court, over which none other can have 'any jurisdiction, if this government should fall then, 'the subject is left without remedy, by any appeal to 'any higher court. *Montesquieu*, *England* must perish 'when the legislative shall become more corrupt than 'the executive. All this from such eminent writers 'must certainly bespeak the highest regard due, as it 'points at the greatest danger, and the saddest conse- 'quences. Consider the evils attending such a scene 'of things, is the language these sages speak. Whilst 'your parliament continues as it ought, that great 'master which might soon be hoped to set at rights all 'less obstructions from any quarter; but if that fails, 'what can you expect to follow but the ruin of the 'machines;—and here these sages, and this writer seem 'at a full stop.—In ruins we are, and there we must 'lie; but Mr. *Locke*, who is never at rest till the sub- 'ject he is treating of is exhausted, and whose com- 'prehension and precision can never enough be ad- 'mired, though he sees and acknowledges the danger, 'distress,

[a] Mod. Univ. Hist. xli. 307.

'distress, and wretchedness of such a case, yet he carries 'his reader a step farther. Suppose the parliament do 'so abuse their trust, exceed their power, and are as so 'many tyrants and leechworms to the people; what 'then is there no remedy? Yes, saith he, there re- 'mains still inherent in the people, a supreme power 'to remove or alter the legislature. In case of such, 'their flagrant abuse of the trust reposed in them, there 'is a forfeiture, and the power devolves to those who 'gave it. This is Mr. *Locke*'s theory, but however 'just it may be, we cannot adopt it, saith this writer, 'because it includes in it a dissolution of the whole 'frame of government; and reduces all the members to 'their original state of equality. Pray how can it be 'just, if it cannot be adopted? Why, if government 'be dissolved, can it not be renewed? How did it begin 'at first? The power in such case devolves to the 'people, who may make such alterations as to them 'seem meet. Begin again, saith Mr. *Locke*, accord- 'ing to the original design of government, as instituted 'by God, the only absolute sovereign and judge of all. '*Salus populi suprema lex esto* [a].'

Let us hear bishop *Burnet* on the Revolution. 'This 'was the progress of that transaction, which was con- 'sidered all *Europe* over as the trial, whether the 'king or the church were like to prevail. The deci- 'sion was as favourable as was possible. The king did 'assume to himself a power to make laws void; and 'to qualify men for employments, whom the law had 'put under such incapacities, that all they did was 'null and void. The sheriff and mayors of towns were 'no legal officers: judges (one of them being a pro- 'fessed papist *Alibon*) who took not the test, were no 'judges: so that the government, and the legal admi- 'nistration

[a] CHRON. No. 1786.

'nistration of it, was broken. A parliament returned 'by such men, was no legal parliament. All this was 'done by virtue of the dispensing power, which changed 'the whole frame of our government, and subjected all 'the laws to the king's pleasure: for upon the same 'pretence of that power, other declarations might 'have come out, voiding any other laws that the court 'found stood in their way; since we had scarce any 'law that was fortified with such clauses, to force the 'execution of it, as those that were laid aside, had in them. 'And when the king pretended that such a sacred point 'of government, that a petition offered in the modestest 'terms, and in the humblest manner possible, calling 'it in question, was made so great a crime, and carried 'so far against men of such eminence; this I confess 'satisfied me that there was a total destruction of our 'constitution avowedly begun, and violently prose'cuted. Here was not jealousies nor fears: the thing 'was open and avowed. This was not a single act of 'illegal violence, but a declared design against the 'whole of our constitution. It was not only the 'judgment of a court of law: the king had now by 'two public acts of state renewed in two successive 'years, openly published his design. This appeared 'such a total subversion, that according to the princi'ples that some of the highest assertors of submission 'and obedience, *Barklay* and *Grotius* had laid down, it 'was now lawful for the nation to look to itself, and 'see to its preservation. And as soon as any man was 'convinced that this was lawful, there remained no'thing, but to look to the prince of *Orange*, who was 'the only person that either could save them, or had 'a right to it: since by all the laws in the world, even 'private as well as public, he that has in him the re'version of any estate, has a right to hinder the pos-

'sessor,

'sessor, if he goes about to destroy that which is to come 'to him after the possessor's death[a].'

When the contest is between a headstrong king, standing by himself, and a set of good ministers, a parliament, and the whole nation, the strife cannot be long-lived. A tyrant can do nothing without a powerful junto of ministers, and an armed force. If the dispute is between a king, surrounded by a set of ministerial tools, and backed by a mercenary army on one side, and on the other, a faithful parliament, and a free people, the command, which parliament has of the purse, will render it difficult for the court to gain their points. But if the contest is between a designing minister, a mercenary army, and a corrupt parliament on one hand, and, on the other, the body of the independent people, the decision may prove difficult, but is most likely to be in favour of liberty, if the people can only unite, and act in concert. For if the cause be unquestionably good, the people will soon have purse, and army, and every thing else in their hands.

Voltaire thinks it would be ridiculous for a citizen of modern *Rome*, to ask the pope to restore consuls, tribunes, a senate, and all the *Roman* republic, or for a modern citizen of *Athens* to propose to the sultan the restoration of the court of *Areopagus*, and the assembly of the people[b]. Such transitions as these may be thought too sudden. And a people debased by inveterate slavery, may be judged unfit for freedom. But surely these considerations have nothing to do with the restoration of independency to the *British* house of commons.

Hugh Capet, to establish himself on the throne of *France*, which he had usurped, granted a great value of

 lands

[a] *Burn.* II. 467.

[b] Ess. sur l'Hist. II. 199.

lands to the nobility of *France*. By this means the crown became poor, and the grandees rich. So that when the king carried on war with the approbation of the grandees, he made a figure. If he began war of his own head, his forces were inconsiderable. And those great vassals thought themselves 'privileged to 'levy war against their king, in case of oppression, or 'even for a bare denial of justice [a].'

Christopher II. king of *Denmark* made some alterations in a monastery, without leave of his bishops, and renewed the plough-tax, which, they alleged, was contrary to his coronation-oath, &c. An immediate insurrection followed, and proclamations were published, inviting all the friends of liberty to join against the king. He was driven from his kingdom, and with great difficulty restored; but never afterwards enjoyed any peace [b].

In a debate during the prosecution of lord *Oxford*, Sir *Watkins Williams Wynne* speaks as follows:

'A civil war I shall grant is a terrible misfortune; 'but it is far from being the most terrible; for I had 'rather see my country engaged in civil war, than see 'it tamely submit but for one year to ministerial bon-'dage; therefore if this country should be reduced to 'the fatal dilemma of being obliged to give up its li-'berties, or engage in a civil war, I hope no true '*Briton* would balance a moment in his choice.'

'Thus his majesty may be prevailed on, to continue 'a bad minister at the head of the administration, not-'withstanding the people's being generally convinced 'that he is every day undermining their liberties, by 'means of a venal and corrupt parliament; and if this 'should

---

[a] *Rap.* I. 223.

[b] MOD. UNIV. HIST. XXXII. 231.

'should be the case, I must conclude that a civil war 'will certainly ensue; or I must form a much more dis'agreeable conclusion, which is, that the people of this 'country are so much degenerated from the virtue and 'courage of their ancestors, that they chuse rather to 'submit tamely to slavery, than to run the risk of ascer'taining their liberties by the sword [a].'

'If the means for preventing slavery have not been 'provided in the first constitution of a country, or from 'the changes of times, corruption of manners, insen'sible encroachments, or violent usurpations of princes, 'have been rendered ineffectual, and the people exposed 'to all the calamities that may be brought upon them 'by the weakness, vices, and malice of the prince, or 'those who govern him, I confess the remedies are more 'difficult and dangerous; but even in these cases they 'must be tried. Nothing can be feared, that is worse 'than what is suffered, or must in a short time fall upon 'those who are in this condition. They who are al'ready fallen into all that is odious, shameful, and mi'serable, cannot justly fear. When things are brought 'to such a pass, the boldest counsels are the most safe; 'and if they must perish who lie still, and they can but 'perish who are more active, the choice is easily made. 'Let the danger be never so great, there is a possibility 'of safety, whilst men have life, hands, arms, and cou'rage to use them; but that people must certainly pe'rish, who tamely suffer themselves to be oppressed, 'either by the injustice, cruelty, and malice of an ill 'magistrate, or by those who prevail upon the vices and 'infirmities of weak princes. It is vain to say, that this 'may give occasion to men of raising tumults, or civil 'war; for though these are evils, yet they are not the

[a] Deb. Com. xiii. 92.

'greatest of evils. Civil war in *Machiavel's* account 'is a *disease*, but tyranny is the *death* of a state. Gentle 'ways are first to be used, and it is best if the work 'can be done by them; but it must not be left undone 'if they fail. It is good to use supplications, advices, 'and remonstrances; but those who have no regard to 'justice, and will not hearken to counsel. must be con-'strained [a].'

This shews clearly the insignificancy of clamouring against ministers, and requesting the dissolution of parliaments, instead of setting ourselves in earnest to restore the constitution. We see the same corrupt or impolitic proceedings going on in the administration of a *Harley*, a *Walpole*, a *Pelham*, a *Pitt*, a *Bute*, a *Grafton*, a *North*; and we see every parliament implicitly obeying the orders of the minister. Some ministers we see more criminal, others less; some parliaments more slavish, others less; but we see all ministers, and all parliaments, the present always excepted guilty, inexcusably guilty, in suffering the continual and increasing prevalency of corruption, from ministry to ministry, and from parliament to parliament. Could we have had every one of our corrupt ministers impeached, and even convicted, would a corrupt parliament filled with their obsequious tools, have punished them? If we did nothing toward a radical cure of grievances, and obliging the succeeding to be honester than the foregoing; what should we have gained by such prosecutions? The greatest part of the *Roman* emperors was massacred, and so are many of our *Asiatic* and *African* tyrants. But did the *Romans*, or do the *Turks*, and the people of *Algiers*, gain any additional liberty by the punishment of their

---

[a] *Sidn.* Disc. on Gov. 434.

their oppressors? We know they do not. Nor shall we by clamouring, nor even by punishing; any more than we stop robbing on the highway by hanging, unless we put it out of the *power* of ministers to go on abusing us, and trampling upon our liberties; and this can only be done by restoring independency to parliament.

'It is true, such as would correct errors, and watch 'that no invasion may be made on liberty, have been 'heretofore called a faction by the persons in power; 'but it is not properly the name, and ought to be given 'to another sort of men. It is wrong to call them the 'faction, who by all dutiful and modest ways promote 'the cause of liberty, as the true means to endear a 'prince to his subjects, and to lay upon them a 'stronger tie, and obligation to preserve his govern'ment. For a people will certainly best love and de'fend that prince, by whom the greatest immunities, 'and most good laws have been granted. They can'not properly be termed the faction, who desire a war 'should be managed upon such a foot of expence as the 'nation is able to bear; who would have the public 'treasure not wasted, the prince not deceived in his 'grants and bargains, who would have the ministry 'watchful and industrious, and who, when they com'plain, are angry with things, and not with persons. 'The name of faction does more truly belong to them, 'who, though the body politic has all the signs of death 'upon it, yet say, all is well; that the riches of the 'nation are not to be exhausted; that there is no mis'government in all its business; that it feels no de'cay; that its œconomy is perfect, and who all the 'while are as arrogant and assuming, as if they had 'saved that very people whom their folly and mad con'duct has in a manner ruined. They may be rather 'termed the faction, who were good patriots out of the 'court, but are better courtiers in it; and who pre'tended to fear excess of power, while it was not com'municated to them; but never think the monarchy 'can be high enough advanced when they are in the 'administration [a].'

'Perhaps nothing can more contribute to restore 'peace and order in a government, than to overlook the 'persons of men, either in contempt or in compassion, 'and to fall to work in earnest upon mending things. 'A man may without imputation of blame profess a 'friendship, and adhere to this or that great man, pre'tending to believe him innocent when accused, and 'consequently join with those who are connected in 'his defence. But can any party be formed, and can 'any be so insolent to go along with them, who shall 'openly declare for such crimes, and for such and such 'corruption and mismanagement? Nor indeed can any 'thing more disappoint the ambitious and wicked de'signs of corrupt men, than to take away their pre'tences and false colours, and to leave them without 'excuse; which you do, when, without expressing 'anger or prejudice to the persons of men, you make 'it manifest that your only aim is to put it out of their 'power, or out of the power of such as will tread in 'their steps hereafter, to bring any farther mischiefs 'upon the commonwealth; and where these measures 'are taken, it is difficult, if not impossible, to form or 'keep up parties that shall combine to protect and 'countenance the vices of the age: for it being the 'interest of much the major part to be well governed, 'where the people plainly see all affairs carried on 'calmly, and without piques and personal enmities, 'they

[a] *Daven.* II. 303.

'they let faction drop, which produces what may be 'called right and perfect government[a].'

It could not be pretended, that an association for restoring the independency of parliament, was a party affair.

If no point be obtained, but redress of a personal injury, or particular grievance, the nation may remain in the same ruinous condition as before. But if independency of parliament were restored, all personal injuries, and particular grievances, would of course be redressed.

Unsuccessful attempts to obtain an enlargement of liberty, have often issued in an abridgment of it. This hazard may be worth running for the sake of a national object; but it is not worth while to risque it for the sake of obtaining redress of a *particular* grievance.

All are not agreed about *particular* grievances. But all are agreed about the necessity of an independent parliament, and the certainty of the ruin which parliamentary corruption must bring on. One would expect an association upon a broad foundation, to attract into its sphere greater numbers, than one set up with any particular view.

A designing ministry desires no better than that the people's attention be engaged about trifling grievances, such as have employed us since the late peace. This gives them an opportunity of wreathing the yoke around our necks, because it gives them a pretence for increasing the military force. Instructing, petitioning, remonstrating, and the like, are good diversion for a court; because they know, that, in such ways, nothing will be done against their power. A grand national association for obtaining an independent parliament

 would

[a] *Daven.* 356.

would make them tremble. For they know, that the nation, if in earnest, would have it, and that with the cessation of their influence in parliament, their power must end.

'The *Romans*, in the Imperial times, destroyed many 'of the monsters who tyrannized over them. But the 'greatest advantage gained by their death was a respite 'from ruin: and the government, which ought to 'have been established by good laws, depending only 'upon the virtue of one man, his life proved no more 'than a lucid interval, and at his death they relapsed 'into the depth of infamy and misery; and in this 'condition they continued till that empire was totally 'subverted. All the kingdoms of the *Arabians*, *Medes*, '*Persians*, *Moors*, and others of the East, are of the 'other sort. Common sense instructs them, that bar-'barous pride, cruelty and madness, grown to extre-'mity, cannot be born: but they have no other way 'than to kill the tyrant, and to do the like to his suc-'cessor, if he fall into the same crimes. Wanting that 'wisdom and valour which is required for the institu-'tion of a good government, they languish in perpetual 'slavery, and propose to themselves nothing better than 'to live under a gentle master, which is a precarious 'life, and little to be valued by men of bravery and 'spirit. But those nations that are more generous, 'who set a higher value upon liberty, and better un-'derstand the ways of preserving it, think it a small 'matter to destroy a tyrant, unless they can also 'destroy the tyranny. They endeavour to do the 'work thoroughly, either by changing the government 'intirely, or reforming it according to the first institu-'tion, and making such good laws as may preserve its 'integrity when reformed. This has been so frequent 'in all the nations, both ancient and modern, with

'whose

'whose actions we are best acquainted, as appears by 'the foregoing examples, and many others that might 'be alleged, if the case were not clear, that there is 'not one of them which will not furnish us with many 'instances; and no one magistracy now in being which 'does not owe its original to some judgment of this 'nature. So that they must either derive their right 'from such actions, or confess they have none at all, 'and leave the nation to their original liberty of setting 'up these magistracies which best please themselves, 'without any restriction or obligation to regard one 'person or family more than another[a].'

I know nothing of war, and therefore can propose nothing concerning the conduct of it; but to wish that it may be avoided if possible. Of all the evils to which human nature is obnoxious, none, excepting fixed slavery, is so formidable as war; and of all wars *civil* war is the most to be dreaded.

When I proposed, p. 428, to draw out a plan for restoration of independency to parliament, I intended to prescribe minutely the steps to be taken for that purpose. But on more mature consideration it occurred to me, that in tracing out this plan I should naturally be led to touch upon some particulars which might alarm the more timorous part of readers, and render them less inclined to join the grand national association. I therefore chose to proceed no farther; but to leave to the wisdom of succeeding times to determine the particular steps to be taken from the association to the obtaining of the great object, excepting what may be learned from the histories and precedents I have here given of associations for such national purposes.

Look

[a] *Sidn.* Disc. on Gov. 439.

Look down, O King of kings, and Ruler of nations, from where thou sittest enthroned high above all heighth, clothed in uncreated majesty, and surrounded with that light to which none can approach, look down upon this once favoured nation, and behold the difficulties and the dangers which now surround us. Rend asunder the thick and gloomy cloud which now hangs over us, big with tempest, and ready to burst upon our heads, and shine forth with brighter beams than those of the meridian sun on this once happy land, once the abode of peace and virtue, the temple of liberty, civil and religious.

Open the eyes of this unthinking people, that they may see the hideous precipice, on the brink of which they stand, and in time regain a station of security for the commonwealth, before it sinks in ruins never more to rise.

Send forth a spirit of wisdom, and of union, of submission to wise and just government, and of courage to resist oppression and tyranny.

Save the virtue of this great multitude, in danger of being utterly destroyed by corruption. Save the protestant religion, for which so many of thy faithful servants have bravely laid down their lives, and from the blaze of the cruel fires which consumed their bodies, ascended to celestial glory. Let not the infernal cloud of popish delusion any more, in this land, obscure the brightness of that system of truth which descended from thy throne, and which shews the way thitherward to every faithful votary of religious truth. Time was when this favoured land was the very bulwark of reformed religion. O let it never lose that glorious title. Let this one country at least possess the inestimable treasure.

Break

Break thou the iron sceptre with which tyrants break and destroy the liberties of mankind. Let the envenomed worms of the earth know that it never was thy intention that they should devour their fellow-worms, their subjects. Assert thy supreme dominion over those who impiously pretend to be thy vicegerents upon earth, to which honour they know Thou hast never called them, and that the unjust authority they assume they have obtained by wicked craft, or by lawless violence, and the effusion of human blood.

Thou art thyself the glorious patron of liberty. Thy intention was, that man should be free. Thy service is perfect freedom. The decrees of the puny tyrants of this world are often impious and rebellious against thy supreme commands, which are all righteous and good, and worthiest to be obeyed. Let the encroaching tyrant, let the corruptor of the people, and the persecutor on account of religious opinions, cease from this land. Let the voice of perjury be no more heard; let the damning bribe be no more seen in this country. Or if any have polluted themselves with the accursed thing which troubleth our camp, may the pangs of conscience seize upon them, may the powers of the world to come amaze and terrify them, and may they, before it be too late, give up the wages of corruption, the price of their betrayed country.

Put it into the hearts of those whose station gives them the power, to restore to the people willingly, and without compulsion, their unalienable rights and privileges. Inspire them with the wise and humane consideration, that, as the shepherds of the people, as the fathers of their country, they are obliged to deny themselves, to mortify their desire of riches, power, and plea-

sure,

ſure, and without waiting for the ſolicitations of the people, they ought to prevent their wiſhes, to offer and hold out to them whatever is for their advantage.

Let the cauſe of civil and religious liberty prove victorious. May the divine preſence be to the defenders of liberty a pillar of light, and of defence, and to the hoſt of the oppreſſors a pillar of cloud, of darkneſs and confuſion. Ariſe, and come forth from thy ſacred ſeat, clothed in all thy terrors. Let thy lightnings enlighten the world. Let thy thunders ſhake the mountains. Let diſmay and horror overwhelm the courage of thine enemies.

In thy hands, O Father and Preſerver of all, doth thy ſervant deſire to leave his King and Country, in the hope that they ſhall be ſafe under thy heavenly protection; and to Thee doth he conſecrate this and all his weak but well-intentioned labours for the good of his fellow-creatures, humbly hoping, that his infirmities ſhall be overlooked, and his offences blotted out; not on account of any merit in himſelf, but through the magnanimity of him who is hereafter to judge the world in righteouſneſs and in mercy.

INDEX.

INDEX.

A.

Addresses,

INDEX.

gerous

B.

Battle,

Dependence

Cromwell,

D.

Electors,

F.

Florence,

Greeks,

Jones,

Tarentum,

M.

O.

P.

ing

Press,

3

Q.

Q.

R.

T.

INDEX.

T.

U.

V.

W.

X.

FINIS.